Start Your Own Interior Design Business and Keep It Growing!

Your Guide to Business Success

By Linda M. Ramsay

Touch of Design ®

475 College Boulevard, Suite 6290
Oceanside, California 92057 U.S.A.
Ordering information in back of the book

Published by:

Copyright © 1994 by Linda M. Ramsay
First Printing 1994
Printed and bound in the United States of America
10 9 8 7 6 5 4 3 2 1

Publisher's Cataloging in Publication
(Prepared by Quality Books, Inc.)

Ramsay, Linda M., 1955—
    Start Your Own Interior Design Business and Keep It Growing!:
    Your Guide to Business Success/Linda M. Ramsay. 1st Edition
    p. cm.
    Includes index.
    Preassigned LCCN: 93-93833.
    ISBN 0-9629918-0-5

    1. Interior decoration firms — United States — Management. 2. New business enterprises. 3. Vocational guidance. 4. Career skills. 5. Schools — Directories. 6. Organizations — Directories. 7. Magazines — Directories.   I. Title.

NK2116.2.R35 1993   729'.068
                                            QBI93-1091

START YOUR OWN INTERIOR DESIGN BUSINESS

and KEEP IT GROWING!

Linda M. Ramsay

Your Guide To Business Success

Table of Contents

Part 3

Location, Location, Location   43

Part 4

Leases, Signs, and Alternate Locations   51

Part 5

Business Equipment and Supplies   59

Part 6

Protecting Your Business   73

Part 11

Expanding and Relocating   115

Part 12

Taxes   119

Part 13

Personnel Considerations   123

Equal Opportunity Laws   132

Part 14

Part 15

Part 22

Commercial Design Jobs

Part 23

Paperwork, Order Expediting, Shipping, and Installation

Part 24

Customer Service

Part 25

Marketing and Promotion

Marketing

Appendix A

Interior Design Programs

FIDER Accredited Programs

Appendix B

Professional Organizations

Appendix C

Industry Magazines, Trade Journals, Book Clubs, and Other Related Magazines

Introduction

"*Your Interior Design and Decorating Information Source*"

The interior design business is a highly competitive, demanding, high energy, vibrant, and at times frustrating business. Today, to have a successful business or to work as a designer or decorator (in essence, to be a successful sales professional) for someone else's business, you must combine extensive business procedures and applications with your creative ability. It is necessary to be familiar with and use the business practices contained in this book. The interior design business environment has never been as complex as it is today. To be successful and grow a business, you must develop and fully understand all of the business skills that are required for a successful business.

Instead of *paying* for your mistakes along the way as they occur and wasting your time and money, read this book and absorb the information contained in it. One of the smallest mistakes (even a slight ordering error, let alone a legal mistake) that you could possibly make will cost many times more than the price of this book. This book will move you in the right direction, page after page, and head you off at the pass *before* you make errors and watch your profits evaporate before your eyes.

People who want to take the risk and start their own businesses are entrepreneurs. The dictionary definition of an entrepreneur is, *an organizer or promoter of an activity, or one that manages and assumes the risk of business.*

Risks are a necessary portion of any future business success. To be a successful business owner, you must be willing to take risks. If you do not have the necessary business management and marketing skills, the risks involved in owning a business are multiplied several times over. Your goal, then, is to minimize these risks.

The goal of this book is to give you comprehensive interior design business knowledge and to teach vital business management skills for those of you who are considering starting your own interior design business. Do not feel discouraged if you feel unqualified or like you lack the confidence to make your business a success. After reviewing and absorbing the information in this book, you will feel more assured and your management skills will be enhanced.

Although this book is targeted at new business owners, the information provided can help already successful businesses double or triple their profits. This book is *invaluable* for struggling or failing businesses, providing them the tools necessary for a fresh start.

Review the table of contents for an overview of what owning and growing an interior design business entails. Several important sections within this book are the marketing and legal sections. If you don't constantly market your business, it will fail. If you don't understand the law of sales and the legalities you must be concerned with, your business will be eaten alive by lawsuits. Many people get started in business without any administrative abilities. And most business failures occur because the business owner lacked the necessary skills. Owners that fail are usually incompetent, lack management training and possess uneven experience.

The demands of the market, not your entrepreneurial enthusiasm, should determine the size and growth of your business. Your business should grow only when you can no longer accomplish your marketing and production goals with your present facilities, staff, and investment. Even in a flourishing company, you will deal with the expensive and complex demands of business growth and expansion.

Operating an interior design business is not easy. You will be faced with many problems and predicaments. Unhappy customers, sales slowdowns, and cost overruns can occur. In today's business atmosphere, lawsuits, competition, and governmental regulations place heavy strains on your efforts to succeed.

You must maintain a positive cash flow for your business to survive. You are in the business to earn money. You want to achieve financial independence and improve your quality of living. In order to provide these benefits, your business must provide a positive cash flow. This book will help you, the entrepreneur, to overcome the problems you will face and to help you to create a successful business.

Since design work usually requires considerable expense, clients want to be sure they are spending their money wisely and that the person they select to do the job will create an outstanding design plan suited to their needs.

What your prospects see in your studio, the picture albums shown them, your portfolio, and your attitude and personality should relay — This is the designer to do the job for me.

Clients must feel that they can rely on the product information provided, and feel confident that you will project *their* personalities with the design job. And they must feel you have the competence to carry the job out from beginning to end.

If you project to the customer that you lack confidence and are no longer enthusiastic about your job, clients will sense this attitude and will not want to hire *you* for the design project.

Meet market needs with your services and the money will follow. If you enjoy being your own boss and don't mind hard work, owning your own interior design business can be an exciting, profitable career.

Disclaimer

This book is designed to provide information about the subject matters covered. Great care has been taken to ensure the accuracy and utility of the information included within this book. It is sold with the understanding that the publisher and the author are not engaged in rendering legal, accounting, or other professional advice. If legal advice or other expert professional advice is required, the services of a competent professional person should be sought. Every effort has been made to make this book as complete as possible.

Neither Touch of Design®, nor the author, Linda Ramsay, assume any responsibility or liability for errors, inaccuracies, omissions, use, application of information, or any other inconsistency herein. The author and Touch of Design® shall have neither liability nor responsibility to any person or entity with respect to any loss or damage caused, or alleged to be caused, directly or indirectly by the information contained in this book.

Therefore, this text should be used only as a general guide and not as the ultimate source on interior design information. Furthermore, this book contains information on interior design products and application current with the printing date. The purpose of this book is to educate on the application of interior design principles.

Any slights against any organizations or manufacturers are unintentional. Readers should consult an attorney or accountant for specific applications to their individual interior design ventures. If you do not wish to be bound by the above, you may return this book in resalable condition to the publisher within 30 days for a full refund.

Part 1

Should You Start Your Own Interior Design Business?

Striking Out and Starting Your Own Business

After spending a few years gaining experience working for a well-run business, you may feel that you could do a better job than your boss. You may be very tired of just collecting a portion of the profit in commissions. Since you are already probably paying for all the mistakes you are making out of your commission, you feel you should just as well add on a bit more work and go ahead and start your own business.

Realize that opportunities do exist for you to go on your own and start your own business. It may be just a matter of courage to get your nerve up to do it.

The truths are it will take you one to two years before you will come out of the red and show a profit with a new business; all of the problems will be tougher than you ever could imagine them to be; all of the costs to start the business will exceed your initial projections; and it will be much harder work than you ever dreamed of to get started and off the ground. If you realize going in that this is the reality of starting a business, you will be far better prepared when the realities hit. Couple these realities with the hard work of running a business, experience, knowledge, and enough capital to survive the start-up phase and you have the potential of making a go of it.

Your goals in starting your own business should be to make as much money as possible, while retaining the money you already have. The errors and problems must be minimized and avoided in order to do this.

The Profile of an Entrepreneur

Entrepreneurs usually have the following characteristics:

- They are usually risk-takers who are willing to take chances; they have the ability to determine the risk factors involved in their decisions.

- They use judgment in weighing the positive and negative points of a proposition. They proceed accordingly, usually with favorable results.

- They have adequate experience in the business they are considering starting up. Even *related* experience may be adequate for success in their endeavor. (Problems arise when a person has no specific or related experience and knows *little* about the business they want to start. This person should gain on the job experience, take all available courses, and read as many books on the subject as she can to gain the lacking experience and knowledge.)

- They have a take-charge type of personality. They are able to make decisions about money. The faster the decisions can be made along the way, the faster the money will come in.

- They are willing to work long, hard hours.

- They have creativity. This includes imagination and all-around abilities for selection of everything from the logo and name to advertising and product selection. You need to be able to visualize the concept of the desired business, and visualize how all of the various parts will come together successfully. Plan the ends and outs of every detail that you can think of, to put into practice later.

Owning and Running Your Own Business

There are many benefits to owning and running your own interior design business. You will reap all of the financial benefits after the initial start-up phase. You will be in control of and responsible for the day-to-day decisions that will make or break your business.

The personal independence and freedom of owning your own business are major benefits. You are now the boss and have no one to boss you around. You come and go as you please. The downside is, if you do not put the time required into your business, it will fail.

All of the creative ideas you've had about merchandising your products and marketing your business may now finally be put to work. If you are a real entrepreneur at heart you will love running your own small business, reaping all of the profits for your business. After the overhead and commissions are paid, the rest of the money is all yours.

Running your own business is much more gratifying and satisfying than working for a large corporation that seems to care less about you. They rarely pat you on the back for the large sales that your work pulls in. You don't hear from the corporate office unless your sales are down. They rarely recognize you and thank you when you are working extremely hard and surpassing the goals. Working for a corporation does not secure your future. Many people work for corporations for many years, expecting the corporation to look out for them later, as they have done for the corporation. There are no guarantees in life. You may quickly be out of a job, given one masked excuse or another, just as you are approaching your retirement years. It is far better to build your own business, whose successes you are able to proudly take credit for and whose failures you have the ability to control.

You will experience pride and prestige in owning and running your own interior design business. People who own their own business are generally highly thought of by society.

By finally taking the plunge into starting your own business you are fulfilling a dream that you may have harbored for many years. Turning a dream into a reality is the most fulfilling aspect of having your own business.

Getting a business started, off the ground, and turned into a success is at best a difficult endeavor. Long hours, research, new information, mistakes, and problems will all have to be dealt with daily. But you will be doing what you want to do.

Depending on where you presently work (a small or larger company), realize that you will be foregoing a regular paycheck, paid holidays and vacations, paid sick leaves, group insurance plans, company retirement and profit sharing plans, and the ability to go home and relax without thinking too much about work at the end of the day.

Your Experience with an Interior Design Business

Do not attempt to start an interior design business before gaining experience in this field. The education and subsequent experience gained by working for someone else (who is, very experienced in this field) will allow you to prevent many costly mistakes.

Try to work in an operation similar to the one you want to start. Do not reveal to the owner of the business that this is your intention; just keep it to yourself. If you reveal this unnecessarily to your employer, you will probably be terminated. He or she will also be very guarded with the information revealed to you, and will keep many things from you, for example. It is not good to mislead your employer, but just keep the desire to start your own business to yourself.

Offer and be willing to do other jobs at your employer's place of business. Learn and make mistakes at their expense, not yours. Be as well rounded as you can be. You may be offered the managers job, and you may be better suited to take this job rather than attempting to start off on your own.

Find out where your strong areas of interest are and find out which areas you need to get educated in *before* attempting to start your own business. Once you start getting your business off the ground, you will not have much time to attempt to educate yourself in your weak areas. Your best sources for gaining needed education are local community colleges for courses in entrepreneurial studies for marketing, record keeping, starting a business, insurance needs, legal issues, etc. Books are published and available for each of these areas. Your local Small Business Administration (SBA) and Service Corps of Retired Executives (SCORE) offer seminars and information for small fees. Take advantage of their experience and knowledge.

Profile of the Successful Businessperson

The successful businessperson:
- Has experience in the field of her business endeavor.

- Is very good at the work she does.

- Has a love for her work.

- Is an ethical person.

- Loves the products and services that she is providing.

- Sells service and product value rather than a "cheap" price.

- Has clearly defined realistic goals, but is not in a hurry to achieve them.

- Plans ahead and is ready in advance.

- Is a "quick study."

- Is detail oriented.

- Is a hard worker.

- Is cool, cautious, and calculates risks carefully.

- Delegates work among and motivates her employees.

- Provides uncompromised service and quality.

- Has good financial perception.

- Expands the business by vertical integration rather than horizontal integration.

- Sticks with one business rather than expanding into and taking on other types of businesses.

Profile of the Unsuccessful Businessperson

The unsuccessful businessperson:
- Doesn't get experience before starting a business.

- Is impulsive.

- Will not test the market before leaping ahead.

- Is overconfident that the business will make it.

- Is in a hurry to grow fast.

- Tends to be overly optimistic.

- Doesn't make prudent decisions.

- Tends to be unhappy in her work.

- Goes for high-risk opportunities.

- Runs more than one business at a time.

- Is diversified, rather than specialized.

- Selects personal preferences, not what will sell.

- Doesn't focus on quality, focuses on "cheap" price.

- Repeats mistakes. Doesn't seem to learn from mistakes the first time they happen.

- May be overly ostentatious.

Ways to Minimize the Risks of Owning Your Own Business

- Avoid taking unnecessary or high-risk gambles that have low potential.

- Use the talents of your employees to perform functions that you might otherwise have subcontracted out.

- Start your business with enough capital.

- If market conditions change, be able to change with them. Don't lock yourself in to a specific plan, be flexible.

- Have backup material, labor, capital, distribution, and management sources ready and available should you need them.

- Constantly request feedback from your customers, suppliers, and employees on ways to improve your business.

Ways to Maximize Your Business Opportunities

- Study and research all aspects of running a small business.

- Ascertain your portion of the interior design market segment.

- Know who your customers are and find out what their needs and habits are.

- Know as much as you can about your competitors.

- Recognize your products and services by the customer wants and needs that they satisfy.

- Protect and keep quiet about your business ideas. Be guarded about who you tell your plans to.

- Keep your business plans flexible and have alternate plans to turn to should your original ideas not pan out.

- Constantly monitor market conditions through your employees, trade publications, and customers.

- Know what your strengths and weaknesses are and work on strengthening your weak areas.

- Network with other people in the interior design field. Become friendly with competitors — both direct and indirect.

The Worst Mistakes Businesses Make
(What You Can Do to Avoid Them)

The following is a list of the most common mistakes that businesses make and how to avoid them.

- **Non separating personal finances from business finances.** When you decide to go ahead and start your own business, immediately open a business checking account. Regardless of the fact that your business is or isn't a corporation, you still need to keep your personal accounts separate from your business account.

- **Starting a business with too little capital.** If you do not start with enough capital, you are placed in a defensive undercapitalized position trying to make a go of it. You need enough initial capital to allow your business to grow into a success. You require money to make more money and allow your business to grow. Starting out you will need extra money for marketing and promotion, start-up costs, inventory, fixtures, samples, paperwork, etc.

- **Not hiring attorneys and accountants in the start-up phase of the business.** Your attorney and accountant need to get you on the right track doing things the way they should be done from the beginning. It is less expensive to hire them and find out what to do and how to correctly do it than to make mistakes and then have to go running to them to correct them. Select an attorney and accountant that you are comfortable working with.

- **Mismanagement of employees.** Correctly categorize your employees from the onset as salaried employees and independent contractors. Learn about payroll taxes and when to pay them. Learn about business insurance — especially worker's compensation. Their are payroll services available to handle payroll for you at a minimal cost. After you get going pretty well, learn to delegate everything you need to have done to someone else, if possible.

- **Selection of a business partner that is doomed to fail.** Review the partnership sections of this book and decide if you really have to have a partner, and how to go about selecting a partner.

- **Business growth mismanagement.** Stay in control of the growth of your business. Stay on top of the profit margin. When the business is growing you should be making more profit. Are you delegating authority or are you attempting to still wear all of the hats? If the latter, you, your employees, and your customers are all suffering. Don't attempt to expand too fast. With careful planning, you can have both the staff and the money to support business expansion and growth. Manage and maintain the growth of your business.

- **Overspending.** Stay in control of your money and don't spend what you really don't have to spend. Put as much money back into the business as you possibly can for as long as you can, to help your business survive and grow.

- **Underemphasizing marketing.** Put a large portion of the money back into your business in the marketing area. Keep in the back of your mind that once you stop marketing, customers will stop coming and calling. Don't make the mistake of using all available money for inventory while overlooking marketing and promotion. Your inventory will sit there forever if you don't have customers coming in to buy it. You need money to advertise to sell your products. Marketing brings in new customers and keeps reminding your old customers about you.

- **Not identifying a market and fitting your products to the market.** Never attempt to fit your products to the market. It just doesn't work. Fill a void in the marketplace. People buy the products that solve their problems and that meet their needs.

- **Not having a business plan.** This is considered the biggest business mistake that can be made. A business plan covers all aspects of your business including all of the above devastating mistakes. You need to establish which direction you are headed with your business and how you are going to get there (goals). Business plans need to be revised periodically, taking into account new growth, new employees, new marketing strategies, and other financial aspects of your business. A business plan is a road map for your business.

Plan to avoid the above mistakes. Think out your plan of action for your business before you start and decide how you are going to deal with each of these potentially devastating mistakes.

Your Potential for Success

Do you fit the entrepreneur profile? If you answer the majority of the following questions with a "yes," the chances of succeeding with a business are good.

- Are you very experienced with and enjoy the interior design business? Does this business really interest you? Is this the business where you can *best* put your interests, abilities, and talents to work? If you really enjoy your work, you will tend to be more successful with it.

- Are you are comfortable with this type of business. Does it "feel" right?

- Are you both physically and mentally healthy? Are you a high-energy type of person? Starting an interior design business is like many other types of businesses. It take long hours at the offset to make it a success. You will be taking the business home with you at night.

- Are you a "people" person? You will need to enjoy all types of people from every economic level.

- Are you a decision maker? You will be making most of the decisions with your interior design business. Sometimes you will be required to make quick decisions.

- Do you have the needed self-motivation that it will take to be successful in running your own business? Are you a self-starter? If you are not strongly motivated, you will probably not be successful. Your motivation and determination to succeed will be what keep you afloat during the slow times.

- Do you enjoy setting goals, obtaining them, and setting more goals for yourself? You should enjoy the effort as much as accomplishing your goals.

- Do you enjoy solving problems? You cannot be afraid of problems and need to have the ability to get right on them immediately while learning from them to help prevent them from happening again.

- Are you very organized? You will need to be with this type of business.

- Does this type of business provides the level of status you are seeking? You may be expecting more status from the ownership of this type of business than the amount of status there actually may be. The benefits may not outweigh all of the hard work and insecurity found in this type of business. You may be better off starting a business that has fewer potential problems.

- Do you have plenty of capital or the means to get capital to stay afloat while you are getting your business off of the ground? Where will you get this capital? Set a limit on the amount of money you will *risk* on your business venture. Does an interior design business meet your investment requirements? Do you have enough money available to start a sound business? Are you comfortable with the amount of risk involved?

- Does an interior design business meet your financial needs? Will you be able to generate enough money from this business to live comfortably several years from now?

- Consider keeping your present job for the next two years and working your own business part time while in the start-up phase.

- Have you selected a prime location for your business, with plenty of walk-by traffic? Is this location near your home?

- Is the interior design business climate experiencing growth, rather than experiencing down sliding?

- Are you good at buying and negotiating prices?

- The ability to account for and keep money under control is vital. Are you profit motivated? Can you spot opportunities for doing things better, faster, and less expensively?

- Is your personality an enthusiastic, positive optimistic one, rather than negative and pessimistic?

- Evaluate the previous work experience, education, and hobbies that you have had. Did you enjoy the marketing, buying, planning, record keeping, management, displaying, and merchandising of the products, etc? What areas did you especially enjoy that you would like to expand on in the future? What were your weak points? Strong points? Are you willing to become better educated and develop your weak points? Are you being realistic about your abilities? Do you expect to delegate these less favorable areas to someone else? (When just starting a business you will be the one performing the vast majority of the required jobs. *You* will be responsible for *everything*.)

- Are you an entrepreneurial, all-around creative type of a person, very interested in constantly marketing your business?

- Are you a self-starter? Can you get the work done without someone hanging over your shoulder cracking the whip? True entrepreneurial types *hate* being bossed around by anybody. They wouldn't have it any other way.

- Are you able to train and keep your decorators motivated to increase their sales monthly?

- Are you willing and able to keep accurate records on your business at all times?

- Having your own business means planning ahead and planning for the unexpected. Do you presently demonstrate these abilities?

- Does your family/spouse agree that this it the right business for you and them to start?

Other ideas:

- Consider starting an interior design business that you can eventually retire from but remain as a consultant because it is run by your children. Set up the business where your whole family can reap the rewards of secure employment with you.

- Consider franchising the business if it should become a successful endeavor.

- Plan the business to include imported products that you can take buying trips to purchase while you see the world.

- Consider setting limitations on the amount of hours you will work on your business and the amount of money you will pour into your business. You do not want to lose your family, social life, and security in the process of attempting to get your business going. Start small.

- An interior design business fits your lifestyle. The hours (after the business is underway) are right for you — early evenings and weekends — if you are making house calls.

To Ensure Success

- Exhibit self-confidence.

- Keep yourself motivated.

- Don't loose your competitive spirit.

- Delegate, delegate, delegate.

- Quit procrastinating.

- Remember: the reason you are in business is *because* of your customers. Don't drive them away from your business by allowing anyone to display a bad attitude toward them.

- Have sufficient product knowledge. Attend those seminars and read the manufacturer's supplied information.

- Stay abreast of new products, presentation, and display materials.

- Subscribe to several trade journals and read them.

- Learn from your mistakes.

- Place value on your time.

- Properly qualify your prospects before you make house calls. Come right out and ask the client if she is shopping for price *or* service.

- Take the correct samples to each consultation.

- Cut down the amount of trips to the client's home or business.

- Spend less time with the client.

- Spend as much time selling as you can. And less time on administration tasks.

- Become comfortable with the business side of the business.

- Learn how to measure for all design products that you have available. Paying an installer for this service is a wasted expense.

- Mark up your products and services sufficiently, allowing you to make a profit.

- Know the cost of your products and services.

- Learn professional sales techniques. Become comfortable asking for the order.

- Always make good use of your time. Sharpen time management skills.

- Streamline the amount of products and services you offer.

- Don't diversify too much. Stick to specializing in only a couple of areas.

- Cut down your overhead wherever you can.

- Constantly prospect for new customers.

Stages of the Life of a Business

Introduction stage:

When you first start a business, you are in the introduction stage. Your business is new and awareness and acknowledgment from potential customers is limited. During the introduction stage your sales will rise very slowly. Due to the relatively small sales volume and accompanying low level of profits, there will be few direct competitors in the introduction stage of development. Because of high origination (business start-up expenses) and extensive marketing costs required for market development, your prices will tend to be high. During this stage, emphasis is on promotion of your business. The following are the characteristics of the introduction stage of your business development:

- Minimal product awareness and acceptance.

- Small sales volume

- Low levels of profit (if any).

- High business start-up expenses and marketing costs.

- High prices.

- Emphasis on promotion of the business.

Growth stage:

The next stage of a new business is the growth stage. This is the market acceptance stage. During this stage, awareness about your business with potential customers increases significantly. Customer acceptance tends to be strong. Sales rise dramatically, and the size of your market expands quickly. There will be a sharp increase in the number of competitors as rivals seek the profit opportunity offered by the business. Business start-up expenses are recaptured, customer areas and customer base become expanded, and businesses tend to shift to sales of name-brand products. These are the characteristics of the growth stage:

- High awareness about your business.

- Customer acceptance of your business.

- Marked increase in sales.

- Strong profits.

- Increase in competition.

- Business start-up expenses are recaptured.

- Move to selective promotion of name brands.

- Expanded customer area and customer base.

- Business becomes more fine tuned and improved in areas of need.

Maturity stage:

As your business reaches the maturity stage, it will enter the period of development that is known as the turbulence period. During this stage, businesses battle their competitors for their market share. This is the "survival of the fittest" time for the market. Marginal producers will now leave the market and fall to the wayside. Sales now level off. Competitors stress brand promotion and concentrate on what is different about their business with products and services. Prices tend to fall and the profit margins gradually shrink. The business is already known within a large market area and it is difficult to get new customers and retain the old ones. Due to the turbulent market conditions, there will be fewer direct competitors. These are the following characteristics of the maturity stage:

- Intense competition with competitors.

- Sales level off.

- Brand names are emphasized.

- Prices decline.

- Profits decline.

- Business is well known throughout the market area.

- Amount of competitors decrease.

Declining stage:

This is the last stage of the business stage of life. Your business reaches its saturation point in the market area and sales begin to fall. The degree of the decline and the final death of the business depend on the market strength of new products that you introduce. During the declining stage there is a decrease in the amount of competitors in the market. The remaining competitors will tend to turn to marketing and promotion to keep sales up. While prices may fall during this stage, there may also be price increases depending on what the market will bear. Some competitors may find that this is an opportune time to make good profits. These are the characteristics of this stage:

- Sales reach their saturation point and fall.

- New promotion of products affect the fall of sales.

- Fewer competitors.

- Remaining competitors switch to marketing and promotion to keep sales coming.

- Prices may shift upward or downward.

- Good profit opportunities may still be available.

Market Research — Researching the Interior Design Market

Market research is a necessary step in the process of starting your own interior design business. Without market research, you do not have a way of determining the size of your potential market, the reaction of people to your products, services, business image, or the prices that people are willing to pay for your products and services. Researching the market helps you to discover the likely size of your market and gives priceless information on how people will respond to your business, products, and services. Market research allows you to calculate the size of the target market, before you invest thousands of dollars.

Market research consists of gathering three distinct categories of data. These are: demographic, informational, and product or service. **Demographic data** detail to you *who and where your customer is*. **Informational data** determine *the need and demand for your product or service*, and *how much people are willing to pay for your products and services*. **Product and service data** provide details on *people's reaction toward design, color, size, shape, styles, business logo, and overall store image*.

Data can be gathered in three ways: historical, experimental, or by using the survey method. The **historical method** consists of *analyzing sales records from past years*. The **experimental method** entails *testing your products or business with a cross section of the market*. The **survey method** is dependable and inexpensive. It involves choosing a random or representative group of your target market and supplying them with a questionnaire to fill out. The questionnaire should be easy to read, short, and easy to understand.

There are sources of information to find more data on interior design businesses. Using this approach to researching the market will give you better than average odds at succeeding once you have decided to go into this business. Strive to find out if there is a large enough market available to draw from for your goods and services. Try to identify other interior design business opportunities in other business areas. Plan and evaluate how you can reach these other market opportunities and capitalize on them.

While market research is time consuming, do not make the mistake of starting a business without taking this necessary planning step. Strive to find out what type of people live in the area, what are their financial circumstances, ages, age of the homes, standard of living, competitors, etc. The more information you can find out before making a large investment of time and money into the business, the greater the possibility for you to put together the right type of successful business for the area.

It is hoped, you will be starting an interior design business with a large loyal customer base already built up to draw from. If you do, you will be cutting down the length of time it will take you to get out of the red and start making a living. Also consider where your present customer base resides when considering a location for your business.

Since market research should be a continual process throughout the life of your business, follow up on jobs by sending out questionnaires to clients about your service and product quality. Allow a section on the questionnaire for the clients to make suggestions on how they think you can do a better job. You must keep in touch with the needs and demands of your customers.

The Competition

The Various Competitors

Who are your interior design competitors? Besides small firms, there are quite a few sources of interior design products. Many stores specialize in one type of product or another or have several. Let's review and analyze the different interior product sources generally available throughout the country.

Department stores   Usually high priced for the limited goods and services available. While they have tremendous buying power, there are more people to pay in their management chain. They have available a limited line of products and cannot "get" an item they don't already have. They generally take a very long time to deliver and employ higher pressure sales professionals that are less-experienced decorators (they do train them, and *some* come in with previous experience). They are learning with each new customer and making major mistakes on the majority of their jobs. So although they charge a lot they absorb the decorator's errors and never seem to turn a truly healthy profit. They generally will try to take care of the customer, as the rest of the store management (who try to always stay clear of the custom decorating, carpeting, and furniture departments) will come raining down on their heads should the customer call them with complaints. Department stores not only accept Visa and Mastercard, but also their own credit cards.

Department store also have their inexpensive ready-made department, accessory department, and some have catalogue shopping. While generally the ready-mades on the shelves are skimpy and cheap looking, the made-to-measure lines are not so chintzy looking. They are fuller and generally made from more expensive fabrics. Customers bring in their own measurements. Generally the salespeople are fairly sharp. They get a lot of practice — fast. They are also trained. This is a lower-pressure (and usually more knowledgeable) salesperson than the custom decorating, carpeting, or furniture department salesperson.

Department store catalogues offer a wide range of window products, area rugs, accessories, and some furniture items at a reasonable price. Many of the items also go on sale regularly.

Franchise stores/vans   Usually high priced for their line of goods and services. They have a monthly franchise fee to pay. They co-op advertise with the main headquarters. Generally a customer is paying for the name and goodwill of the company. They generally have only a limited line of products, and usually can't get what they don't carry. Franchise companies are usually well organized. The main headquarters does not appreciate customer complaints and strives to maintain customer goodwill. They tell you how to run *your* company and how to handle customer complaints. They provide training on how to run their decorating business, but expect you to be somewhat experienced in decorating when you take over the reins. Usually higher-pressure sales professionals (they have to be to survive with their pricing). Franchise companies usually accept Visa and Mastercard.

Chain stores   High priced to moderately priced. Familiar sources are blinds stores, hard-surface window treatment shops, wallpaper stores, floor covering stores, and furniture stores. Usually higher pressure sales professionals. Some of these are limited to the lines and fabrics that they have available, while others can order other products.

Interior design firms   High-priced to moderately priced independently owned shops and stores. Can generally get whatever the customer would like. Uses a full range of sources and contractors. Striving to build repeat business by quality service and the use of quality ideas and products. Usually hire decorators and designers that are experienced. If not, they generally have the jobs reviewed and remeasured before specifying items. Usually accept Visa and Mastercard.

Discount interior stores   Usually independently owned, moderate to lower-priced interior product sources. These may come in the form of discounted interior fabric stores with or without decorators on staff, the discounted flooring store with salespeople, the discounted furniture store, the discounted paint and wallpaper store with its various lines of window treatments. They may be able to get other lines besides what they show and sell. They usually offer a measuring service for the customer. Usually accept Visa and Mastercard.

Catalogue stores   These come in the form of independent membership (pay a few bucks a year to join) and nonmembership stores. They are usually a very reasonable source for a customer to order from for all types on interior design products. They can and do get a wide range of products. If a customer wants a particular product that he doesn't have the information for, they will try and get it. Customers shop other sources and select what they want. They bring in the item number, color number, and manufacturing or distributing source and give this to the catalogue store. Some catalogue stores will measure for the customer, others will not. They usually take Visa and Mastercard.

Workrooms   Many drapery workrooms will sell to customers at a price slightly over wholesale labor. The fabrics are generally discounted additionally. They usually have a fair selection of fabric or they can order from any fabric source. They generally do not accept Visa and Mastercard as their mainstay is not retail but wholesale. But they don't turn down sales either. Generally, customers must bring in their measurements just as designers and decorators do. They may have a commercial salesperson or other decorator on staff that will measure for the customer for a measuring charge.

Factors to Use in Analyzing the Competition

Most businesses have some competition. Some interior design firms do the complete interior, while others specialize in window coverings or floor coverings.

Even though you may have a few competitors operating a similar business, you should not feel that you will not be successful. Availability of competition may mean that there is room for growth in the interior design area in the community you are considering. **Consider the following factors when analyzing each competitor, both direct and indirect:**

The competition:
- Who are your competitors? Determine your direct competition — those who have almost exactly the same type of interior design firm — and indirect competition — competition such as paint stores, furniture stores, wall covering shops, etc., that sell some of the same products that you will also carry.

- What are their strong points?

- What are their weak points? Determine their weak points and capitalize on these. Do a better job than they do in their weak areas.

- In what ways is your company better than the competition?

- What does/will your company offer that is unique?

- Investigate your competition and determine *why* they are successful or *why* they are unsuccessful.

Location:
- Where are your competitors located? If they are not doing a good job overall, locating your business by theirs is favorable. If they are heavy competition overall, locate in another part of the community. Where are they located? In a shopping center? On a main thoroughfare?

- Are they drawing customers from nearby large retailers?

- How much auto traffic passes their business? Foot traffic?

- Is their storefront highly visible?

- Is their store easily accessible? Enough parking spaces?

Outside store image:
- How does the store appear overall from the outside?

- Do they have window display area? Do they maximize on their window displays?

- What type of signs do they use? What type of signs does the community allow?

Inside store image:
- What type of image does the interior of the store or studio project? Is the interior decorated so that it make you feel welcome and comfortable to come in off of the street and just browse? Does the store *feel* snobbish? Is the interior clean? How is the layout and traffic flow of the store? How large is the store?

Salespeople and staff:
- Do the sales people make customers feel welcome? Are these educated interior designers and decorators with years of experience or are these salespeople with limited knowledge and experience?

- How many people does the business employ? Are they paid by salary or commission?

- Do the salespeople employ a soft sell (low pressure) or a hard sell (high pressure) when dealing with customers?

- How much product knowledge do the salespeople have? Do they really know the technical ins and outs of what they are selling?

Advertising and promotion:

- What advertising and marketing methods does the competition employ for promotion of its company?

- How is everything displayed? Easy to get to and look at?

- What quality of products does the store carry?

- How does the store price its products and services? Are the products discounted at a percentage off the retail price or do they use a cost-plus pricing strategy?

- What advertising methods do they employ?

- Does the company keep much inventory on hand? Do they offer sales prices and promotions on items that they stock?

Products and service:

- What products and services do they offer?

- Do they insist on installing everything they sell or can the customer order and install some of the products?

- Do they strive to immediately install the products as they become available or do they try to install everything at once (holding up the order for a small missing item)? How fast do they service a customer on a service request? Do the salespeople return phone calls promptly?

- Are their past customers happy with their service? Do they retain customers on a mailing list and keep them aware that they would like to continue doing business with them?

- What are the payment policies? How much of a down payment is required to start the order? Does the company carry its own paper? Does it accept Mastercard and Visa?

After determining the above factors for each of your competitors, decide why you think the company is really successful. How could the company be even more successful? If you are going to compete with this company, how are you going to do a better job?

Gather information from competitors and suppliers:

Find out about your competitors' pricing, sales, brochures, business practices, and business style. Not all of this information needs to be gleaned undercover. Some people (especially older people — usually very experienced) do not mind sharing their knowledge and helping you out by giving you realistic information. Sharing their vast experience and being considered as an expert is satisfying to their ego. They were once in the same boat — about to embark on starting their own business. You may not be perceived as a threat at all, especially if you emphasize that your business will be located in another distant city.

Let the owner know about the type of interior design business that you are considering, and ask for his input and advice in this area. Pay him a visit and tell him that you are interested in starting a similar business. You may find out that he is thinking of selling the business and wouldn't mind training you for running his thriving business! **Some of the vital questions to ask an owner of a successful interior design business are:**

- How long has he been in the interior design business?

- What experience and background does he consider vital to your success? What major functions does the owner perform for the business now? Many years later?

- Does the business employ soft selling or hard selling?

- How much help do the vendors actually provide? How do you get the vendors to help you with co-op advertising and provide other support? From what suppliers does the company buy the majority of its carpets, flooring, fabrics, window coverings, etc.?

- How much capital does the owner consider necessary today for a start-up venture similar to his own? How much capital must be kept in reserve? What are the major monthly overhead expenses (payroll, rent, utilities, phone, advertising and marketing, insurance, legal help, samples, etc.)?

- What are the major problem areas that you should expect?

- What kind of profit is it reasonable to expect to make in a business such as this today? How long will it take you to get there? What avenue should you take to get there the quickest?

- What advertising methods have worked the best in the past? In the present? What does the owner recommend?

- What major factors are vital to be successful in this business?

- What level of sales is realistic to expect at the end of the first year? The second year? The third year?

If you are able to get this knowledge from one or two successful interior design business owners, you will have reaped a gold mine of information. Many advertising dollars will be rescued, much of your time in trial and errors will be saved, and you will have learned a great deal.

No, it is not easy to call and ask for an appointment to talk to a successful business owner. Just go right into the business and openly admire the business with the salespeople and owner. Ask if the owner is around and ask to speak to him. Compliment him on what a nice business he has. Start the questions by telling him that you to would like to have a business like this, but located in a nearby town (at least 35 miles away). Be nice and tell them that you certainly would appreciate any words of wisdom that they might have to offer you. Then slowly and subtly start the questioning process. The owner's body language and way he answers the questions will tell you when to back off and stop. Be assertive and get as much information as you possibly can.

If you are getting mostly negative answers from the owner of the business, he may be trying to discourage you — feeling the threat of competition. Realize where he is coming from and find another company with another owner who is more open to providing you with the needed information.

If you are just not nervy enough to try this approach (you may not have enough nerve to start your own business either), then try to work for a successful business owner. You may or may not choose to tell him that in the distant future you want to start your own interior design business. See the section on *Your Experience with an Interior Design Business* to see what approach to take. You would simply ask him one question a day until you have enough information, while seeing firsthand how he runs a successful interior design business.

Contact suppliers and vendors that you would like to use in the future and ask to meet with them. Invite them out for lunch. Explain that you haven't decided to open your own business yet, that, you are simply testing the water at this point. Realize that they do have a vested interest — they would like you to become a customer and buy their products — whether you survive in business or not. Vital questions to ask them are:

- Where do they see the interior design field going in the future? What areas do they expect to see grow? Does the field in growth look optimistic? If the field for your area is oversaturated and has little prospect of future growth, do not waste your time and money attempting a start-up.

- Ask about their feelings on which areas are lacking in interior design businesses, and what would they consider a good location? They also know which businesses are available for sale.

How to Compete with the Competition

- Be competitive with your pricing of your products and services.

- Provide high-quality customer service. Return customer telephone calls in a timely manner. Get back to the customer with the promised information.

- Make sure your employees have adequate product knowledge in addition to comprehensive interior design knowledge.

- Stay up-to-date with current trends through seminars, workshops, magazines, books, etc.

- Get more publicity for your advertising dollar.

- Plan effective promotions.

- Don't give your customer too much information regarding measurements, fabric suppliers, etc. Don't make it easy to be *shopped*.

- Check out fabric samples only *after* the customer has given you a deposit for her order. Let her borrow them only to match up other items. It is better to tell her that you will order a cutting for her to work with. This buys you time until the sample arrives and then if you are shopped, it is too late for the customer to cancel.

- Try not to give quotes over the phone. Attempt to get the customer to come in to talk with you, and then you make an in-home appointment to meet her at home.

- Emphasize the quality service, design expertise, and information you provide.

- For do-it-yourselfer customers, place emphasis on having window treatments installed professionally.

Marketing Questions to Answer Before Starting Your Business

If your interior design firm is to be successful, it must satisfy the needs and desires of its present and potential customers. You must make *sound* buying decisions, know where to buy, what to buy, how much to buy, and how to place an order. To do this, you should be familiar with old and new products. Stock enough products and have a good working relationship with your vendors. When pricing your goods and services, understand the market forces affecting your business.

The following questions need to be answered before starting your business. They will help you to analyze your operation from the marketing viewpoint. The answers will determine what way you advertise for business.

Know the strengths and weaknesses of your products and operation. Make decisions on how to handle problems before they appear. The success of your business depends on your management skills and correct planning. You will have to adapt your business to new markets, product changes, and be flexible and innovative to keep your business growing.

Methods for marketing plan evaluation:
- How will you know that your customers like the line of products you have selected?

- What method will you use to evaluate sales?

- What method will you use to determine correct pricing?

- How will you determine if the location of the firm is "right"?

- How will you evaluate personnel performance?

- What methods will you use in contacting customers to find out how they feel about your services?

- Will you make your own deliveries or will you use delivery services to deliver noninstalled merchandise?

Determining how to price goods and services (answer these questions before making any pricing decisions):

- Do you understand the market forces affecting your pricing system?

- What price range will your line of merchandise fall in? High, medium, or low? What quality of merchandise will you be providing?

- Do you know the top level that your customers will pay for some of your products?

- Will you price your goods and services below market, at market, or above market?

- What price *must* you charge to make a profit?

- Which of your products are price sensitive to your customers? How high can you price *these products* without turning off your customers?

- What price is the customer willing to pay?

- Will the set prices cover full costs on each sale?

- Will you set definite markups for each product?

- Will you set markups for different product categories?

- Will you use a one-price policy rather than bargain the price with the customer?

- Are regular repeat sales throughout the year better than one annual large sale?

- What part do you want price to pay in your overall retailing plans?

- What will you keep in stock? What is the price range of your stock?

- Will you take credit cards such as Visa or Mastercard? Will you *raise* all of your prices to cover the extra charges for a merchant account and processing fees? Visa and Mastercard will not allow you to charge a customer more *during* a transaction if the customer puts the purchase on a credit card.

- Will your business use unusual pricing because of your competitors?

- What products will attract customers when placed on sale?

- Will you use leader tactics in advertising to get the customers in the door? How about loss leader pricing on some items?

- Will you lower some products' prices to attract customers? Do you know at what point, with price lowering, customers will become suspicious and hesitant?

- Have you provided for discounts and allowances?

- Will coupons, rebates, markdowns, or special sales methods be employed?

- How will you respond to special pricing by your competitors?

- Do you keep track of your competitors' sales? Do you know when they normally have sales? If you do, you might find a trend and be able to beat them to sales.

- Will you be influenced by competitors' price shifts?

- Will you offer discounts for quantity purchases or to particular groups of buyers?

- Do you know which products will be slow movers and which ones will be fast movers? Will you consider this when making pricing decisions?

- What is your policy on when to take markdowns? How large will the markdowns be?

- Will your customers expect sales at certain times of the year such as the holidays?

Pricing restrictions:

- Do any of your suppliers have a minimum price standard at which their goods may be sold?

- Does your particular state have fair-trade practice acts that require you to mark up your merchandise by a minimum percentage?

- What are your state regulation regarding length of term for advertising of "close-out" sales? How about two-for-one sales, etc.?

- Do you know all of the state regulations regarding your business?

- Will you issue rain checks for advertised inventory that is sold out?

Controlling inventory and processing orders:

- Who is responsible for receiving and controlling inventory at your firm?

- What transportation methods will be used in delivering ordered merchandise?

- What duties in receiving the inventory must be performed during a merchandise delivery?

- How will the merchandise be stored? Displayed? Controlled?

- What will be your procedure in handling damaged goods?

- How will orders be processed?

- What will be the plan of action should there be a shortage or back order of products?

- Who will you notify about the problem?

- What type of inspection is made of received goods to determine quality and quantity?

- How will you know when you should reorder stock goods and how much will you reorder?

- Where will you display the merchandise?

- How will you organize the samples so that all are easily found when needed?

Customer service:
- What services do your customers expect?

- Where does your repeat business usually come from?

- What is the usual reason for losing customers?

- How are customers usually approached? What is usually said by the salesperson?

- Is there easy access and adequate customer parking for your business?

- What services will you offer? What services do your competitors offer? Are you offering minimum services to compare favorably with your competition or are you offering extra services?

- What services are you and your competitors not offering that customers would like?

- Do you offer extra services at certain times of the year, such as Christmas time? Are there extra services you could offer during certain times of the year that your customers would appreciate? You might offer layaway, gift certificates, and gift wrapping for accessories during Christmas, Mother's Day, etc.

- What is the policy about refused or returned merchandise? Custom-made items?

- What are the hours that the business will be open? Will it be closed Sundays? What holidays? Will you accommodate a customer coming to the studio at off hours?

Services:
- For noninstalled items, will you have your own delivery vehicles or will you subcontract out this service? Will you buy or lease company vehicles?

- How much will you charge for the delivery service?

- Will you work the price of delivery into the price of the item and offer "free" delivery?

- What are your policies for returns? Returns of custom merchandise?

- Will you make charitable contributions to various community organizations, clubs, ads in yearbooks, donations for school functions, etc.?

- Will you join the local chamber of commerce, merchant's association, Better Business Bureau, or other local organizations?

Store displays:
- Will products be displayed to maximize their appeal in your store?

- Where in your store will products be displayed?

- Will you be using window displays?

- Which of your products have unusual eye appeal and will be impressive if used in displays?

- If you are using multitiered stands or shelving, do you know which shelves are the most eye-catching?

- Will attention-attracting accessories be displayed so that other nearby items will have attention called to them also?

- How often will the displays be changed? Will they be changed with the seasons?

- What are your impulse items? Will these impulse items be placed in high-traffic areas?

- On window treatment displays will you price out the total look as shown in the display, or will the customer have to inquire as to the approximate price?

- Will prices be easy to see on most of your displayed products?

Credit:

- Will you be offering credit? If so, what type of credit?

- How much credit can you carry and still keep your business afloat at any given time?

- Have you planned your credit program with the help of your accountant or attorney?

- Will you carry your own paper on accounts receivables? What will be the determining factors on accepting or rejecting credit? For what time periods? What amounts?

- Have you contacted local finance companies to see if you can workout a credit plan with them for credit customers?

- Have you shopped around and applied for a Visa or Mastercard merchant account? Do you realize the costs involved?

- Do you know about the Fair Credit Reporting Act?

- Do you know about truth-in-lending legislation?

Management:

- Have you developed a set operational plan for the year?

- Do your plans consider creative methods to problem solving?

- Are your plans realistic?

- How will you know when your plans have been achieved?

- Do you have a system for setting aside money to meet quarterly tax obligations?

Organization:

- Have you clearly stated job descriptions and who is responsible for what?

- Will your organizational plans minimize duplication of efforts and maximize the use of each employee's strong points?

- How will you rate your employees for promotions and salary increases? Will you clearly define the guidelines for your employees?

- Do your commission rates or pay rates meet your competitor's rate of pay?

- Will a training program help your employees do a superior job?

- Will you encourage and pay for ongoing education and seminars attended by your employees? For relevant books and reading material?

- Will more experienced employees help train the newer employees?

- What are your working conditions?

- What are your leadership skills for setting examples for your employees? Do you frequently provide encouragement? Praise? Criticism? Do you listen to complaints? Set examples of how others should be treated? Are you impartial?

- Are you aware of the rules regarding the Fair Labor Standards Act as it applies to minimum wages, overtime, and child labor?

- Are you careful to avoid *any* type of discrimination in your employment practices?

- What methods will you use to motivate your employees?

- How will you minimize shoplifting and employee thefts?

Communication:

- How will you effectively communicate with your employees?

- Will you hold regular meetings for all personnel?

- Will you have an employee bulletin board for items needing to be posted?

- Will all employees receive an employee handbook outlining all rules and regulations?

- Are you easily approachable?

Finances:

- Have you decided on a accounting system to use?

- What records are needed to maintain control?

- Which records should you keep to assist you in meeting tax obligations in a timely manner?

- Will your sales records give you the important information you need to make sound decisions?

- Will you be able to separate your cash sales from your charge sales?

- Can you break down your sales by department? By merchandise classification?

- Do you have a system to evaluate each salesperson's performance?

- Will your inventory records give you the important information you need to make accurate decisions?

- How will you know how much you have invested in merchandise without having a physical inventory?

- What is the difference between inventory value at cost and at market value? Will you be able to tell which one shows a loss in the period earned? Which one preserves cash?

- Do you understand the differences in the cost method of inventory accounting versus the retail method of inventory accounting?

- Have you found an accounting method that will show you the inventory shortages in the year?

Accounting and expense records:

- Will your expense records give you the important information you need to make accurate decisions?

- What expense items do you have the most control over?

- Will the records be in enough detail to show you where the money is actually going?

- Will you deduct those expenses not necessary to the successful operation of your business?

- Can you effectively use the information on your profit and loss statement and balance sheet?

- Will you analyze monthly financial statements?

- Will you analyze your financial statements in terms of how you did last year and to see if you met this year's goals?

- Will you be undercapitalized starting out?

- Have you borrowed more than you can *easily* pay back?

- Are there ways you can improve your profit circumstances by improving your gross margin?

- Will you use the information within your financial statements to prepare a cash budget?

Insurance:

- Will you have adequate insurance coverage?

- Will you carry up-to-date fire coverage on your building equipment, and inventory?

- Will your liability insurance cover bodily injuries in addition to libel and slander suits?

- Are you acquainted with your obligations to employees under common law and worker's compensation?

- Will you buy insurance from one agent, rather than several agents, opening the risk of gaps and controversy over who is responsible should an accident occur?

- Have you discussed insurance coverage with your insurance agent and found out the most economical ways to cover your business such as umbrella policies, proper classifications of employees under worker's compensation, cutting back on seasonal insurance coverage, etc.?

- Has the insurance agent discussed business interruption insurance or criminal insurance with you?

- Will you have employee benefits available? Will you provide group health, group life, disability, or retirement insurance?

Part 2

Should You Start a New Business, Buy an Existing Business, or Buy a Franchise Package?

A new business, an existing business, and a franchise package all have their positive and negative points. In the following areas weigh the negative against the positive and decide which fits your personality, drive, and abilities before starting or buying an existing business or franchise package.

Starting a New Interior Design Business

After looking around at available existing businesses, you may decide that what is available is too antiquated, run down, has an old style and image, is poorly located, or seems to have little potential. You may simply not be willing to pay for an overinflated perception of what their business's goodwill is worth. Some business owners feel that their businesses are worth much more than they really are. The new owner of the business must be able to buy the business at a price where she will be able to make a living plus have a return for her investment. If as a prospective owner you are unable to do that, it is best to struggle for a few months and come out ahead later by starting a new business.

If you opt to start a new business, you must be far more experienced in all of the required areas than if you buy an existing business where the owner is happy to train you and show you exactly how the business functions.

Starting a new interior design business versus purchasing an existing business or franchise package is a difficult proposition involving a large amount of risk.

Much time beforehand, will need to be spent in marketing analysis, deciding on a location, interviewing business owners and vendors, learning a bookkeeping system, and selecting everything from a name and logo to samples, equipment, and fixtures.

All the potentially fatal problems that can come up for your business must be foreseen and headed off before they are allowed to damage your business.

If you are unable to find a business that you can mold to the image you are striving to achieve, you'll need to start from scratch and start a new business.

Advantages to Starting a New Interior Design Business

- You can start the business with the style and concept that you want to project, rather than using someone else's ideas, look, and feel. You thus eliminate having to deal with someone else's debts, negative image, problems, old samples, and old equipment.

- The location of the business, the name, logo, equipment, fixtures, samples, and accessories are selected by you.

- You get to hire the employees of your choice. You will not have to rid your new company of problem employees whose personalities you are unable to adjust to or relate to.

- Since you are starting fresh, you will not have the added expense of paying for the previous company's goodwill or paying a monthly franchise fee.

- When you put the whole package together you get to feel the challenge and subsequent pride and accomplishment of the feat.

Disadvantages to Starting a New Interior Design Business

- Everything must be researched, planned, shopped for, and put together by you. Sometimes, due to inexperience in marketing, accounting, purchasing and merchandising, mistakes are made.

- You are starting from square one. You must put everything together and tread through the red for awhile before (many months later) you start to show a profit. It is very stressful to keep throwing money out, keeping the bills and advertising covered without knowing if your company will survive. You may end up just tossing away a large quantity of money.

- The process of putting a business package together involves numerous elements such as site selection, sample selection, setting up an accounting system, working with an attorney and accountant, shopping for a merchant account, planning your advertising, and pricing your products and services. Everything is new, difficult, time consuming, and expensive. It is easy to become discouraged before you have gotten started.

- Because you are just starting out, almost every start-up cost must be paid in full as you go. You have not yet established the credit and longevity that businesses you work with require. Little money and credit are available from banks and lenders.

Strategy to Use to Achieve Success in Starting a New Business

- Gain experience in the interior design and decorating field before you start your own business. Try to work in a company similar to the one you want to start. Learn at the other company's expense and avoid costly errors in your own business later.

- Decide how much money you are going to invest in making a go of the new business, and stick with that amount. Use as much available credit from vendors and manufacturers as you can.

- Realize that your salary will be tight for the next couple of years. Now is not the time to redecorate your home and buy a new car. Most all of the profit will have to be put back into the business for promotions, inventory, samples, and displays to build a stable base for your business.

- Analyze and study the industry before delving into a new business. Talk to as many people as you can about their businesses and their opinions of your new business venture. Reading trade publications and researching the community will give you an overall opinion of the interior design industry and community at the time you want to start up.

- Start the business on a part-time basis out of your home before you quit your present job, if possible. Discover whether you really want to be in business for yourself, handling all of the administrative details besides planning and selling. Find out whether you will make money in this area before investing everything into it.

- Find out why operations similar to the one you would like to have are successful or unsuccessful. Emulate their success by using the same approach. If they are unsuccessful, don't make the same mistakes.

- Make a business plan. Find out your errors and weak areas on paper before you start making mistakes in your business.

Buying an Existing Interior Design Business

The easiest way to start an interior design business is to buy someone's existing business. This is also the safest way to start a business and is more likely to be a success than if you start your own business. You will also save much time and money on the start-up phases of a new business and building that business to a profit point.

If you do not have much experience in the interior design field, buy an existing business and have the owner train you in the day-to-day operations. Shop around and find the business that comes closest to the style of business you are seeking to project. It is preferable to work for the business, try it out, and get a feel for it before making a commitment to purchase the business.

When you purchase an existing interior design business, you are in essence purchasing someone else's reputation, goodwill, image, and style.

Find out about available interior design businesses for sale by reading the newspaper's classified business opportunity sections, the classified sections of interior design trade journals, contacting business brokers and real estate salespeople, and by asking interior design sales representatives if they know of any interior design businesses for sale.

Advantages to Buying an Existing Business

- Some of your customer base is already in place, saving you time and money.

- If the business has been for sale for awhile or if the owner is ill or wants to leave the area, the existing business may be a good deal.

- Many potential start-up mistakes are eliminated. The owner probably made them for you, long ago.

- The location may be good; the sales are growing every year; the overall look and style of the business may be workable for you.

- The owner is probably happy to train you in order to sell his or her business. The existing employees may be well trained and know how to run the operation almost as well as the owner. You will acquire the established discounts that have been built up with volume over time, and the bank will work with you on the existing line of credit.

- The present lease may have been set up long ago and be very favorable compared to the ones available at present.

- The seller of the business may be happy to carry paper on the business for you at a favorable interest rate for both of you.

- Financing is easier to obtain on an existing business with previous records than on a new business.

- If the business is presently making a profit, when you take over the reins it should still make a profit.

- You are able to review the marketing techniques that have been used in the past to see what did and did not work for the business.

Disadvantages of Buying an Existing Business

- It takes time to find the right business to buy. Realize that 30 percent of all businesses, if personally approached, are probably for sale — if the terms are favorable to the seller. If you do not want to come right out and ask the owner if the business is for sale, ask him if he knows of a business like his that is for sale. If he is contemplating selling, he will speak right up and say that *his* is for sale, or he knows of another for sale.

Most businesses change hands among people in the same business. You will probably not see the business you want advertised or listed with a business broker. This is why it is so important to get a relationship established with your manufacturer's reps. They know which business is for sale, in trouble, or may be available soon. Let them know that you are in the market.

A business may be "for sale" and not advertised because the owner may not want the customers or the employees to know of its availability until the transaction is under way.

Do approach several business brokers and keep checking the businesses for sale area of your newspaper in case a business you would like to have is advertised.

Call the sellers and ask for the location, price, terms, age of the business, and the reason why the business is being sold. If the information sounds like what you are looking for, make an appointment to meet with the owner or broker to delve deeper into the details about the business opportunity.

Look for clues in existing businesses that tell you that they might be for sale. Some of these clues include lack of pride in the store or studio's appearance, low inventory, inconsistent advertising and promotion efforts, and poorly trained employees.

When a business owner is in distress with his business, he may be thinking of just going out of business rather than selling the existing business. He may feel disillusioned with the business or may not realize that someone like you would pay money to walk in and take the business off of his hands. Not everyone is a businessperson.

- The price of the business may be too high. You may go ahead and buy the business and find out later that the price was inflated. The business isn't really as good as you expected.

- The reputation of the business may not be as good as you thought it was. In fact, the business's reputation may be pretty bad. A bad reputation may be why the owner sold, and may be costly or near impossible for you to turn around.

- The location of the business may be in the old downtown area and the shops and larger stores are relocating to malls and other centers. There may be shops sitting empty nearby that couldn't survive or made the move to the newer locations.

- The existing owner may know something that you don't. He or she may have heard (probably from a rep) that a major interior design chain or other competition is about to start up in the area. A massive layoff at a large company in the community may be rumored or be a well-known fact. The owner (feigning ignorance and fearing for survival) gets out before it becomes public knowledge.

- The fixtures, equipment, Visa and Mastercard terminals, samples, etc., are probably worn out and out of style if the business is several years old or more. You will probably need to do some replacing right away.

- The lease may be ready to expire. The existing owner realizes this and knows that the renewal terms of the lease will probably not be to his liking and will choose to bail out now, selling the business, rather than moving or going out of business.

- The monthly debt on the existing business may be built up quite high. You will inherit this with the new business.

- The business may come with employees that you do not wish to retain under your new ownership. Employee problems may be the real reason the owner wishes to sell.

- It may take most of your available cash to buy the business, leaving you short on marketing money.

- There may be potential lawsuits looming against the business.

Factors to Determine *Before* Purchasing an Existing Business

- Why does the owner want to sell the business? She will probably tell you that she is moving, divorcing, retiring, having health problems, wants to cash in the business value, or has partner disputes. The real reason is probably because business is down, she wants to branch off into a better opportunity, bad management, bad location, she needs money, the business is losing money, competition is tough, the area is being rezoned, or auto and pedestrian traffic patterns are changing. Make the owner state in writing the reason she is selling so that you do have legal recourse later, should you find out the real, undisclosed reason for the owner selling the business.

- Is this the type of business that you want to have?

- Is the seller willing to train you and help you in the early stages of the business?

- Will the employees stay with the business? What seems to be their attitude?

- Are the asking price and terms realistic? Can you afford the price and terms? If not, what can you offer in the way of a reduced price and flexible terms?

- Is current pricing on products and services competitive?

- Is the inventory current and resalable? How much of the inventory is not resalable? Will the owner reduce the price due to unresalable and old inventory?

- Are there ways to cut the cost of the goods further?

- Will the suppliers continue to work with you? On the same terms?

- What are the fixed expenses? Are there ways to cut the fixed expenses down?

- What are the terms of the lease? Is the lease transferrable? At what cost? Is the leasing term expiring soon?

- What changes need to be made to the business immediately? Three months from now? Six months from now? Can you afford these changes?

- How much more will you have to spend to promote the business initially?

- What are the worst things that could happen? Do you have the money to cover the worst case scenario? Can you afford the potential problems that can and probably will happen?

- How much is the seller collecting in salary, personal expenses, and perks? Can you support yourself and cover your debts with this same amount?

- Is your understanding of the company's profitability realistic?

- What position in terms of cash will you be in after you take over the business? In three months from now? In six months from now?

- What sales trends show up in the records?

- Compared to the overall interior design market, has this business done well?

- What problems has the business had in the past? Present problems?

- Will the current and previous customers accept a change of ownership? Do you foresee *any* problems?

- Does the business have a good reputation? Is the existing customer base loyal?

- Is the risk of taking over the business worth the investment?

- If the business reaches its capacity, what is the projected end result?

- Are there potential lawsuits looming against the business?

- Does the business have liens placed against it from creditors with outstanding debts? Make sure the business is free and clear. Check with the secretary of state in your state to see if liens have been filed against the business.

- Are employee problems the real reason the owner wishes to sell?

Exchange Information Between Buyer and Seller:

In order to show the owner your strong interest in purchasing their business, present him with a personal financial statement to show your ability to purchase the business. Personal financial statement forms are available in stationery and office supply stores or in computer software packages. Don't reveal all of your capital resources immediately, unless you want to pay full price for the business.

To show your expertise in the business, provide the seller with a resume of your experience, education, and background.

Prepare and sign a statement stating that any information provided by the seller about the business will be held in confidence.

Negotiating benefits are available to you, if you are prepared and informed enough to ask for them.

Information about the existing business must be provided by the seller — usually with great reluctance. This is especially true if you are still considering buying the business and have not yet made an offer to purchase it. If you provided the above information to the seller, he will probably provide the desired information.

Make an offer on the contingency that if what the seller says is true, then you offer to buy the business. You may discover that the sales projections previously quoted do not match the IRS records. Beware of purchasing a business where the owner will not provide all of the needed information. Unwillingness to provide you with all necessary information indicates that there *are problems* with the business. These problems are probably not minor ones. Reconsider whether you want to buy the business.

You may be faced with the possibility that the owner has not kept accurate records about his business. If the owner doesn't have accurate records, he is unable to provide you with a factual picture of the business. Lower the price you are willing to pay for purchasing the business, due to the owner's inability to substantiate his claims about the business.

You need to be provided with information about the business's past and present. With this information, you will be able to fairly ascertain the future of the business. **The information you need to get from the seller to analyze the business is:**

- Past sales for the last three years. Data should show what was sold for each month and by which decorator. If the owner didn't keep accurate records, some of the information may be obtained through sales tax reports and IRS statements. If you are unable to obtain this information, you will not be able to realistically project the future sales of the business. When you are checking the sales figures, look at two sources and compare them against each other.

- An expense statement about the business. This would include rent, utilities, telephone, payroll, advertising, etc. Data for this information are usually listed in the profit and loss statements of the business. Compare the figures against the year-end tax statements and the business's checking account.

- Cost of goods sold. When provided with this information, you will be able to determine the store's gross profit (which is the money available to pay expenses after the merchandise has been paid for). Again, if the existing records provided by the business are unclear in this area, check the invoices from the suppliers of the goods. Combine this data with the business's expenses and you are able to determine the overall health of the business. **Make sure to receive accurate records for both the cost of goods sold and expenses.**

Note: if the owner has more than one location, he may have enhanced the gross profit picture of one of the locations by showing the other location paying some of the invoices. By understating the actual amount of invoices and their costs, this will drastically improve the business's net profit and make the records very inaccurate.

- If the business is a sole-proprietor or a partnership, you must be provided with information by the owners showing their personal income. This is the net profit left after paying all expenses of the business. This information is found in the owner's IRS statements. If he wants to sell the business to you, this information must be provided to you.

- Past history of the business. Who were the original owners; what major events have occurred that have caused sales to rise or fall; different advertising methods used and the results; marketing information and customer demographics (profile of their customers); suppliers used — their strong and weak points; employees; banking relationships; legal status of the business; any business problems. From a legal standpoint, it is important that this information is in a written form and signed by the sellers of the business. Chances are, if signed by the sellers, the information will not be exaggerated and will be closer to the truth. If the information is in a written form, it may be used to substantiate any legal claims that you may have later against the business.

- A list of the assets and their estimated worth. This information is needed later for tax and depreciation purposes. The asset list would include cost price of inventory (any stock that is salable); leasehold improvements (interior and exterior improvements to walls, floors, lighting, etc.); fixtures (shelving, displays, counters, etc.); equipment (cash registers, computers, copiers, safe, desks, etc.); signs (exterior and interior); business vehicles (usually for delivery or leased autos for the business); real estate (the seller may keep the title of the building and lease you the space); accounts receivable; supplies, customer lists, patents, trademarks.

- Leasing contract. In order to buy a business that is leased, be sure that the lease is transferable or assignable to you; whether it is transferable in its present form; whether the lease needs to be renegotiated and if so at what terms; what are the terms of the remaining lease; is there a renewal option; whether it is a percentage lease and if so, how is it calculated; whether this is a triple-net lease (very common in shopping centers and malls — where the lessee pays *all* costs, including property taxes, insurance, heating and air-conditioning repair and upkeep, and common-area maintenance); use clauses to cover things you can and cannot do, or hours and days you *must* be open (*common* in larger malls).
  Make sure that the lease is favorable to you and at your terms. The seller has copies of this information and is obligated to provide you with the information. The leasing arrangement is *very* important for you to examine and investigate.

Note: the present owner may be bogged down with the terms of the present leasing agreement, and want to unload the present business and start back up elsewhere with a new name and less restrictive lease.

- Asking price and terms of purchasing the business. Realize that you and the seller are looking at the asking price from opposite viewpoints. The seller is thinking, *How much can I get for the business? What is the business really worth? What price shall I ask for the business? What price and terms will I accept? How much shall I pad the price, so I can come down?*
  The buyer is thinking, *How much is the business worth? The price seems high, I don't think I can afford to buy this business. Is it better to start a new business? What problems am I buying with this business? Will the seller come down on his price? Will I be able to support the price in extra sales?*
  Realize where the owner is coming from. The owner has probably determined the price impulsively and really doesn't have much to show that will support the asking price. During good economic times, businesses sell for more; during bad economic times, businesses sell for less. How motivated is the seller? If the seller is truly motivated, he will probably be willing to take less. The price really consists of three elements: the down payment, the terms, and the security of the sale.

The owner may have determined the price by using the *multiplier method*. The gross monthly sales of a business is multiplied by anywhere from three to ten times after tax annual earnings, plus the cost of the inventory. If the seller has used this method to determine the price of his business, realize that this is only an approximate idea of what the business is worth.

Book value is another method of determining the value of a business. Book value is the difference between the company's assets and liabilities, or the net worth of the business. This approach to pricing a business has a major problem: all fixed assets are shown by their depreciated value rather than by the cost of replacing them. Replacement costs of assets are an asset's true value. If the business has been in operation for more than five years, the assets may have been completely depreciated. The assets may still be usable and in good condition, so using book value to determine the price of the business wouldn't give you a true value of the business.

The preferred method to use to determine whether a business is priced correctly is to consider the business's *potential earning power*. Potential earning power includes profit, while also including the income the owner can make and other fringe benefits such as an auto, medical insurance, travel, and entertainment. To determine the potential earning power of a business, you need to get your hands on accurate records. Regardless of what the owner says about "skimming" money and not showing it in the records, work off of the proven figures in the books.

Once you have determined the business's potential earning power, consider whether you can increase sales. Adjust the figures accordingly to decide whether or not this business is the right one for you to buy. Determine what expenses will decrease and get a grasp on the ones that will increase.

To determine what the business is worth and the price you should pay for it, calculate what you are presently earning working for someone else's business, and what you could expect to earn from the business, if you bought it, in the near future. If you see a significant difference in the two figures — your present salary versus the potential money netted with the acquisition of the new business — then your plan to buy the business may be very viable and can help justify your paying a high price.

You have the right to expect that as a business owner you will be receiving a significantly higher salary. You are taking a large risk and investing money in the venture. You need to earn a return on your investment. Later, the investment should provide you with a good income and good resale value when you sell the business. When a business has a realistic price on it, you can expect to get all of your investment back within five years, or a twenty percent annual return on your money and a good salary.

The next step is to determine how much it would cost you to set up a brand-new business the way you really want it. You should actually price the new business in a similar location with a similar setup. Now compare the asking price of the business with the cost of setting up a similar business. By determining the cost of setting up a new business with the asking price of the existing business, you are checking the value of the existing business. Determine what it would cost to build a new business up to the sales level and profit margin of the existing business.

With the purchase of the existing business, there is a built-in following of customers; the business has proven sales and profit. The negative points are that the business may be antiquated, all assets may be fairly worn out, inventory may be old, and the business image may be questionable. *Be sure that the sales are high enough to cover the note, other debts, and your salary.* If not, you are going to lose out on the deal.

Consider the method of payment for the business. Will the owner take back a note for a portion of the purchase price of the business? If so, the value of the business may increase. The less money you have to come up with for a down payment, the more value the business has for you. **Take the following points into consideration when deciding to purchase a business:**

- Most businesses can be purchased for twenty-five percent down with the seller carrying the rest of the loan.

- Most businesses are not sold for the asking price and original terms offered. Both buyer and seller must have a meeting of the minds somewhere between each other's price and terms, for a sale to happen.

- You should be able to get an interest rate that is slightly lower from the owner than your bank would charge for the same loan.

- The note may be interest-only with an entire balloon payment amount due in five years or may be a term of five to seven years with both principal and interest added in.

- You will probably use the business as security for the note. But you could use other assets as security for the note instead.

- If you can't get the seller to come down on the asking price, get him to meet you halfway on the terms of the sale.

- Quality businesses for sale are always in high demand and are in limited supply.

- Low quality, nearly failing businesses are always available to be had — usually cheap. The question is, can you turn the business into a winner in a short time?

- Even though the business may be older and the assets have seen better days, you may be able to give it a jump start and get it thriving once again. Have a plan for how you are going to turn the business around if you buy it.

- Get the owner to carry a second trust deed on the business. Pay off the second trust deed over a few years, and keep the owner on the hook and still interested in the success of the business.

- At the time of sale, prorate rent, telephone, utilities, employees' salaries, and insurance.

Buying an Existing Interior Design Business

Before you actually buy a business, you will need to make many decisions and do some serious analysis. You want the best deal and terms possible. The owner wants the highest price obtainable and wants to sell the business on his or her terms. The buyer and seller usually have different motivations, objectives, and perspectives on wanting to make a buy-sell transaction.

- Realize that you are motivated and excited about buying a business. Keep your eyes open and don't overlook important details in the excitement.

- Try to find out the real reason the owner wants to sell the business. It may not be the reason she is telling you. The owner may be over stressed, not realizing the profit or personal satisfaction she envisioned, or may feel very tied down. People's interests do change; they may simply want to do something else now or travel.

  Note: If the business is the enjoyable money maker that the owners are probably projecting to you, the owner could simply hire a manager to run the business for them.

- You must find the right business to buy.

- An accountant should analyze the provided business information to make a sound decision about going ahead with the purchase. The best records for an accountant to review are the bank statements, sales tax returns, and income tax returns. These records would probably reflect the minimum sales the business has made for the period, as most people tend to understate, rather than overstate records for tax purposes. The safest route to take to make sure that you are looking at the actual filed records is to get them from the government. Check the property tax statement filed with the tax accessor for assets of the business.

- After your accountant analyzes the records, decide if the asking price is realistic.

- Ask for employee contracts and review them to see the terms the employees are hired under.

- The negotiation phase begins. The buyer and seller must now resolve any discrepancies and differences and negotiate the terms and price of the business.

- When everyone is in agreement, then a contract is signed. The escrow phase begins.

During this process, many things are going to arise along the way. More decisions and negotiations will have to be reached.

How to Negotiate Successfully with a Seller

From the onset when working with a seller, try to be positive and upbeat, rather than pessimistic and negative. Do not put the seller on the defensive, but encourage him to provide you with the information you need to make a decision about purchasing the business. Always try to go right to the source and work with who will actually be making the final decisions on your negotiations. **Follow these points while proceeding with your negotiations:**

- Determine as quickly as possible why the owner wants to sell the business. If you are able to determine the motivation and reasons why the owner wants to sell, your negotiations can be tailored to fit the owners in some areas; the owner may bend slightly more in your favor in other directions. The owner may be burned out, ill, or want to move as quickly as possible from the area. If so, he may be willing to reduce the price.

  Other owners may be just fishing to see if there is a possibility of someone paying their illusionary price. They are not serious sellers.

- Realize that the business is probably not perfect. There are some flaws and that is probably why it is up for sale. As you start to look around, you will soon spot the businesses that look like ones you could make a go of and other businesses that seem doomed for failure.

- Proceed with negotiations to buy the business in a *timely* manner. Don't rush the owner, but do not be slow in reacting when asked to supply needed paperwork.

- Make reasonable offers to purchase the business. If you make unreasonable offers that offend the owner, you will destroy his trust, put him on the defensive, and create a tense atmosphere between both of you. The owner may feel insulted and decide not to bend an inch on the negotiations and asking price. He may not even want to sell the business to you, let alone train you to take over.

  If the price does seem excessive to you, ask the owner to please justify and explain how and why he arrived at the asking price. Have him list the assets and his perceived value. When an owner starts listing his assets, it is hard to justify an overpriced business, and he may just come down to meet you part way once he sees that the price does seem out of line. The negotiations may become simpler after that.

- Get in writing all seller warranties that the owner is claiming. For example: owner knows of no zoning changes or pending lawsuits and he owns all assets free and clear.

- Get in writing all seller obligations and risk after escrow closes. For example: owner will train you and work for you for a specific period of time, will pay certain expenses, etc.

- Include an attorney fee stipulation for who will pay the legal fees should either party go to court over a legal dispute. Have the losing party pay the attorney fees.

- Include an arbitration clause stating that in the event of a legal dispute, both parties agree to arbitration and agree to be bound by rules of American Arbitration System.

- Hang around the business you would like to purchase. Talk to suppliers, customers, and employees. Find out as much as you can about the business's negative points and positive points. Don't tell what you are going to do to improve the business and improve sales. If you do, the seller may feel insulted and become hard to work with, or the seller may implement your ideas and not sell the business.

- Make the seller feel like he is the expert and is very much appreciated during the days that he trains you. Act like you know what you are doing, but appreciate all the help that the seller will give you.

How to Take Over an Existing Business

- Listen to what the seller has to say. She knows all about the business. Ask her to stay and train you for a period of time.

- Discuss the business with customers. Get their opinions. They are the reason you are in business.

- Make new changes slowly, one at a time.

- Determine the crucial areas of the business and go to work on them immediately.

- Minimize conflicts with employees by keeping a low profile at first. Discuss their areas of concern with them. Ask for their opinions, but do not make them feel that they are very much in control.

- Start on the worst problem areas and solve them one at a time.

- Have a written plan and timetable to follow.

- Make contact with suppliers you intend on working with. Establish rapport with them.

- Don't immediately jump in and change the name of the business.

- Spread out your expenditures. Wisely decide where your limited funds will be spent.

- Get the employees excited about the new business, its image, and you by projecting pride and enthusiasm for owning the business. If they like you and what you are doing they will work harder and try harder.

Buying a Franchise Business

Buying a franchise is the easiest way to start your own interior design business and involves less overall risk than starting a new business. Essentially, you buy a prepackaged concept, pay a monthly fee, and operate your business under the contract set out by the franchisor.

Name recognition is an important valued benefit of the franchise package. You gain instant credibility. Due to national advertising, prospects probably have heard of the franchise company. Unfortunately, the higher degree of name recognition and acceptance, the higher the price of the franchise opportunity.

Starting up a business under a franchise system will not guarantee you success, but will certainly reduce your risks. The franchisor has made many of the mistakes that will come up before you and troubleshoots the operation, before you are involved. He has put together the package that has been successful for him.

Franchisors usually provide training, have a complete prepackaged image for your business, help you with the site selection and store design, and supply you with a plan to run your new franchise business.

The downside to buying a franchise is that it is expensive and you are not independent. You must adhere to the rules of the contract. Before venturing into buying a franchise operation, make sure to completely check out the operation.

Thanks to Federal Trade Commission Disclosure Requirements, effective October 21, 1979, the Basic Disclosure Document must disclose the twenty different categories of information to potential buyers of a franchise:

1.   Name of the franchisor.

2.   Franchisor's directors and officers, and their experience.

3.   Franchisor's business background.

4.   Past litigation.

5.   Past bankruptcies.

6.   Description of the franchise.

7.   Amount of up-front money required by a potential franchisee.

8.   Monthly or continuing required franchise fees.

9.   Any associated parties the franchisee is required/advised to do business with.

10.   Any purchasing commitments.

11.   Amounts of revenues collected by franchisor for franchisee purchases.

12.   Any available financing.

13.   Any sales constraints.

14.   Personal participation requirements of the franchisee in the operation of the franchise.

15.   Terms of termination, cancellation, and renewal of the franchise.

16.   Number of franchises and company owned outlets, their locations, and other statistics.

17.   Selected sites.

18.   Training programs.

19.   Public figure interest in the franchise.

20.   Franchisor's financial information.

Advantages to Buying a Franchise Business

- You get name recognition and a concept that usually works fairly well. You consequently will usually have immediate business.

- Use of a system that has already proven to work. The risks of failure are minimized more than if you start a new business or buy an existing one. Your chances of success are improved. The franchisor has made the mistakes for you and now knows the better course of action to take in all areas. Consequently, you will be reducing tremendously a portion of your start-up costs.

- You receive training on exactly how to run the business. A complete blueprint on how to run the business is laid out for you. By following the plan, you avoid expensive mistakes. The training (usually from one to six weeks) may be at your new site, or at the headquarters of the franchisor.

- Expert company and staff support. You will receive ongoing assistance, recommendations, and suggestions from the headquarters and from the field representatives that will be visiting you regularly. You will receive newsletters, training manuals (for yourself and employees), and have regular seminars to attend. Affordable legal assistance, accounting, cost controlling, and marketing support is usually provided. If you were to subcontract for these services you would pay much more.

- Franchise businesses are set up on a consistent accounting system, buying system, and inventory system customized to your exact operation. With a franchise system you will also be reporting to them regularly on their forms so they can track everything you do.

- You will receive national advertising and marketing assistance. They will come in and actually study the demographics of the area and do a marketing and site survey.

- The image of the company is planned and usually already well known through advertising efforts. If you are going to buy a franchise operation, it is preferable to go with the company that is nationally known rather than the unknown company that is offering you its packaging concept. Pick up those customers that will call you due to name recognition from the franchise name, since you are paying substantially to have a franchise operation.

- The interior and the exterior of the store is planned out for you. Layout of fixtures and displays is consistent with the next operation. You essentially get a turnkey operation. Take over when you are actually ready to start the business operating.

- The franchisor will negotiate the lease *for you*. If you are not comfortable working out the terms with the landlord, the franchisor's legal department will handle the details (it is hoped to your advantage).

- Less capital may be required. Financial assistance may be available to applicants with good credit and collateral. Normally, you will make periodic payments instead of a large down payment for the initial franchise fee, inventory, and other expenses to start the business. If you are not financially credible, you will not receive financial assistance and may not be allowed to become a franchisee.

- Suppliers are already set up for you. Products may or may not be more expensive. You may or may not be required to buy the products from the suggested suppliers. You may have better purchasing power due to the volume purchasing of the franchise.

- You will receive higher profits when you sell the business. Once your business has a proven track record, the business can be easily sold.

Disadvantages to Buying a Franchise Business

- There may be long-term liabilities. To keep the front-end costs down, the franchisor may require the franchisee to pay for a portion of equipment, facilities cost, or franchise fees over a specific period of time. Should your business fail or be sold, you still have to make the payments.

- Ownership of the franchise may be indeterminate. After you buy the franchise, you find out that you really don't own much. Most of the assets are leased (equipment and real property) and your franchise fee pays for privileges, not assets. Recoverable assets are restricted.

- Because of the royalty fee and the preselected products that you must sell, the pricing of goods and services offered for sale is not competitive with pricing of your competitors. If the customer shops around, you will not get the sale, unless she wants to buy your recognized name and image.

- Hidden or masqueraded start-up costs. These start-up costs may include the one-time-only franchise fee, lease-hold improvements, and real estate purchases.

- You are managed and not in control of the decisions and operations of the business. You will really be and feel like an employee of your own business.

- The name, image, logo, products, pricing concepts, and store policies will be standardized and probably not be the ones you would select for a business that you would start from scratch.

- You will lose your business flexibility, creativity (advertising, display, image, name, logo, etc.), and authority of having a business that is solely yours.

- You will be *required* to work long hours. Any business you start at the onset will demand that you put in enough time to get the business off the ground. The franchisor may command you to work a certain number of hours per week.

- Franchise operations are expensive to own and operate. If you have experience already and will try and get the experience and education in your weak areas, starting a new business is the preferable, much less-expensive way to go.

- Franchise operations have a monthly royalty fee. This fee ranges from two percent to ten percent of your gross receipts. If you had your own operation, this would be profit for you.

- You may be required to pay an advertising co-op fee for advertising.

- There may be hidden equipment costs. All equipment must be uniform from one franchise to the next. To control the equipment you use, the franchisor will require you to purchase the equipment from them.

- The franchise contract tells you exactly how you must run the business. In general, franchise contracts are very restrictive and consistent with each of the franchisees. If you do not like to feel controlled in virtually everything you do regarding the business, this is not the business for you. The franchisor probably has the capital and legal means to back up their lengthy contract if a dispute arises. If sales are going good, you would probably try to get along and go along with the operation. If sales are bad, potential problems with the operation are going to arise.

- Business market capability is confined to your assigned geographical area. Your rights extend only to the area specified in the contract. You will not be able to work someone else's area. If you had your own business, you could expand into other areas at will. You could develop chain or franchise operations nationally if you chose to.

- Should the franchisor go out of business, you are still liable for your financial obligations.

How to Find Out About Available Franchise Packages

Your local bookstore or library carries annual franchise books that list the top or current franchise operations by category. Review the book by category and description to find if any of the franchise operations offered appeal to you.

Write to the companies for their information and literature packages. Try to find a franchise operation that will match as closely as possible the operation you want to set up.

Franchise operations are regulated by law. Federal Trade Commission Rule 436 mandates that the franchisor is required to furnish a potential franchisee a full disclosure statement. This is also known as the *Uniform Offering Circular*. This statement, coupled with the franchise contract, must be presented to you ten days before you pay any money or any contracts are signed. Failure to supply these documents results in the franchisor being fined up to $10,000 per day. Because of negligence in the past, the government now keeps a closer watch and regulates franchise businesses.

When considering the purchase of a franchise, keep accurate dated records of all conversations in person or over the phone with the representatives of the franchisor. You may need these records later to document a dispute that may come up.

Realize that the franchisor's representative will present the franchise opportunity in the most positive way possible. The potential earnings that the franchisor is claiming to you *must* have a reasonable basis to support the figures thanks to the Federal Trade Commission. The franchisor must provide the data to support their claims in projected profits to you. And if you do request the data, the claims presented to you must be in a similar geographical area as the one you are considering.

Consider the worst possible case scenario concerning this presented data. Can you still succeed if your sales do not meet projections? What if the expenses of running the business are higher than projected? When discussing the acquisition of a franchise with the franchisor's representative, cover these following points:

- What is the franchisor's position in the industry? Is it a large or small company?

- What are the capital requirements for running this type of business?

- Is this a recession-proof business not susceptible to economic fluctuations?

- What is the number of franchises presently in operation and their locations.

- What is the national and regional system size?

- How long has the company been selling franchises? When was the initial store first formed?

- What is the growth rate of the franchisor?

- Does the size of the franchise operation give each franchisee mass buying power?

- Who is the main competition?

- Does the franchise have name recognition? How well known is the franchise?

- Does the franchisee receive a protected trade area? How large is the protected area?

- What is the success ratio of the franchise? How many franchisees have not been successful and have gone out of business? Why did they fail?

- Have any of the franchisees ever sued the franchisor? Why did they sue? What was the outcome of the suit?

- If disputes between the franchisor and the franchisee arise, how are they usually resolved?

- How much are the franchises really making in actual profits? Compare this information against the franchisor's pro forma or financial assumption sheet.

- Exactly what does the franchise package include? What does the training consist of? Is there field assistance on site? Someone to answer questions over the phone? Is there a training program to attend?

- Does the franchise package include exterior and interior store design, layout, marketing, site selection, demographics and market analysis, and needed construction?

- What does the franchisor offer in the way of support? Motivational incentives?

- With regard to the initial capital that is required for a deposit to buy the franchise package, where is this money used?

- How much extra money is actually needed beyond the original investment to get the business off of the ground? For the first year?

- How much per month are the royalties? What do you receive in exchange for the royalty check? Is the money going back into the business? Are some of the royalties paid back out in the form of stocks and dividends?

- Does the corporate office have advertising programs that are paid for out of the royalty fees?

- Do the franchisees in the area pay an association fees that is used as an advertising fund? Do the franchisees advertise as one group?

- Does the franchisor sponsor programs? Are the franchisees required to participate?

- Are you assigned a particular advertising territory that you must stay within? How are you protected from another franchisor infringing on your territory?

- How many more locations are planned to be added? Where? How close to this one?

- What new concepts for the franchise are planned for the future? Any new products? Is the advertising going to be the same?

- Is the pricing competitive for all products offered? What are the products?

- What happens if I want to sell or terminate the business? What if I decide to renew the franchise agreement?

- Does the company ever terminate franchise agreements? Why?

- What happens if I have other merchandise and use other suppliers? What are the potential problems with the franchisor?

- Is there any financing available? What are the terms?

- What is the company's current financial condition?

- Who are the principals of the company? Are they from the interior design industry? Who owns the company?

- Number of hours daily and weekly required to run the business?

- Number of employees needed to adequately run the business?

- What are the inventory requirements?

Get answers to the above questions to make a sound decision about making a purchase of a franchise. Beware if the representative doesn't want to cooperate or take the time to answer your questions. You will pay plenty over the long haul for a franchise. Settle for a quality franchise. **Some of the tip-offs that the franchise you are considering may not be a good one to buy:**

- Refusal by the representative to supply a list of all of the franchises in operation.

- Interest in separating you from your money as quickly as possible.

- Insisting that you put down a deposit immediately to secure a location or territory.

- Trying to make you feel anxious about losing out on the territory if you don't move on the deal immediately.

- If they avoid or change the subject when you ask the above questions.

- Insistence that you do not need to waste your money to have an attorney look at the contract.

Talk to Other Franchise Owners of the *Same* Franchise

If you're dealing with a quality franchisor, they will not hesitate to supply you with a list of the existing franchisees. Make personal visits to as many of the nearby franchisees as possible. Call up a few others. If you are friendly, letting them know that you were given their name to contact by the franchisor's sales representative, they will probably be very willing to talk to you. Try to set an appointment that would be convenient for you to visit the franchisee. Get right to the point and ask about your concerns. They will be able to relate to your questions; they were once standing in the same spot as you. Let them know that the fact that you even contacted them will not be divulged to the sales representative of the franchisor or to anyone else. Let them know that you cannot afford to fail financially with the business and would appreciate that they be honest with their answers to your questions. Key questions to ask an existing franchisee:

- How has it been to work with the franchisor? Have they been helpful or do they tend to find fault? Do you feel that they are an honest company?

- Do you consider the figures in the pro forma statements to be accurate? Or do the figures tend to be under- or overstated?

- Are you making the amount of sales that you were expecting to make? Is the amount of money you are making what you projected?

- What type of assistance did you receive from the company when starting up? Did they follow through and deliver on *everything* that they said they would initially? In what areas do you feel they are lacking in their performance?

- Are they still providing assistance and training as needed for your company? Does the amount of support and assistance justify the high royalty fees?

- Do you feel that the pricing of the products and services is competitive in the marketplace? Is the quality above or below your closest competitors?

- Do the advertising, public relations, and promotional programs provided by the company work well? How do you feel about their cost to you? Is the price fair in light of the results?

- What are the negative points about the franchisor? Would you buy the franchise again if you were in my position?

- Is the contract easy to work with? Is there something in the contract that I should really take note of and try to negotiate or reconsider?

- How much money do you really feel is needed to be successful with the franchise?

- When you first opened, were their any significant problems that came up that you didn't expect?

- What major problems are you faced with today?

- Are their any franchisees that you know about that wish they had not invested in the franchise?

- How long have you had the franchise? Did you start it up at this location? Why did you opt to start a franchise rather than start a new business or buy an existing business?

- Is the net income enough for all of the negatives you must deal with?

How to Check Out the Franchisor

In order to check out the franchisor you need to find out if the franchise company is publicly held or privately held. A publicly held company is one that has its stock sold on one of the stock exchanges. A privately held company is one that is owned by private investors.

If the company is publicly held, your information search is relatively easy. Call the company and ask for an annual report and a 10-K report. The 10-K report will offer much information on who is involved with the franchise company, what type of business they are in or were in, whether or not there are pending lawsuits against the company, and the financial situation of the company. You will note that some of the above information is also on the disclosure statement that was required by law to be provided.

If the company is privately held, have a Dun and Bradstreet report run on the company by your bank. The bank may or may not charge for this service, but it's worth it. Also contact the Better Business Bureau, your state agencies that are concerned with franchise companies, the Federal Trade Commission, your area consumer fraud department, and your local chamber of commerce.

Franchise Up-Front and Royalty Fees

The negative aspects of owning a franchise business are the up-front costs, monthly royalty fees, and the restrictive contract that you must sign. Again, the advantage to a franchise business is the reduced risk you are faced with by owning a proven enterprise. You must trade one for the other when going ahead with buying a franchise package. Decide if the price of the royalty fees and the restrictive contract outweigh the merits of having a known, proven concept.

Determine what is included in the package deal. Is it an entire package? An entire package is the whole business virtually set up and ready to go. You use their program, logo, name, etc.

Add up what it would cost you to start a similar new business. Use this projected figure and compare it against the money that is required of you up-front to buy the franchise package. Compare other companies' franchise packages against each other. Then negotiate with the franchisor to get the price down. Is the area saturated with this type of franchise already, or does the franchisor want to get into the area as soon as possible? This would be a key negotiating point. They may allow you to spread your up-front fees out over a longer period of time with a low interest rate.

The biggest concern is the monthly royalty fee that must be paid to the franchisor. The fee typically varies from three percent to six percent. Realize that since you are opting for an easier way to start a business with a proven concept, you are opting to give away net profit that would otherwise be yours. How much profit do you really think you will be left with? You need to be rewarded for the stress, long hours, lean years, risks, pressures, problems, etc. Do not line everyone else's pockets, from your landlord to your suppliers, without lining your own pockets as well.

Franchise Contracts

Franchise contracts usually consist of numerous pages written by attorneys in legalese to protect the franchise operation. Laws regarding franchises today have toned down what can and cannot be requested of prospective franchisees.

Hire an attorney to review your contract. Find one that is familiar with franchise contracts who may point out the positive and negative features. Your attorney can negotiate and attempt to change any disagreeable points for you. After both parties have reached agreement, have *your* attorney rewrite the areas that you have come to terms on. Anything that comes up verbally during the negotiations that are not written down in the contract should be written out and included in the contract by your attorney, also. **The important points to be considered when reviewing the contract are:**

● What will you get for your money?

● Must you participate in company promotional programs that will cost you extra money?

● Is it required by the franchisor that you must purchase your supplies and merchandise from the franchisor?

● What do the continuing support, services, and training consist of?

● What are the restrictions you must abide by?

● Why would the franchisor terminate your contract?

● Are you able to sell, terminate, or transfer your franchisee agreement to someone else? What are the rules?

● When does the franchise contract expire? What is the renewal or buy-back procedure?

Last Points to Consider Before Purchasing a Franchise

- Is an interior design business the business you really want to have? Does the franchise business offered fit your wants?

- Can you afford the required fees?

- Can you work with this company? How about the individual people?

- Are the existing franchisees happy?

- How long have they been in business? How long have they been franchising? What is their reputation?

- Will you be able to abide by their rules and regulations? How about being supervised by the headquarters? Audited? Questioned over every discrepancy?

- Can you succeed in starting your own business? Do you have enough experience and knowledge? Do you need the ongoing support of a franchise company?

- Is it a fair price to pay to have the business set up? How about the price for name recognition?

- What did your attorney think about the contract? What was her opinion overall?

- Is this a realistic thing for you to do? Are your projections practical?

- Will you be happy with the projected income? Have you checked out these figures and do you feel that they are realistic?

- Is the selected location a good one?

Part 3

Location, Location, Location

Selection of the Right Community

The location will affect all aspects of your retail operation. It could mean the difference between your firm's success or failure if you are attempting to capture a large portion of drive-by or walk-by customers.

The first thing to do is to define your firm's operation in terms of the objectives you are trying to achieve. Write down these objectives. Define the demographics of various locations in terms of age of the surrounding population, income, family size, surrounding competition, and traffic patterns in the areas of consideration. Defining these factors is vital to selection of a successful location.

When you spot a tentative location, use the demographic data and check several more aspects of the location to ensure your satisfaction and success at the selected site.

Beware of being in too much of a hurry when making a site location. Selecting the right site takes time, patience, perseverance, and careful analysis. Don't make the mistake of *settling* for a location that lacks several qualities that you need. It is better to *hold off* opening your business than to *settle* for an inferior location that may put you out of business very quickly.

One of the key decisions that will ensure your success or failure is the location you select for your business. As the familiar saying goes: location, location, location, is *everything* to your business. A good location is the site where your business can make the most money. A desirable location with a large customer base to draw from, will help a struggling business succeed; an undesirable location with a limited customer base will *allow* a potentially successful business to fail. **These are the factors and questions to consider when selecting the community in which to open your business:**

- Decide if you will be going to your customers, or if will they be coming in to your business, or both. Which of the two will happen more often?

- Where do you and your family want to live?

- Determine if there is *available* opportunity for growth in the community. Is the community thriving economically; are there good locations available for your type of business; what is the competition in the area? Select a growing community, rather than a community that shows weak development.

- Is the community supported by several industries rather than one or two large industries that could lay off people by the thousands and cause the whole community economic distress?

- *Who* is your target market customer? Where are your customers located?

- Are you attempting to target only one community? If so, locate in the center of the community. If you are attempting to reach other surrounding communities, locate on the outskirts of town so both customer bases have easy access to you, and you have easy access to them.

- What is the tax base for the city or town? Adjacent cities can vary widely on the tax basis they charge businesses.

- What is the community's laws about exterior signs? Some communities have very strict policies concerning size and display of signs. Signs are a very important advertising medium for an interior design business. You must constantly strive to remind potential customers of your business. Heavy restrictions by a community about sign placements will severely cut down your business.

- Will prospective employees be able to afford housing within a reasonable distance to the location?

How to Determine the Health and Potential of a Community

- Is the community growing, prospering, or stagnant? Do you see a surge of large chain stores (grocery, department, discount) opening or planning to open in the community? Large chain stores extensively study sites and communities before moving ahead to open up in new areas.

- The demographic profile of the area fits the type of customer you are seeking for your business. The income and consumer awareness of interior design match the type of target customer you are pursuing. Analyze the residents' ages, spendable income (do they have much money left after paying for their housing costs and food?), economic level, etc. Note that even if the community is comprised largely of seniors, they may have all the furniture they need, but are excellent customers for floor coverings, wall coverings, and window coverings. They usually have the money and appreciate quality.

- Local industries are thriving and growing rather than downsizing. There are jobs available.

- Real estate values in the area are on the upswing or holding their value. There is new construction in residential homes and commercial businesses.

- There are *few* vacancies in commercial locations. All of the surrounding business seem to be doing well.

If these factors are or seem negative in the community you are considering, reconsider locating your business there. You need *everything* in your favor when opening a business. It is difficult enough starting a business without starting it in a negative economic climate.

The local chamber of commerce and local banks can supply you with information on the growth or decline of the area.

How to Analyze the *Economic* Potential of a Community

- Write to the U.S. Department of Commerce, Bureau of the Census, to obtain a detailed business census report of *individual home furnishings or drapery, curtains, and upholstery stores* for your state or metropolitan area.
  This information will tell you how many stores there are of this type in the United States, the national average sales of these stores, and how many customers patronize these types of establishments.

- Gather census data on the population of the community.

- Look through the yellow pages of the phone book of the community. How many *other* interior design businesses like your are already listed in the phone book?

- *Divide* the number of adults into the number of existing interior design businesses like yours. *Compare* the net number against the amount of customers listed in the census data report information on individual home furnishings or drapery, curtains, and upholstery stores.
  Does the community appear as if it has an overabundance of available customers or does it look as if there aren't enough customers to go around?

- Talk to suppliers and business owners in the interior design market (can be in related businesses) to get their opinions about adding another interior design business to the community.

- Investigate the competition. Does each competitor appear to be growing or declining with their amount of business? What condition (appearance) is their studio or store in? Do they *seem* to have enough advertising dollars? Are they putting their advertising and marketing money to the best use? What type of people does the competition employ — professionals or *inadequately* trained people with limited knowledge?

- What quality of advertising is available in the community for your use? Is it affordable and cost-effective? Ask around or phone small businesses that use the various available advertising methods; ask about response to the ads.

- If you are adding an interior design business to a community with several other interior design businesses, how will your business be an improvement over the other existing interior design firms?

Even if the community shows an overabundance of interior design businesses like yours, if the existing businesses are not putting their marketing and advertising efforts to their best use and are employing inexperienced people, you may *easily* be able to take over the market and put them right out of business.

Deciding on an *Exact* Location

- Determine where all your *major* competition is located. Mark the locations on a map. Don't locate a new, struggling business near a popular established interior design business of the same type. You *will* have serious trouble competing.

  Look for a site that is located near a large shopping center, on a busy street, or in a smaller shopping center in an area not already saturated with competition.

  If the competition doesn't have its act together, is not treating its customers well, is excessively charging for its products and services, etc., locating nearby can actually work to your advantage (if your business improves on their drawbacks). Your business can capitalize on their built-up customer following and advertising dollars.

- Select a location that is easy to find and highly visible. If you skip these two factors, prospective customers will not be able to find you.

- A site that has abundant walk-by traffic is *highly* preferable to one that has only drive-by traffic. If you can effectively decorate the windows and keep the displays current, you will find people make an effort to take a look at what you are displaying for the next design trend.

- Drive-by traffic will save you a great deal of money in marketing and advertising. You should actually count the cars during different periods of the day to see how many cars are going by. Compare rush hours to slack times of the day. The types of people driving by should also be considered. Pick a poor drive-by location and you will only get customers by spending advertising dollars or those who are referred by other customers.

  Compare the various sites you are considering with each other. Which site has more drive-by and foot traffic? Select the site that has the largest amount of traffic going by (foot and cars) that is affordable for your company.

- Keep the rent of the space under ten percent of your estimated sales. Some landlords will require you to pay a percentage of your sales. Therefore, your monthly rent will be a flat rate, a percentage of gross sales over a certain set amount, or a combination of the three. Ask the owner for several months free rent for the desired site.

- Your business location should be *easily* accessible for customers and deliveries. Make sure that the site you select can have large trucks deliver at that location.

- Determine how successful other businesses in the immediate area are. Do some research. Find out if a business similar to yours *has been* or is still in business in the vicinity of the desired location. How did the business do? How is it doing? Learn from the mistakes of others. If a few businesses in the area are failing, this may not be a good location.

- Find out how good a deal on the rent or lease you can make with the owner. Review the leasing section of this book.

- Determine if any governmental zoning and ordinances will affect the location. Don't get stuck paying fines because the building you have selected doesn't meet building and zoning regulations.

Evaluation of the Business Site

Retail Compatibility:
Most businesses starting out in their first year of operation are *limited* in their available promotion and advertising dollars. You need to locate your business near other businesses that will be compatible with and generate traffic for your store or studio. Do not locate your business near other businesses that will compete with or clash with your operation.

If you are picking a mall location, you need to locate in the area of the mall that will be conducive to the type of goods you are selling. Locate near other furniture stores, wallpaper stores, or bathroom and bedroom accessory shops. These stores carry related goods, but not necessarily exactly the same products that you sell. If there are areas of the mall where lines form, such as outside movie theaters or restaurants, this is an ideal location if you have exciting and innovative window displays for people to inspect while waiting. Have a holder attached to your door that holds flyers and brochures for potential customers to take with them.

Merchant Associations:
Merchant associations can be very effective in promoting your business. Be sure to look into the available associations at your site location. You may be able to participate in cooperative advertising, group insurance plans, and collective security measures. Together the association as a whole is a strong entity to work and lobby together for needed community improvements. Ask other store owners in the immediate site location about the available merchant associations in the area.

Merchant associations can be effective in promoting stores using common themes or events during holiday seasons. Together, several stores will be able to draw more customers than one attempting to do it alone.

Find out how many members the association has; who the officers are; how often the group meets; what the yearly dues are; and what the association has been able to accomplish in the past year. Ask for a copy of the last meeting's minutes before you sign up. Also inquire how many members showed up at the meeting.

If you find out there isn't a merchant association or there is an ineffective one in the area of your desired location, that is a possible sign that the shopping center or mall is in a declining state. The obvious signs will probably be visible — trash and litter strewn about, vacant storefronts, parking area in disrepair, and other obvious signs. Take these as warning signs for you to select *another* site location for your store or studio.

Zoning and Planning:
Check the desired area zoning commission for the latest mapping of the site and surrounding location that you are strongly considering. Most zoning commissions, boards, and economic and regional development committees plan several years in advance. **Ask these questions of the zoning commission:**

- What restrictions, currently or in the future, are there that could hinder or limit your type of operation?

- What future construction or changes in the area's traffic or construction of new highways will be taking place in the future that may hamper traffic at the desired site location?

- Are there any expected zoning changes in the future that would limit your operation or probably encourage competitors to move in and compete with you in your desired area?

Landlord Considerations:

Ask the store owners in the shopping center, mall, immediate area, or the desired site location (if they haven't yet moved out) just how *responsive* the landlord is regarding the needs of other merchants. By talking with the present and previous tenants you will gain valuable information such as why they moved, how their business is actually doing, if they will renew their leases, and if they could rent from this landlord again, would they? Some landlords actually hinder a store's operation rather than help it.

- Does the landlord do the required maintenance or repairs in a timely manner? Does the landlord spend the necessary money to keep up the property, or does he or she seem *unwilling or unable* to spend the money required to do so?

- Does the landlord care to whom or to what type of business operation he or she rents adjacent storefronts to? Will the landlord put a direct competitor in the same mall or center? Your business's future may be impaired if the landlord will not cooperate in helping your business succeed.

- Are there sign placement and size restrictions levied by the landlord? Any other policies that will hamper marketing plans?

- Is the landlord easy or hard to work with? Are there seemingly unnecessary rules and regulations?

- Does the landlord return phone calls in a timely manner? Do you have to stay on top of him or her to get anything done? Does the landlord collect the rent and not appear until the next month's rent day? Is the landlord sympathetic to the needs and desire of the tenants? Just how supportive is the landlord toward new ideas?

Available Sources of Help for Site Location:

If your desired site location is a highly populated area (more than 125,000 people), the local chamber of commerce should have a division devoted to assisting prospective business owners, free of charge, with site locations.

The Small Business Administration (SBA) has field offices throughout the United States. The SBA provides free counseling assistance, guidance, information, and literature to help you make a qualified decision about site location. It is located under the U.S. government section of your telephone book.

Consultants are available for hire to analyze and select the best of several locations. If you do your homework ahead of time and provide them with several possibilities, rather than have them do all of the legwork for you, the cost of their services will be much less.

Local bankers are in the position to know what areas are good ones to set up businesses in and which areas to avoid. They know which ones are high on survival and which ones are high in failure.

Area real estate professionals can also provide you with information on locations. Take their information and realize that they are paid on commission and will probably be somewhat biased.

Location Description:

- Appearance of overall surrounding area.

- Appearance of actual site.

- Terms of the lease.

- Room for expansion.

- Type of traffic — auto and foot and what type of people are passing by.

- Amount of auto traffic.

- Access to public transportation.

- Available parking.

- Easy accessibility.

- Easy to find.

- Access to suppliers and warehousing of deliveries.

- Site advantages.

- Site disadvantages.

Building Information:
- History of occupants.

- Problems occupants faced.

- Physical condition of the building — interior and exterior.

- Necessary repairs required — who will do them, you or the landlord?

- Interior layout and traffic patterns.

- Floor covering.

- Interior lighting and exterior lighting.

- Heating and air conditioning.

- Exterior sign requirements and limitations.

- Fire protection.

- Security system.

- Present color scheme.

- Present wall covering — how easy is it to change?

- Available equipment.

- Equipment needed.

Area Economics:
- What are the main sources of income for the area?

- Will the business flow be steady or seasonal?

- Growth of area — new industries, new homes, new roads.

- Activity in and out of the general area.

Population:

- General levels of income.

- Average income.

- Is the population growing or decreasing?

- General age groups.

- Population educational levels.

- Employment and unemployment patterns.

- Quantity of homes owned and rented in the area.

- Population changes.

Competition:

- Main competitors.

- Number of competitors — direct and indirect.

- Size of main competitors.

- General customer opinion of competitors.

- History of failed competitors for the area — who failed and why?

Other Things to Consider:

- How much space do you actually need for your business?

- Are the available parking spaces adequate for your needs?

- Is the lighting sufficient?

- If the desired location is secluded, will your advertising expenses be considerably higher?

- Will the desired area supply you with the required employees?

- How is the fire and police protection for the area?

- Is the available sanitation or utility supply sufficient?

- Does the site have adequate exterior lighting to show display windows and make your location visible at night?

- Are there public rest rooms available in the area?

- Is the location easy to find; does it have easy access for cars and delivery trucks?

- Does the site have exterior awnings to provide shelter during bad weather?

- Will crime insurance be prohibitively expensive for the location?

- Are the adjacent stores locked into seasonal business or year-around business?

- Is the location convenient to your home?

- Are the target market customers you are seeking located nearby?

- Does the area have a population dense enough to support your business?

Part 4

Leases, Signs, and Alternate Locations

Leases

Leasing property is a good alternative to buying property because you do not have to come up with a large down payment when you purchase real estate. You are also not stuck with a property that you may have difficulty selling later. On the other hand, you will not be building any equity in the property, the lease amount may be raised, or you may be out on the street looking for a new site. With leasing property, as with buying real estate, there are specific tax advantages available.

Before you go ahead and sign a lease, be sure to check the future zoning plans for the immediate area of the desired site location. Decide how long you will want to keep your operation at the selected site.

- Are you planning to operate your business at the location indefinitely or for a certain number of years?

- Is there room for expansion at the selected location?

- Is the lease agreement flexible, allowing you to have an option to renew after a specific time period?

- Is the lease of a limited, realistic time period that may be canceled if you should decide that the location is not the right one?

- Is the rent based on sales volume or is it a fixed amount every month?

- Are you receiving as much protection from the lease as the owner of the property? Or is it completely one-sided?

- Can the site be sublet?

- Be sure that any and all promises from the owner about property improvements, repairs, construction, decorating, alterations, and maintenance are in writing.

- Will you be able to obtain a zoning "certificate of occupancy" for your type of business?

- What licenses will you need to operate an interior design businesses at this location?

Types of Leases

- **Gross leases:** The tenant of the building pays a flat monthly rate. The landlord pays for the expenses to keep the building in operation. These expenses include repairs, taxes, and insurance. Normally the utilities are charged to the tenant on a separate bill from the landlord or the tenant is billed by the utility company. This type of lease is usually found in residential rentals, and may be found in office space.

- **Net lease:** The most common method to use in a office lease. Tenants pay for most or all of the operating costs and property taxes in addition to the base rent.

■ **Net, net leases:** Tenants also pay for ordinary repairs and maintenance, insurance, operating costs and property taxes.

■ **Net, net, net (triple net leases):** Usually found on industrial properties and in shopping centers. Tenants pay all of the costs of operating the building and capital improvements. All building repairs are included (maintenance may be on a *required* regular schedule with a licensed contractor doing the work).

■ **Percentage leases:** Usually found in shopping centers and used only for the leasing of retail space. In addition to one of the above leasing arrangements (usually the net, net, net lease), the tenant must also pay a percentage of the gross sales to the landlord when a certain level of sales is reached. Be sure to note how the percentage lease is calculated when you consider this arrangement. Is there a minimum amount that must be paid monthly should you not make your quotas?

How to Negotiate a Lease

One of the most important contracts an owner of a business will be required to sign is the lease for the building. The key points to consider *before* signing a lease are outlined below.

● How long is the term of the lease? Typical leases for buildings run between three to ten years in term. This is usually a negotiable point with the landlord. Set a specific time limit on when the lease starts and when it actually ends. Define within the contract what happens if the space isn't ready by the move-in date. How much will the landlord deduct for your inability to use the space? Make sure that you don't give an exact final date on vacating your present premises.

● How much is the rental payment per month? Rents for commercial buildings are usually determined by the annual cost per square foot of the interior space. (See the preceding section on types of leases for information on the various leases and the way rental rates are determined.)

● How *soon* will the rent be raised? How *much* will the rent be raised? Leases usually have an escalation clause built into them to protect the landlord against rising costs of ownership. Some of the escalation clauses are in the form of step-ups and others simply pass on the extra costs to the tenant. A common escalation clause for leases is to tie in the rent raises with the consumer price index or other comparable price index.

   If the tenant has already agreed to pay for the escalation of the property taxes and other operating taxes, the tenant should not agree to also pay the total portion of the increase of the price index. Be very careful here if the building is a new one and the landlord does not have previous years' figures to compare the costs against.

● May I sublease the space? Understandably you will need to find a suitable tenant for the space. Determine that if the space is sublet, *who* will be the recipient of an overpayment in rent, should that occur.

● Can the lease be renewed? At what terms? Have a clause written into the leasing agreement guaranteeing that you get the first rights of renewal at a favorable rental rate when your lease expires. Realize that you must give written notice to exercise this right or the right of renewal will automatically lapse. If it is a long-term lease, give notice about a year ahead. For shorter term leases, several months ahead would be sufficient. Unless you take steps to terminate a lease, it may be set up to automatically renew. Some companies prefer to set up their leases with an automatic renewal to prevent the lease from canceling beneath them, leaving them without a building to occupy.

● Who pays the insurance on the building? The building landlord should carry a comprehensive insurance policy that covers liability for common areas including the lobbies, stairways, and elevators. This policy should also provide casualty insurance for the building. Landlords generally demand that tenants provide their own insurance for claims that can occur during the course of business activities. Be sure that there is enough coverage to cover everything without any gaps.

- Who pays for improvements? This is an area of negotiation. Landlords today expect to provide or pay for the carpeting, partitions, painting, lighting, etc. Some of your needs will be provided and some won't. Negotiate. If the landlord feels that he or she is going to lose you over the improvement allowance, he will probably increase the improvement allowance to keep you, especially if there is abundant space available. Sometimes they are happy to provide the materials, but are unhappy about providing the installation with today's high cost of labor. Get estimates for the costs involved before approaching the landlord with the requests.

  If the improvements are generally going to improve the space (and are to be completed in a neutral color scheme) for future tenants, the landlord will be much more receptive to paying for them.

- Who owns the improvements? Even if you pay for the improvements, if they are attached to the building, generally they become the property of the landlord. Exterior signs, air-conditioning units, heaters, lighting, shelving, and cabinets are all subject to ownership questions after they become attached to the building.

- During the improvements stage, is the space rent free? If the improvement stage will take some time, this will cost the landlord some money while waiting for you to occupy the space.

- Purpose for which the site or premises will be used. Is the intended purpose the premises is to be used for, satisfactory to the leasing terms?

- What building services are covered with the lease? What maintenance is the landlord willing to provide? How much gas and electricity are you allowed to use? How often may you run the heating and air conditioning? At what temperatures? Any cleaning services provided? How often will the building be cleaned? Does this include your space or just the common areas?

- What happens if the landlord declares bankruptcy? To prevent being at the mercy of the note holder and having your lease declared void, have a standard recognition or nondisturbance clause inserted into your lease. You do not want to be at the mercy of someone demanding to double the original rent.

- Is there a clause in the lease to protect you from the landlord placing questionable tenants nearby? What about competitors? How about tenants that are noisy? Businesses with disreputable images? Businesses that use chemicals? Zoning laws generally offer some protection from landlords placing inharmonious businesses near each other. Write in the contract that you do not want another interior design business that sells similar products near your business — preferably not in the same shopping center.

- Include the rights and the obligations of both parties in the contract.

To find an ideal site, drive around and attempt to locate a desirable location. The lessor or real estate company representing available properties will have signs displayed with information on *whom* you should contact for information on the property.

Contact a real estate broker who specializes in commercial property. Let her know what you are looking for in terms of size, location, and type of space. Give information on possible sites you have seen. Agents are usually informed about leasing property and may help you negotiate better terms, at no extra cost to you.

Since leases are written in legal language (legalese) to protect the owner, have a lawyer review the lease for your protection.

Before signing a lease, negotiate every possible provision in the lease contract, including the amount of rent, length of the lease, maintenance of the property, leasehold allowances for improvements, and use clauses. If the property has been vacant for a while, the landlord may offer some very positive concessions in order to fill the space. After the lease is signed, the landlord will not be in favor of offering anything extra. Ask for tenant improvement allowances to finish the space and incentives in free rent. For example: lease the space for three years and get six months free; lease for five years, get one year free. Have the landlord give you the incentives now, not later.

Try to negotiate an option clause for renewal later, or negotiate the longest lease you can get, *if* you feel that the business will be successful and will still be in business a couple of years from now. The advantage to a longer lease or an option clause is that the rent will stay constant and you will not lose your lease after a short period of time.

If you are willing to opt for a lease of five years or longer, owners will usually pay for some of your improvements.

If the desired site is located in a developing shopping center where few sites have been filled in proportion to those available, consider the risk of starting a new business in a new development that doesn't yet have many repeat customers. It takes a while for a shopping center to get going and to get a large flow of customers. Do you want to struggle with those problems in addition to all the problems of starting a new business? You need as many positive factors in your favor as you can get to survive the start-up phase.

Some shopping centers have constant turnover of businesses that are unable to survive. Investigate the reasons various businesses have left the center *before* signing a lease.

Even though it may cost more, the advantages of locating in an existing shopping center with a history of successful long-term tenants cannot be overestimated.

Lease Considerations

Note the following points when leasing space:
- Hire an attorney to review the contract if possible.

- Use correct names and signatures of all parties involved in the agreement.

- Write a complete description of the leased space.

- Remeasure the space and be sure that the quoted square footage is accurate. Is all space useable, or are the common areas added in?

- What are the sign requirements and limitations for the area? Do you need permission before erecting signs?

- Realize that you will be bound to the terms of the written lease agreement.

- Terms of the lease. Ideally, strive for a series of short-term, one-year leases with options to renew three times, or lease with an option to purchase.

- The rental payment. How is it calculated?

- Is there an option to renew later?

- Describe how the space is to be used.

- Any free or reduced rent?

- Allowance for tenant improvements?

- Are you to pay the real estate taxes, insurance, utilities (individually metered?), janitorial services, and maintenance?

- Is the parking adequate for your needs?

- Who takes care of the common areas?

- Can the lease be assigned or sublet? Add these options to the lease for your protection.

- Add a provision that protects your rental rates should the landlord sell the building.

- Who owns and pays for fixtures, alterations, and repairs?

- Are there any limitations on use for the space? Should you need to sublet, you want to keep this as open as possible.

- What are the provisions in case of late payment penalties and interest?

- Can you cancel the lease if the premises are damaged due to flood, earthquake, etc.?

- Ask for moving expenses, as you might get them. Do they have space planning help available?

- Is a security deposit required?

- Do you have to prepay the rent?

- Include a clause on using arbitration should a dispute between the lessor and lessee arise. Include who shall pay the attorney fees for the party that prevails in the decision.

- Clearly define all rights and obligations for all parties to the contract.

Exterior Signs

Before signing a lease for space, find out about any sign regulations for the area. Consider the following points:

- What exactly can you do regarding signs? How many signs are you allowed? Size restraints?

- Where can signs be placed where they will be highly visible?

- What type of signs are you allowed?

- Who owns the signs once they are affixed to the building? Pole or other means of display?

Purchasing Commercial Real Estate

Realize that there is no *standard real estate contract*. Every point in a real estate contract is *negotiable*. Additional points and language may be inserted to protect your position as a buyer (or as a seller). Changes may be typed or handwritten into the contract, or placed on an additional sheet of paper (an addendum) referenced within the contract.

Consider leasing property with an option to buy, rather than jumping in and making an outright purchase of real property. It is better to be *sure* that a business will make it and the location is truly a good one, before making the big commitment. With a usual lease for an option to buy, the lessee puts up some option money, say $1,000 to $2,000, for the option. The lessee must exercise a decision to buy the property within a stated amount of time, at stated terms, and at a stated purchase amount. If you do not go ahead and purchase the real property, you forfeit the option money. Some leases will include a portion of the monthly lease to be allocated toward your down payment, others will not allocate any of it.

Have an attorney draw up a purchase agreement (also called a sales agreement, contract of sale, offer, binder, preliminary sales agreement, earnest money deposit, or deposit receipt) when you initially want to purchase commercial real estate. Do not expect to supply the details and fine points of the purchase later. Supply the details when you make an offer to buy the property.

Generally, preliminary offers or purchase agreements are binding contracts. Do not sign a preliminary contract without having an attorney double-check if for you. The attorney needs to verify that it is not a binding contract, and you can get back the deposit under certain circumstances.

The purchase agreement should cover all details and elements of the purchase and be very specific; it is then signed by both the buyer and seller.

The purchase agreement should be signed by the legal owner of the property. If the agreement is signed by an agent of the owner or the executor of the owner, seek a real estate attorney's advice. If the owner of the property is a corporation, ask to see the board of directors decree showing that the person signing the purchase agreement actually has the authority to do so. Here are the points that should be covered in a purchase agreement to alleviate future problems:

- Purchase price of the property.

- *Legal description* of the real property to be sold. If in doubt about the legal description, have the owner supply a survey that shows exactly the boundaries of the property.

- Include a complete description of all fixtures and personal property that are included. If items are attached to the building, they are considered to be fixtures. Again this is a negotiable point. Simply list the items that stay with the property and those that don't.

- If *time is of the essence* in the acquisition of the property, say so. If you need the property as soon as possible and not receiving it by a certain time will cause you to suffer, have your attorney draft a *liquidated damage clause* in the purchase agreement. This type of clause will require the owner to pay you damages for every day escrow finalization and possession of the property is held up or delayed.

- Type of deed and title confirmation (insurance) will you receive at close of escrow.

- Conditions of the building that are guaranteed. Get warranties for the building in writing. Include a section within the contract called *warranties and representations*. Include any statements about the building's condition, use, zoning, etc., that the owner has made verbally and in writing. If the statements should be false, you are sitting in a better legal position.

- Proration of the taxes, utility bills, and payment.

- Conditions of use and any restrictions for the building. Is the building and accompanying land subject to zoning regulations, building and safety codes, private building and use restrictions, or easements for utilities, sidewalks, and streets that limit your use of the premises? Be sure to cover yourself, in the event that restrictions you were unaware of (that prevent using the building as you intended) should be uncovered during the escrow period.

- Include contingency clauses to protect your rights as a buyer. If you or the owner of the property cannot or will not meet the conditions within the purchase agreement, within the stated periods of time, you have the right to cancel the contract without any loss of deposit money.

   The inspection report on the building may come back extremely negative and you will not be willing to pay the quoted price to buy the building. You may be unable to qualify for the loan to finance the purchase of the building or you may need to make a contingency agreement that on the sale of your present property, you will purchase this new property.

Office Space as a Business Base

For a low-cost alternative to a large store front and an alternative to having your business in your home, consider leasing turnkey office space. This is a great way to keep the overhead down while you are seeing if your business is going to succeed.

Depending on the area you reside in, here are some of the usual amenities that are available with an office space package. With an office space package, you pay for the extra services only if you use them.

- Low rent, flexible short-term leases.

- Average size range of 100 square feet to 200 square feet.

- Usually well lighted, plenty of windows, modern styling.

- Include copy and fax machines.

- Include multi-line phone and answer machine.

- Computer systems and laser printers.

- Contemporary desks and furnishings.

- Nicely furnished reception area.

- Conference rooms.

- Usually located in easy access areas to the freeways.

- Can share use of receptionist.

Using Your Home as a Business Base

You may need to start your new business in your home rather than rush out and open a store or studio. Your car or van may have to be the base for showing products and samples. You may retain a post office box rather inexpensively, for all correspondence. A business phone line may be installed in your home.

Overhead will be vastly lowered by starting this way. Starting out of your home will also allow you to find out if this is a business for you to pursue. After you gain some experience in running your own business, the business has grown, and your customer base is built up, you may want to go ahead and open a studio or a store.

Low-Cost Location Alternatives

- Work out of your home and use a van as your business base.

- Set up a co-op studio with other decorators. Share samples and all overhead. If you advertise together, rotate the leads. Each decorator should be on a floor time schedule. Otherwise, hire a coordinator to screen the calls and distribute the personal leads and rotate all other leads.

- Rent space in a related home furnishing product store. For example, you could share space with a carpet/flooring store. For you customers that require carpet and floor coverings, receive a commission from the carpeting/flooring operation. Other related areas include furniture stores, accessory shops, florist shops, gift shops, and greeting card shops. You may own and run the other business or share rent with another business owner. Sharing space with another high-traffic business gets the customer in the door to examine what you have to offer.

Part 5

Business Equipment and Supplies

Office Furniture — Buy, Lease, or Rent

Instead of a large cash outlay and a major commitment to keeping your office furniture, consider renting or leasing it. By renting or leasing furniture and making payments consistently, you boost your credit rating with banks. When you rent or lease furniture, you sign a written contract with one of several options:

- **Rent-to-rent** for expected short time spans. Sign and set up the contract to run month-to-month. You will *never* own an interest in the furniture.

- **Rent-to-own** furniture for longer time periods. Most rental contracts have a purchase option. At the end of your contract, you'll *own* the furniture. You may also be allowed (according to the terms of the contract) to buy the furniture earlier, at a guaranteed price.

  If you change your mind during a rent-to-own contract, you are able to cancel the contract after an initial minimum period (usually four months) and return the furniture.

- **Leasing,** these contracts are like rental contracts, except they're for a specified certain time period. With leasing, you generally do not have cancellation, return, or exchange privileges. Lease payments may be lower than rental payments. Buy-out terms may also be available (so that you will own the furniture at the end of the lease).

Since you are purchasing the furniture over time, you must pay a premium. Find out what that premium is in actual costs. Weigh these costs against the benefits of buying the furniture outright.

Why Rent or Lease?

- Helps your cash flow. Save your capital for other necessary expenses. Instead of requiring a down payment, monthly fees, and interest, leasing requires only a security deposit and a monthly payment.

- Saves your credit line. Capital and credit are left free and available.

- Saves on taxes. Rental payments are usually fully tax deductible as a business expense. Since your company doesn't own the furniture, you won't have to pay property taxes on the furniture.

Review the contract for these key points:
- Will you own the furniture when the contract is up?

- Can you buy the furniture early? Before the contract is completed? Will the remaining payments be discounted? Will the payments you have already made be applied to the purchase?

- Can the contract be terminated before the specified term is up? When? How much notice is required?

- What's the total price you are actually paying? Are there any surcharges, late charges, etc.? Who pays for delivery and pick-up? How much is the required security deposit?

- How are the payments calculated? Is there a balloon payment at the end of the contract?

- Does the firm offer a design service to work with you?

- How fast is the delivery?

- What is the maintenance agreement? Maintenance is the responsibility of the renting/leasing company. When you buy, your warranty is usually good for only a limited time. When you rent or lease, the warranty is good for the duration of the contract.

- Is there flexibility with exchanges? If you tire of a piece, is it readily exchangeable?

- Is there relocation assistance? Is relocation assistance available at no cost or at a lower cost than it would cost to move the furniture?

Telephone Systems

Selection of a telephone distributor:

The telephone trade was deregulated in the late 1960s. Consequently the telephone industry has been flooded with companies entering this field. The careful selection of the telephone equipment supplier is actually more important than the selection of the *right* telephone equipment.

Just as in any other type of business, the telephone supplier business has some companies that are poorly managed and barely hanging on financially. These companies are not going to follow through and provide service problems arise once your system is in place.

Select a telephone distributor that specializes in only a couple of systems, rather than a supplier that carries many. Usually a company that specializes will have parts available, *know* how to fix the system, and service will cost you less in the long run, because the technician knows how to fix the system quickly.

When you are shopping for your telephone system, consider the following before you decide which company to give your business to:

- How long has the telephone supplier has been in business?

- Check the credit of a company you are considering doing business with by contacting Dun and Bradstreet.

- Call the phone system manufacturer to find out what type of association the telephone equipment manufacturer and the distributor (supplier to you) *have*.

- Ask the telephone distributor for its financial statement (they may or may not provide it).

- Check with the Better Business Bureau in the geographical area where the telephone distributor does business.

- Ask how *many* servicepeople are available for service of the particular system you are considering.

- Are parts readily available? At what price? Do they have to order parts or are they stocked and ready for emergencies?

- Ask for references and check them.

- Most problems that arise from a telephone system are caused by poor quality initial installations.

● Does the telephone distributor provide training for your employees so your company can get the most out of the system?

Selection of a telephone system:

When shopping for a telephone system (as with computer systems), it is very important to select one that can grow as your company grows. You will pay a higher price later to replace a poorly selected system if you are not careful about your initial selection. Select an expandable and upgradeable system that you can add on to later. Initially ask if you can upgrade your selection without replacing the very expensive station equipment.

Software driven telephone systems can save your company up to 20 percent on telephone bills. Software systems offer management capabilities that will help control the costs of the telephone network connected to your system and they will print out information on how your system is actually being used by your employees. Plan enough lines to allow use of a modem and a fax machine line. As with most other equipment, you will get what you are willing to pay for.

Cellular Phones

Cellular phones, whether mounted in your car or the carry-around type, are a great tool for designers to use their driving time to make quick telephone calls to customers, the studio, suppliers, etc. Cellular phones will increase your productivity and therefore your income. Small businesses that maximize and put to use the majority of their available time during the day are able to compete successfully against larger businesses. If you have a portable cellular phone that you carry around with you, the days of making repeated return calls to connect with people attempting to get a hold of you are gone. Experts predict that within the next ten years cellular phones will be a standard feature on most new automobiles.

Because cellular phones and cordless telephones are like miniature radio stations, they transmit messages through airwaves instead of wires as regular telephones. Anyone can tune into the frequency being used and listen in on the conversation. Do not ever assume that your conversation is private. And there is not a way to tell if your conversation is being monitored. Never give out a credit card number or other confidential information while using a cellular or a cordless telephone.

Selection of a cellular telephone distributor:

As with the selection of a business telephone system, the careful selection of your cellular telephone supplier is crucial to your satisfaction or dissatisfaction with the supplied service, should a problem arise in the future.

Many cellular telephone suppliers get into the business in hopes of turning a quick profit. They do not intend to be there for you when a problem comes up. Most of these suppliers depend on the fees paid by the telephone service carrier when a new subscriber signs up for service. Usually this type of cellular phone supplier does not have in-house service available. In essence, what they do is mobilize a batch of new customers, get them signed up for telephone service, collect the fees, and move on when the first complaints start coming in.

Since getting stung by one of these companies will cost you a lot in the long run, it is best to go with larger, firmly established cellular suppliers that care about their reputation and are attempting to build their business off of referrals from happy customers.

Larger companies also have a wider range of equipment available and can customize your installation as needed. They usually stock parts and have in-house service available for customers. The three types of cellular phones available are:

● The type that are found permanently installed in automobiles.

● Transportable cellular phones that can be connected to a specialized battery pack in an automobile and that can also be used outside the automobile.

● Portable cellular phones that are available in sizes small enough to carry in your briefcase.

As with many types of equipment, cellular phones have gotten less expensive in the past few years. Today, basic cellular phones can be found on sale for under $500. Several years ago the starting price was $2,000.

Unfortunately, the negative point about cellular phones is the monthly service fees. Your fee will vary from $30 with minimum usage, up to hundreds of dollars with excessive use. The average monthly charge is around $100.

As a business owner wanting to maximize available time, and be out in the field, rather than in the studio, you will have to weigh the costs of the phone against time lost not having a phone available and decide if it is feasible for your business.

Selection of a Copier

Copiers are very complex machines that can have problems due to dust, failure of a moving part, timing, the positioning of the image, or with the darkness or lightness of the image.

When you purchase a copier, heavily weigh the cost of a service contract or preventative contract against potential problems with the copier that can come up. Have the copier cleaned regularly — every six months with medium volume to help extend the life of the machine. Ask yourself the most important question before shopping for a copier:

■ **How many copies will you be making monthly?**

Buy the copier according to how many copies you plan to make. For lighter weight copy volume, buy a machine that is geared for lighter weight volume. For heavy-weight copy volume, buy a heavy-duty machine. Once a copier is purchased, expect your volume of copies to rise at least 20 percent.

Other questions to consider:
● How much are you spending at outside copy machines? About how many copies do you make?

● How much volume to you anticipate? Plan according to the next two years.

● Double the anticipated volume above and buy a machine according to that number.

Weigh all costs:
Consider the cost of the machine and supplies (toner and paper) versus the cost of having the copies made elsewhere. Examine these tradeoffs:

● Price of the copier.

● Operating costs (cost per copy).

● Speed of output (number of copies per minute).

● Functions (can the copier reduce and enlarge?).

● Durability, expected life span.

● Reliability.

● Service (availability, cost, response time).

Should You Buy or Lease a Copier?
Ask your copier dealer about the advantages of leasing the copier rather than buying it. Leasing will probably offer tax advantages. Buy-out purchases of the copier at the end of the lease may be attractive. Examine the tax implications and the cash-flow disadvantages of buying the equipment outright.

Fax Machines

Fax is short for facsimile. All fax machines do basically the same thing. They send a copy of a document over the phone lines to a destination. Fax machines are only slightly different from standard photocopy machines. The exception is the original stays at the source and the copy arrives at the destination.

Fax machines (like all other equipment) come in many different variations. These differences are the various available options. Evaluate these options and decide what is best for your business. Will the lower end, slower model serve your purposes, or do you really need the more expensive, faster and option-laden model? Or can you easily add a fax board to your computer system for a low-cost alternative?

Select your business fax machine according to your anticipated company needs. Many of the options you can afford to do without or simply don't need. If you suspect that you won't be using the machine much, buy a less-expensive, less option-laden model. As with most equipment decisions, you will find price, quality, speed and convenience are trade-offs.

Modems:

Fax machines communicate with each other through modems. Modems are the same tools computers use to communicate over phone lines. Presently there are two types of modems available — 4,800 and the faster 9,600 bits per second (bps). With the 4,800 bps it will take approximately thirty seconds to transmit a letter-size document. With the 9,600 bps it will take the same letter only about twenty seconds to be transmitted to its destination.

If you will frequently transmit multiple page documents, the faster 9,600 bps is the fax for you. If you expect to do infrequent single-page documents, the 4,800 bps will be sufficient for your needs. Determine how your phone company bills you. If the phone company bills you by the full minute, the less-expensive 4,800 bps is *clearly* the best way to go. If you are billed in increments of seconds, the time you actually use, the faster modem is the correct selection.

When making a fax machine selection, other considerations are the scanning width, feeder capacity, and printing method.

The scanning width determines how much of a document can be read. Most scanners can read letter-size and computer printout size. A few can read 11"- x - 17" ledger-size paper. Naturally you have to pay quite a bit more to get the ledger size. Some machines are designed for European designations which have slightly different page sizes. Use of these types of machines will cause loss of margins.

Feeder capacity is an important consideration when you send multi-page documents. Less-expensive, lower-end fax machines may have as few as a single-sheet or as much as ten-page document feeders while the more expensive heavy-duty machines can hold up to fifty pages.

Output:

Thermal printing is the more common form of fax output. With the thermal printing method, points of heat are fired at heat-sensitive paper to produce the image. Thermal printing is a less-expensive process with poor type quality, and flimsy (expensive) paper that will discolor and fade rapidly. On any faxed documents that you may need for future reference, photocopy the fax document immediately.

Thermal transfer fires the heat at a ribbon, and the ribbon then prints on the paper. The type quality is slightly higher than thermal printing. The process requires specially treated, expensive paper.

Plain paper copiers or laser printing faxes are the top of the line, more expensive type of fax machines. The type quality is very high and the paper used is the same inexpensive kind that photocopiers use. Unfortunately, plain paper fax machines require lots of upkeep. Toner cartridges and drums need frequent replacements (according to their amount of use).

Options:

The auto-dialer is a convenient option to consider. This feature allows you to enter the telephone numbers of the document recipients into the machines's memory and have the machine dial the numbers and initiate transmission automatically. If you do not buy a fax with this option, you will need to dial with a telephone handset or keypad and wait to hear the fax tone.

Most auto-dialers come with automatic redial, delayed transmission, sequential dialing, and short-code dialing. Automatic redial is an important option to consider for faxing orders to vendors since it will keep dialing the number until a connection is made.

Delayed transmission allows you to program the machine to send your documents at a certain time so that you can take advantage of the off-peak phone rates.

Sequential dialing allows you to individually program the fax for a stack of documents, all with different destinations at different times.

Short-code dialing lets you store several of your most commonly used numbers in memory that may be quickly accessed by the touch of one or two buttons.

Polling combines the above functions and allows a central fax (usually located in a central office) to call your fax and retrieve any documents being held for the central fax. This is a good feature for a central office that may have a constant busy signal on its fax. The central office calls when its line is free.

Security features:

Access codes allow you to control who is using the fax, at what time, and where they are faxing to.

Secure mailbox features allows you to establish a secure mailbox where the document can be stored, and will only be printed when the correct access code is punched in. If you have a number of confidential documents that you don't want read by anyone else, this is an option for you.

Normal or fine mode:

Standard fax machines are able to transmit in normal or fine mode. Normal mode handles regular text, while fine mode is used for graphic images and higher resolution documents. Fine mode requires more transmission time.

If you want to transmit photographs you will need a fax machine capable of printing a half-tone. The half-tone mode will provide you with sixteen shades of gray. Without this option, pictures will be transmitted in high-contrast black and white.

Error detection and correction:

Error detection is a standard feature for most fax machines. Transmissions will be cut off if line interference causes more than 15 percent corruption of the data being transmitted. More advanced models will have an end-of-transmission printout informing you which of the transmitted pages were corrupted with data errors of more than 15 percent, and need to be retransmitted.

The most advanced models have error correction features or systems. These systems check the incoming transmission by lines or blocks. If any errors are spotted by the system a retransmission is requested.

Memory:

Amount of memory is another consideration. Adequate memory will allow you to send the same document to several different destinations without having to re-feed the same document into the fax. Memory lets you establish confidential mailboxes and allows you to set up a broadcast network.

Should you desire to send information to a number of distant destinations, broadcasting will be an important feature for you to have. Broadcasting allows you to send the document to the fax that is closer to the other destinations. The closer fax then does the transmitting to the other machines, thus cutting down on long distance phone charges.

Computer Systems

What can computerization do for you? That depends on the short- and long-term goals that you have for your business. You need to decide what you want to accomplish through the use of a computer. A computer system can:

• Organize and store records (i.e., names, addresses, and phone numbers stored in a database form).

- Recover a single piece of information from stored records (i.e., the telephone number of a particular customer).

- Perform mathematical computations quickly and accurately (i.e., projections of business growth over a certain period of time).

- Make changes easily and quickly.

- Print out information or word processed work.

- Execute the same function the same way every time (i.e., print out the same letter repeatedly).

The purchase of one or more personal computers and several software packages, while requiring a large investment, will usually pay for itself in a very short time. With the acquisition of an adequate system, a few employees are needed, rather than many. Database management, accounting, inventory, payroll, spreadsheet, planning, word processing, desktop publishing, and CAD (computer-aided design and drafting) can be combined to increase productivity, in addition to creating and giving the impression of a larger, well-established, successful company.

After analyzing your individual application needs, consider the computer investment in terms of the payback period, depreciation, tax advantages, and the possible increase in your management capabilities.

Consider hiring a computer consultant to help you make a correct selection and evaluation of your computer and software system requirements. Have the consultant or your software vendor train everyone who will be using the hardware and software.

Prepare a list of all business procedures that you are performing manually that you wish to convert to a computerized system. Convert each task one at a time. Once you have mastered the new task on the computer system, move on to mastering the next. Trying to do them all at once will overwhelm a beginning computer user and disrupt your work flow.

Be sure to train more than one employee on the operation of your particular system. Once you get your system up and running you will tend to rely on it. The absence of an employee due to illness or termination can be disastrous without another employee ready to take over on the system.

Data can be destroyed by unanticipated disasters (fire, water, power changes, magnetic fields, or employee interference) and can result in high costs to recreate. To prevent loss of data, keep regular back-up copies of all data. Store and copies in a safe place away from your business. Identify all data, programs and documents that are needed for all required tasks during recuperation from a disaster.

If you decide that your business needs a computer system, plan to spend the time and money necessary to make its installation and operation successful. Use a computer in the areas that will save you money and increase your company's productivity.

If you are unsure whether to spend the money to become computerized or do not want to make the investment immediately, consider renting time on someone else's computer. It is the most economical way to proceed when you have only a small amount of data processing to do or want to be sure that computers are *right* for you and your business. Purchase a computer when you are sure it can pay for itself.

The single largest expense for a computer system is not the hardware or the software. It is your time. Spend a small amount of time at the start before you buy software and hardware in the evaluation, negotiation, preparation, installation, and training, or spend a much larger amount of time later, toiling with inadequate hardware and software that won't do the required job.

Computer and Software Terms

Application programs	Software engineered to perform a particular function (i.e. word processing, accounting, database, payroll, accounts receivable, inventory, etc.).
Bit	A binary digit (bit) is the smallest storage unit for data in a computer.
Byte	Amount of space required to store a single character. A byte generally represents eight binary digits (bits).

Compilers/ interpreters	Software that translates programs to machine language that the CPU can perform.
CPU	Central processing unit. The CPU is the "thinking" or "brain" part of the computer and performs calculations, administers the flow of data within the computer, performs the software program's instructions, and controls other hardware components.
CRT monitor	Cathode ray tube. Refers to the display monitor.
Disk drive	The device that allows the computer to receive or give data to or from a disk. Disk drives are either hard drives or floppy drives.
Floppy drive	Disk drive that writes data to, or receives data from, floppy diskettes. Floppy drives come in 5 ¼", or 3 ½" size.
Hard drive	Mass storage device usually located internally in the computer.
Input devices	Unit used to enter data into the system for processing. Input devices normally used with keyboard and CRT (display monitor).
Megabyte (Mb)	024 kilobytes (1,048,576 bytes) of storage space.
Memory	Temporary data storage area.
Output devices	These display data. Normal output device is a printer.
Main memory	The storage area easily accessible to the CPU. When purchasing a computer system the memory is usually measured in bytes (i.e., 80K = 80,000 bytes).
Memory storage	Non-main memory storage. Storage of memory through devices such as disks, diskettes, and magnetic tape. Make sure that all memory storage devices are labeled with their contents as you use them.
Modem	Hardware that permits a computer to communicate with other computers via the telephone lines. Modems may be internal or external.
Monitor	Display screen (CRT) for the computer. Monitors come in several types: monochrome; CGA (color graphics adapter); EGA (enhanced graphics adapter); VGA (video graphics array).
Mother board	The computer's main circuit board. All other boards attach to the mother board.
MHz	Megahertz. Operating speed, or clock speed, is measured in MHz. The higher the number, the faster the speed of the computer.
Operating system software	Software that tells the hardware how to run.
Parallel port	A plug-in area to connect parallel devices, such as printers, to the computer.
Power supply	The element that supplies electrical current to the computer. Power supply is measured in watts. The higher the watts, the more internal add-ons the computer can handle.
Printer	Output device to print entered data from the computer. The print quality of printers ranges from the low-end dot matrix to high-end laser and postscript printers.

RAM   Stands for random access memory. Located in the CPU and measured in Ks. RAM is used to temporarily store all the information necessary for the CPU to do its job. RAM is erased when the computer's power is turned off.

ROM   A program stored in the computer memory that cannot be changed by the computer operator or an externally introduced program. ROM is permanent and is not erased when the computer's power is turned off.

Serial port   Similar to a parallel port, but used to connect a mouse or modem to the computer.

Scanner   Optical device used to transfer pictures, photographs, and images from paper to the computer screen. The images can be incorporated into text or drawings on the computer and printed out.

Software   Computer programs. The set of instructions that tell the computer to do what you bought it for.

Terminal   Usually consists of a keyboard used to enter data into the computer and a CRT display monitor (screen).

Decisions to Make When Purchasing a Computer System:

- Your business needs.

- What you can spend.

- Required software.

- How much memory is needed with both RAM and ROM.

- What type of disk drives.

- Type of keyboard.

- Type of display monitor (CRT).

- Expansion ability.

Software

Since computer systems are bought around required software, we will start our discussion with software.

DOS:

For IBM computers or IBM compatible computers, DOS is the standard operating system to run other software off of. DOS also has more compatible software than any other operating system. DOS consists of the command processor, the file and input-output system, and the utilities. DOS controls the interactions amount the CPU, disk drive, keyboard, video monitor, and the printer.

The command processor is the part of the operating system that interacts with the user. The utilities part of the system takes care of tasks such as disk and file management.

As with other operating systems, DOS uses a hierarchical file management system. The DOS file system consists of files and directories. The file COMMAND.COM manages the file system.

Spreadsheet software:

Spreadsheet software consist of rows and columns made up of individual "cells" that data are entered into. The ability of spreadsheets to quickly perform intense mathematical calculations has experienced rapid growth recently. Spreadsheet software allows you to calculate mathematical "what if" situations, project growth, and determine present value of diverse inventory. Data can be entered, changed, graphed, and recorded. Popular programs include Lotus 1-2-3, Excel, and Quattro Pro.

Graphs, pie charts, and bar charts can be created with the application of financial information. Charting allows company management to project what lies ahead and help aid in their decision-making processes.

Database software:

Database software is used primarily for storage and retrieval of large amounts of information. It is usually used to track inventory, production, purchasing habits of customers, mailing lists, and vendor lists.

Once data have been entered, the data (now called a record) may be used to pull up customers' similar data — whether it is *all* the customers who purchased carpet, all customers with the same zip code, or all customers who spent over $2,000 with your firm for the year. The most popular database programs are Dbase IV, Rapidfile,and Paradox.

Accounting software:

Accounting software programs are widely used by design businesses. Accounting programs have the ability to take care of your day-to-day accounting and financial needs of your business. Accounting programs keep track of credits and debits, issue checks, calculate depreciation, and will print out detailed accounting of transactions. Computer stored accounting and financial data allow businesses fast retrieval of business financial data.

Word processing software:

The most basic software programs and probably the most widely used even in design offices are word processing programs. With word processing, you are able to get rid of the typewriter and the correction fluid. Word processing programs allow you to type, change, copy, and revise your documents whenever you desire. You are able to move paragraphs, edit typos, reuse portions of text from other documents, and spell-check and find new words with the aid of the thesaurus.

Design firms use word processing to write letters, create direct mail pieces, write reports, prepare bids, etc. The two most popular word processing programs are WordPerfect and Microsoft Word.

Desktop publishing:

Desktop publishing is the combination of text and graphics on paper. The combination of a desktop publishing program with a laser printer can be very effective for a small firm. Generally a desktop publishing program contains all of the features of a good word processor and a number of different size and types of lettering and numbers. Text can be printed out in columns if desired or wrapped around illustrations and photographs. Outside typesetting is no longer needed. Laser printers are used to output the final hard copy from which copies can be made or offset printed.

Desktop publishing programs are priceless to firms that want to create their own brochures and mailing pieces and save money while doing so. Many advertising agencies, magazines, and newspapers do their work with PageMaker, Quark XPress, and Ventura Publisher.

CAD (computer-aided design):

CAD is a tool to use for designing on the computer. Shapes, spaces, and furniture can easily be changed and changed again. You only need to draw the images one time and they can be moved, sized, duplicated, or manipulated at will. A CAD system consists of a computer, software, and plotter.

Normally, because of the expense (several thousand dollars), CAD is found with larger interior design firms. Smaller firms find it hard to absorb the initial set-up expense of a CAD system. CAD systems require a considerable amount of time to learn and become comfortable with.

Interior design financial management and bookkeeping software:

Software packages that include project management, job cost analysis, and accounting systems are available for interior design firms for around $1,000. Software can also be used to specify furniture, fabrics, fixtures, etc. This type of software allows you to catalog objects on floor plans while adding as involved description of the item as you wish. It is difficult to overlook a needed product or item (the software tells you that you forgot to account for an item) and the software takes a count and adds the cost of each item into the total price.

One company that appears to offer a comprehensive package is Systems Integrated Solutions, 517 Glenwood Ave., Suite. H, Menlo Park, CA 94025, (415) 324-1055.

Shopping for Software

Use the following guidelines when shopping for software for your business. Realize that once the software is opened it may not be returned unless it is defective. Software varies widely in quality. And price is no indication of the quality.

- Decide what you need the software to do. Let your applications determine both the hardware and the software that you buy. Decide which needed features are mandatory and which are desired, but optional.

- Let the person who will be using the software have a say in its selection. If you involve these people in the selection process, they will probably cooperate fully when it comes time to set up and use the system.

- Ask several salespeople what software they recommend according to your needs.

- Ask the salesperson why one type of software is preferred over another.

- Determine if the program has all of the features you need. If not, you may have to supplement the program with another program — a costly and sometimes complicated proposition.

- Have the software program *extensively and slowly* demonstrated for you by the salesperson.

- Try the software program out *yourself* before purchasing.

- Computer magazines publish articles about the pros and cons of the various popular software packages. Local community colleges or adult education classes may offer inexpensive courses in the most popular programs. Check to see what support programs are available, if you are torn between which program to buy.

- Ask the salesperson which are the better software manufacturers for after-purchase support, should a problem arise — chances are you *will* be occasionally phoning them with various questions and problems.

- Do the manufacturer and the software vendor have a good reputation for follow-through? For supplying a quality software package? How long has the vendor been in business? Are they going to stay in business?

- Select software that has a "help" person available via the phone. The company you bought the software from should have a support person (800 number) available for you to talk to and willing to walk you through the steps of the problem you are having.

- Attend computer courses and ask fellow students what software programs they like, and why.

- Employ a computer consultant *before* deciding which software to buy. If you save money by making a better purchase, then it is money well spent. Computer consultants are readily available to help should you run into any difficulty with your software or hardware.

- Order and read the software manuals.

- Is the software user-friendly? Unless you are a computer whiz, chances are it is going to take some time for you to learn the program adequately. Once the program is mastered, you will gain tremendous leverage in terms of increased productivity with a limited number of employees.

- Will the software work with a hard disk or multiple users when you are ready to upgrade your computer system?

- If security features are important to you (i.e., passwords, user identification codes), select the software accordingly.

- Can the data be changed once entered? How easily? Can the program be adapted by rewriting the instructions to fit your needs? Will the vendor change the instructions for a charge? How much is the charge?

- Ask for names and telephone numbers of other purchasers of the same software and call them for their opinions.

Purchasing Computers and Printers for Your Interior Design Business

When you narrow down your software needs, you will have narrowed down what type of computer to purchase. Most software is written for a specific type of computer.

When you purchase a computer for your interior design business make a wise decision about who you buy your system from. The selection of the computer system should have the ability to grow along with your business. Do not just consider the price of the system. While price is vital, an adaptable system that can be used for a few years is even more significant. Select a computer dealer that will work with your business over a long period of time and provide support as needed. The dealer should also be willing to help you refine your system as your business expands and grows. The correct selection of compatible hardware and software is extremely important.

- Decide what functions the computer needs to be able to perform for your business. These functions should step up productivity for your business.

- Does the selected hardware have sufficient processing ability to meet your requirements within acceptable time frames?

- Work with computer suppliers and vendors that are reputable and established. Make sure that they willingly will provide you with ongoing support and service.

- Buy the best system for your company's needs. Make sure that the model may be upgraded as computer technology progresses and your business needs progress. Can you add additional memory? Plug in additional disk drives? Upgrade from a single-user to a multi-user system? Network several computers?

- If you purchase the wrong computer system for your business, it may not be able to be upgraded or may become outdated quickly.

- Select a personal computer and a single-user accounting software package that will also support future multiple users in a network system. A network system allows information to be shared so that several users can simultaneously access customer information or work at different tasks such as accounting, billing, product receiving, order checking, faxing documents, and communicating with credit bureaus simultaneously.

- Does the dealer provide computer and software training for the systems you have selected for your employees? If you don't take advantage of training, chances are you will only be making use of about 65 percent of your software's capability, many tasks will be unnecessarily repeated, and you will have many more errors than you would have if the employees working with the computer had been trained. Lack of training for your system will cost you much more money and you will have many unhappy customers due to the errors that could have been eliminated.

- Don't purchase a system that has just come out. Instead buy something else or wait until the bugs get worked out at someone's elses expense.

- Ask if there are any shipping or installation costs, and what are the perceived maintenance costs for the selected system.

- Who sets up the system? If you are a beginning computer user, purchase the system from a source that provides on-site set-up. Check the hardware manual to be sure your selected location meets the system's requirements for temperature, humidity, and electrical power.

- What type of warranty does the dealer and manufacturer offer?

- When the system breaks down, how long will it take to be fixed? Who does the repairs? On site or off site? Plan on setting aside about 25 percent of the cost of the system for the first three years to cover the costs of maintaining the system. A hidden cost of repair is the down time you suffer while having the system repaired.

- Make your computer system final payment contingent upon successful installation of all hardware and software.

Desktop Publishing and Laser Printers

A laser printer is a wise selection for a business to produce professional typeset looking documents (i.e., for letters, advertising, and graphics).

The most important features about laser printers are that they are able to produce a high-resolution image. This image is described as "dots per inch." The more dots per inch, the better the printing quality.

The combination of a laser printer and desktop publishing are rapidly changing printing technology. The combination allows for typeset quality printing on a computer with the output camera-ready.

With the more sophisticated desktop publishing systems, entire page layouts (illustrations and all) can be scanned into a computer and printed out on the laser printer.

Previously, with regular typesetting, should mistakes occur or the copy need to be changed, you were dealing with a costly proposition. Today copy can be key stroked and composed on a computer and output with a laser printer in traditional phototype.This method combines the advantages of high-resolution phototype with cost-saving convenience and versatility of desktop formation.

Required Business Supplies

When setting up your interior design business, you will need the following supplies for your office and equipment.

Desk:

- Paper clips (large and small sizes)
- Adhesive tape
- Scissors
- Pens and pencils
- Staplers (large and small size)
- Staples
- Hole punch (to add supplier information to notebooks)
- Pencil sharpener
- Markers (highlighters and regular black)
- Calculator, preferably one that prints out on tape
- Paper for calculator
- Stamps or postal meter
- Postage scale for mailing items

- Mailing envelopes and boxes
- Packing materials, and tape
- Address card file
- Message books
- Push pins
- Pens and pencils
- Notebook binders
- Accounting forms and ledgers
- Copier paper
- Copier toner
- Large manila envelopes
- Stick-on notes
- Printer labels
- Inventory tags
- Sale signs
- Scrap paper pads

- Correction fluid
- Typing/printer paper
- Letterhead, business cards, and envelopes
- Typewriter ribbons and correction tape
- Extension cords
- Computer and printer furniture
- Modem
- Printer supplies (according to what type you have)
- Computer diskettes and diskette holders
- "In" baskets for desk tops
- Self inking stamps
- Gluesticks

Drafting Equipment

- Basic drafting table.

- Drafting machine to mount to the drafting table for calculating different degrees and drawing lines or can substitute basic parallel straight edge or drafting triangle.

- Basic blueprint machine or access to a blueprint printing service.

- Drafting supplies: rulers, triangles, scales, templates, drafting tape, lead sharpeners, lead holders, lead pointers, erasers, paper supplies (vellum drafting paper, printing paper, sepia paper), etc.

Part 6

Protecting Your Business

When starting a business you must plan to protect your business in these various areas:

- Shoplifting
- Employee theft
- Bad check writers
- Bank deposits
- Safes
- Audit of books by IRS
- Locks
- Access to keys
- Alarm system
- Employee bonding insurance
- Cash exposure
- Check, credit card handling
- Cash register controls
- Sales procedure

- Robbery
- Interior and exterior lighting
- Visibility through exterior windows
- Controls on checking in merchandise
- Merchandise protection from damage
- Price tag controls
- Employee theft
- After hours safety
- Trash handling
- Injuries, accidents
- Liability insurance
- Casualty insurance
- Property and fire insurance

Security Systems

Security professionals advocate certain procedures and guidelines to maintain a secure business situation. Use the following guidelines to improve the effectiveness and control to the access and security of your business.

Install a security system:
- Security systems have fallen in price. Watch the sale price between competing security companies. Have a system installed that is monitored by the security system's main office. For a few hundred dollars and a $20 to $30 a month monitoring fee, you can have a relatively secure system installed that is monitored. They call you when the alarm is set off by an intruder or accidentally, and ask you your code word. Once you give the correct code word you are cleared. If you don't answer the phone or give an incorrect code word, the police are called by the security company. The police come out ready to face a burglar.

  Depending on your locale, you will probably have to pay a $25 yearly permit fee to the police department. Security systems are great deterrents to burglars.

  The security company will tell you that the decals and the exterior signs that show you have a security system are about 75 percent of the deterrent for the burglar. He naturally would rather break in somewhere else that doesn't have a security system.

- Security systems that are not monitored are also deterrents to burglars. They sound an alarm just like the monitored systems. Unfortunately, your neighbors may or may not hear the alarm and may or may not call the police when they hear it. Have the speakers mounted on the exterior of the building so the alarm will be heard.

Maintaining control of keys:

- Select one person to be responsible for authorizing and distributing keys to your building.

- Maintain control records of key numbers, door numbers, whom the key is checked out to, the date key is issued, the dates keys are returned, and signatures of the persons the keys are returned to.

- Place *all* key records in a safe or a locked file cabinet.

- Label all keys and identify individual keys by their sequence number. Cross reference what lock the key goes to by the key numbers, in a legend located in the key record.

- Place all undistributed keys in a locked key cabinet, safe, or locked file cabinet.

- Have keys made up only as they are needed. Do not keep excess copies of keys on hand. Keep extra keys to a minimum.

- Lock up and keep *all* original keys as originals, not ever to be distributed. Should keys become lost or should you become locked out of the locked area or cabinet, use master keys to back you up. Do not make the mistake of locking up the master key in the locked safe or file cabinet that the key goes to.

- Make copies of keys from the originals, not from the copies. A key made from a worn copy will never work as well as a key made from the original that hasn't been used.

- Have all of your key copies stamped Do Not Duplicate. Professional locksmiths *will not* copy keys that are marked in this manner.

Identify and discuss security measures with staff/owners:

- Before opening your business, or a major expansion or move, have all key people responsible or in charge of maintaining security have a meeting on necessary security measures to be taken. Invite your locksmith and main security person to attend and give input to the discussion.

- Do not use the more common key ways (hole in the lock cylinder). If you use the common cylinders, they can be easily duplicated by most anyone with the most basic knowledge of locks and keys. Make gaining access to your locks more difficult.

- If you use more uncommon key ways, most keys will not fit into the lock and will not turn. Order your locks with unfamiliar key ways. If the locks are already in place, have your locksmith retrofit the old locks with new cylinders.

- Purchase high security keys and cylinders. They are more costly, but will offer much better protection. If you value your property, money, checks, business information, customer records, and mailing lists left on the premises, this is actually good value for the money spent.

- You may desire to have certain areas of your business more secure than other areas. It is a smart idea to add extra security to the exterior doors, accounting areas, personnel, and executive offices where your safe and vital records are stored, rather than worry about interior spaces that house samples and store fixtures.

Maintain locks and cylinders:

- Regularly maintain locks and cylinders. Regular lubrication will make locks work smoother.

- Don't force a lock. If you have to apply heavy pressure, it needs to be fixed. Locks are designed to work smoothly. Force a lock or put off fixing it and it will break at a most inopportune time.

Customer Theft Prevention

- Place small items in a locked case or near the cash register.

- Use adequate personnel to cover the store if you sell merchandise.

- Price all store merchandise by machine or rubber stamp.

- Use large tags that are hard to remove.

- Keep receiving door locked until shipments arrive.

- Use adequate store lighting.

- Use signs (shoplifters will be prosecuted, and *do prosecute*) and mirrors to deter shoplifters.

Employee Embezzlement Prevention

Unfortunately, as a business owner you need to take steps to ensure that your employees will not steal from you. **Use the following guidelines to help ensure that this doesn't happen to your business:**

- Set good examples for your employees to follow.

- Hold your employees accountable. Clearly define their duties.

- Have adequate accounting systems set up. Use good internal control. Make it easy to catch problems and discrepancies when they occur.

- Use numbered sales invoices.

- Let only one employee use the cash register.

- Have distinct separation of duties for employees.

- Check references of all people you hire.

- Bond employees by buying bonding insurance.

- Monitor bank deposits.

- Do not sign blank checks.

- Check the numbered sequence of checks.

- Watch for clues: Watch sales returns, unusual large debt write-offs, decrease in sales, inventory shortages, unrecorded sales, profit declines, increase in accounts receivables.

- Deposit customer checks daily.

- Keep a minimum of cash on hand.

- Watch for employees parking near the back door.

- Let only authorized employees place prices on merchandise.

- Watch for overrings. Items are rung up and sold to the customer for more on the cash register, re-rung at the correct price, and the difference pocketed.

- Do secondary checks on incoming shipments and confirm that what was recorded what was actually received.

- Keep tight control over keys. Change locks when employees who had access to keys leave.

Part 7

The Business Plan

A business plan performs several functions. A business plan helps the prospective business owner see if her ideas and plans are reasonable, possible, and viable. A business plan is a written guideline to follow that outlines the objectives, policies, timetables, functions, future goals, and strategies to use and follow for your business. A business plan shows where you are and where you want to end up. The plan will guide your firm during periods of growth, slow periods, and during long-term expansion.

Business plans are *extremely* important to help you obtain financing from any source. They must have accurate information on your business history, and your business future. It will provide the information to support this. A business plan will also show lenders and other professionals that you do have the managerial abilities to accomplish your final objectives.

Creating a business plan allows you to set goals and objectives. You are able to communicate these goals and objectives along with the strategies that will allow you to achieve them. All marketing procedures should be based on the written plan. Personal management skills for marketing, financing, and employee relations will also be developed more fully. If initial objectives and goals are not met, the business plan can be reviewed and used as a guide to help you meet the plans, goals, and objectives.

With a business plan the process is broken down into easier to manage steps. You gather and analyze information. A business plan may be an ideal place for you to make and learn from your mistakes — on paper — not with dollars.

Results of proper business planning:

- Business objectives are organized.

- The priorities of the business are laid out.

- Business and marketing strategies are outlined.

- The business timetable is outlined.

- Potential problems tend to show up during a business plan analysis, and their solutions may be contemplated before they occur.

- Financial goals are defined and communicated.

- Business activities, jobs, and responsibilities are defined and can be delegated at this point.

- Provides documentation for bankers and other professionals.

- Will help you build your management team.

- Helps prospective business owners evolve their managerial abilities.

Business Plan Outline

To create a viable business plan, it is necessary to take the time and the necessary steps to research and make decisions on all areas outlined below. Do a business plan outline before creating the final business plan.

Business idea:

- What type of interior design business do I want to have: Retail, wholesale, service, or a combination?

- What type of opportunity is it? Will it be year-around, seasonal, part-time, an expansion plan, or a new business?

- Why does this business promise to be successful?

Marketing plan:

- Who are your potential customers?

- How will you entice your target market customer and keep your share of the market?

- What will be your marketing territory?

- What methods will you use with marketing to achieve financial goals?

- What does the future of the interior design market look like?

- Is anything happening locally that could affect an interior design business, either positively or negatively?

Promotion:

- Advertising methods and plans. How will you promote sales?

- How much is your projected budget for advertising?

- Do you have co-op advertising plans with vendors and other related small businesses?

- What special promotions at various times of the year do you have planned?

- What type of window displays will you be using?

- What type of interior displays and other promotional methods will you use?

Competition:

- Who are your main competitors?

- Are the competitors progressing with their businesses?

- What are your competitors' weak points? Strong points?

- What competitor strong points should you employ in your business?

- How are you going to gain your share of the market? What methods will you use?

Products and services:

- What lines of various products are you going to select and carry? Why these lines over others?

- What services will you provide?

- Do you have a list of projected suppliers and their terms?

- Who will be the best suppliers? Why?

- What inventory will you have on hand when the business opens? How soon will you add other inventory?

- How will you price your products and services?

- What will be your discount policy? How about markdowns on older merchandise that isn't selling well?

- What will be your inventory, warehousing, and delivery systems?

The business operation:

- Where do you plan to locate the business? What factors and features influenced you for the location selection?

- Any advantages or disadvantages to this location?

- Does the selected building reinforce your marketing plans?

- Size of the location. Any advantages or disadvantages with size?

- What leasehold improvements will the landlord pay for? What are the leasehold improvements you will have to pay for?

- Have you planning the lighting of the location? Interior and exterior?

- Have you determined the layout of the location? Draw a floor plan and note fixture locations, electrical outlets, windows, etc.

- What image are you trying to project? What methods will you use to project this image and personality of your business?

- What color scheme will you use for the image?

- What are the projected hours and days of operation?

- Are there any special licenses and permits needed in your location?

- Will any regulations affect your business?

- Have you addressed future product capabilities that will either help or hinder your business?

Financial plan:

- Who will manage your finances?

- Who will do the record keeping?

- What are the monthly financial goals for the first year? Total for the first year? Quarterly for the second and third years?

- What is the projected monthly cash flow for the first year?

- Amount of money projected that will be needed for start-up? What will you use the money for?

- What is the source of the needed money? Method you will use to repay the money? How will you secure the loan?

- What will it cost to support your business for the first eighteen months?

- What sales volume will you need to make a profit during the first three years?

- What will be the break-even point?

- What are your growth and expansion plans and opportunities? Additional plans to add merchandise for the first year, second year, third year?

- What are your limitations financially? What are your projected assets, liabilities, and net worth at the time you will open?

- What will be the capital value of your equipment?

- What areas are you weak in? Where will you use consultants and specialists? What areas are potential employees weak in?

- What special talents will be an asset for the business? What special talents do your potential employees possess?

- What will be your monthly personal financial needs? What will be your yearly financial needs?

- Create pro formas, profit and loss statements, and balance sheets for the projected business.

- Create projected cash flow statements.

- What are the gross sales and profit projections for the first, second, and third years?

Personnel:
- What is the history of labor use for the business?

- What are your anticipated labor needs?

- Who will manage the business? Their qualifications? Weak points or limitations? Strong points?

- How soon will you recruit other designers or decorators? What will be the required qualifications regarding experience and education? How will you pay them? Will they be on commission only? Salary plus commission? What is their job description?

- Will you be hiring a studio assistant immediately? What will be the qualifications that you will require? How much will be the salary? Will the studio assistant also get a percentage of gross sales?

- Will you be willing to provide training? What type?

- What are your plans for employee hiring? Salary? Training? Supervision? Are you offering employee benefits? What type?

- How often will you be evaluating your staff? What will you base the evaluation on?

- Are you going to offer in-house contests and other means to motivate your staff with sales goals?

Administrative procedures:
- Business accounting system. Will you hire an accountant or attempt to do your own books?

- Who will file the required government reports?

- How will you control your business expenses?

- Will you have a petty cash account?

- How much business insurance will you have and where will you get it?

- Will you be hiring an attorney and an accountant to set you up and get you on the right track initially?

- What type of business structure (legal form of ownership) will you use for your business?

- What national organizations will you join? Local organizations?

- What collateral will you use for your business?

Customer service:
- Will you be offering Visa and Mastercard services?

- What procedure will you use for cancellations and refunds?

- Are you going to offer any free services?

Time schedules:
- What are you including in the time schedule?

- What is the projected time period for each of your business priorities?

- Who will take care of each priority?

- At what intervals will large amounts of money be needed? What will the money be used for?

The Business Plan

After outlining the business plan carefully and completely, you are now ready to proceed on to actually creating a business plan. Follow the business plan procedure step-by-step in the order shown below to create a viable business plan.

Cover sheet:
- Name of business.

- Name of owner(s).

- Home/business addresses and telephone numbers of owner(s).

- Date business plan is to be presented.

First sheet:
- Statement of business purpose.

- Name and address of business.

- Amount of financing sought.

- Purpose of financing (what will the money be used for).

- Statement of profit potential.

Section 1: Description of business (discuss in detail):
- Business description and the products or services you will provide.

- History of the business, if it is an existing one. Major successes and achievements to date.

- Your work experience.

- Projected growth possibilities and why you believe that the business will be successful.

- Affix a statistical summary of the interior design industry (in general) and correlate it to your market area.

Section 2: Marketing plan (describe in detail):
- Who are your potential customers? What is the description of your target-market customer? How are you going to entice them to your business, motivate them to buy, and how will you promote repeated business?

- Who is the competition? How is the competition doing? In what way will your business be superior to the competition? What is the share of market you expect to receive for your firm.

- Discuss your niche in the marketplace.

- What are your marketing/promotional plans? What will be your selling methods? Who will you use for suppliers? What do the selected suppliers have to offer your business? What are your purchasing plans?

- Where will the business be located? What are the positive features of that particular location? Why did you select that location? How will you lay out your business? How will the selected location help you with your marketing and promotion of the business?

- What equipment is required?

Section 3: Organization plan (describe in detail):
- Who will be your management personnel? What are their job descriptions? What are their qualifications, weak points, and strong points? What is the innovative ability of the management team? What are their salaries for the first three years? Attach resumes, references, and any employment agreements.

- Discuss your expected labor requirements. How many employees will you need? What are their job descriptions? Who are they? What are their qualifications, weak points, and strong points? Will they be employees or independent contractors? Who will train them? Who will supervise them? Attach resumes, references, and any employment agreements.

- Discuss the consultants and nonbusiness associates who will make up a portion of your management team. What specialist or consultant services will you need to subcontract? What will each of them provide for you?

- What is the legal structure of the business? How will the selected legal structure benefit the business? If a corporation, who are the officers?

- How will you manage business finances and record keeping? Who will do it?

- What licenses, permits, and regulations will affect your business?

Section 4: Financial plan (discuss in detail):
- Include the application form (from the financial source you are presenting the business plan to) and the expected effect of loan report to show your plans for the use of the financing.

- Carefully answer each question in brief sentences on the application and expected effect of loan report.

- Description of accounting principles and accounting firm used.

- Attach copies of tax returns.

Summary: Summarize the business plan (in two to three paragraphs):
- Paragraph 1: Summarize the description of the business. Include the name and address of the business, type of business, the offered products and services, the names and addresses of the principals, amount of money sought, and the purposes that the money will be used for.

- Paragraph 2: Summarize your marketing and promotional plans. Portray your potential market and how you will attract this market. Describe your competition and your superior selling methods.

- Paragraph 3: Summarize your organizational plan in terms of management personnel, employees, and the business legal structure.

Financial Data: Include the following financial reports (be very thorough):
- Sources and application for financing (this shows how much money is needed and sources of funding).

- Capital equipment list (list of all equipment owned by the company that could be used to secure the loan).

- Beginning balance sheet (shows the up-to-date assets, liabilities, and net worth of the business).

- Break-even analysis (how much you have to sell for the business to break even and cover monthly expenses).

- Annual projected income statement and explanatory notes (these show sales, costs of goods sold, gross profit, expenses, and net profit for the first three years).

- Monthly projected income statements (these show estimated income for the first year monthly, and quarterly for the second and third years).

- Monthly and quarterly cash flow projections and explanatory notes (these show the expected business cash flow).

Business Plan Evaluation

Once you have set yourself up for business and opened your doors, it is imperative to stay on track with your business plan and projections. This is done by periodically evaluating where you appear to be heading as compared with your original business plan. If you are going off in another direction, a careful evaluation of the business plan can help you get back on track. You may find that you need to revise your business plan to fit your business. The initial planning may have been off base with your original projections and ideas.

Part 8

Forms of Ownership

Legal Forms of Businesses

Before starting your interior design business, decide what legal form your business will take. The legal form selected will affect taxes and personal liability. There are three different legal structures to take: sole proprietor, partnership, and corporation. Regardless of the legal form selected for your business, as a business owner you will still risk liability for everything you own and have. Work with a CPA and/or a business attorney (preferably a business/tax attorney) in deciding which legal form to take. **Factors to consider when selecting one legal form over another:**

- Any legal restrictions.

- The need to borrow capital.

- Better tax advantages.

- Liability concerns.

- Number of people associated in the business venture.

- Division of company earnings.

Sole Proprietorship (ONE PERSON BUSINESS)

Small businesses usually start out as sole proprietors or partnerships and progress to corporations later. A sole proprietorship is the simplest and easiest legal structure to start a business with. It is also the least expensive of the three legal forms. You are simply required to file a fictitious name statement at the local courthouse and obtain a business license from your city or county. If there are zoning problems, you may need to hire an attorney to help you with zoning changes.

The disadvantage to being a sole proprietor is that *you* are solely responsible for any liabilities of your business. Creditors of your business can and will sue you, personally, to recover any debts owed by your firm. Any income generated by your firm is your personal income. Income taxes will be based on the profits generated by your firm.

Advantages to starting a business as a sole proprietor:
- Easy business organization to start.

- More freedom than other organizations.

- The owner has absolute authority over his or her business.

- The owner maintains maximum control over the business.

- All profits from the business go to the owner.

- There are tax advantages for small companies because earnings are personally taxed. Use Schedule C on individual tax forms.

- There are social security advantages.

- The owner can discontinue the business at will.

Disadvantages to starting a business as a sole proprietor:
- There is unlimited liability.

- The owner may have limited resources.

- The rate of growth of the company corresponds with the amount of personal efforts of the owner/owners.

- A death or illness can jeopardize the business.

- Personal matters can be easily intermixed with company business.

- Ability to retain professional management is more difficult.

Partnerships

Partnerships are *similar* to a sole proprietorship with regard to personal liability and taxation. A partnership may be formed by an oral agreement between two or more persons. Legal fees are higher than those of a sole proprietor, but less than forming a corporation.

A partnership consists of two or more people sharing a common interest in the business. All of the partners share the ownership of the business along with the risks, personal liability, and the profits. All partners of the partnership also have unlimited liability. Any claim made against any member of the partnership is a claim against *all* of the partners.

Partnerships are *dangerous*. Like marriages, most of them do not work out. If you are opting to form a partnership, select a partner or partners who have business talents that are different than your own. Let them contribute in a major way to the business, but in areas that you are weak in.

The possibility of finding another person or persons who will contribute the time, interest, expectations, effort, money, etc., to the business and be compatible with you in personality and business style is extremely remote. Most partnerships start out with high expectations and an optimistic attitude among the partners and end up dissolved later (in or out of court with mounting legal fees). At the time you are putting the business together a partnership may seem and feel like it is the right route to take. You may feel that you need that extra support and comfort of having a partner by your side. Consider *finding* (use any avenue that you can) the money the partner would contribute, take courses to brush up on your weak points, and hire out some of the work that would be performed by your partner. If you don't, you will probably end up paying dearly in the end.

Partnerships are usually started by friends, former colleagues, and relatives. Because of these close ties, a split up of a partnership may be as painful as a divorce. Like a divorce, a split up of a partnership will usually cause hurt feelings, bitterness, misunderstandings, and anger toward one another.

The need for each partner to contribute equal amounts of time and energy is far more important than each partner contributing the same amount of money to the business. Time off should be available in equal portions for each partner. In a start-up business, each partner should be willing and able to do a little bit of everything. If you have a partner unwilling to do his share of the drudgery, hard feelings, friction, and anger develop, and the failure of the partnership is imminent. This is why it is necessary to spell out in writing exactly what is expected from each partner when starting a business.

How much money each partner will invest and the source of the money should also be in writing. During the periods of restricted income, the amount of money each partner will forfeit should be discussed and written down in a record. Partners should also note, in writing, their individual goals and aspirations for the company concerning marketing and management.

By noting all of the above in writing, you are able to foresee problems before they arise. If problems are resolved before they appear, you will not have to face a solution under stress later that may lead to bad feelings, anger, and the eventual dissolution of the partnership. If you survive and you have been in business for awhile, writing all plans out is still the way to go.

If the partnership should need to be dissolved later, who did what, why the partnership actually failed, and all records of the ongoing decisions of the business may be examined and the reason determined for the partnership failure. If you don't write down the decisions as they are made, when the partnership fails no one will agree on who actually made the failing decisions.

If you still think that a partnership is the way for you to go, find a partner/partners who you know you can get along with, be very careful in the selection of your partner/partners, and always retain 51 percent of the partnership for personal control. Additionally, you must be a partner-type person. You will not be able to run the whole show, only your portion of it. Partners must cooperate with each other on each and every decision. In other words, are you very independent? If so, forget it!

Advantages to forming a partnership:

- Talented people with diverse talents can work together complementing each other's weak points.

- More capital is available for partnerships than for sole proprietorships.

Disadvantages to forming a partnership:

- Unlimited liability.

- All partners are responsible for other partners' business actions.

- All owners share control of the business.

- Disputes may arise among owners of the business.

- Should a partner die, withdraw, or go bankrupt, the partnership may terminate under state law. Under federal income taxes, the partnership lives on.

- It may be difficult to get rid of an incompatible partner.

- The line of authority is unclear.

Guidelines to Use For Partner Selection

- Select a partner with strong talents and skills in the areas that you are lacking.

- Select a personality that meshes well with yours. Can you brainstorm together? Do you trust this person? Are you better together as a unit than you are individually?

- Are your goals for the business similar? If you don't share common ideas on where the business should go or how it should be operated, you won't work well together.

- Define what *specific* jobs each of you will be responsible for.

- Can you agree on how money will be spent? This is a key area of concern (just like marriage).

- Do you agree on the amount of money to be taken out of the business and used as your salaries?

- Can you communicate well?

- Do you have the same degree of motivation? Otherwise, you and your partner will be constantly irritated.

- Put in writing everything agreed on.

Partnership Agreement

A partnership agreement should consist of some key elements. Have the partnership agreement in writing in case of a dissolution. Use the key points below as a guide to forming your partnership agreement.

- Name and address of your company.

- Legal description of the business/type of business.

- Term of the partnership.

- Partners' names; their share of ownership; their financial contribution.

- Duration of the partnership.

- Restrictions on expenditures by all partners.

- What avenue your partnership will take to obtain needed money in the future.

- Duties and responsibilities of each partner concerning the business.

- Amount of salaries for each partner.

- Division of profit and losses.

- Buy-sell agreement should be drawn up by an attorney if the business is sold later. How will it be sold? Under what terms?

- Method of liquidation of the business in the event that a buyout by the partner doesn't occur or the business needs to be dissolved for any reason.

- Restrictions and provisions on ownership transfers, additions, or forced withdrawal of any partners.

- Value method to be used to determine the business's value in the event of death, disability, or a partner wanting to leave or retire from the business.

- Insurance coverage to cover any partner's death or disability. The insurance money should be used to buy out the dead or disabled partner's interest. Talk to a qualified insurance agent to discuss the amount and type of plan you will need.

- Arrangements to update or amend the partnership agreement regularly.

- How will disputes among partners be handled?

- Distribution of assets on dissolution.

- Dated signatures of partners and their spouses.

Corporations

A corporation is an artificial body — a legal entity. Forming a corporation does offer some benefits, if it is properly formed and maintained. Corporate shareholders' personal liability is limited and there is continuity of the corporate entity. Creditors may look only to the corporate assets to collect on monies owed. Shareholders may be held personally liable if they sign guarantees for the corporation or agree to pay corporate debts, in the event the corporation can't. Any debts not guaranteed become the liabilities of the corporation. When the corporation terminates and liquidates, the corporate shareholders are not personally liable for debts owed to creditors even if the corporation is unable to pay.

Banks, landlords, and other sophisticated people associated with during the course of business may ask you to sign personally, to give your personal guarantee that *you* will repay or pay any money owed. If you sign guarantees, you will not be able to hide behind the corporate veil concerning your debts. Always sign in corporate capacity (corporation name) rather than in your personal name to limit liability to the corporation.

Corporations are expensive to form. Consult with an attorney about what form of corporation your business should take. The amount of paperwork required by the government is extensive and stockholder meetings must be held regularly. If you form a corporation, always retain 51 percent of the corporation for personal control.

For potential product liability suits, make sure that corporate policies and rules are strictly followed, otherwise the corporate veil can be pierced and corporate officers and managers can be held personally liable for liabilities.

The board of directors is the governing body of a corporation. The board of directors consists of shareholders (elected by shareholders) and usually several managers (outsiders), who are in charge of managing the company.

Incorporate your business name. Call the secretary of state's office to see if the desired business name is available for use.

Advantages to forming a corporation:
- Limited liability for stockholders for larger businesses. Liability *may not* be limited for stockholders of smaller companies.

- Easiest business form to use to raise larger amounts of capital.

- Stock shares can be easily transferred to another person or entity.

- Business purposes may be separated into different corporations.

- Death of a shareholder will not affect the corporation.

- Unlimited life.

Disadvantages to forming a corporation:
- Owner/owners of a corporation may have a false sense of security should something go wrong.

- More expensive organization to form and maintain annually (legal and accounting expenses).

- Corporations pay more taxes (depending on the type).

- Franchise tax fees must be paid and filings dealing with security laws and the establishment of the corporation must be filed annually in most states.

- Power of owner/owners is limited due to the corporate charter.

- Owner/owners have less freedom involving business activities. The corporate managing body and the board of directors make the business decisions.

- Legal formalities must be followed if the corporation is to be maintained. Closely regulated.

- Control and management are governed by the majority stockholders.

Sub-Chapter S Corporations

A Sub-chapter S corporation (also called a Sub S corporation or an "S corp") combines the positive features of corporations with the tax advantages of the sole proprietor or partnership. Sub S corporations are taxed like a partnership, while still allowing corporate protection against liabilities and debts. There is no double taxation; the corporate tax is erased. All profits and losses pass through to the stockholders. Some of the qualifiers for your business to form a Sub S corporation are:

- Shareholders must be U.S. residents or citizens (domestic corporation).

- Sub S corporations cannot have more than thirty five shareholders.

- Sub S corporations can have only individuals, estates, or certain types of trusts as their shareholders. Partnerships and other corporations (artificial entities) are excluded.

- Only one class of stock may be issued. Generally this type is voting stock.

- Nonresident aliens may *not* hold stock in the corporation.

To maintain a Sub-chapter S corporation:
- Records and books of the Sub S corporation must be maintained on an annual basis.

- As with other corporations, Sub S corporations must meet the corporate formal requirements mandated by state law. Included are minutes from meetings and the election of board of directors and officers.

Part 9

Business Start-Up Costs and Sources of Capital

Business Start-Up Costs

You need to be very realistic when determining how much money you need to start a business. If you underestimate how much capital you will need, you will run out in a very short period of time, and if you do not have any ways to get more capital, you will soon be out of business.

The stress of trying to survive undercapitalized is hard to deal with. Undercapitalization is probably the primary reason that most businesses fail today. They didn't plan on all of the costs of having and sustaining a business during its growth period.

You may find that you do not have as much money to start the operation as you would like. You may need to retain your present job and work the new business on a part-time basis. Start small and find out if the business will really succeed. Don't get discouraged and throw your dreams out the window if you have limited resources or means to get the money for your business. Save money while gaining the knowledge and experience needed to go forth and start your own business.

Capital Needs for Start-Up Costs

As you gather information on the costs of starting your business, fill out the following two work sheets to gain a perspective on the amount of money you will need to start and hold in reserve while getting your business through the start-up phase. Determine the approximate date capital will be needed for *each* expense, so that you will have access to the right amount when it is needed.

$_____ **The down payment.** If purchasing an existing business or starting a franchise. Confirm amount with seller of the business or franchisor.

_____ **Inventory.** To get an accurate estimate of this figure, check with suppliers, vendors, and wholesalers. They may offer you sixty to ninety days to pay for the items.

_____ **Needed construction improvements.** These improvements include construction, signs, and everything needed to be done by a contractor to get the store interior and exterior ready to open.

_____ **Fixtures and equipment.** All items needed for display, interior signs, Mastercard and Visa equipment, cash registers, desks, chairs, etc.

_____ **All deposits.** Deposits include rent, telephone, utilities, sales tax, etc. Call and get amounts for each.

_____ **Business stationery.** Call around to various printers and compare pricing on several items.

_____ **Cleaning equipment and supplies.** Starting up, you will probably need to do your own cleaning. Later, you can hire a janitorial company.

_____ **All permits and licenses.** Call your city office to determine their requirements for interior design businesses.

_____ **Incorporation fees.** If you decide to incorporate early on. Call your attorney to determine his or her charges for incorporation.

_____ **Legal, accounting, bookkeeping, and insurance costs.**

_____ **Advertising expenses.** Interview the various advertising media available for the community to determine what methods you are going to use to launch your business initially.

_____ **Staff payroll.** If possible hire a studio coordinator immediately. Place your decorators and designers on commission with a weekly draw check. Starting out you may need to be the only designer. Have fellow designer friends work out of your studio on commission with their own leads and some of your leads.

_____ **Add an additional 10 percent** (minimum) **of the total for unforseen expenses.**

Capital Needed in Reserve for Operating Expenses (Overhead)

Estimate the monthly amount for each of these major expenses. Multiply the monthly amount by the factor shown to determine what amount of money you will need to hold in reserve. Unless stated otherwise, for a new business multiply by two. Determine the approximate date capital will be needed for *each* expense, so that you will have access to the right amount of capital when it is needed.

_____ **Staff salaries.** Multiply by two for an existing business or franchise. Multiply by three for a new business.

_____ **Owner salaries.** Multiply by one for an existing business or franchise.

_____ **Payroll taxes.** Multiply by one for an existing business or franchise.

_____ **Rent.** Multiply by one for an existing business or franchise.

_____ **Utilities.** Multiply by one for an existing business or franchise.

_____ **Telephone.** Multiply by one for an existing business or franchise.

_____ **Advertising.** Multiply by two for an existing business or franchise. Multiply by three for a new business.

_____ **Auto expenses.** Multiply by one for an existing business or franchise.

_____ **Office/store supplies.** Multiply by one for an existing business or franchise.

_____ **Leases on all office equipment.** Multiply by one for an existing business or franchise.

_____ **Travel/entertainment expenses.** Multiply by one for an existing business or franchise.

_____ **Bad debts.** Multiply by one for an existing business or franchise.

_____ **Interest and principle on borrowed money.** Multiply by two for an existing business or franchise. Multiply by three for a new business.

_____ **Association and professional dues.** Multiply by one for an existing business or franchise.

_____ **Other expenses.** Multiply by two for an existing business or franchise. Multiply by three for a new business.

Even if a business isn't generating any income, the overhead expenses must be added in as they are constant.

Financing a New Business

Many businesses fail because the owners do not acquire adequate capital to keep them running during the start-up phase. Most of the time, this is due to poor planning, not a lack of funds. Before attempting to start your own business, make sure that you have enough affordable and easily accessible capital.

After determining the amount of capital required for start-up costs and the amount of capital held in reserve, you will have an accurate idea of the capital requirements for the start-up of your business.

After you determine how much capital you require, you need to *find* affordable capital to fund your business venture. All capital has a price — some stiffer than others. The price may not be reflected in interest rates or other miscellaneous charges, but may be reflected in the degree of control you agree to give up. Make sure that you are willing to pay the high price of loss of control and independence. Look around and find a capital source you can afford. Generally, new businesses will not make a profit the first six months to a year. Therefore, *avoid* loans with short repayment periods. Determine the date you will require the capital. Money must be available *when* you need it.

Sources of Capital

Money to start a business may be obtained from various sources. Depending on your credit and its condition, the availability of financing will vary. The older the business and its ability to show profit, the more money will be available to borrow. You will find that money is more readily available for tangible goods such as equipment and real estate than is available for overhead expenses.

Since you are probably concerned with finding capital to start a business, listed below are the sources for you to consider to obtain financing:

- **Your own savings accounts.** If you do not have at least *some* money of your own to invest and risk on your new business, you will have a difficult time borrowing from other people.

  Usually people who are anxious to strike out on their own and have their own business save up some of the money to finance their own business. The funds obtained this way become the equity you have in your business. Ideally this equity continues to grow with the life of your business.

- **Take out a home equity loan on your house.**

- **Mortgage your home or other large asset.**

- **Take out a loan on your life insurance policy.**

- **Take an early payoff on a company pension plan.**

- **Ask family and friends.** Family and friends are usually the easiest to persuade. Make sure that you will be able to repay them. When borrowing from family and friends, make sure that they are in a financial position where they will not be ruined if you are unable to pay them back.

  Decide if you are going to simply pay them interest, or if they will own a portion of your business. Have legal agreements made up showing how you will repay the loan.

- **Obtain and use credit cards with lower interest rates.** Have the amounts for the credit cards you already have increased *before* you state that you are starting a new business. Put what expenditures that you can on the credit cards. Take cash advances at your credit card cash advance interest rate for the rest. This type of credit usually has a substantially higher interest rate than other capital sources.

- **Banks.** Not many banks will loan money to new businesses in the start-up phase. If you find one that will, the loan will have many restrictions attached to it. Banks like to see financial records showing how the business will repay the loan. They will also require collateral for their loan. This collateral will probably be in the form of a second trust deed on your home. You will also probably be required to have a financially able co-signer for the loan. Banks do not feel that the positives outweigh the negatives when dealing with small businesses. See section on borrowing from banks for more information.

- **Finance companies.** If the interest rate and other circumstances are met, some finance companies will lend small businesses money. You will pay more points and a higher interest rate here, but if you have few other alternatives, this may be the way for you to go.

- Consider forming **a partnership** (silent or active). Both of you put up and/or borrow a portion of the money. For money advanced by silent partners, pay a reasonable interest rate for the use of their money.

- Consider forming **a corporation** and selling shares in your corporation. Your business does not have to be a public company to sell shares. Make private sales to individuals. The investors will have to believe that they will be able to get their investment back, either in the form of dividends or equity growth.

- Contact the **Small Business Administration** and other government groups that sponsor small businesses (see below).

- **Request credit from suppliers, vendors, manufacturers, distributors, and wholesalers.** Available trade credit will vary from thirty days to six months. They may charge a service charge for any credit extension beyond thirty days. After you establish credibility with the trade (established through a good working relationship and prompt payment of your bills) you will see that credit is easily obtained through these sources.

- **Use deposits on orders and letters of guarantee.**

- **Lease everything possible** (instead of purchasing) through leasing companies.

- **Use venture capitalists.** Venture capitalists demand a high rate of return for money lent. Only the smaller venture capital companies will do business with small businesses starting up as they require high capital appreciation. They are found in the yellow pages under investment firms, financing, and loans and in newspaper classified ads or from referrals from other lenders.

  Be prepared to sell venture capitalists on your business idea and supply a professional business plan for their review. They will provide money as a silent partner rather than as a lender. They will want a controlling interest in your company (could be 51 percent or more). Be sure that you are *willing* to give up financial and possibly management control of your business. Have an attorney draft and review any documents required to obtain money from a venture capitalist.

- **Purchase a seller-financed existing business.** Most sellers of existing businesses will finance their loans for you. You will generally be required to come up with a 20 percent to 30 percent down payment and may end up with loan terms that you can get at the bank. This is a preferred way to go for someone with little capital available to invest in a start-up company. The seller may want out of the business and the interest rate available from you in carrying the paper of the loan will be better than what saving term accounts have to offer if the loan was paid in full to the owner.

If you cannot show a way to repay the money, you will have difficulty borrowing it anywhere, even if you have collateral to back up the loan.

Small Business Administration (SBA)

The **U.S. Small Business Administration (SBA)** operated by the federal government, sponsors small businesses. The Small Business Administration largely functions as a guarantor of loans for small businesses supplied through commercial banks (up to $500,000). On occasion it will make direct loans to business owners. Presently, its direct loans are limited to handicapped persons and Vietnam veterans. Some banks will work with the SBA and others will not.

Massive amounts of paperwork to guarantee the loan is required by the SBA. Because of the time-consuming amount of paperwork and your lack of credibility (because you couldn't obtain the loan on your own merits from the bank), some banks will just not work with an SBA-secured loan. The SBA also has heavy requirements that must be met before considering whether to secure the loan for you. The advantage to an SBA guaranteed loan is the length of term you have to pay it back.

To qualify under an SBA program, you need to meet the following criteria:
- The proposed business will be the primary source of income for your family.

- You are unable to obtain financing elsewhere.

- You have at least 20 percent of your money invested in the business venture. This 20 percent can be in the form of collateral.

- You are able to show a reasonable chance of repaying the loan with the business.

- Your business concept is solid and viable.

- You have the capability and experience to succeed in the proposed business.

- You are of good character.

- You agree not to discriminate with the business on the basis of race, creed, color, or national origin.

The SBA's mission statement is to "*stimulate and foster economic development through small business.*" It will help you start a business and help you over the growth hurdles of existing businesses. Representatives will counsel and assist you with business development, finances, contracts, and advocacy, *free of charge, if you are a small business.* The business must be "*independently owned and operated and not dominant in its field.*" The business must meet size and volume standards as determined by the Standard Industrial Code. Your business will likely fall in the category of a small business.

The SBA provides management assistance. They sponsor courses, workshops, provide counseling, and provide very informative booklets. They work directly with SCORE (Service Corps of Retired Executives). SCORE is an organization of 13,000 volunteer business executives.

Visit an SBA office (every large city has one) or call (800) 368-5855 for more information and get some direction from their loan officers on the best way for you to go on obtaining financing for your business venture. SBA may or may not be right for you.

Your local SBA office can supply you with a list of small business investment companies (SBICs). These companies are licensed by the SBA and can supply you with equity capital to finance your business if you are unable to obtain capital elsewhere. These companies are usually more willing to take a bigger risk than other lending sources.

Borrowing Money from Banks

When you borrow money from banks and credit lenders, you will not have to repay it through a reduction in ownership of your business.

Expect to come up with 50 percent of the money you require from your own sources. You must have 50 percent of the needed equity for the business for a bank to consider loaning you the rest. Be willing to secure a bank loan with your personal and business assets. Have a co-signer lined up to sign as a source of repayment for the loan if you fail.

If you feel that this is an avenue that you are going to attempt, have a professional business plan to present to the bank.

When ready to borrow money, design your loan proposal so that it will fit into the type of categories that banks use when determining whether they will accept or veto a loan proposal.

Banks will expect you to be of good character and require the following questions to be answered. These are easy if you have taken the time to develop a business plan.

- How much money does the business need?

- Why do you need the loan?

- How will you repay the loan?

- How long do you need it?

- How soon do you need the loan?

- On *what* will the money be spent?

If they are convinced of your ability to repay a loan, banks, will place certain restrictions on the lending of their capital. Your loan will also be supplied with a variable or floating interest rate. As their costs rise, so does your interest rate. Interest rates charged by banks are connected to the prime rate, or the rate charged by the bank to preferred customers. As the prime rate changes, so will the variable interest rate on your loan. The following restrictions apply when you borrow money from a bank:

- You must file a periodic report about your business.

- You may not borrowing any more money with the bank or elsewhere.

- Limitations are placed on your salary and your employees' salaries.

- You must personally guarantee that you will repay the loan, signed in your name, not your corporation's name.

- You must have a non-interest-bearing checking account for your business account so the bank can make extra money without having to pay you interest.

The following conditions can be negotiated with a bank on obtaining a loan:

- **The interest rate of the loan.** Try to get a variable loan rate that will not exceed 3 percent above prime rate. If you are providing collateral for the loan, try to get an even lower interest rate. Have a ceiling amount placed on the interest rate.

- **Term of the loan.** Request a time period with monthly amounts that you can reasonably afford to pay back. Consider having lower monthly payments with a balloon payment at the end of the loan.

- **No prepayment penalties.** If you get the chance to refinance the loan elsewhere, if interest rates fall or you decide to sell the business, you want to be able to pay back the loan without a penalty.

Types of Loans

Short-term loans

Short-term loans are usually for less than one year, but may extend to two to three years. They are used for seasonal money needs, when emergencies arise, when good deals on inventory arise, and to pay for accounts receivables on a short-term basis. With short-term loans, banks usually require you to be fully paid up and out of debt at least thirty days a year. Within the short-term loan category, there are several different classifications:

- **Line of credit:**
A very simple way to borrow money from a bank. A predetermined amount of money is available for a company to use as needed during a specific period of time. Interest is paid only on the amount of money used during this period (up to two years), but other banking fees, usually about .5 percent to 1 percent, are charged for the availability of the funds that may or may not be used. Banks will sometimes waive the fee if a company keeps a compensating balance in its account (an amount of money that must be kept on deposit at the bank during the loan period).

  - **Nonbinding line of credit:** This form of credit is less expensive, but if your company isn't doing well, there is a strong possibility that your available credit will dissolve before your eyes. During hard economic times, banks may run into cash flow problems and eliminate your available credit. The sudden loss of available credit may be avoided if you are willing to pay a premium commitment fee — usually 2 percent. With payment of this fee, the loan becomes committed and available when you need it.

  - **Revolving line of credit:** This type of credit demands that your line of credit, debts, and payback are reviewed yearly, but does not require that you be paid up for thirty days a year at the bank. This is not unlike your credit card system. As you make purchases, your available credit diminishes; as you repay your account, your credit again rises. Revolving lines of credit are usually paid back in monthly installments of interest plus principal.

- **Inventory loan:**
Some banks prefer to give you a more informal inventory loan (usually of six- to nine-months duration) to big-ticket retailers rather than a line of credit. An inventory loan is a short-term loan to carry inventory. The bank uses the inventory as its collateral. This is also know as "flooring" or "floor planning." Money is available to be borrowed as needed, and repayment of the loan occurs in installments as the inventory is sold. Again this type of loan requires a period of thirty days a year where all debts are paid.

- **Commercial loan:**
This type of loan cuts down bookkeeping time for both the borrower and the lender. Commercial loans are time loans that are repaid in a lump sum at the end of the duration of the loan (usually three to six months). Commercial loans are usually used to fund inventory, but can be used for other reasons if the bank agrees. The bank will question how your company will be in the position to repay the loan in one lump sum at the duration of the loan. An extensive credit check will be done on your company.

- **Accounts receivable financing:**
Much of a company's capital may be tied up in accounts receivables. Banks convert accounts receivables into needed cash. The accounts that banks will consider for accounts receivable financing are those with good credit with accounts that are less than sixty days overdue. Banks will generally loan you up to 65 to 80 percent of the account receivable's face value, to be repaid as the money is paid by the customer. Generally, the actual payment check you receive from the customer is handed over to the bank. The bank divides the check and deposits your portion into your account. Any loan amount that is still outstanding is charged interest. This type of loan is usually written for one year, although depending on the bank you may be placed on a revolving account. With a revolving account you are reviewed yearly and the account must be renewed yearly. The bank will continue to advance funds against your accounts receivables. A minimum amount to loan may be set by the bank due to the costs the bank incurs in handling these loans for you.

- **Factoring:**
Accounts receivables are bought outright from you at a discounted rate from a bank or factoring company. This is an expensive way to borrow money (higher than most of your other options). You accounts receivables may be deeply discounted from their face value. Accounts receivables are purchased without recourse. The bank or factoring company assumes the risk (you are no longer involved in any way) and makes all of the collection efforts. You can have your factoring plan set up to notify your customers that their account has been sold, or set up so that your customer is not notified and is unaware that their

account has been sold. Banks and factoring companies will pick and choose which accounts receivable are credit worthy enough for them to buy.

Medium-Term Loans

Medium-term loans are usually of a duration of one to five years and normally require collateral. Equipment, fixtures, furniture, remodeling, and expansion are all usually done under a medium-term loan. If you are just starting a business, banks may require you to come up with additional collateral in addition to the assets you are borrowing money to pay for. Banks making medium-term loans may assess operating restrictions on your company. You may be required to maintain a certain amount of working capital or a specific ratio of assets and liabilities. Limits may be levied on the distribution of dividends and/or on other company debts. Terms are negotiable and will vary from one bank to the next. Shop around. Below are summaries of the two types of medium-term loans available:

- **Term loan:**
  Term loans are usually written for five years or for the life of the asset. If the loan is only for five years, the asset may be refinanced at the end of the loan. This type of loan provides from 80 percent to 90 percent of the costs of the assets. Term loans are usually set up to require quarterly installments of principal plus interest. The principal amount will remain consistent with the interest declining over the term of the loan. Installment payments on the loan are higher at the beginning of the loan and lower at the end of the loan. The repayment schedule can be adapted to your cash flow needs.

- **Monthly payment business loan:**
  This is an adaptation of the term loan. Instead of making the payments quarterly, you make them monthly. Try and set it up with the bank so the payments are equal for the life of the loan. Equal monthly payments are usually easier to handle than large quarterly payments.

Long-Term Loans

Long-term loans are usually five years or longer in length. These loans are hard to get and are not usually sought unless you need to borrow money for real estate, expansion, acquisitions, and start-ups for new businesses. These are the different types of long-term loans available:

- **Commercial and industrial mortgages:**
  Usually available if the building you are leasing becomes available for you to buy. Banks and other lenders will lend you up to 75 percent of the building's appraised value. The mortgage may be written up in various forms geared to the appraised value of the real property, your company's long-range plans and profit projections, and the terms of the bank you are dealing with. The longest term loan that you will get is for twenty-five years, to be paid back in monthly installments. More true to form is the five- to ten-year loan with affordable monthly payments that will have a large balloon payment of the entire amount owed when the loan comes to term. Most companies refinance the loan when the balloon payment is looming in the near future.

- **Real estate loan:**
  This type of loan is borrowed against already owned real property. Money may be borrowed to expand a business or to make other business acquisitions. If your property has appreciated in value substantially and the money borrowed is almost guaranteed to show substantial profits, this may be the way for you to go. You are adding a second mortgage against your equity and good credit. You may be paying a lower interest first mortgage. Another alternative is a "wraparound mortgage." A wraparound mortgage is nearly identical to a second mortgage except that the bank receives all of the mortgage payments and then pays the first mortgage after the second mortgage is satisfied.

- **Personal loan:**

  Personal loans are given on the basis of personal collateral, marketable securities, savings passbooks, and certificates of deposits. This is usually an easier type of loan to qualify for and get, than a business loan.

- **Asset-based loan:**

  This is also known as a leverage buyout or takeover. This type of loan is new to small businesses; in the past it was predominantly used by large corporations. The main company's assets are used to finance the takeover. Almost all of the company's assets may be used as collateral for this maneuver. All assets combined will amount to 70 percent of the acquisition costs. Your company will be charged prime rate by the bank plus 2 percent to 3 percent. Banks will levy operating restrictions and keep close watch on your assets. Terms will vary from bank to bank.

- **Start-up loan:**

  Banks want to see start-up companies with most of the capital needed coming from your own personal funds. You will need to take out personal loans and tap any partners you have for their share of the funds. It is possible to get a loan from the bank's venture capital specialists. Through the Small Business Administration program that guarantees loans for small businesses, 90 percent of the loan will be guaranteed. Small Business Administration guarantees demand a vast amount of paperwork that the banks do not look fondly on. Also, depending on the economic climate, the SBA may or may not be in a position to guarantee small business loans. Some banks participate in the SBA's Certification Program, and are able to put these packages together for you when the backing is available through the SBA, so shop around.

Writing a Loan Proposal

The main idea to project to your banker or lender is how the money you want to borrow will enhance the worth of your company. Loan proposals actually consist of eight different categories.

A preliminary to writing a loan proposal is a well put together business plan. If you have written an accurate business plan, your work is almost done. You are aiming your loan proposal at a different audience, so you are simply adapting your business plan to fit.

If you are unsure of which way to go, work with the lending officer at the bank on the information and the form that this information should be provided. They realize that your forte is your business, not writing loan proposals and business plans. They will expect the needed information to be provided in the required time frame. Try to put the package together and present it in one trip for a professional presentation.

When working out your loan proposal, be realistic and frank about your plans and figures. Bankers sometimes have solutions and experience should you run into trouble and will work with you to try to work things out favorably for you. **These are the various categories that must be addressed in this order for a loan proposal:**

- **Summary:**

  Start your proposal with a summary on the first page. Include your name and title, company name and logo, company address and telephone number, type of business, amount of money needed, reason for needing the money, and how you plan to repay the loan.

- **Profiles of the business's owners and management:**

  Include a paragraph on each owner and top manager. Describe background, education, achievements, skills, areas of expertise, and experience relating to the business. The more business-related experience and education that you can list here, the better. Make sure each key person appears very qualified.

- **Business description:**

  Provide a business overview of legal structure, length of time you have been in business, business assets, and number of employees. Describe what you sell, what markets you sell to, your customers, and your competitors. Give a description of and amount of present inventory on hand, how old is it, how popular it is (marketability — preferably not faddish), and how often your inventory turns over.

Include an accounting of your accounts receivable and your accounts payable. Describe and show individual amounts of your accounts receivables. List any foreseeable expenses.

Your banker will be looking for accounts receivables to be under sixty days old and spread out among many customers rather than just a few customers.

- ## Business projections:
Using your present and past growth as indicators, project the future growth of your business. Describe what you will do to obtain this growth within the next year, the next three years, and the next five years. Describe alternative plans and the course of action you will take should your growth projections fall short of your plans. Work out a practical timetable to achieve your goals and projections.

- ## Financial statement:
Assemble income statements and balance sheets for the past three years. Include current figures and make your projections for one year, three years, and five years. Figures on these sheets need to be very accurate. To establish credibility, have your figures and records audited and verified. At the very least have the figures reviewed and verified by your accountant before presenting them to your banker for a loan proposal. You will need to furnish two sets of projected balance sheets, with two sets of income and cash flow statements. One set should show projections of what will happen if your company *does* receive the loan, with the other set projecting what will happen if your company *doesn't* receive the loan.

Realize that your projected growth will be measured against published industry standards, so be realistic and don't over- or underestimate expenses anywhere.

Provide income tax statements for the past three years, even if you were not in business at that time. Your personal financial credibility is also on the line. Credit reports will be run not only for the business itself, but for all of the principals of the business.

- ## Purpose of the loan:
What are you going to use the money for? Describe and spell out what the actual use and end result expected will be by receiving the loan.

- ## Amount of money needed:
Determine and state the amount of money needed to achieve your projections and goals. Support the figure with estimate sheets and documentation from suppliers, media sources, etc. Also have last year's figures from similar or the same sources to present. Determine the actual amount needed and ask for it. Remember that bankers will compare the amount you request and the figures you use to support it to published industry standards.

- ## Method of repayment:
Match your assets to the type of loan you are attempting to get. The asset should last as long as the duration of the loan. The proposed assets should be able to generate capital, which will be used as repayment funds. If you increase your sales, cut your costs, or increase your efficiency, you should increase your capital. Your projected balance sheet should define the ability of your company to meet the interest payments and the capability to repay the principal from your net profits. Spell out an alternative plan for repayment if your first plan fails. You will have to personally guarantee the loan if your first plan fails. Again, the review by the accountant will verify if your plan is viable.

Part 10

Management and Financial Considerations

Hire an accountant and business attorney when starting your new business. The accountant will help you avoid mistakes that you are sure to make without the proper financial counseling. The accountant will set your accounting system up in an organized, usable manner. Although it will cost you money, you will save money in the long run.

You should use a business attorney to help you decide what business form to take, review any contracts you consider signing, and draw up any needed contracts for your business.

Accountants and Certified Public Accountants (CPAs)

A good accountant can help erase many obstacles, costs, and potential problems by supporting you with accurate and timely data.

A certified public accountant (CPA) serves as your business and financial guide, helping you to use your resources more effectively. CPAs help you to achieve maximum success and profitability with your business. They help you to make sound business decisions, to solve business problems, and to communicate effectively with other professionals and governmental agencies connected with your financial life.

To become a certified public accountant, a CPA has to meet significant educational standards, work a minimum of two years for a public accounting firm, pass a difficult examination, and meet state licensing requirements. CPAs must also meet continuing education requirements.

You do not need to know how to draft final balance sheets and other related financial statements, but you should be able to interpret them. When financial statements and financial records arrive, review them. Have your accountant teach you how to interpret them and use the information. Have your accountant demonstrate how the data and information can assist your company.

Since creative people are usually the worst when it comes to the financial record-keeping aspects of the business, start your business with professional help. **A CPA will create and oversee a system that will meet your business requirements. A CPA can:**

- Help you select the proper organizational structure for your business.

- Prepare annual tax returns.

- Do tax planning and recommend tax-saving strategies.

- Monitor tax law changes that may affect you.

- Prepare financial statements according to the needs of your business. Help you to understand and use these financial statements to your benefit. Help you with business projections, budgets, and goals.

- Prepare quarterly financial statements and payroll tax reports.

- Design and help select software for your record-keeping and accounting needs to fit your business and/or personal financial affairs.

- Work with you and your management team to plan your business strategies and help to solve your business problems.

- Help you with decisions about whether to lease or buy and expansion decisions.

- Serve as your advocate in tax matters. Should you be audited by the IRS, the Franchise Tax Board, or another governmental agency, your CPA can represent you.

Set Financial Objectives for Your New Business

Decide and write down what you want to make for the first year and again for the next five years. Beware of setting your financial objectives too high for the first and second years. These are the difficult years for starting a business. You actually will probably just stay financially afloat during this period.

Bank or Savings and Loan Selection

Shop around for a bank or savings and loan for your business, just like you shop for everything else. You may find that savings and loans have a lot of services free to offer your business. They do differ in their charges, what they will provide you, and whether they want DBA (doing business as) business accounts.

- What are the minimum balances that must be maintained to get free services?

- Are there monthly charges for savings accounts?

- Is there a charge for *each deposit made*?

- How is the interest compounded? What is the rate and the yield?

- What services do they have available? At what cost?

- What can they offer you in a loan or line of credit?

- Is there a free checking if a minimum savings account balance is maintained?

Business Checking Account

Do not make the mistake of using your personal checking account for your business transactions. You need a separate business checking account for accurate record keeping and substantiation of your business deductions for income tax purposes. Banks do differ in what they charge for checking accounts. Call around and price compare banks and savings and loans that are near your business. **Use the following points for comparisons:**

- Is there a *monthly charge* for the checking account? How about if you maintain a minimum balance?

- What is the charge for checks? With maintenance of a minimum balance?

- Is there a charge for *each deposit made*?

- Is there a charge for each check *deposited*? A charge for out-of-state checks deposited?

- Is there a charge for each check *written*?

- Is there a charge for *returned* checks?

- Is *interest* paid on the checking account balance?

Will Your Interior Design Business Make You Money?

To answer this question, you must estimate sales, gross profit, expenses, etc. Combine the estimated figures with the information gleaned while discussing your potential business with business owners and suppliers in the interior design industry. If you are buying an existing interior design business or franchise, the estimated figures are available for your information and the potential success rate is much higher.

The following are the real determining elements that will likely ensure success or failure. Adequately cover these areas and your chances of having a successful interior design or decorating business are greatly improved.

- **Economy of the community.**

- **Location.**

- **Adequate financing.**

- **Experience.**

Note: An interior design or decorating business is relatively easy to start. Showing a profit and staying in business is a more difficult achievement.

Ways to Cut Down Costs of Doing Business

There are two ways to increase profits in business: increase sales or cut down costs. These are methods of cutting down costs of doing business:

- Analyze where are you spending your money.

- Have a timely record-keeping system.

- Reduce your costs for installation, delivery, and shipping.

- Select products that are manufactured and distributed closer to your locale and are less expensive.

- Evaluate your marketing costs. Select *smarter* ways that give you a higher return for your money.

- Get your management team to work on cutting costs of doing business.

- Outline a budget and stick to it.

Business Capital Shortages

After you have been in business awhile, you may find that you require additional business capital. This does not mean that your business is struggling. Successful businesses need extra capital from time to time. In growing businesses you may need to finance growth to sustain the greater customer demand for your products and services. Here are some of the typical reasons why you may require additional capital for your business. If you properly planned for your business needs, you will avoid the first three reasons for needing extra capital.

- **Business plan *improperly* estimated capital requirements.**

- **Unanticipated company growth.**

- Inventory needs to be increased.

- Need to purchase company assets.

- Excessive unpaid accounts receivables.

Sources of additional capital:
- Commercial banks.

- Small Business Administration.

- Partnerships.

- Make a public offering.

- Venture capitalists.

- Obtain and use supplier credit.

- Have orders prepaid.

- Use deposits for orders to partially pay for goods.

- Obtain accounts receivables.

- Use bonds and other debt vehicles.

- Home equity loans.

- Use your credit cards.

- Use personal savings.

- Borrow from family and friends.

Visa and Mastercard Merchant Accounts

If you want to increase your gross sales by thirty percent to fifty percent, the best means are Visa and Mastercard transactions.

Visa and Mastercard transactions have changed tremendously in the past few years. Now, almost every merchant that offers these accounts has a computer terminal to read the credit card or key in credit card numbers. A printer then prints out a receipt. The merchant is freed from making a phone call to get the authorization number and writing out a credit card receipt. Some banks still offer their credit card services via their telephone lines (transaction fee per call). But it appears that the phone line transactions will be phased out in the future. Presently, if you opt for the transaction via the phone lines, you will pay a slightly higher interest rate in addition to the higher transaction fee per call.

The bank of your choice will electronically be deposited with the amount of the transaction transmitted via your terminal.

Because of heavy abuses, Visa and Mastercard merchant accounts are not easy to get. This is especially true if you have questionable credit, no storefront, are new in business, are transient in nature, or are a non-homeowner (can easily pick up and leave town).

It may seem that everybody appears to have merchant accounts — the TV is full of "infomercials" (long commercials) asking you to call up and order via your Visa or Mastercard. Some of these companies are shady, some pay very high interest rates up to 20 percent, and some actually have their accounts in other countries.

Rates and service charges vary tremendously within this business. You would probably assume that the lower rates would be available through the commercial banks, but this is not so. Commercial banks are more afraid than ever to deal with you, and charge very high rates for everything. Banks want to put you on a sliding scale for a percentage rate for the amount of your average item and for the amount of transactions that you do. If you go through a bank, you will be required to have an account with them.

It is far better to go through a Visa and Mastercard broker and shop their rates against each other. An unknowledgeable person who does not shop around will *easily* pay a higher interest rate, a higher monthly service charge, higher fees per transaction, and will definitely pay too much to obtain the transaction terminal and printer. After shopping the various rates available through brokers, if you are a very credible applicant, try to get the lowest price offered down even further. The representative will want to know who offered you the lowest rate and will probably know what bank the brokerage works through for that rate and for the credit level of the person who they are working with. Some of the companies guarantee to match or give the lowest rate; there is some flexibility in the interest rate, equipment charges and the initial application fee. A service charge of $5 per month and a per transaction fee of 20 cents would be hard to beat, but it may be possible.

Brokers will try to find out how much in gross sales you expect to do each month — the less the better, believe it or not. They are so afraid that you are going to go wild with the amount of transactions and money amounts, and they have to guarantee the Visa and Mastercard holders' accounts. If you go over the projected sales that you and the rep arrive at initially, they want to be immediately notified. They don't want any surprises.

Visa and Mastercard now want to know about what is the average transaction amount to expect from you. Anything more and they are red flagged to call you and discuss the transaction with you. They are only protecting themselves.

Whether you go through a bank or go with a broker, they will check you out carefully. A picture of the exterior and interior of the store, any stock, etc., will be taken. You will be required to submit your past year's taxes, samples of sales flyers, write-ups about your company, press releases, banking information, trade references, etc. They want to be sure that you are credible. You will be charged a fee of at least $100 just to apply for this service.

In recent times, some supposedly reputable people have taken all the credit card numbers that they have a record of (past sales) and rung them up on their terminal (which almost immediately credits the business bank account tied into it) and have taken off with all of the money.

Some brokerages will try to tell you that your good credit doesn't matter, that because of your newness in the business, you are working out of your home, etc., you have no choice but to pay *outlandishly* high fees, leasing, and service charges. A quality broker (the one you can trust to work with) will immediately run your TRW (credit report) before they even spend the smallest time with you to see if they can even help you. You will find out that your credit is everything.

If you are in a position to buy the equipment rather than lease it, do it. You will pay about three times the price to lease it. The equipment company will still stand behind it and fix it as needed, if you buy it. The price on the equipment will also vary widely. There are various brands and levels of quality for the equipment.

A printer is optional and expensive. If you expect to do few sales (but in large amounts), you might opt to write out the receipts by hand for small items you sell in the store. On your sales contracts for custom-made items you will be noting the use of the credit card and that is the only receipt you will need. As you grow and the more smaller items you sell, you may be in a better position to add the printer later. Get your broker to throw in (at no extra charge to you) a hand printer (remember the ones they used at every store, inserting the credit card and making an imprint). This will work for a while, without too much effort and without an extra expense since you are just starting out. Have them throw in several hundred receipts and give you the inexpensive source to buy more.

After extensively checking your credit and giving their approval, the brokerage will program your terminal for you. The terminal can be programmed for your city only or may be programmed (at no extra charge, so grab it) for the whole country. You are free to take your terminal to trade shows around the country and perform immediate transactions right there. Today you may not think that you need that special programming, but if you don't do it now, and want it later, you will pay to have the terminal reprogrammed.

Finally, the representative will come out and setup your equipment in your place of business and give you a demonstration on its use.

Be sure to take *special* care of any and all customers that pay through their credit card accounts. If more than a couple of customers call the credit card telephone number for their Visa and Mastercards and complain (called charge backs) in any way about you not taking care of a cancellation or a credit due them, your bank or broker source will cut off your account. After you are cut off from your current bank or broker, you are forced to go out and get your Visa/Mastercard merchant account elsewhere at a higher interest rate and service charge.

Note: If your brokerage or the bank backing the merchant account should go out of business, Visa and Mastercard will reassign you to another.

The following is what you should try to use as a guideline on your fees and charges to know if you are receiving a fair deal or someone is attempting to overcharge you. Paying slightly more or less is still okay. This is what Touch of Design agreed to pay after careful shopping:

Initial application fee (nonrefundable):	$100.
Interest rate:	2%
Monthly service charge for bank statement:	5.00
Per each transaction fee:	.20
High quality terminal, purchase:	750.
Printer, purchase (approximately):	400.
Lease terminal, monthly:	30.
Lease printer, monthly:	20.

Note: Since many more small businesses fail than succeed, and since many companies buy their equipment outright, you can find barely used equipment for less money than you can buy brand new from a brokerage or bank (let alone lease from these sources). The equipment simply needs to be reprogrammed for your business and bank accounts. Since most of the companies you will be contacting make a large amount of money selling you the equipment, they won't want to use your used equipment. But, some reputable companies will reprogram the equipment for $100 to $200. It may be worth it to you. Obviously, the company that simply reprograms the terminal is not going to be willing to service it or guarantee its performance in any way should anything go wrong with the equipment. Chances are, the equipment you buy will be barely used — probably from a company that never quite got off the ground.

Accounts Receivable

Client Records

Every customer who has retained your services or has ordered merchandise should have a client account card to track what they have paid and what they owe. A client record or account card should include an ongoing record of debits and payments. Send a copy of this record as your invoice or along with your invoice when you bill your customer.

Across the top of the card:
• Name (last name first), address, work and home telephone number. List across the top of the card.

In column form from the left to the right:
• Date of each sale for product or services.

• Product and/or service rendered.

• Paid column (when the client pays for that portion, mark paid in the column).

- Debits column. When the client pays for that portion, show a debit for the amount paid.

- Credits column. When a client makes a payment on the account, the credit column is credited with the payment amount.

- Balance column. Shows the balance of the account every time an item is debited or credited.

Invoicing Your Customer for Accounts Receivables

As a designer, you should not send an invoice to a client or collect payment for the job until the portion of the job you are billing for is completed to the customer's satisfaction. This also means that all parts of that portion of the job have been supplied and any related service requests have been completed.

Since you are in business to make money, it is important to have a billing system that provides for immediate collection the day of installation or for a system for billing once the job or portion of the job is completed. You should have invoices sent out within ten days of completion for smaller jobs and a monthly statement of completed goods and services for larger jobs.

Small companies or any company in business to make money cannot afford to have many accounts receivables. To ensure collection you need to attempt collection immediately and proceed with alternate collection plans for clients that do not pay or put off paying their accounts payables. See the section in this book on collection agencies and small claims court.

One way to ensure prompt payment is to charge interest on overdue accounts receivables. Print on the invoice, *Payment net 30 days. Late payments will be charged a fee of 2% per month* (or whatever amount you choose to charge). Then do it!

Have three-part invoices designed at a print shop with your business logo, address, and terms. Review Common Pricing and Purchasing Terms in this section for ways to write out pricing terms if you are willing to provide a discount for prompt payment.

The top sheet of the invoice is usually white, the middle sheet yellow and the bottom sheet is pink. Mail or give the top two parts of your invoice to the customer. Keep the bottom sheet for your records. Or photocopy the invoice if your customer requests a three-part invoice.

When the customer pays her bill, have her return the second sheet of the invoice with a check (yellow sheet). Match this sheet to the bottom sheet you retained and marked them both paid.

If the customer doesn't pay the bill within thirty days, rebill the customer. For collection problems review the collection problem section of this book.

If the job is ongoing and the customer is not paying you, stop working on the job. Let them know that work will resume when you are paid in full for the job. Write a stop work clause in your contracts, *that should the customer exceed the payment period, the job will stop, and in order for the job to resume, the rest of the job must be paid in full before delivery or installation.*

Accounts Payable

Accounts payable are not any *less* important than accounts receivables, if you would like to continue to stay in business and keep working with your suppliers.

To stay on top of your accounts payable, you need to work out a system to stay on top of the situation. Use the following system for staying on the bill-paying track:

- **Have time-frame targets.** Pay all bills within forty-five days after receiving them. Also aim to collect all accounts receivables within thirty days. You will not always pay and be paid during this time frame — just use it as your target so you keep up your cash reserves at all times.

- **Keep your paperwork organized.** Stay in track of particulars, especially due dates of your bills.

    - Date each invoice with the date they arrive.
    - File each invoice according to the due date of payment.

- ■ Stagger payments out over days and weeks. Get them out of the way sooner if the money is available to pay them and other expenses are expected.

- ● **Give your financial commitments priorities.** Which bills are the most important to be paid on time? Write a note to others explaining that you need to put them on the forty-five day plan. If you need to pay your payments with the forty-five day plan, let your vendors know that. They now know when to expect the bill. The bill is now not considered overdue. If they know what to expect, they will be happy with you and will want to continue the relationship.

- ● If you see the warning signs that you don't have the money to cover your bills, get on the phone and call your slow-paying customers and request that they immediately pay their bill.

Source Invoicing

An invoice is a billing statement. As a designer you will receive invoices from your suppliers or manufacturers for supplied goods and services, and you will send invoices to clients for payment of your supplied goods and services.

Suppliers do not generally waste much time in billing you. The billing statement usually arrives before merchandise shipments. Once the invoice arrives it is imperative that it is once again checked against the open purchase order for correct pricing. People do make mistakes. Be sure to note if any extra discounts are available if the invoice is paid promptly (within ten days.). Review the section on pricing and purchasing terms in this book.

Accounting Terms

A/R	Purchases by customers on account.
A/P	Purchases by business on account.
Accrual accounting	Revenue and expenses are recorded at the time they are earned or incurred.
Accounts payable	What a business owes creditors.
Accounts receivable	What creditors owe a business.
Assets	All resources (tangible or intangible), measured monetarily, that are owned by a business. Types of asset are: current assets, fixed assets, other assets.
Balance sheet	Report showing the assets, liabilities, and capital for a specific date.
BE	Break even. Revenues are the same as or equal expenses.
Capital	Owner's equity. Rights or claims to assets by owner/owners.
Capital statement	Report showing a summary of the changes in capital for a specific period of time.
Cash accounting	Revenue and expenses are recorded when they are actually collected.
Cost	The amount agreed upon by both buyer and seller.
Depreciation	Gradual wearing out of buildings and equipment over time. They lose their ability to provide useful service due to age and usage.
Drawing account	Remove money from business account/accounts for personal use. Acts like an expense because it decreases capital.

Equities	All rights or claims to assets of the firm. The two principal equities are liabilities and capital.
Expenses	Monies spent by firm toward creating revenue. Used up assets.
Income statement	Shows the summary of revenue and expenses for a specific period of time.
Investments	Acts like capital. They increase capital.
Liabilities	Rights or claims to asset by creditors.
NI	Revenues are greater than expenses. Stands for net income.
NL	Expenses are greater than revenue. Stands for net loss.
On account	Pay in the future.
Revenues	Monies to the business by customers for goods and services.

Record Keeping

Every interior design business needs a easy but precise record-keeping system. Record keeping may be done by hand with the use of journals (book of original entry) or with a computer system. Whichever type of record-keeping system you decide to use, it should be designed and planned by your CPA. Select a system where that you can simply double-check your figures to catch errors early and easily. In the yellow pages under *Business forms* you will find bookkeeping systems. One Write Systems (and probably others) have a representative that will come to you, demonstrate, set you up, and sell you appropriate systems for your needs. Your bank may also offer the same system (at probably the same price), but you will not get the same one-on-one help you will with a representative.

Record only *necessary* information. You can easily get bogged down and never seem to get around to doing your record keeping if the system you choose to use is to complex and time consuming. You need to do your record keeping regularly and keep all of your records up to date so that you know how your business is doing at all times. Detailed record keeping is vital for you to how your business is doing financially and is required for federal and state taxes.

How complex your record-keeping system will need to be will be determined by the size, volume of sales, capability of hiring and retaining accounting help, and the intricacies of your firm's operation.

These are the usual records that you will need with your accounting system. Some of them can be combined into one record. Have your accountant tailor a simple system for your business needs.

- **Customer's record** (on their folder)

- **Sales journal**

- **Purchase journals**

- **Quarterly cash receipts journal**

- **Quarterly cash disbursements journal**

- **Petty cash journal**

- **Accounts receivables ledger**

- **Accounts payable ledger**

- **General ledger**

- **General journal**

To be more accurate with your record-keeping system, use the *accrual method of accounting*. The accrual basis will tell you not only the money that you took in and the money you paid out, but what is owed to you, or what your owe. With the cash method of accounting you record money only when you receive it, and only when you pay it out in accounts payable. You don't account for what is owed to you or what you owe until money exchanges hands. Sales tax must be maintained on the accrual basis. **Follow these simple rules for better record keeping:**

- Assets = liabilities + capital
  (owns)   (owes)   (net worth)

- KIS — keep it simple!

- The record-keeping system needs to be consistent.

- Use a double-entry system. This way you are able to balance every transaction. If you did it right it balances.

- Use a calculator with a tape to check your numbers when you don't balance. If the balance difference is divisible by "nine", you have transposed a number.

- Put small notes around numbers to help you remember what they are.

- Set up columns for more common expenditures. Use a miscellaneous column for uncommon expenses (make a small note, labeling the item in the column).

- Make a chart of accounts. List all the categories. Consistently list items by the same name throughout the year.

- Be timely.

- Deposit all income from the business (cash also), then write checks to pay the bills.

- Pay for all business costs by check or with your petty cash fund.

- Separate your business checking account from your personal checking account.

- Pay yourself a salary rather than constantly dipping into your company's funds.

- Request a month-end cutoff statement from your bank on the same date as you do accounting.

- Use a spread sheet system — spread the checks to their appropriate categories.

- Place a check number on all bill stubs.

- Make a yearly log of all months at the end of the year to do a comparison.

- Current account receivables are thirty, sixty, ninety days. Anything over one hundred and twenty days should be sent to a collection agency. Keep notes in your ledger on what is going on with these accounts.

- The three ways to increase capital: investments, revenue, and net income.

- The three ways to decrease capital: expenses, drawing, and net loss.

The major accounting reports for businesses are the **balance sheet, the income statement, and the capital statement**. These should be prepared by your accountant or CPA They show the financial condition of the business.

Sales Journal or Sales Record

Keep a simple journal of all business transactions. This record will tell you how well you are doing and is also needed for tax purposes. Purchase an 8 ½" x 11" notebook or ledger and use one or more pages for each month (depends on how much business you are doing). Across the top of each page mark off ten columns, reading from left to right. Make the third, fourth, and fifth columns wide enough to contain the customer's name, a description of supplied merchandise, and a description of supplied services.

- Date of invoice.

- P.O. invoice number.

- Sold to.

- Amount of retainer or deposit and check number.

- Brief description of merchandise and quantity (pattern, color, source).

- Source or vendor.

- Services provided.

- Sales amount without sales tax.

- Amount of sales tax.

- Total amount of sale.

- Projected costs.

- Amount billed.

- Amount received.

- Date received.

At the end of each month or at another regular interval, send ongoing customers a statement keeping them apprised of their balance due and payments received.

Purchase Journals

For *each* vendor or supplier of goods and services you will need to create a purchase journal to track vital information. The purchase journal should list purchase information and supplementary information relating to the order. In a column format from left to right, label and record the following information:

- Date of order.

- Supplier or vendor.

- Purchase order number.

- Item.

- Receiving date.

- Selling price of the item, service, labor.

- Cost of item, service, labor.

- Freight costs.

- Work order number.

- Labor vendor for work order (all labor vendors have a purchase journal cross referencing the same information).

- Installer (all installers have a purchase journal cross referencing the same information).

- Sales tax.

- Customer's balance for vendor-ordered goods.

- Date payment received from customer.

- Payment amount from customer.

- Date vendor or source paid.

- Amount paid to vendor or source.

- Company balance with vendor.

Quarterly Cash Receipt Journal

This journal is used for your quarterly reports. Information is recorded after you have been billed for the total costs of all merchandise and shipping. Across the top of the page of your ledger mark off and label ten columns, reading from left to right:

- Bank deposits.

- Payments on account.

- Total sale.

- Amount of sales tax.

- Job costs.

- Use tax.

- Payments received.

Break-Even Point or Analysis

You are in business to make a profit. Making a profit will not only improve your standard of living, but will also provide the area with economic growth, employment opportunities, and long-term wealth. The break-even point shows you how to make a profit by increasing the contrast between income and expenses.

A profit is the amount of the gross income that is left after all the expenses are paid. A loss occurs when the expenses are more than the income. To determine if your are making a profit, you must employ a break-even analysis. **The break-even point occurs when total expenses equal total gross income.** The two types of expenses are the fixed costs and variable costs. Fixed costs are the costs that must be paid every month, regardless if you make any sales (salaries, interest charges, rent or mortgage payments, equipment costs). Variable costs are the costs that are directly related to the sale of the products and services (commissions, subcontractors, product costs, marketing and advertising costs). As your gross sales increase, your variable expenses increase. If your break-even point is too high, you will lose money. With your profit and loss statements, you should be able to project a break-even point with 50 percent or less of your anticipated business.

To determine you business profit, you should receive timely profit and loss statements from your accountant that list your company's sales and expenses. By reviewing these you can determine whether your fixed or variable costs are excessive. You can also determine if it is likely that you *can* make a profit.

Cash Flow Analysis

Cash flow analyses are prepared monthly by your accountant. You need to review and understand it. A cash flow analysis will show you how much money you have available, how much is needed for a specific period of time, and when you will require additional cash. A cash flow analysis will help you prepare for future problems. If you can see that you are going to run short of funds down the line, you can plan how you are going to get the needed funds, before it is too late.

Cash flow analyses will only show cash income and cash expenses. It should display actual expenses and income for six months and project at least twenty-four months ahead.

Staff Salaries

When determining how much an employee is going to cost your company, factor in these additional benefits:

- Social Security insurance.

- Unemployment taxes.

- Worker's compensation insurance.

- Vacation and holiday pay.

- Sick pay.

- Company costs for group health insurance and dental insurance.

- Company costs for group life insurance and disability insurance.

- Pension or profit-sharing plans.

- Educational seminars and courses (highly recommended, but optional).

- Payment for employee professional dues (optional).

Paychex

Paychex is a publicly held company that provides a comprehensive payroll and payroll tax preparation service to more than 100,000 small to medium-sized companies nationwide. This is an extremely affordable service that includes payroll tax return preparation. Each company that signs up to work with Paychex is assigned to a fully trained payroll specialist. The specialist coordinates the services to meet each client's needs. The following are standard Paychex services:

Each pay period the following is prepared:
- Payroll checks with employee earnings statements.
- Payroll journal
- Departmental earnings and deduction summary
- Client time sheet
- Required payroll deduction registers

Every deposit period:
- Written notification of all required federal, state, and local payroll tax deposits, including the tax deposit amount and due date.

Every Quarter:
- 941 quarterly return
- State unemployment insurance return
- State quarterly wage return
- Required tax deposits for federal unemployment insurance
- Required local tax return and deposit notices
- Detailed employee earnings history
- Quarterly report of wages
- Year to date report of wages

At year-end:
- Employer and employee W-2 forms
- W-3 transmittal of income and tax statement
- State and local reconciliation form
- 940 federal unemployment insurance return
- Supporting detail for the year's payroll

All of the above is included in their one low price. They don't charge extra for anything except delivery. There's no extra charge for conversion to their service, new hires, for checks, W-2's, completed quarterly returns, etc. This is the way to go if you want to cut down payroll headaches for a very inexpensive price. Contact Paychex Corporate Headquarters, 911 Panorama Trail South, P.O. Box 25397, Rochester, NY 14625-9986. Highly recommended.

Part 11

Expanding and Relocating

Should You Expand Your Operation?

To accomplish long-term cash flow, business growth is required. You can expand your business by finding new markets for your products and services, enhancing your marketing attempts, and providing support products and services.

Evaluate what made your present customers purchase your products and services. *Who* is your target customer? Survey similar markets with *like* target markets (demographics). I.e., if a certain type of person is constantly buying from you, target other nearby areas with similar customers.

Your management team should constantly brainstorm and investigate new ways to keep your company out there in front of prospective customers. Consider hiring an advertising agency or public relations firm to assist you with marketing. They will provide you with new ideas and skills to carry out effective marketing plans. Some of these agencies will allow you to simply pay them a portion of the new business they help you acquire as their fee. This way you pay for what you *actually* get.

Consider products and services you can easily spin-off on and add to your present line of products and services. Know what your competition's weak spots are with their products and services, and add those to your line.

If your present operation is successful, you may consider adding another branch store. This carries as much risk as opening your initial operation. There will be different types of problems and challenges that you did not encounter the first time around. Approximately half of all expansion efforts fail within five years of their opening. If you are able to succeed with your growth plans, your compensation will probably be excellent.

The advantages to expansion are that you are able to spread your expenses between more than one operation. Some of the expenses that may be shared include bookkeeping, insurance (business interruption), advertising, delivery, and warehousing costs. You will receive better discounts from your suppliers for larger volume purchases.

Adding another operation allows you to immediately multiply equity and status in your business. Equity in your business may actually double because of the addition of a second operation. With additional operations you are able to easily spot your strong points with one store and your weak spots in another — allowing you to accentuate the strong points in both stores and eliminate the weak.

Adding a second operation gives you more ammunition to fight your competition. Sometimes it is better to expand your business on the outskirts of your area when opportunities become available, than to let your competitors enter your territory. Place an operation fairly near the first one (easy to manage) and discourage your competition from moving in on your customer base.

Realize that your new branch operation could attack in on your own customer base from your original store and grab some of its profits. Give careful consideration to site selection to help eliminate this problem. Don't suspend plans to expand to a certain area because a competitor has moved in. Turn the presence of a competitor where you want to expand to a benefit. You may have the *better* operation and may be able to grab their customer base if their quality of work and service is not satisfying their customers.

If the location you are considering is located in a shopping center of any size or is located near a shopping center with storefronts available for lease, contact the leasing agent for demographic information on the area. The leasing agent usually has a packet of information to send out.

You will be provided with information on population, race, age groups, income, education level, marital status, age of area, number of children, number of home owners, number of renters, home value, number of autos per family, etc. Another source for this information is the U.S. Census Bureau.

Use the demographic information to calculate your branch operation's approximate gross sales. Take the per capita expenditure for your type of product. Find out how many customers reside in the territory you are considering and multiply the number of customers by the average purchases your current customers make.

As an owner and probable manager, you will now have to delegate duties. You will no longer have the time and energy to do it all. Do not make the mistake of neglecting your initial operation while starting the one. Put out fires at each location as they arise. Don't put them on hold until they are out of control. If you don't have extra time and great health to devote to an expansion project, don't go forward with one.

Try and give your expansion project a slightly different style. Don't use the exact same product mix, layout, samples, displays, etc. Rather, tailor your new store to fit your new group of target customers. Are they more upscale as a whole? More family oriented? Do they mostly work in a specific industry? What is that industry?

When Should You Expand Your Operation?

Just because your operation may be humming along smoothly making you money, this should not be the sole factor causing you to take the plunge and expand into another store. Simply duplicating your present operation in another city will not necessarily guarantee satisfactory results. More stores will not ensure more financial growth for your business.

If you should have the right situation arise where you *do* want to go ahead and add another location, realize that doing so will probably not double your present income. There will be the *possibility of improving* your present income over a period of time. By adding another location, you *will* be building equity in your business. Your business will increase in its present value.

You may feel that you should add another location. The business *is* there and your ego demands that you go ahead and add another store. The prospects of doing so may be exciting and may help breathe life into your existing business with exciting marketing plans to help get the other location thriving. If you carefully consider the location of the new business it is hoped as you did with the first you may easily achieve large financial rewards by opening up a store in another location. One location may bring in an adequate living, but two would help you live very comfortably — this is especially true in the case of a partnership setup where the money is going into more than one pocket. Make sure the time is right, the location is superb, you really do have enough time and energy to go ahead with an expansion plan, and all negative points are carefully weighed against all positive points.

Do not locate your new store too near your present store or you will be taking business from your existing store and giving it to your new store, while paying double overhead for the same customer. Locating your new store in a distant city will make it difficult for you to travel between your various locations. You will spend virtually most of your precious (and stretched thin) time on the road in your car, talking on your car phone. Things can get out of control when businesses are too far apart and you may end up later back at square one — with one location you can easily manage and control. **These are the various ways to expand your existing business:**

- **Expand at your present location.** Add more inventory, take on more lines. Add more space — if the location next door should come available at favorable terms and the timing is right, take it.

- **Add one or more locations.** Build more businesses (cookie cutter approach) just like your existing one.

- **Open a similar business.** Pick related products or higher quality products than the ones you carry presently. Go into manufacturing your own window treatments, accessories, reupholstery, etc. Become a wholesaler at one location and a retailer at your other location.

- **Set up a franchise operation to copy your successful business.** If your image, ideas, and marketing plans are great ones, this may be just the way for you to expand.

- **Sell your business and buy an existing, more luxurious and impressive business.** Since you now have the experience it takes to run a business, you may now be in a position to have the interior design business of your dreams.

Things to Consider About Expanding Your Business

- How organized and well-run is your present operation? Get your existing operation humming along smoothly and profitably before considering any expansion efforts. You will not have time later, once expansion is underway, to refine your operation.

- Can you make quick, accurate decisions? Are you a problem-solver that can head off problems immediately before they get out of control?

- Are you proficient enough to run another location or a larger operation? Can you handle the extra stress and pressure?

- Can your present business be affordably copied elsewhere? How smoothly is your present operation running and what is its financial condition?

- Is there enough demand for the products you carry or want to carry at the location you are considering?

- What is the projected economy? Does the interior design industry as a whole project a healthy economy or are sales down everywhere?

- Will the expected financial gain outweigh the time, energy, and investment expenditure?

- Do you have enough experience in running a business to take on other locations? Your present system of operations will have to become very refined, organized, and easy to teach to less-experienced managers.

- Are there qualified people available for your new business? Your choice of management for distant locations will make or break your new operation.

- Do you have the skills needed to recruit, train, delegate, fire, and motivate your employees from *afar?*

If considering franchising your business:
- Do you have the available financing to put together a franchise operation?

- Is there really enough available profit for the franchisee to pay your percentage each month and still make an adequate profit?

- Will the image of your franchise operation attract potential franchisees?

- Can you standardize your operation? Each new location should be more efficient than the last.

- Are there other *similar* successful franchise operations?

Relocating Your Business

At some point you may decide to relocate your business. You may be located in a dying area of the city, your lease may be up and you are unable to renew at favorable terms, or a newer and nicer location may be available for your more affluent business.

If you are faced with relocation of your business try to improve on what you have presently in pass-by traffic, quality of the building, a more prestigious neighborhood, etc. Attempt to capture as many new customers as you can to add to your existing customer base. Get rid of anything that is not adding to your business. Put more attention on the areas of your business that are really working and expand in these areas.

First and foremost preserve your existing customers. They must be brought with you to your new location. They are the base of income that you need in order to pick up the pieces and keep your income coming in without missing a beat.

In order to preserve these customers you need to **tell them repeatedly that you are moving — when and where.** Do this by sending letters, reminding them in flyers, calling them up, reminding them when they come in to your store, and posting signs on the door of your store and in the store before it is relocated. Start months in advance. Put a notice in the newspaper inviting anyone interested to come to an open house and a grand opening sale at your new location. Use the relocation as an idea for a fantastic sale. On all notices and flyers, include a map pinpointing your new address.

Realize that if the new location is too far away you are going to lose many customers. Some customers will always be loyal to you; others, usually the ones you *thought* would be loyal, will be the first ones you will lose. It might be better to expand into another location than lose most of your customer base.

Try to plan your relocation with closing one door and opening the other. Make sure you are continuously available for customers.

Part 12

Taxes

Internal Revenue Service (IRS)

The IRS keeps a careful eye on small businesses in two primary areas. Their main concerns are businesses that don't make payroll tax deposits and for those that identify employees as independent contractors, when they are really employees. If you are careful with these two areas, the chances of getting into trouble with the IRS are vastly reduced. The IRS is very concerned about collecting what is owed to it.

IRS investigators come right into businesses and audit books if they suspect wrongdoing. Collectors start their investigation by finding out who had authority in the business to pay taxes. This is determined by examining records to see who makes the financial decisions for the business. They focus on the person or persons who had check-signing authority and the people with corporate titles. Then they decide who of their targeted group acted "willfully" in preventing the IRS from receiving payroll taxes. Willful means that you knew that you owed payroll taxes, but for some reason didn't pay them. If you are found to be the responsible party, you will receive a notice and a tax bill. The determination can be appealed. Appealing will buy you time, interest will not accrue, and the decision *may* be reversed in the process. Hire a tax attorney to represent you with the appeal. Should it be determined after the appeal that you do owe the money, plus penalties, you still have several options:

- Pay the payroll taxes plus the penalties. Set up an installment plan or try to reduce your liability through an IRS program called an Offer in Compromise, which allows you to get off with paying only a portion of the amount assessed.

- Sue the IRS in federal court. All payroll penalties can be brought before a federal court. To start the process, you must pay a small portion of the taxes due. The amount you must pay is the only the amount for one employee's payroll tax for one quarter of any pay period. File a suit seeking a refund for the taxes paid on the grounds that you were not responsible.

- File for bankruptcy. You won't be able to cancel all of a payroll penalty with a Chapter 7 bankruptcy, but you can include the penalty in a repayment plan with a Chapter 13 bankruptcy.

Misclassifying employees as independent contractors is the other major problem that businesses easily encounter with the IRS. If you call your workers independent contractors you may be audited to see if this is correct. Review the independent contractor section in the personnel section for the criteria to follow with an independent contractor classification.

If you are audited and found to have misclassified your workers as independent contractors, the IRS will assess you not only the payroll taxes that should have been paid, but also any of the employee's unpaid income taxes. The penalties can be as much as 50 percent of the workers' total wages received.

Federal Filings and Forms

Hire a CPA and a tax advisor to help you stay current with all necessary federal filings and forms. Below is the list of federal filings you must make to stay in business.

Employer identification number:

If you have formed a corporation or partnership or are a sole proprietorship with employees, obtain a taxpayer identification number by filling out Form SS-4, Application for Employer Identification Number. This form is available from the Internal Revenue Service. For sole proprietors without employees, you are able to use your social security number for identifying purposes. This number is your employer identification number and is to be shown on all business tax documents including tax returns. If your legal structure is a partnership or a corporation rather than a sole proprietor, you will need to obtain a separate tax identification for the corresponding legal structure of your business. To apply for a separate number, use the IRS Form SS-4. Also available from the IRS is a business tax kit, which covers all of the various taxes your new business is responsible for.

Necessary filings for firms that have employees:

- Form W-2: Employer's Wage and Tax Statement.

- Form W-3: Transmittal of Income and Tax Statements.

- Form W-4: Employee's Withholding Allowance Certificate.

- Form 501: Federal Tax Deposit Form. Used for withholding income and FICA (Social Security) deposits.

- Form 940: Employer's Annual Unemployment Tax Return.

- Form 941: Employer's Quarterly Federal Tax Return.

- Form 1099: Information Returns.

- Social security taxes, quarterly.

Federal Income Tax Filings

Businesses must file income tax forms. The type of forms needed to be filed will differ depending on the form of your business. Below is a listing of the legal formations and what forms they must file:

Sole proprietors	Schedule C, Form 1040 Schedule SE, Form 1040
Partnerships	Schedule K, Form 1065 Schedule E, Form 1040
Corporations	Form 1120
Sub S corporations	Form 1120S
Private corporations	Form 1120

State Filings

State forms required will vary with the state. Most states will require:

- Employer identification number (EIN)

- Sale and use tax certificates

- Registration of corporations

- Employee withholding reports

- State unemployment taxes

- State income taxes

City/County Filings

Every location is different. Some cities and counties are extremely strict, while others are very lenient. Check with your chamber of commerce and city offices to see what you must file for your business. Usually when you file for sale and use tax certificates you will be requested to fill out the city or county sales tax licenses so that they can also collect their share of taxes. If it is not offered to you at the board of equalization, then check with your city offices to find out where you need to go to fill one out.

Check with your city about zoning before you apply for a city license. If you are caught operating a business in a residential zone or a noncommercial zone you may be fined. If you want to do this and know that you are in violation, keep a low profile and do not tell neighbors that you are operating out of your home and do not tell your customers where you live. Naturally, no customers will ever be coming to your house. You will always have to go to them. Usually cities will allow you to operate a low-key business out of your home. If you do not accept deliveries at your residence and do not have employees and clients coming and going, they will usually issue you a license. Anonymously call and inquire over the phone before you go down to the city and alert them to what you are going to do.

Payroll Taxes

If you have employees working for your business, you must file Form 941, Employer's Quarterly Federal Tax Return, every three months and Form 940, Employer's Annual Federal Unemployment Tax Return, once a year.

Every payroll period you must withhold federal income tax and FICA (social security and medicare) contributions. The amount of federal income tax withheld is determined by how many deductions employees claim on their W-4. The FICA contribution is a percentage of the employee's gross earnings, which employers must equal with their contribution. Employers pay the tax by depositing the money with a bank qualified as a depository for federal taxes. Employers withhold the tax every pay period, but deposit it only quarterly.

Sales Tax

To sell goods to customers, you must obtain a resale permit from your local board of equalization. A resale permit allows the retailer or designer to defer the sales tax to the time when they resell the goods to the consumer. The consumer then pays sales tax on the selling price, not the designer's cost or net price. If you sell a customer goods and don't collect sales tax, you will still have to pay it to your state and city.

States vary on sales tax percentage and sales tax law. When you apply for a resale permit, you will find out the percentage of tax and the state's procedures.

A **note** of caution: if you tell the agency that you are going to be making big sales monthly, they will have you post a bond, accordingly. If you tell them you are just starting out and don't expect too much in the way of sales, you may not have to post a bond at all! Everyone thinks (and hopes) they are going to start off really making the sales. It doesn't usually happen that way. So tone it down and be realistic. If they see you are making a large gross in sales, they will ask you for the bond anyway. Another reason to tone it down is so that you only have to pay the tax annually, rather than quarterly. Again, if the board of equalization sees that you are selling a lot, they will convert you over to the quarterly plan.

California sale and use tax regulations:

Terms vary from state to state, so read the information given to you when you apply for your resale number:

Merchandise or goods are taxable. Fees charged in connection with acquiring and providing furnishings or other tangible personal property are taxable if purchases are made. Fabrication labor is labor used to make a new article, or labor used to change the form of an existing article. Charges for this type of labor are taxable, even if the customer furnishes the materials. Stain-repellant finishes and fire proofing are also taxable.

Labor, consultations, layouts, design fees, installations, supervision of labor, and shipping are not taxable. But if you have built the labor into the price of the goods, the whole package becomes taxable. Repair labor, which is labor used to repair, refinish, or restore pre-existing property to its original state and use, is not taxable. Billings for exempt fees should be listed separately from fees related to sales of personal property.

Deliveries charges are exempt if all of the following are met: if the deliveries are separately listed, delivery is made by a facility other than that of the decorator (common carrier or contract carrier), charges to the client for delivery not to exceed the amount paid to the carrier, and charges are for transportation *directly* to the client. If you deliver property by your own facilities, or sell it for a delivered price, tax applies to the delivery charge.

The retailer may segregate in his records the sales price of materials and findings, fabrication charges, and exempt labor charges. The total sales less the exempt labor would be reported as taxable. Or, an alternate method may be used: 80 percent of the total labor charge may be claimed as exempt labor. The remaining 20 percent will be considered to represent taxable fabrication labor and findings.

Merchandise that you purchase for resale and divert to another use is subject to use tax measured by your purchase price. This includes merchandise taken home from your business for personal use or given or donated to others or organizations. If you know that you will not be reselling the merchandise at the time of the purchase, do not use a resale number to make the purchase. Purchases of supplies and store equipment for your business or use are taxable.

Any person who secures a seller's permit from the board of equalization ostensibly to conduct a legitimate business enterprise, but who in reality has no intention of doing so and uses the permit to give a resale certificate for purposes of evading payment of the tax is guilty of a misdemeanor.

As a seller you are required by the California Sales and Use Tax Law (probably the same in most states) to keep adequate records showing:

- Gross receipts from sales of all tangible personal property (including any services that are a part of the sale) whether you regard the receipts as taxable or nontaxable.

- All deductions allowed by law and claimed in filing your returns.

- The total purchase price of all tangible personal property purchased for sale or consumption.

These records must include (and be kept for four years):
- The normal books of account.

- All bills, receipts, invoices, cash register tapes, or other documents of original entry supporting the entries in the books of account.

- All schedules or working papers used in connection with the preparation of tax returns.

Part 13

Personnel Considerations

Consultants and Specialists

Most people venturing out and starting their own business are entrepreneurial types. They are usually multi-talented types of personalities. Even so, few people have all the knowledge and skills needed to do everything for their business.

Evaluate your strong and weak points to see in what areas you will need to hire consultants and specialists. If you can honestly answer yes to the various questions below, you may be able to perform those particular duties yourself. If you answer no to some of the questions, plan to get more education and experience, or hire a consultant or specialist for that particular area. Before you jump into starting a business, learn how ready you really are.

General organization and management:

- Are you very experienced in the interior design field? In the areas you will be specializing in?

- Do you know if it is better for you to open a new business or buy an existing one?

- Are you able to determine what legal form of business is better for you to use?

- Can you make the necessary business filings yourself?

- Do you know how to select a successful location for your business?

- Do you have an idea of what building site improvements will cost?

- Can you handle the negotiations regarding the lease or purchase of a business site?

- Can you make informed office equipment decisions?

- Can you efficiently plan the interior layout for your business?

- Can you plan for receiving of products?

- Do you know how to provide warehousing and delivery of products?

- Do you know where to find quality employees?

- Can you hire the needed employees yourself?

- Are you able to develop job descriptions for each employee position?

- Do you know how to determine employee salaries, wages, and benefits?

- Can you produce an effective employee training program?

- Are you experienced with supervising other people?

- Do you know how to evaluate an employee's performance?

- What methods will you use to motivate employees?

- Do you know how to plan work schedules for employees?

- Can you develop and administer company policy?

- Can you produce a comprehensive security plan?

- Do you know a business attorney and an accountant that you are comfortable working with regarding business matters?

- Are you skilled at deciphering contracts and familiar with legalese?

- Are you familiar with government regulations that may affect your business?

- Can you develop an effective customer service plan to keep customers happy?

Marketing management:

- Can you find your target market customers and develop a profile of their purchasing habits?

- Can you evaluate and analyze your competition?

- What sales techniques will you employ?

- Can you design, develop, and manage a marketing and sales promotion plan?

- Can you produce marketing strategies for your business?

- Do you have a marketing evaluation plan to determine that your marketing decisions are sound and effective?

- Do you know where to get help and where to get your questions answered about various advertising ideas?

- Do you have the skills to conduct market research?

- Can you produce an effective public relations plan?

- Can you produce a merchandise purchasing plan?

- Do you have experience in purchasing?

- Do you know how to select and work with suppliers?

- Are you familiar with interior design pricing procedures?

- Do you know how to take inventory?

Financial management:

- Can you produce your own business plan?

- Can you produce your own loan proposal packages?

- Can you set up, implement, and manage a record keeping and information system?

- Do you have the ability to evaluate business records and finances?

- Can you produce your own financial statements and reports?

- Do you know how to produce profit and loss statements?

- Are you skilled in long- and short-term planning and goal setting?

- Do you have an idea of how much money is needed in business start-up costs?

- Can you determine what your cash flow requirements will be?

- Do you know how to figure depreciation?

- Can you administer your taxation program for your business?

- Have you checked with your suppliers to see how much credit they will extend you?

- Do you know how to determine how much financing is needed for your business?

- Have you checked to see how much money is available for you to borrow?

- Are you able to determine whether or not the business will be profitable?

- Do you have the skills to handle customer billing and collections?

- Will you extend credit to your customers? What type? Will you offer Visa or Mastercard?

- What criteria will you use to evaluate a customer's credit worthiness?

- Do you have the necessary skills to manage credit accounts?

- Are you able to make informed decisions regarding various insurances?

The Ideal Management Team

If you do not possess all of the skills needed above then you will either have to master these skills or hire the necessary talent to help your business. The required business professional help is listed below. Some of these individuals you will want permanently on your staff, while others you will hire as the need arises. When hiring anyone, always check their credentials, their past performance, and their references.

Each member of your team should have a definite area of expertise and specific duties to perform. Give team members a job description that details their company responsibilities and accurately specifies the control they have with the company. If each member of your team knows what his or her responsibilities are, then they will function together more effectively.

Surround yourself with capable people who are able to make sound decisions and who come up with creative, innovative ideas for your business. When you have a strong management team you are able to see both sides of an issue, and make better decisions. Your management team should participate in company strategies, organizing, directing, supervising, and making company decisions.

Contracted help:
- Business attorney

- Accountant (CPA)

- Bankers

- Consultants

- Advertising agency

- Public relations agency

Staff members:
- Board of directors (corporations)

- Chief executive officer (CEO)

- Business manager

- Marketing director

- Installation/project manager

Design Staff Positions

Chief executive officer (CEO)	The staff person who oversees the company. Usually this will be the person who started the company.
Business manager	The number of management positions depends on the size of the company. You may be the manager when you first start off (you will wear many hats). Later you may add a business manager to oversee all aspects of management for your firm. This person will oversee all financial aspects, schedule personnel, make final decisions, work with the orders and problems, and will work with the company's accountant, bookkeeper, attorney, etc.
Administrative assistant	Manages the office. Does all routine office work and assists the business manager in all aspects. Select a person with strong secretarial, bookkeeping, and computer skills.
Marketing director	Key position and key person to market, promote, and bring your firm design contracts. This person makes decisions on all aspects of marketing and advertising and works with outside public relation firms, media, graphic artists, and any other marketing-related professional or business that works to help with the marketing and promotion of the business.
Human resources manager	Also known as a personnel manager. Controls and oversees all personnel functions, problems, hires, fires, in charge of training, is the salary and benefit administrator, and handles all aspects of employee relations.
Studio coordinator	In charge of greeting customers over the phone or in the studio (select a warm, friendly person) and finding and showing customers various products (if the customer comes back in to take another look at the sample). Additionally, sets appointments, tracks orders and problems, reports all difficult problems to the business manager or the installation manager, can do installation scheduling if installers are in-house, oversees and manages the studio library, provides customer service, and does whatever

she can to work with the assistant designer in aiding the designer. Works to ensure jobs go in smoothly and customers are satisfied.

Try to keep studio coordinators busy working on mailings during their idle times. They can save the designer's time by filling out customer address information on job jackets, work orders, and purchase orders, leaving the designer to fill in the vital details of the order.

Because of the large scope and visible position that a studio coordinator has, theirs should definitely be paid a salary plus a percentage of the company gross sales to help ensure that they will do the best job possible to keep customers happy.

Head designer

Generally the person who created the company. While you will still serve customers, you are the mentor, overseeing and working with the designers under you to make sure they know exactly how to handle each design situation.

Designers

Should be added as your company grows. They are under the head designer but have a lot of leeway in working with customers and handling all aspects of *business as usual*-type jobs.

Assistant designers

Depending on how many designers you have (it is much less-expensive to cut down on the number of designers and have several assistants), you will need to have a couple of assistant designers. Assistant designers have been to design school (a great place to find them) or are otherwise trained in interior design. Assistant designers usually use this position as a stepping stone to gain experience before moving on to designer position. They set appointments, track orders and problems, and report all problems to the designer or business manager.

Installation/project manager

As your company grows larger, add this position. He will take a large weight off the business manager and the studio coordinator's shoulders. This person is in charge of all aspects of overseeing projects and installations. After the order is tracked by the coordinator or the assistant designer, he takes over on problem areas and coordinates everything, making sure customers are satisfied with their installations when the job is completed.

Always let a seasoned installation manager preview jobs at the start. He knows where costs can be cut and to how to correctly plan installations of items and window treatments. He can coordinate the job to make your company appear very proficient and professional.

Draftsperson/ renderer

This is the individual who does illustrations and who drafts and draws plans for the design firm. Try to hire a person that is very capable in all areas so you only need to hire one person.

Bookkeeper

The bookkeeper may work exclusively for your firm or work as a subcontractor. Bookkeepers keep your books organized and keep you on target for accounts payable and accounts receivable.

Independent contractors

Hired on a per need basis depending on the scope of the job. These include contractors, subcontractors, craftspeople, artists, illustrators, etc.

Job Descriptions

Write a thorough job description for each position you are filling. Outline all duties, responsibilities, required education, talents and abilities, and work experience for each position. Use the following as an outline to write a job description for each required position:

- **Job title.** Name of position.

- **Required education, talents and abilities, work experience.** List the minimum requirements you will accept for the position. List the desired requirements that the ideal candidate would possess.

- **Job responsibilities.** List duties and obligations that the position includes.

- **Possibilities of future job opportunities.** Describe how the person holding the specific position for a period of time may have other growth opportunities available in the future. Realistically, project when these growth opportunities might arise. I.e., an assistant designer might expect to rise to a designer level after several years of experience. Do you promote from within? Are you likely to fill an open designer position with another seasoned designer from another company?

- **Automobile usage and insurance requirements.** Since federal law prohibits you from asking applicants whether or not they have a car, spell it out here if they must provide their own auto and auto insurance. Describe what coverages are mandatory. Have employees provide required proof of insurance coverages.

- **Travel and schedule conditions.** If the position will require the applicant to travel long distances frequently, say so. If the applicant is required to work every weekend and work late hours frequently, spell it out. Some applicants have families that are important to them and you will waste your time if you don't let them know at the onset what the scheduling and traveling requirements are. The employee will quit when forced to make a choice. And you will start at the beginning.

- **Salary/commission structure.** What amount will you pay for the position. Salary only? Salary plus commission? Salary plus a percentage of the gross sales? Straight commission? Outline when the employee will be paid: weekly, bi-weekly, monthly, semi-annually, or annually (percentage of gross sales). Explain when raises are to be expected and what they are based on.

- **Benefits.** Are you offering company health, life, disability insurances? Profit-sharing or retirement plans? Employee discounts, paid vacation, and sick days?

- **Vacation, holiday, and sick days.** Usually two weeks paid vacation is provided, three weeks for long-term employees. Explain when an employee is eligible to take his or her vacation. Plan around peak operating periods when you need all your employees on the job. Several sick days a year are generally provided.

Develop Your Own Personnel Manual

Company policies need to be written down for employees to see and refer to as needed. If your company is larger than four employees, ideally you should write and distribute a personnel manual. A personnel manual addresses common important issues and questions. Some of these typical questions pertain to salary raises, personnel reviews, vacation pay, holidays, available benefits, leaves of absences, and other situations that will affect employee morale. Nonavailability of the information can force your company into lawsuits with unhappy employees.

A personnel manual will keep your employees informed about company rules and policies. Should certain situations arise, management has a personnel manual to back up enforcement of company regulations and policies.

After you compile your personnel manual, have your attorney review it before you distribute it to your employees. Your personnel manual will be considered legally binding if a dispute or an accusation about unfair employment practices should arise. **Use the following as an outline for your personnel manual:**

- **Welcome message** from the owner of the company.

- **Description of the company, history of the company and company objectives.**

- **Equal opportunity statement:** Write a statement that says your company will not discriminate in hiring, promoting, pay scale, or benefits due to age, religion, sex, national origin, race, or color.

- **Pre-employment credit investigations:** Let your potential employees know that you will run a credit check on them. It is easy to determine who is a stable person and who is unstable by running a credit check.

- **Drug testing/polygraph examinations:** What is your policy about random drug testing and polygraph examinations? By law you cannot make a polygraph a condition of employment. If money should be missing, you can *ask* the employees to take a polygraph. But a person can refuse and you can't force them to take a polygraph. The person who refuses to take a polygraph will look suspicious in the eyes of some.

- **Employee status:** Give definitions of a full-time employee, a part-time employee, a temporary employee, and exempt and nonexempt employees. Describe what employee benefits are available for each description.

- **Career opportunities within the company.**

- **Work hours:** Describe a typical work week and length of lunch hours and other breaks. At what rate of pay is overtime paid? Note the cutoff points for each pay period. Describe how an employee reports time worked.

- **Available training programs.**

- **Meetings/seminars:** What do you require here? Are you going to hold frequent meetings where employees cannot take a vacation during the scheduled time? Are you going to require that your employees attend seminars and other training to keep themselves current on new products and information?

- **Sign-in system:** Insist that hourly employees sign themselves in personally every time. In the event that the employee is unable to sign in, have him or her ask a manager to sign the time card. You need to be strict. Make sure that the employees do not sign in too early or out to late. Have them adhere to their schedule.

- **Pay periods:** Do you pay monthly, semi-monthly, or weekly? How is the pay computed?

- **Overtime pay:** Do you pay overtime after an eight-hour period or after a forty-hour work week? How much overtime is paid on a holiday? Is overtime a requirement of employment?

- **Reimbursement for expenses:** State what expenses you will reimburse and what ones you won't. Will you be paying mileage expenses, or paying for gasoline? Or will employees claim their own expenses on their income taxes.

- **Probationary periods:** State the probation period (probation periods are usually thirty to ninety days) during which you can dismiss an employee without cause.

- **Benefits:** State the available benefits and when an employee becomes eligible to start receiving them. Define what portion of the benefits the company pays and what portion the employee pays. Is there a pension or profit-sharing plan available? When is the employee eligible for the plan?

- **Performance reviews and pay raises:** Reviews are usually done on an annual or semi-annual basis (usually near the anniversary of the hire date). Raises are not mandatory, but they're essential for employee morale and if you want to keep your employees doing a better job.

- **Holidays:** What holidays are paid holidays? How long must an employee have to work for the company before becoming entitled to paid holidays? For employees of different faiths, what holidays are you willing to pay for and recognize? At what rate of pay are holidays paid?

- **Vacations:** Outline length of vacations and how long an employee must work to get a base vacation. How much longer must the employee work to get a longer vacation? Vacation policies should be as outlined in publications from the Bureau of Labor Statistics. Define how an employee must take his or her vacation: all at once, a few days at a time, or a day at a time. At separation from the company, will the employee receive accrued vacation pay?

- **Personal time off or sick leave:** Describe how to report absences. Typically businesses offer six to ten days a year for personal leave and/or sick leave. You may opt to pay only for sick time off with proof from a doctor for illnesses. Specify the length of personal leaves.

- **Company parking guidelines.**

- **Accident and safety prevention procedures.**

- **Policy about hiring relatives or allowing intimate relationships among employees:** Will you allow married couples to work for your company? Does one of the parties have to quit? Inflexibility in this area isn't readily accepted by employees.

- **Physical examinations:** State that you have the right to require a physical examination at the company's expense as a condition of hiring the employee.

- **Bereavement pay:** A typical period of paid bereavement is from three to five days with pay in the event of the death of an immediate family member.

- **Disability leaves:** Federal law requires that companies allow time off for pregnancy leaves equal to leaves allowed for male disabilities. Specify a period of time (sixty to ninety days) where a disabled worker is guaranteed his or her job. Reserve the right to have a company paid doctor's examination.

- **Severance pay:** State how severance pay is determined. Usually a week's pay is allowed for every three years. If an employee is terminated, he or she should not be eligible for severance pay.

- **Emergency shut downs:** You should guarantee partial wages in the event that the store is closed due to an unforseen event.

- **Jury duty:** Time off for jury duty is required by law. Depending on the state that you live in, you may be required to pay all or a portion of your employee's wages.

- **Employee merchandise purchases:** What discount are you going to extend to your employees for purchases?

- **Dress code:** Specify what is and is not acceptable for a professional appearance.

- **Outside employment:** Do you allow your full-time employees to work a second job? How about your part-timers?

- **Noncompetition agreement:** Get your employees to sign a noncompetition agreement stating that they will not go work for your competition in your same city. You will probably *not* be able to enforce this, but your employees may not know this.

- **Telephones:** Have your employees pay for the long distance phone calls they make for nonbusiness reasons.

- **Confidentiality agreement:** Protect your marketing secrets and game plans. Have your employees sign an agreement that they will not divulge anything about your company to your competition.

- **Company social events.**

- **Complaint procedures.**

- **Conflicts among decorators over customers:** This is an important area to spell out to keep peace among the decorators. See the section on lead rotation.

- **Personnel file access:** Can the employees ask to see their personnel files? How frequently?

Ways to Find Potential Employees

- **Contact area design schools for apprentices or referrals.** Inexpensive. Good source for inexpensive assistants that are trained in theory but lack on-the-job experience. They haven't yet picked up bad habits from other companies that conflict with your company's policies.

- **Competitors' employees.** Inexpensive. Employee may be trained and ready to go. But the competitor may have hard feelings.

- **Help-wanted signs posted on your place of business.** Inexpensive. *Many* nonqualified people may apply.

- **Newspaper classified advertisements.** Relatively inexpensive. You may be flooded with applicants. Get ready to screen the masses.

- **Word of mouth.** Inexpensive. May or may not be effective.

- **Employment agencies.** Employment agencies screen the applicants for you. This will be an expensive means of obtaining a designer or decorator.

- **Employee referrals.** Inexpensive. One of your other designers may know a highly qualified designer to recommend.

- **Family and relatives.** Inexpensive. But you may never get rid of a family member that doesn't fit in with your business. Hiring a family member may create problems within the family.

Hiring the "Right" Employees

Hiring the right employees is crucial to the survival of your business. With correct employee selection from the onset, you will cut the cost and liability that comes from hiring and then firing employees that don't fit your needs. Keep the following ideas in mind when you make those hiring decisions:

- You need to create a team of people that will work well and that will fit with your company style.

- Select people that will give you *maximum production.*

- Hire people that are competent in necessary skills and experienced to do the job. Ability to do the job, while important, should not be the sole criterion for selection of an individual to fill a job slot.

Have the ability to recognize success factors within individuals to accomplish selection of qualified job applicants. Don't hire people that are capable of doing the job, but hire people who will *do* the job. Consider these factors about job applicants you are considering:

- Does the job applicant have the necessary skills, knowledge, training, and experience required to do the job that she is being considered for?

- How driven is this person to succeed? Are you getting the feeling that if you hire this person she will *not* stay long?

- For designers and decorators: Can this person really sell? Does the applicant have a track record of a high closing ratio and providing quality service to customers?

- Does the prospective employee reflect the image that you are projecting or attempting to project with your company? Is her style of doing business consistent with the way you do business?

Equal Opportunity Laws

Equal opportunity laws protect applicants from unfair discrimination. Be very careful to consider *all* applicants on their professional qualification and appropriateness for the position.

As an employer hiring employees be aware of what you can ask an applicant and what you cannot ask. If you violate the laws, you are opening up yourself and your company for a discrimination lawsuit. What was considered fair to ask in previous years, is not fair to ask today. To do so is to be in violation of equal opportunity laws.

Do not ask (either in writing or verbally) **an applicant about:**

- Marital status.

- Maiden name.

- Spouse's maiden name.

- Spouse's or other relative's employment.

- His or her age, unless you write a statement on the application that age discrimination is illegal.

- His or her birthplace, race, origin, weight, height, hair color, or eye color. You cannot request a photograph, either. You may *not* inquire about an applicant's race, birth, or physical characteristics. To do so would indicate that you were in the position to discriminate against certain ethnic groups.

- Whether or not he or she has children.

- Home ownership.

- Automobile ownership (does he or she have one?).

- His or her credit rating.

- His or her religion.

- His or her relatives.

- The method or date of acquiring citizenship.

- His or her means of mastering a foreign language.

- Participation in nonprofessional organizations or other extracurricular activities.

- Any arrests. You *can* ask if the applicant was ever convicted of a crime.

- Whether he or she has ever been refused bonding.

- Past salaries and bonuses with other employers.

Additionally:

- Be sure that any tests administered to test applicants reflect the skills required for the particular job position.

- Do not provide fringe benefits only to "heads of households" or "principal wage earners." Make them available for each employee.

- Treat pregnancy/childbirth as you would any other temporary disability.

Employees' Rights to Privacy

The Privacy Act of 1974 has established the Private Protection Study Committee. This committee recommends that all employers use the following guidelines for employee privacy:

- Make employees aware of exactly what records are kept about them. Permit employees upon request to see these records and copy them if desired. Exceptions to this would be certain management records.

- Make corrections to any records that an employee or former employee believes are inaccurate, or record why these changes were not made. If the request to amend the records are denied, the employee should be notified of the reason for refusal. If the employee disagrees with the reasons for the refusal to change the records, he should be allowed to insert a statement of his disagreement in the records. Clearly note the disputed areas within the records. Send a copy of the disputed statement to any employee-specified persons that have already received information from the files.

- Allow employees to make additions, changes, or corrections to job records that are believed to be inaccurate or incomplete. Anyone affected by the changes to the records should be notified.

- Do not release any information about an employee without his or her consent. Information about employment dates, position held, and salary is acceptable information to be given out without an employee's consent.

- Do not use an applicant's criminal conviction record unless mandated by law that this record must be reviewed.

Independent Contractor or Employee?

Any worker that received earnings for services is either an employee or an independent contractor. Whether a person is an employee or an independent contractor depends on the circumstances in each case plus statutory provisions. You have to decide how you are going to classify your decorators. Independent contractors must fill out an IRS W-9 form and a 1099 Misc. form instead of a W-2 form.

The question is, are you able to classify your decorators as independent contractors, thus saving your company a great deal of money in payroll taxes, pensions, group health insurance, social security, unemployment taxes, and worker's compensation insurance?

Here is the IRS definition of an employee and an independent contractor:
Employee: A worker that performs such services subject to the will and control of an employer, both as to what shall be done and how it shall be done.

Independent contractor: A classification of workers hired to do specific jobs over which the person hiring has no right to control the manner in which the work is done. The workers generally have a distinct trade or business that is offered to the public, and are often paid a lump sum amount for the complete job.

Some state jurisdictions follow common-law rule regarding who is classified as an independent contractor. Other state jurisdictions have statutory provisions that may or may not reinstate common-law rule.

Common-law rule: Every worker who performs services subject to the will and control of an employer is an employee for the purposes of federal payroll taxes.

The employer must have the capability to direct and control the work, say what work is to be done, the way the work is to be done, when the work is to be done, and where the work is to be done. The employer must have the right to control the performance of the person doing the work. Employer's may also have the right to fire the employee. The employer must also furnish tools and a place to do the job.

The IRS is levying very stiff fines, rules, and penalties in the area of misclassification of workers. It is especially taking a long, serious look at small businesses. It seems that small businesses don't know the classification criteria as well as larger companies and are not in compliance with the IRS standards regarding independent contractor classifications.

An independent contractor actually works for himself. They are considered in business for themselves in the IRS's eyes. The key factors in classifying a worker as an independent contractor in the IRS's view are that the employer *has no right to control* the worker and *no right to direct* the manner in which the job is completed.

Worker Classification

Below are a list of factors to consider in classifying a worker.

Independent contractor:

Training	No training is needed to start and complete the job.
Business integration	Only temporary and usually minor integration with the person's services.
Assignment of job	Free to assign anyone to do the required work.
Supervision	Personally supervises, hires, fires, pays the people doing the work.
Work hours	Able to set own hours. Free to work when they choose. If the business has specific hours, they may have to follow suit.
Work site	Worker is able to perform work at site of his or her choosing.
Work sequence	Worker decides in what order to do the needed work.
Reporting	Is not required to provide written or oral reports of progress.
Method of payment	Paid by the job, not by the hour.
Expense accounts	Expenses are pre-estimated before the start of the job.
Risk of financial loss	Runs risks of profits and losses.
Availability to others	Available to work for anyone else doing the same or other type of work.
Termination	Must complete jobs contracted for. Incomplete jobs will result in liability in damages for worker.

Employee:

Training	Training is available and may be necessary before beginning the job.
Business integration	Under the control of the employer.
Assignment of job	Worker must do the work personally.
Supervision	Under the employer's supervision, whether direct or indirect.
Work hours	Employer decides and sets the hours.
Work site	May be restrictions on *where* the work must be completed.
Work sequence	Employer determines the order in which the work must be done.
Reporting	Worker must report back to the employer about work progress.

Method of payment   Preset plan on payment by the hour, day, week, month.

Expense accounts   Employer pays expenses as they arise.

Risk of financial loss   No risk of loss to worker.

Availability to others   Not available due to mutual agreement not to work elsewhere.

Termination   Worker has right to terminate employment without suffering any recourse from employer.

If you do not follow the rules closely, you are taking a chance that you will be audited and your independent contractor status strictly questioned. This idea may not bother you now, but if a decorator is a disgruntled ex-employee, you may be faced with problems with the IRS. Potential disaster by misclassification is very weighted against you.

If you are unsure which classification to use for your worker, submit a Form SS-8 to your IRS district office. The form provides information for use in determining whether a worker is an employee for federal taxes and income tax withholding. The IRS will officially determine for you whether your worker is an employee or an independent contractor. Of course, most workers will be classified as an employee if the IRS is asked to make the determination.

Classifying Decorators as Independent Contractors

If you can follow the rules below closely, you may be able to classify your decorators as independent contractors and come out way ahead financially. Work closely with your business attorney and accountant and heed their advice on this subject.

- Have your decorator sign a written agreement (contract) drawn up by your attorney. Include the following in the agreement:

  - A statement that decorators are not entitled to any employee benefit programs.

  - A joint severability clause holding that if a portion of the agreement is canceled out, the rest of the contract is still valid.

  - Assent that decorators are able to work elsewhere at any time.

- Independent contractors services must be available to the general public. An independent contractor is free to obtain her own jobs. She is not free to take your leads and use them for another company or for herself. If she wants to work for the general public, make sure she does it with her own or someone else's samples, not your company's samples.

- For classification as an independent contractor, the decorator technically will have to set her own appointments. You can hand her a lead slip, but it is up to her to decide when she wants to make the call or meet with the customer in the studio. You absolutely cannot tell her that she has to go on that appointment on that date at that time.

- You cannot tell independent contractors how to do their job. It is up to them to decide how to get the job done. If you hire experienced decorators and require them to read our book, *Secrets of Success for Today's Interior Designers and Decorators,* and they want to work for you in the future, then most of the training will be covered.

- Independent contractors do not have to account for their actions to you. They do not have to supply you with a written report of their work. On leads that you supply (that they set up) ask them to explain the results of the call on the lead slip, and have the slips returned to you for tracking purposes.

- Independent contractors are expected to supply their own equipment, briefcases, calculators, etc. Technically, they are to supply their own samples. You can probably let them borrow or rent samples from your store as needed and satisfy the IRS since this involves tons of samples of all types. Basically, they supply everything that they need to get the job done. You should be safe in supplying your company forms for fabrication and ordering purposes. Since they are working and doing the job on the behalf of your company, they can use your forms.

- You cannot demand or even request that decorators work floor time. I would let them know that if they don't put in floor time, they shouldn't expect to see many leads, as the leads that walk in or call go to the decorator that has voluntarily been scheduled to work that slot. On leads that come in when more than one decorator is present, and not written in on the voluntary schedule, the leads should be rotated among the decorators present. If a decorator doesn't show up as voluntarily scheduled for floor time, the leads should go to the decorators present. If no decorators are present, the leads should be rotated.

- You cannot demand or request that decorators work weekends or nights. They are free to do the job when they choose to do it. You are also free not to use them in the future if they are not doing the job to your satisfaction. Independent contractor status makes it easy for you not to keep certain decorators. Just don't give them leads anymore.

If you misclassify your employee as an independent contractor, IRS levies penalties. The penalty will range from the amounts that should have been withheld to two time the amount. Criminal penalties can be much stiffer, especially if you are incorporated — up to a $100,000 fine, one year in prison, or both. Usually the IRS will waive the penalties if you agree to comply and correctly classify your employees in the future.

If you are hesitant about which way to go with your employees or independent contractors, contact the IRS and fill out form SS-8.

Hiring Designers and Decorators

When you are ready to add designers or decorators to your interior design firm, you will be concerned about whether to hire an experienced decorator with product knowledge that you train to sell, or to hire a professional salesperson that you train to sell interior design products and services.

Since customers are the reason you are in business, consider the customer's point of view when selecting salespeople. Customers feel overall product and decorating knowledge to be of prime importance. Send a so-called decorator out to their home who doesn't know what she is talking about, or to see a customer that may have good general knowledge about available products, and the customer will be quickly turned off by your inexperienced decorator. To make sure that decorators have adequate product knowledge to work with, make a list of each product that you carry with its feature and benefits.

Having a meeting once a week to discuss one product at a time is another alternative to use to get your salespeople trained thoroughly on the products you carry. Make use of your suppliers' sales representatives and their product knowledge. Have them do their job. That is what they are there for — to make sure that your people have adequate knowledge to sell their products, comfortably (they of course are also on commission).

Do not hire decorators who say they will get back to a customer and never do! You need salespeople who will follow through on any question or request that they are asked by your customers. When interviewing decorators to hire for your firm, make this very clear. You will not tolerate decorators that will not follow up and follow through on requests, questions, or orders. If you want your company to lose credibility, hire undependable salespeople.

A quality decorator is one that will recognize the right product to show her customers to fit their perceived wants and recognize their true needs. In order to do this, the decorator must have adequate product knowledge and education.

A customer has to be able to bond and mesh with the decorator in personality and feel that the decorator is her ally concerning her proposed interior design job. Customers need to feel that if something goes wrong with their job, the decorator is going to be on their side when attempting to resolve any problems.

Customers want to work with decorators who are current with design style, know what the current trends are in interior design, have the ability to recognize faddish styling, and know what is on the way out of style.

Willingness to share and discuss trends, styling, and market knowledge with their customer is important. Attend trade shows and subscribe to trade publications to help your decorators stay current with the market.

Creativity and imagination are attributes that customers find important when selecting a decorator or designer to work with. The decorator has to quickly sum up what existing furnishings she will be working with, combine all other elements that can't be controlled together, and come up with an exciting, creative, imaginative interior to fit her customer's personality. Good decorators (salespeople) have ideas that work. Photograph, recognize, and share at your sales meetings quality ideas that decorators discover or complete for their customers.

Professional salespeople *prefer* to be on commission or a portion of commission rather than on straight salary. They know that if they make a real effort they can make good money. Offer a draw against commission so that there is money coming in weekly while the decorator is waiting for jobs to be completed and paid for by customers.

If there is going to be a rather long period of time from when the decorator starts working and will finally see a commission check, consider starting decorators on a salary guarantee that tapers off when the commission checks start coming in. If you have decorators drawing against commissions and make them pay back the initial draw money they collected while waiting for their first jobs to be completed, it will be a long time before they will make any real money. They will get discouraged, be unable to live on the draw check amount for an extended period of time, and quit. They will then take your operational secrets down the road and share them with another company. Keep your decorators happy if you want to keep them working for you.

Fair Employment Practices

The Civil Rights Act of 1964, Title VII, prohibits discrimination in employment on the basis of race, color, religion, sex, or national origin. Under Title VII, it is an unlawful employment practice for any employer to make decisions to hire, discharge, compensate, or establish the terms, conditions, or privileges of employment for any employee based on these categories. Follow this procedure when seeking to hire new employees:

Hiring and promoting:
- Write a job description of the position. Set work hours, wages, and commissions. Determine employee fringe benefits.

- Recruit and hire from the cultural mix of your location. Be sure to include women and minorities that are living in the area in proportion to the amount of employees you have. Consider all qualified people for the position.

- Use only tests to measure qualities that will be needed on the job. Tests for promotions should also reflect the needed skills of the job position.

- Verify the applicant's education and employment references. Ask for written permission from the applicant to authorize previous employers and schools to release information verifying reference information.

After hiring:
- Cancel any ads you had placed for the position to be filled.

- Have the employee fill out a federal withholding exemption form W-4. All forms are available through IRS offices.

- Discuss all company policies and procedures. Outline pay days and when the employee is eligible for worker's compensation and other benefits.

- Start a personnel file for the new employee. Include all documents that the employee has signed (including any employment contract).

During employment:
● Include a statement of earnings and deductions with each pay period. Issue paychecks at scheduled dates as allowed by your state.

Consistent job performance records:
● Be very thorough with keeping *objective* records of all employee's performances. Spell out any problems, dates, places, and in the case of any confrontation, any witnesses.

● Keep a record of all pay raises, promotions, courses taken by employees to improve their knowledge, address changes, and number of exemptions claimed on IRS W-4 forms.

● Issue an annual statement of earnings as required by state and federal laws.

● If you keep regular records, instead of waiting for a bad situation to arise and then starting to document everything, you will appear *credible* in court. Be sure to also keep records consistently on all other employees. Otherwise, it appears that you singled out the employee in question. Be objective.

● Send quarterly and annual statements of salaries paid and deductions made. Follow the specifications on depositing withholding taxes and insurance premiums.

The Hiring Process

Use the following guidelines for successful employee selection for your company. The ultimate goals are to take the time to make a careful employee selection and select a person who will both work out and be the most successful candidate for the position.

Have all prospects fill out an application and ask to see a resume and portfolio.

Pre-interview:
Begin the hiring process by conducting a pre-interview. Analyze the responsibilities of the job and discuss the way your company conducts business. Identify *who* the prospective employee will be directly reporting to and *who* are the decision makers within your company structure.

Interview:
● Carefully look at and listen to the applicant.

● Allow time for the applicant to ask you questions after you have thoroughly questioned and interviewed him or her.

● Take thorough notes.

● Listen to your sixth sense about your feelings concerning the individual.

● Ask questions that the applicant has to elaborate on. Don't ask questions that can easily be answered with a simple yes or no answer.

● Objectively listen to the answers to all of your questions and to the way they are answered. Restate the answers given back to the applicant using the same wording and terminology, to be sure that you understand his or her response to the question.

● Don't prematurely decide for or against the applicant during the interview process. Rather, gather all information and wait to make a final determination.

- Use silence to get the applicant to start talking and opening up. Several seconds of silence are uncomfortable to an applicant sitting there during an interview. The pressure is on them to start talking. By using this technique you are pressuring your applicant to give you a more complete response to the question asked.

Post-interview:

Check references before extending an offer of employment. Before extending your offer of employment, decide what terms you are offering the applicant. Also decide how much room you have for negotiating salary, commissions, time off, and other conditions. Ask the applicant these final questions (even if you have already asked them before):

- Can you do the job?

- Will you do the job?

- How will you do the job?

- Do you feel that you will readily fit into the company structure?

Hiring employees:

When you hire a new employee, **inform** her that she is being hired on a three-month probationary period. If you do this, you will save yourself much stress and possible legal problems later. If the new employee isn't a good fit, doesn't work out, or if her performance fails to meet your company's expectations, you are able to easily terminate her during the three-month probationary period. Set out specific dates for agreed-upon goals ahead of time. Also preschedule reviews to follow up and discuss the new employee's progression from the beginning.

Should it become evident that termination is eminent due to the employee not meeting the company's objectives, terminate her with a written statement that states: "The company's goals or objectives are not presently being met and the employee has this additional time period (state a period of thirty to sixty days) to improve her performance. If the employee's performance is not improved within this stated time period, termination of the employee will result."

Informing nonsuccessful job applicants:

Within one week after making your employee selection for the job opening, inform the nonsuccessful job applicants of your decision not to hire them by letter or by a phone call.

- Be very polite, short and to the point.

- Thank the nonsuccessful job applicant for his or her interest in applying for the position.

- State that the position has been filled and wish them luck on further job hunting endeavors.

- It is considered best not to tell the applicant why he or she did *not* receive the job.

New employee's job transition:

Give your new employee a smooth transition to starting the new job. Emphasize the employee's strengths and discuss her weak points or areas where she needs improvement. Provide assistance in developing her weaker areas. Help your new employee feel comfortable with her new business environment.

Terminating an Employee

Termination is hard on both the employer and the employee. To avoid future repercussions, the termination must be handled correctly and carefully. Strive to maintain your employee's dignity, while following the correct procedure to avoid a wrongful termination lawsuit by the terminated employee.

A wrongful termination suit can cost your company extreme amounts of money, stress, and years of litigation. But on the other hand, to delay termination for fear of a lawsuit may be detrimental to the health of your company in productivity, low morale among fellow co-workers, loss of sales, poor service provided by the employee in question, and a negative attitude from the employee that tends to spread like wildfire among the co-workers.

A poorly handled termination of an employee may motivate the employee to retaliate against your company and against other employees of your company.

Be extremely careful, consider what your employee's probable reaction will be, and prepare in advance how you are going to terminate the employee. Consult with your business attorney about each termination in question, buy law books on the subject from law book stores (and read them) and *carefully* proceed. **Follow legal rules on termination to the letter.** Usually an employee will be terminated from a company for the following reasons:

- **Poor chemistry.** The employee does not fit in with other employees, management, and owners of the company.

- **Politics.** The employee is not a team player. Does his or her own thing without regard to the company style and image that the company is attempting to preserve or create.

- **Dislike of job.** Employee does not like the job, but makes no effort to find another one and move on.

- **Reduction in communication.** The employee attempts to stay in the background and becomes progressively hard to work with and communicate with.

- **Poor attitude and work habits.** The employee has a poor attitude and poor work habits, and there is a danger that other employees are or and may be affected.

- **Decline in sales or production.** The employee's sales or production have declined over a period of time. The employee may not even be aware of the descent.

- **Not meeting sales or production goals.** The employee is not meeting preset company goals and objectives. Personal employee career goals are not compatible with the company's objectives and goals.

Termination Guidelines

Once you decide the employee in question must go, devise a plan to carry out the termination. Ideally, you should start the termination plan six months ahead of the actual termination date. If a six-month period is out of the question, plan the termination over a three-month period that entails monthly follow-up and review meetings with the employee.

During every monthly meeting, remind the employee that termination will occur if the required improvements haven't been made by a specific date. Document all conversations and correspondence with the employee and put all documentation in your safe, locked file cabinet, or keep at your home, rather than in an accessible place at your business location. Keep all documentation and evidence for the future, should the employee decide to take action at a future date and time.

For proper documentation, include the date, time, place, a summary of the review, and whenever possible have the employee sign the summary. Should the employee refuse to sign the review documentation, have a witness present for the next review session that will verify what actually occurred and was discussed at the review.

If your company has a personnel department, the personnel manager should sign the review documentation along with the manager giving the review.

If you feel that there is no way you can hold out for a three-month period, you may decide to terminate the employee in a shorter time period. Carefully weigh all of the consequences of proceeding with a shorter time period.

If there is termination for cause (stealing, sabotage, or revealing company secrets), you may suspend or fire the employee immediately. Before proceeding to take action on an employee for cause, take some time to cool off and calm down before taking suspension or termination proceedings. Do not do it when angry. Remember your every word, procedure, and action needs to hold up in court.

If you are suspending the employee, let the employee know that following an investigation of the matter, termination may immediately result. Be sure to have a witness present and sign documentation of the suspension or termination.

Present a copy of the suspension or termination documentation to the employee at the time of the suspension or termination.

Make an attempt to preserve the employee's honor, regarding the reason for termination. Doing so will go a long way in preventing reprisals by the employee with lawsuits or other types of retaliation against your company. Ideally, you want the employee to just walk away.

An alternative to termination would be to set the employee's goals to unattainable levels, thus motivating the employee to just give up and quit.

Use the following as a guideline *only* for termination of an employee. Again, seek an attorney's advice and buy law books on unlawful termination to make sure that the attorney has not skipped a vital point of termination of an employee that may come back to haunt you later.

- Hold employee reviews in a private room or another location out of view and earshot of other employees.

- Interview any employee with unsatisfactory service. Issue several written reviews of warning in *advance* of the termination.

- Have an exit interview with the terminated employee. Let the employee know within the first few minutes of the review that he or she is being terminated.

- At the exit interview be prepared for a wide range of emotions to surface from the terminated employee. If you suspect the employee will act violently, have the exit interview in a setting where other people are nearby. The terminated employees that remain calm and controlled are usually the ones to file wrongful termination suits later.

- Allow the terminated employee to ask questions and express his or her feelings.

- At the exit interview, state your decision and the exact reasons for the termination or dismissal. You do not need to justify or defend your decision. If you have had the previous reviews leading up to the dismissal, the employee already knows your reasons. Record the reasons (factually) in the job performance records.

- Discuss severance and benefit arrangements with the employee. Since the employee may be in a state of shock and not concentrating on what you are saying, present the information in a letter format or ask him or her to take notes.

- Give the terminated employee a copy of his or her severance agreement, termination notice, etc.

- Have the employee's benefit package ready at the exit interview. Let him or her know how long the insurance will be in effect.

- Provide the terminated employee with information about unemployment benefits. Doing so will make the employee feel that you are attempting to make the best of a bad situation.

- Request a forwarding address from the terminated employee.

- Act positive and confident with the terminated employee that he or she will be able to find employment elsewhere. Attempt to preserve the employee's self-esteem.

- Encourage the employee to follow up with your personnel department for information on finding a job. Also ask the personnel department to contact the dismissed employee periodically to see how he or she is doing with a job search, and attempt to help the ex-employee if possible.

- Have the employee clean out his or her desk while you watch him or her separate your property from their own.

- Escort the terminated employee out of the building and to his or her automobile.

- Collect all of your property from your employee's automobile and arrange to pick up any samples, etc., from the employee's house.

- Write up a summary of the reason the employee was dismissed. Write the statement in a non-discriminatory manner.

- Place the documented exit interview in the ex-employee's file and hold another copy at another location. Should another employee question the reason why the ex-employee was terminated, he or she should be allowed to read the statement for the dismissal.

- Pay all wages due within the specified time period. If severance pay was promised, pay it.

- Job performance records must be consistent. Records must be available on other employees besides the one to be terminated or laid off. Again, records must be written in an objective manner.

- If contacted by worker's compensation, disability insurance, or unemployment insurance offices, answer all correspondence promptly.

- Let fellow employees know that the employee does not work for your company anymore and should they see the employee loitering around, to notify management.

Employee Agreements

As a business owner, you need to protect yourself against future lawsuits from employees that do not work out. You can be held liable for promises made with employees that do not perform as expected. Have your business attorney design a statement for your company.

Have new employees sign a statement, similar to the following statement, to protect you and your business, should the employee need to be terminated or reminded of the terms they were hired under:

This is a legal record. Do not sign this agreement unless you have read and understand the entire agreement and agree with the contents herein.

I, (employee's name,) who have been hired as an employee of (employer's name), (the company name) as of (date), hereby certify that:

I understand that I am not being hired for any specific period of time. Even though I will be paid my wages on a (weekly, monthly, commission) basis, I understand that this does not mean that I am to be hired for a specific period of time.

Since I understand that I am not to be hired for any specific period of time, I will be an employee at will and can be terminated at any time, with or without cause, for any basis that does not violate a public policy of this state. I also understand that I may leave this job at any time for any reason provided I give at least two weeks notice to the personnel office.

I understand that company policy requires me to be hired as an employee at will and that this policy cannot be changed except in a written statement signed by me and the (assigned officer) of (name of company).

I have been given a chance to make inquiries regarding company rules and my position as an employee at will. No representative of (employer name) has made any commitments or other statements to me that imply that I will be employed under any other terms other than those stated herein.

I agree that all conflicts associated with my employment with this company or the termination thereof shall be presented to arbitration before an arbitrator who is a member of the American Arbitration Association. I understand that I may be represented by an attorney in such proceedings and I agree that arbitration shall be the only means of settling all disputes relating to my employment with the company or the termination thereof.

This document is executed at (city name), (state), County of (name of county) on (date).

Note: Never use the word "permanent." Legally, this means the employees can work for you for the rest of their life, if they desire!

Compensation Policy Governing Designers/Decorators

Have new employees sign a compensation agreement similar to the following. Have your business attorney design a statement for your company.

1. According to (company name)'s policy, there is a thirty-day probationary period for new designers/decorators. During this probationary period, no advances against commissions will be paid. After thirty days an advance against this commission arrangement can be made providing the designer/decorator can generate such net sales volume and gross profit dollars that the commission will exceed the advance. Designers/decorators who qualify will be put on a standard bi-weekly advance of $400 (or whatever amount) per week.

2. Designer/decorator commissions will be paid only upon total completion of each sale.

3. Designers/decorators will call only on prospects provided by (company name), or generated through (company name). Any other house calls or appointments performed for any other company or party will be considered a conflict or interest and will result in the termination of the designer/decorator.

4. Contract sales are bid at the highest selling price allowed as the recommended regular price. The lowest selling price will be determined by the company in each individual case.

5. Any direct expense to the company as a result of mis-measurement or commitment made by designer/decorator but not recorded on the sales agreement will be charged against designer/decorator commissions.

6. Upon termination, designers/decorators will receive all current commissions that exceed the total of the advances for the operating period. Any over amounts will be paid upon the completed installation of each outstanding sale. The designer/decorator shall be required to return all sales agreements, samples, leads, contacts, price lists, and any other materials belonging to (company's name). Any samples or materials not returned to (company's name) upon termination shall be charged against future monies owed to the designer/decorator.

7. Commissions are as follows: List the percentage that you will pay for the individual products that you carry (break down the products individually, and list the corresponding commissions or compensation):

   10 percent of gross amount on all drapery, soft window treatments, bedspreads, accessories.
   7 percent of gross amount on all carpeting and flooring, etc.

This compensation agreement governing designers/decorators of (company's name) has been reviewed by me, and I agree to the contents herein. I have acknowledged and received a copy of the executed agreement.

_____   _____
Designer/decorator's signature   Officer of the company's signature
                                        For (company's name)

_____   _____
Date   Date

Designer/Decorator Acknowledgment

Have new designer/decorator employees sign an acknowledgment similar to the following:

As an employee of (company name), I understand and agree to the following:

1. I will not change a price or consummate a sale for any merchandise or service before the beginning of a sale date.

2. Appointments scheduled before the end of a sale period must be completed within ten days after the end of the sale period. Customer's name, date, and deposit or method of payment must be included herein.

3. I agree to complete *all* paperwork required to complete a sale within five business days.

4. I agree to study and review all products until I am very knowledgeable about all the products and services carried by (company's name).

5. I will carry and be prepared to show customers not only sale-priced products, but regular retail products as well at all times.

6. I will give my customers, both verbally and in writing, a realistically estimated delivery date on all sales agreements.

7. Every customer must sign a three-day right-to-cancel form as required by federal law with each sales agreement.

8. I work only for (company's name) and agree to show and sell products only for (company's name).

9. I understand that I may not charge a customer for any product or service unless I have a correct price list to work from.

I further understand that compliance with this policy is a condition of my employment with (company's name) and that if I violate any terms herein, I may be terminated.

_____
Signed by designer/decorator

_____
Date

Designers and Decorators on Commission

For best use of your cash flow, pay your design staff on commission when the job is completed to the customer's satisfaction, after the customer pays the bill.

Most commissioned salespersons will not work for you unless they receive a draw check (advance on commission payments). Many firms pay only minimum wage as a draw or $200 or so a week against commissions earned.

In order to receive full commission, prices charged must fall in the pricing guidelines that will allow you to pay full commission. If the prices charged are below the pricing guidelines, the commissioned salesperson should receive less commission for the sale.

All charges for errors should be charged back at your cost to the commissioned salesperson who made the error. Although this seems brutal when it happens to you as a sales professional, there is no way that a small company can absorb the mistakes made by a less-experienced decorator or designer. If the company did absorb mistakes, salespeople would not quickly learn from the mistakes they made, and the company would quickly go out of business, or never make a profit on most design jobs. There is no better way for people to gain experience than to pay for the mistakes they have made. Let them know when you hire them that this is the case. Otherwise they will find it an extremely bitter pill to take later, when they have their commissions docked; they may quit on the spot and attempt to sue you for the money lost due to their negligence. Be fair. If it is not clear as to who is at fault, do not make the commissioned person pay for it. If the mistake is 50 percent their error and 50 percent the workroom or installer's error dock the commissioned person only for their fair share.

If a designer should leave or be terminated from your company, have him or her pay back any overpayment of his or her draw payment.

Always review your decorators at regular intervals. Set goals for them to achieve in gross sale amounts monthly, quarterly, and yearly, and track how they are doing with these goals. Also track their closing ratio versus the amount of leads they are provided.

Ledgers for Commissioned Sales Professionals

All decorators should keep documentation of their sales in a ledger, which serves as an on-going record. It is set up in a column format from left to right: the sale's date, who the decorator made the sale to, the customer's address, telephone number, a description of the merchandise, services rendered, a total of the sale without sales tax added in, their rate of commission for that type of sale, and a column for any adjustments taken (either for the job delivering late, or decorator errors).

The record is extremely important to ensure that the decorator gets paid for all sales made. Since commissioned sales professionals are paid only when the sale is completed, commissions do not get paid in the order they are sold. Sales are easily overlooked or paid to the wrong decorator.

As the decorator gets credited against his or her draw or commission paid for each sale, he or she should go back and write "paid" and the date of payment in the ledger. Any missing commission payments for completed sales should be brought, in writing to the attention of the company bookkeeper or accounting manager for them to track. If decorators do not track payment of their sales, some of their pay will get overlooked or paid to the wrong decorator.

Note: The ledger also serves as a mailing list of past customers for the decorator. Encourage the decorator to type this information on a computer data base so that the customer's name and address can easily be converted and printed in a label format.

Noncompetitive Agreements

Ideally, every employer wants to have his employees sign a noncompetitive agreement, where they agree not to go down the street and reveal company secrets to a competitor, or go out and start their own company. An employer can have an employee sign a *covenant not to compete* or a *noncompeting agreement.*

Unfortunately, while you can try to make an employee *think* he or she is agreeing not to compete against you for a specific period of time (six months to two years, usually), noncompetitive agreements are almost always not enforceable. It is extremely difficult, depending on the state (they usually don't hold up in court), and expensive in legal fees to attempt to prevent an employee from obtaining employment in the career in which they have education and experience. Noncompetitive agreements cannot be enforced if they impose undue hardship on the employee.

The law will usually prevent employees from purposely harming an employer even if the employee has not signed a covenant not to compete.

Not hiring a qualified applicant who has signed a noncompetitive agreement with a previous employer is not the most intelligent business decision. A better decision is to seek a business attorney's advice and have the attorney draw up an agreement (have every employee sign one even if they *say* they haven't signed a noncompetitive agreement elsewhere) that releases your company of any responsibility, placing any and all liability on the employee should a lawsuit be brought against the employee by a previous employer.

Employee Leasing

Employee leasing is a relatively new concept for personnel and benefit administration of small businesses. Employee leasing firms help businesses fight the high costs of company health insurance, personnel administration, and compliance with complex governmental regulations. Employee leasing is designed to elevate businesses to a higher level of personnel management than they are capable of supplying themselves. Businesses need help in managing increasingly complicated employee matters such as payroll, payroll taxes, medical benefits administration, worker's compensation claims management, immigration compliance, etc.

By the use of employee leasing, a business *selects* its desired employees, has them hired by the employee leasing company, and the leasing company leases the employees back to the business. The leasing company becomes the employee of record for tax and insurance purposes, and the business owner/owners become on-site manager and supervisor. The business owner now has only **one** check to write per pay period — a large one to the leasing company. This check covers payroll, taxes, benefits, and administrative fees and the employee leasing company handles all of the details. The use of an employee leasing company allows the business to concentrate on what it does best: sell products and services. With the use of employee leasing you acquire quite a few pluses:

- It provides higher quality benefit packages. This includes affordable company provided health insurance (comprehensive group major medical and HMOs), credit union, term life insurance, short- and long-term disability, dental care, vision care, group discount plans, training libraries, employee assistance plan, emergency travel fund, etc.

- With your better benefits package, you are able to attract a better quality employee that will stay longer with your company.

- A leasing company takes care of payroll, OSHA, INS, EEOC, COBRA, immigration law, and other governmental regulations.

- All claims processing for worker's compensation, unemployment insurance, garnishments, etc., are taken care of for you.

- Provides a professional human resource department for you.

- Will reduce your accounting costs.

- Ongoing advice that can help you eliminate wrongful termination suits or negligent acts in the work place.

- Reliable payroll processing, delivery, and payroll records.

- Handling W-4's and W-2's.

- Quarterly reports.

- Comprehensive payroll deductions.

- Reconciliation of payroll accounts.

- Legal responsibility for audits transferred.

- Provides employees with assistance with employment-related problems.

- Professional employee handbook and introduction, procedures, and policies.

- Human resource records administration and management.

- Statutory protection is extended to employees.

- Up-to-date advice on labor regulations and workers' rights, work site safety, employee wellness, etc.

- Smoother insurance processing.

- Employees can be moved to another employee-leased company, without loss of their benefits.

- Correct termination procedures for disciplinary reasons or layoffs.

Naturally, all of this service does not come without a cost to a business. Contact the National Staff Leasing Association (NSLA), 1735 North Lynn, Ste. #950, Rosslyn, Virginia 22209. NSLA is the trade association for employee leasing and standard-setting organization for the employee leasing industry. They can provide more employee leasing information and employee leasing firms in your locale. Consider using an employee leasing operation to make your life much easier!

Part 14

Pricing Products and Services

Pricing can and will affect your company image and your company growth. Buyers have preconceived ideas about product and service value. Depending on their income levels, buyers are willing to pay only so much to obtain goods and services. When pricing products and services (after you add in your overhead) you may find it hard to believe that most people will actually pay the price necessary to make a profit. Sellers who feel this way have the tendency to keep their prices down at a lower level because they just don't think they will make many sales at the higher price.

Realize that it is far easier to cut your expenses and costs than to increase your sales. If you sell more goods you increase your costs. If you are able to lower your costs, your profits will increase even if you are making the same amount of sales. Marketing and obtaining additional customers is expensive in both time and money.

In order to guarantee that profits continue for your company, regularly analyze what is happening with your business. Carefully study your sales and what it cost you to make them. You may need to increase the prices on some merchandise or services. The analysis may show that you really need to add to or decrease your line of products and services.

When pricing goods and services, realize that the pricing structure selected must account for designer's time and overhead expenses, and a degree of profit for the firm. Design firms' overhead expenses generally are about one and a half to three times what the employees cost in salaries and benefits. Unless you are fully aware of the amount of money required to run your firm and make a profit, it is very easy to shortchange your company with pricing.

As a business owner, you must decide what your time is worth. The determining factors are: amount of education, degree of skill, professional reputation, job experience, where the business is located, your need or lack of need for money, and your level of confidence.

Usually when a customer pays an hourly design fee, he or she is billed at a rate of two and a half to four times what the designer working on the project costs the firm. Usually only a portion of the designer's time is billed to the customer. It is hard to recover all of the time spent on any project.

Job Estimating

Before you determine what the price structure should be for a design job, consider the following additional points:

- **The extent of the job.** Is the job small or large, low or high liability and profit risk? Is this the type of job you and your design firm are used to doing? If so, you will be able to do it faster, easier, and less-expensively than you would if you took on a specialized project that you are unfamiliar with and have to spend a lot of time researching.

- **The exact services required to complete the job.**

- **How fast the job needs to be completed.**

- *Who* **will be doing the work and what will he or she cost you** in time and money

- **Is the customer hard to please with quality and workmanship?** If you don't know, talk to the customer and find out how her previous jobs went with other design firm. Some customers can never be pleased. They will find a problem after a problem for you to service. This will frustrate you and consume all of the job profits.

- **How easy or difficult is the customer/company to work with.** Are they decision makers or people who just cannot make up their mind (and who will use up hours of your time in the decision-making process). You also want to avoid having to make repeated presentations (and having to repeatedly educate prospects on design theory and products) to individuals who have a stake in approving the project. Insist on having everyone involved in the decision present at the same time for the presentation.

- **What other companies are competing for the job?** Do you expect (from past history) them to come in lower or higher than your company?

- **Consider unanticipated costs and expenses.** These must be considered (and the price must be padded to compensate for them) before you arrive at a price to charge the client. Once the contract is signed, the designer must perform at the agreed price.

- **How much outside help will you need to employ for the job?** Will you need consultants or legal or technical advisors? Is this business as usual, or are you and your firm venturing into new territory on this project?

- **Are there special governmental regulations or codes that will be involved with the job?** You will have to take time to research the regulations and codes and make sure that you are in compliance.

Common Pricing and Purchasing Terms

Cash discount	See Terms of Sale. Bonus discount given to companies that promptly pay their bills. This type of discount is shown on the invoice like this; 2/10 net 30 (days). In other words, if you pay the account balance within ten days, you receive an additional 2 percent discount off of the invoice price. If you are not able to pay within ten days, the full balance is due in thirty days. Discount amounts may vary.
COD	Payment for the merchandise at the time of delivery. It may be necessary to do this on initial orders where you haven't established your credit and want a timely delivery, until you have built up some credit with the supplier.
Cost price	The actual price the designer must pay to buy the goods from the manufacturer or distributor for the goods. Since small firms do not usually buy frequently or in quantity from the same vendor, the cost price is usually less than 50 percent off.
Discount	The percentage a retail outlet subtracts from the retail price to get the wholesale price they'll pay for merchandise. Price reduction is usually shown in a percentage off of the price. A full or whole discount is 50 percent off of the suggested retail price. Because of low volume or inability to stock inventory, most designers will receive a reduction of anywhere from 10 percent to 50 percent off of the list price.
FOB	This term means "freight, or free, on board." These initials with the city name immediately following them indicate the point to which the seller will pay the freight. If the customer is to pay freight, the notation would read FOB, his city. If the goods are lost or damaged in transit, the person who holds the title of the goods would be the responsible party. Legally, title changes hands at the FOB point.
FOB destination	"Free on board to the destination." In other words, the manufacturer is spelling out his liability and responsibility for the goods to be shipped. In FOB destination, the manufacturer is responsible (and still owns the goods until they reach their intended destination) for the risk of transporting the goods to the design firm and is also responsible for payment for the shipping.

FOB factory "Free on board from the factory." In the case of FOB factory, the purchaser of the goods is responsible and subsequently *owns* the goods when the goods are loaded into the truck from the manufacturing facility. What this means is that the designer pays for all transportation costs and accepts the risk of the goods to the design firm.

FOB factory, freight prepaid The manufacturer is responsible for payment of the freight or shipping, but the purchaser becomes the owner and is responsible for the risk once the goods are loaded in the truck.

Gross margin Amount of difference between the cost price and selling price.

Keystone/keystoning Common industry term meaning 50 percent discount.

List price The asking price (to the consumer) for the goods suggested by the manufacturer. Means the same as suggested retail price.

Markdown A "sale" price or reduction on inventory and ordered goods.

Markup The percentage a retail outlet adds to the wholesale price it pays for any item.

Multiple discounts A progression of discounts off of the list or suggested retail price generally for larger orders. These are shown in this way: 50/5. Calculate this by first taking a 50 percent discount and then take another 5 percent discount. Do not make the mistake of adding 50 percent plus 5 percent. This will be incorrect. First take a 50 percent discount and then take another 5 percent discount. Sometimes for *very* large orders, an additional discount 50/5/5 will be given. Again each discount is calculated off of the previous resulting balance.

Net price Has the same meaning as wholesale price. Usually a 50 percent discount off of the suggested retail price.

Price list These come in two forms: the suggested retail price or list price and the net or cost price list to the designer. Designers should *always* determine what price list they are working off of, before quoting a price to the customer or estimating a job. Pick up the phone and call if you are not sure. The results of discounting a cost or net price will be disastrous.

Pro forma For the first order to a supplier when there isn't any credit established, to keep the order on schedule, it may be necessary to pay the supplier in full or make partial payment before they will ship you the merchandise. Once you order several times or they establish your credit rating, suppliers will probably extend credit.

Quantity discount A discount larger than 50 percent off the list price, usually due to a large quantity purchase all at once.

Retail price The price the retailer decides to charge for the goods.

Selling price Actual quoted or sold price for the goods to the consumer. This price may be higher or lower than the manufacturer's list or suggested retail price.

Trade discounts Given to people in the trade by local retail stores and establishments, out of courtesy to the trade, since you are reselling the item to a customer. These are generally not large discounts, usually from 10 percent to 40 percent.

Terms of sale See Cash Discount. 2/10/30 is the same as 2 percent, 10 days, net 30. Either term on your invoice indicates to the buyer that you will receive a 2 percent discount if payment is made within ten days, and full payment is expected within thirty days. If you do not want to offer a discount, but simply want full payment within a specified period, write Net 10 days or Net 30 days on the invoice. Discount amounts will vary.

Suggested retail price   The asking price for the goods (to the consumer) suggested by the manufacturer. Means the same as list price.

Wholesale price   Has the same meaning as net price. Usually a 50 percent discount off of the suggested retail price.

The Federal Trade Commission (FTC) oversees the price that manufacturers can charge a retailer (price discrimination) and other deceptive practices among businesses.

A manufacturer is not allowed to charge "*like*" companies different prices for their goods. All like firms, those that purchase similar amounts of goods yearly, or companies that are stocking dealers, must be offered the same pricing from the manufacturer. Naturally, a stocking dealer is going to receive a greater discount than a small interior design firm that only occasionally places an order from the manufacturer.

A designer, on the other hand, can charge whatever the market will bear — either less or more than the suggested retail price.

Usually, small design firms are not in the position to annually purchase large quantities of goods from a manufacturer. Consequently, smaller design firms or those that purchase in less volume, will not usually purchase enough to receive 50 percent off of the suggested retail price.

The Federal Trade Commission also oversee practices by competing businesses that restrict competition among businesses. Practices are prohibited where businesses engage in "*price fixing.*" Price fixing occurs when businesses agree to sell only the goods and services at the same set price. Review the Uniform Commercial Code for rules and regulations that businesses must follow.

How Much Should You Charge Per Hour for Service?

If you are just starting out in this business, you need to be competitive with your hourly fees for services. The initial hourly rates that you charge for services will bring your customers in or drive them away. Below is a listing of the factors to consider when deciding what to charge per hour:

- *What are other competitive companies charging per hour for services only? What is their policy when the customer is making purchases also?*

   Pick up the phone and pose as a customer interviewing a design firm to do a large job. Ask them for brochures and price lists. Have information sent to your friend's house. Get on their mailing lists for sales. Use a fictitious name. Find out about pending sales as they come up. By this means you will find out a lot about your competition, about their sales strategies and products carried. When a prospect mentions that so and so has this or that sale going on, offering 50 percent off on these same products, you will know if it's the same product, if it includes installation, etc.

   Unless you are well known in your area, with a reputation as the place to use for interior decorating, you are going to need to be competitive in pricing for products and services. If you are well-known, you still must realize that people are going to pay only so much to buy their products and services from you. Experiment with different rates per hour, until you hit the rate that seems to work for your company and your customers.

- *Are you just starting out in this business or are you very well-known and experienced?*

   If you are learning this business as you go along, and are still learning from your mistakes, you should charge less than the going rate in your area. Beware of undervaluing yourself and charging too little. You don't want prospects to question your ability. How much talent do you really have? If you are very talented, although still relatively inexperienced, you may be able to justify charging more. Get as much public visibility as you can through seminars, press releases, and public displays of treatments, using use before and after photographs. Get your name out there. Before long, people in your area will recognize your name and be familiar with it.

   If you are very experienced, having worked at other companies for years and are now venturing out on your own, you will have a following to fall back on. Consequently you can and will be able to charge the going rate for your services.

- *How much do you need to generate in gross sales dollars?*

    How many new customers do you need to generate regularly to meet your financial goals? Depending on the time of the year and how busy you are, your need to take on new customers at a rock-bottom price will vary.

    If you are fairly busy, and don't really feel interested in the proposed job, the customer, and the amount of money you will be making, you are more readily able to pass on certain jobs, than if you are worried about making the overhead for the month.

    The busier you are, the better you will feel. It's not a good feeling to sit there and *wait* for customers to come in or call when you are not busy.

Methods for Pricing Products and Services:

- **Flat fee basis.** The design company specifies a specific amount of money to cover the job, except for reimbursement of expenses. Consultations for planning and specifications only. *No merchandise purchasing.* Do not work with flat fee rates until you are relatively experienced and can safely project how *long* a certain type of project will take. The designer must be very aware of overhead costs for the firm when quoting a flat fee. It is easy to miss the mark and be put out of business by underbidding jobs. If you go over or under the allotted time or the product's costs you estimated, you are bound by the price quoted and the agreed-upon design concept. Any changes will consume any profits. If you determine the majority of your time will be used in planning and execution of design boards with only a small amount of purchasing, or the purchasing is to be done less-expensively elsewhere, this is the way to charge.

- **Flat fee plus percentage of gross costs basis.** Flat fee for design work, expenses, time, and materials plus a markup on *costs* of purchases. Consultations for planning and specifications. All merchandise is specified at the designer's cost or net plus any expenses incurred. The designer then adds a certain percentage (such as 5 percent to 10 percent for larger purchases, 30 percent to 50 percent for smaller purchases) to the gross costs, for her fee. Review the flat fee basis above; the same rules apply.

- **Hourly rate or time basis.** May also be a per diem basis. Fee is based on actual time designer and staff spent on the job. Used for consultations when no purchases are made. Usually billed to the customer at two and a half to four times the designer's hourly wage. Any other expenses incurred to do the design work, travel, shipping, paperwork handling, and materials are also charged to the customer in addition to the hourly rate. Time logs must be kept to prove the time spent, if it becomes necessary. To keep the client secure with this arrangement, place a limit in the contract on the amount of time that you will use for the services. Used both in commercial and residential jobs.

- **Hourly rate plus percentage basis.** Charge an hourly fee (as above) plus a percentage of the retail expenditures. This works well for smaller jobs. With larger jobs, a percentage of the retail can quickly become exorbitant. Used both in commercial and residential jobs.

- **Cost-plus markup basis.** The cost price has a percentage amount marked up or added to the cost of goods to reach the selling price. The percentage marked up must cover overhead costs and allow for a suitable profit margin. This method ignores the consumer demand and the competition with pricing of the product. Products should have a minimum of 50 percent markup. Most products should be 100 percent markup (what the traffic will bear). Reinforce to your decorators that if the profit falls below 40 percent markup, no commissions will be paid. This method should be used in combination with a flat or hourly fee to ensure that the firm will make a profit. Very common pricing method with both commercial and residential jobs.

- **Percentage of *cost* of purchases basis.** The designer is paid by the percentage markup on the cost of all furnishings and services he or she purchase for the client. All merchandise is specified at the designer's cost or net plus any expenses incurred. The designer then adds a certain percentage (such as 10 percent to 20 percent for larger purchases, 30 percent to 50 percent for smaller purchases) to the gross costs, for their fee. This fee structure is only feasible for larger purchases.

- **Perceived value pricing basis.** This method of pricing is based on the buyer's wants and needs, not on the cost of the product. This type of pricing is used when the price is determined by what the target market will *pay* for the goods and services. This basis is usually used when you have severe competition, or when there is not any competition.

- **Full retail price basis.** Charge for services and furnishings at full retail price. Consider this basis if the job is relatively small (either commercial or residential). Not recommended if the job demands a lot of job planning and supervision, design work, drafting, and specification writing.

- **Percentage off retail price basis.** Very common pricing method for very organized stores and firms with buying power, and few delivery and shipping problems. Not recommended if the job demands a lot of job planning and supervision, design work, drafting, and specification writing (POs and work orders).

- **Square footage basis.** This is calculated by multiplying a set amount times the square footage involved in the project (e.g. $1.50, $1.75 per square foot). Use this method after doing a few of the same type of jobs so you are able to review and determine *accurately* an average square footage price. This can be a highly profitable way to charge for your services. A common method for commercial jobs.

- **Combination of the above methods.** In order to ensure a profit, it is usually necessary for design firms with large overhead to use a combination of the above pricing structures.

When you price out a job, it is safest to use several of the above methods and compare them against each other to make sure that you haven't under figured the job. The safest way to charge and ensure you make a profit for a job is to analyze and determine all projected costs. The jobs that will have higher profits for your company will use a combination of the above methods, such as a small percentage off retail plus an hourly rate. Research how other design firms in the area are charging. They are your competition. While you do not want to emulate them, customers will be calling to compare pricing. If you are too different (or appear much higher), you probably won't get jobs from shoppers.

Always ask for a retainer (advance or deposit on a portion of the job), or on retail priced jobs a deposit for items ordered (at least one-third) to get you started on the project.

Residential customers (due to competing retail competition) may resist paying a flat or hourly rate for a designer or decorator's time. Retail establishments offer "free" consultations and estimates and a discounted sale price for the same or similar products you are offering. Frequently, residential customers (due to customer indecisiveness) will take more of your time than a higher paid commercial job will.

Pricing Products

When pricing your products, weigh *supply versus demand* before making a decision on what markup to use. Price is relative to the value of the item. Where does the price fit into the overall perception of value in regard to quality, design, and provided service?

- What do you want the pricing structure to accomplish?

- Are you simply attempting to survive? Or are you after maximum profits?

- Are you striving for market share leadership? Or product quality leadership?

- How will the price point you select affect your competitors?

- If you select the wrong method of pricing for your location, how much will this cost you in dollar amounts plus other costs?

Pricing Factors

Before you determine how you are going to charge for your products and services, consider each of the following points in depth:

- Costs.

- Customer perceived value.

- Current market pricing.

- Manufacturer's suggested retail prices.

- Pricing your products at a consistent markup over cost.

- Supply and demand.

- The competition.

- Present economy.

- Added value laden bonuses.

- Pricing some products at a loss leader to get customers in the door.

- Quantity discounts.

- Being the discount leader, or following the discount leader in pricing.

- Decision on whether your company will be a leader or follower of trends.

- The inclusion or exclusion of freight costs in the pricing.

- The inclusion or exclusion of design, measuring, or installation costs in the pricing.

Determining How to Price Your Goods and Services (answer these questions before making any pricing decisions. This information is provided in the Business Plan Preparation section):

- Do you understand the market forces affecting your pricing system?

- What price range will your line of merchandise fall in? High, medium, or low? What quality of merchandise will you be providing?

- Do you know the top level that your customers will pay for some of your products?

- Will you price your goods and services below market, at market, or above market?

- What price *must* you charge to make a profit?

- Which of your products are price sensitive to your customers? How high can you price *these products* without turning off your customers?

- What price is the customer willing to pay?

- Will the set prices cover full costs on each sale?

- Will you set definite markups for each product?

- Will you set markups for different product categories?

- Will you use a one-price policy rather than bargaining the price with the customer?

- Are regular, repeat customer sales better than one large annual sale?

- Are regular repeat sales throughout the year better than one annual large sale?

- What part do you want price to pay in your overall retailing plans?

- What will you keep in stock? What is the price range of your stock?

- Will you take credit cards such as Visa and Mastercard? Will you *raise* all of your prices to cover the extra charges for a merchant account and processing fees? Visa and Mastercard will not allow you to charge a customer more *during* a transaction if the customer puts the purchase on a credit card.

- Will your business use unusual pricing because of your competitors?

- What products will attract customers when placed on sale?

- Will you use leader tactics in advertising to get the customers in the door? How about loss leader pricing on some items?

- Will you lower some products' prices to attract customers? Do you know at what point customers will become suspicious and hesitant?
- Have you provided for discounts and allowances?

- Will coupons, rebates, markdowns, or special sales methods be employed?

- How will you respond to special pricing by your competitors?

- Do you calendar and track your competitors' sales? Do you know when they normally have sales? If you do, you might find a trend and be able to beat them to sales.

- Will you be influenced by competitors' price shifts?

- Will you offer discounts for quantity purchases or to particular groups of buyers?

- Do you know which products will be slow movers and which ones will be fast movers? Will you consider this when making pricing decisions?

- What is your policy on when to take markdowns? How large will the markdowns be?

- Will your customers expect sales at certain times of the year, such as the holidays?

Pricing Restrictions:

- Do any of your suppliers have a minimum price standard at which their goods may be sold?

- Does your particular state have fair trade practice acts that dictate the you must mark up your merchandise by a minimum percentage?

- What are your state regulations regarding length of term for advertising of "close-out" sales? How about two-for-one sales, etc.?

- Do you know all of the state regulations regarding your business?

- Will you issue rain checks for advertised inventory that is sold out?

Part 15

Insurance

Disclaimer:
Use the following information as a guideline, only. **I am not an insurance broker** (insurance agent, only), **nor has this section been written by an insurance broker. I am not attempting to give you** *any* **legal or insurance advice. Use the following information as guidelines for what is** *probably* **necessary, <u>seek a business attorney and an insurance brokers advice for your individual company's needs,</u> buy legal, financial books, and insurance books on the laws in your state on the various following subjects (written by attorneys, accountants, insurance brokers), and research material at your local law libraries for absolute information on any given subject. Touch of Design nor I will accept responsible for any misinformation or any misconstrued information, herein. The information in this section is simply an** *approximate* **overview of what to expect.**

Businesses need to purchase insurance to transfer risk. Proper insurance coverage will allow you to stay in business should a catastrophe occur.

There are many types of insurance available to businesses. A business can easily become insurance poor if insurance is purchased for every conceivable occupance. The basic types of essential insurance are covered in this section.

One reason for joining interior design associations and other business associations is for the group insurance plans that are available. Some of the available insurance will still be relatively expensive. Before proceeding to buy through a regular insurance agent, check to see what your options are.

Insurance Agents

Insurance agents vary, as do designers and decorators. Naturally, you want the best you can find, with also the most competitive prices. When shopping for an insurance and an insurance agent, include the following:

● Check around for competitive bids for your policies.

● Check the insurance agent's reputation, integrity, and rating.

● Has the agent made any errors with you in the past and did not give you the best possible advice or coverage for the money?

● Has the agent been successful in recovering compensation for past losses?

● Does the agent foresee any problem regarding settlement of any foreseeable losses?

● Measure the level of protection and valuation of the insurance offered.

● Evaluate the most important coverages needed to determine if you are spending your insurance money in the best possible way.

● Examine deductible amounts to determine if they are affordable and realistic.

● Can you reduce your premiums by installing sprinklers, security systems, and fire extinguishers?

A quality insurance agent should be accommodating and be willing to provide the following:

- A thorough evaluation of your personal and business insurance needs.

- Comparison of insurance alternatives. If a multi-line broker, a comparison between companies.

- Help in negotiation with the insurance company via telephone calls and letters.

- Help in the business establishment of easy procedures for insurance paperwork.

- Help and service with processing of claims.

- Competent advice on loss prevention.

- Guidelines for you to follow to comply with the Occupational Safety and Health Act and the Environmental Protection Act.

- An annual review of your insurance coverage.

Insurance Companies Ratings

Insurance companies are rated by a company called Best's Advance Report according to a list of criteria. When selecting an insurance company, you want one with the best rating possible. Here is a list of Best's ratings. To check a rating for an insurance company that you are unfamiliar with call, Best's Advance Report, (201) 439-2200. Be sure to ask the quoting agent what insurance company he or she is quoting.

A+	superior
A and A-	excellent
B+	very good
B and B-	good
C+	fairly good
C and C-	fair

Guidelines for Insurance Coverage

Follow the guidelines below to avoid underinsuring or overinsuring your business:
- Use only one insurance agent, if possible. Be realistic and honest with him or her.

- Make sure that your name is on the policy correctly.

- Keep complete records of past insurance policies, losses, premiums paid, and any loss recoveries. It may help you get better insurance at a lower price should you change agencies.

- Read your legal contracts such as leases, deliveries, and contracts to determine what your actual legal liability is.

- Purchase replacement cost value.

- Assess valuable antiques and art work (for sale or not) in addition to your studio inventory.

- Determine just how a business interruption, loss of a key employee, or gross mismanagement would affect your business.

- Predict your product liability to consumers, other users, and even nonusers.

- Realize that only a portion of the risks your business faces is insurable. You can buy insurance for some risks and not for others. Your agent will help determine what can be covered.

- Do what you can to prevent losses from occurring. Keep the cost of any losses that do occur as low as possible.

- Buy coverage for the large potential losses, and don't worry about insurance for the small things. Pay for the small things as they come up. It will be expensive to cover them with insurance.

- Use as high a deductible as you can afford.

- Do not become underinsured.

- Get appraisals for real estate periodically so you are not underinsured, and will be able to prove actual losses should they occur.

- Avoid overlapping or duplication of insurance policies.

- Put only a very responsible person in charge of company insurance program.

- If you work out of your residence, your homeowner's or renter's policy will not cover your business equipment, supplies, or inventory should any losses occur. Add special riders or an individual business policy to cover business losses at your residence.

- Make photographic records of what you own, should a loss occur and you expect insurance to cover the loss.

- If start-up funds are limited, check to see if you can break the premium up into several payments.

- Check to see what indemnification you can procure should your leased building be condemned.

Insurance Company Policies

Insurance companies are obviously in the business to make lots of money. If you don't carefully examine the fine print of the policy, you may think you are covered, when you are not. Work with your agent to review the fine print and help compare coverage, from one company to another. Below are some insurance company "tricky terms" and other explanations to watch for, before *needing and expecting to* collect from a claim:

Actual cash value. The replacement cost on the date of the loss, minus depreciation to cover physical deterioration and wear and tear of the destroyed property.

Repair and replacement endorsement (replacement value). This endorsement provides for payment sufficient to actually replace or repair your damaged prices at current market prices. Always request replacement value.

The policy was never legally assigned to you. Policies cannot be assigned without the insurance companies authorization. If you purchase insured property, be sure that all contractual insurance assignments are taken care of. Be sure that you have a signed letter from the insurance company stating that all is taken care of, or purchase new insurance for the business.

You don't have an insurable interest. You must suffer a direct financial loss from the insured property's damage to collect any money. Inform the supplier of your ownership interest at the time you make the insurance purchase and let them know when and if changes occur.

You violated your warranty/representation. Your insurance application for coverage will invoke warranties, or facts you guarantee to be true, representations, declarations that the insurance supplier counts on. Any warranty or material representation that proves false might result in your policy being voided, retroactively.

The insurance company is not obligated. Should the insurance contract and its underwriting be in disagreement, the underwriting rules. Get it in writing from the insurance supplier, not from your agent. Should changes in your circumstances come up, don't rely on the insurance broker to relay the news; write the insurance supplier yourself and have them write you a letter.

You breached the policy. Should you violate a policy term or condition, you coverage will be suspended until you correct the violation. Reinstate the policy. Do not assume since you corrected the problem, the insurance is automatically back in force.

You have duplicate coverage. If you purchase a second policy to insure property, you must have the written permission from the first insurance supplier or an endorsement for additional insurance on the first contract. Even so, you can only collect what the property is worth, not more. Each insurance company will pay a portion of the claim.

Agreed-upon endorsement. A signed, written endorsement by both the insured and the insurance agent agreeing about the actual cash value of your property. This must be done before a disaster strikes and must be renewed once a year. This is used in the case when you have co-insurance and are not in agreement on the actual value of your property.

Building laws coverage. Most cities will not allow you to leave unburned portions of a building standing. You will probably have to tear down the unburned portions and completely start over with a new building. When you go to plan the new building, check to see if the codes are not different now than when the initial building was built. The building becomes much more expensive to replace. This endorsement will cover the additional costs of a new building, demolition of the old building, and construction of the nondestroyed parts of the old building. Unless you purchase this endorsement, you will not be covered with your regular insurance policy.

Employee Benefit Coverage

Insurance coverages may be purchased to cover employees for group life insurance, group health insurance, disability insurance, and retirement income. Buy key-man insurance to protect against financial loss should a valuable employee or partner die.

By having available extra benefits such as life and health insurance, employees will feel that your company is a more valuable place to work than most and will tend to stay longer.

Consult with your accountant or financial advisor about setting up company retirement and profit-sharing plans.

Group Life Insurance:

If you pay group insurance premiums and cover all employees up to $50,000, the cost of the premium is deductible for federal income tax purposes, and the benefit value is not taxable income to your employees.

Group life insurance is readily available at low rates even if there are ten or fewer employees in your group.

If the employer opts to pay part of the cost of the group insurance, state laws require that 75 percent of the employees must elect coverage for the plan to qualify as group insurance.

Should an employee leave the company, group plans allow the employee to convert group insurance coverage to a private plan, at the going rate for their age, without a medical exam, within thirty days after leaving the job.

Group Health Insurance:

Group health insurance costs less and provides more ample coverage and benefits for the employee than individual contracts will.

If the employer pays the entire cost of the premium, individual employees cannot be dropped from a group plan unless the entire group policy is canceled.

Disability Insurance:

Worker's compensation insurance pays an employee only for time lost because of work injuries and work-related sickness. It will not pay for time lost because of disabilities incurred off the job. Available at a low premium is insurance to replace the lost income of workers who suffer short-term or long-term disability *not* related to work.

Coverage is available that will provide employees with an income for life in case of permanent disability resulting from work-related sickness or accident.

Retirement Income:

For self-employed persons, income tax deductions are allowed for funds used for retirement for you and your employees through plans of insurance or annuities approved for use under the Employees Retirement Income Security Act of 1974.

Annuity contracts may provide for variable payments in the hope of giving the annuitants some protection against the effects of inflation. An annuity, whether fixed or variable, can provide retirement income that is guaranteed for life.

Additionally, Individual Retirement Accounts (IRAs), Keogh plans, and other plans are available for retirement planning. Check with your accountant, banker, or financial planner to find out what the latest information and on how to qualify for these plans, what are the contribution limits, and how to set them up.

Business Insurance

When you have your own business, four types of insurance coverage are necessary. They are fire insurance, liability insurance, automobile insurance, and worker's compensation insurance.

- Should you have several insurance policies to cover the same property, you will only be able to collect the actual cash value of the property. All of the insurers will divide the actual cash value in proportion with each other and pay their individual portion.

- You can buy insurance for property that you do not own. In order to do this you are required to have an interest — an insurable or financial interest in the property *when* a loss occurs.

- You need *not* have the financial interest when the coverage is taken out on the property.
    When the property is sold, you may not assign the insurance policy along with the property unless you have prior permission from the insurer.

Fire Insurance

In addition to regular fire insurance, you may want to add other perils such as windstorm, hail, smoke, explosion, vandalism, and malicious mischief at a relatively low cost.

- In order to insure the loss by fire of accounts, bills, currency, deeds, evidence of debt, money, and security, you will need to take out additional special coverage.

● Should the possibility of a fire hazard become increased (such as sub-letting a portion of your space to a business that is more hazardous) the insurance company may cancel coverage for losses *not* originating from the increased hazard even if you have faithfully paid the insurance premium.

Property Comprehensive Insurance:

Generally with comprehensive insurance your best buy is one of the all-risk contracts offering replacement cost value, which offers very broad coverage for the money. Areas usually covered are: real property (optional), personal property (optional), loss of income, extra expenses, personal property off of premises, exterior signs, and credit card slips. These packages can usually be expended to cover newly acquired real property (180 days), newly acquired personal property (up to thirty days at new location), trees, shrubs, plants, lawns, valuable papers and records, personal effects, accounts receivable, debris removal, pollution clean-up, and fire department service charge.

Fire Insurance Compensation:

Should you suffer a loss, your insurance company will compensate you or indemnify you by:

● Paying the actual cash value of the property at the time of the loss.

● Repairing the affected property with material of same or like materials.

● Removing and taking the affected property at the agreed or appraised value and reimbursing you for your losses.

● Should an insured building become vacant or unoccupied for more than sixty consecutive days, insurance coverage will be suspended *unless* you have a special endorsement to your policy canceling this provision.

● If you are found to have misrepresented or concealed facts to your insurer about any material fact or circumstance concerning your insurance or the interest of the insured, the policy may automatically become void.

● In the event of a property loss you must take all reasonable means to protect the affected property from further loss or run the risk of having your insurance coverage canceled.

● To recover for a loss, you must furnish within sixty days (unless the insurance company grants you an extension) a complete inventory of the damaged, destroyed, and undamaged property showing in detail quantities, costs, actual cash value, and the amount of loss claimed.

● Should a disagreement arise regarding the amount of the loss, the question of the value of the loss may be resolved through special appraisal procedures provided in the fire insurance policy.

● Upon canceling an insurance policy, your policy will be prorated and any balance of the insurance premium will be returned to you. Your insurance company may also cancel the policy at any time by giving you a five-day written notice.

● You need to insure 80 percent to 90 percent of the value of the property. This is known as a co-insurance clause. If your insurance coverage is less than this, you cannot collect the full amount of your loss. The amount of recovery is in proportion to the percentage of the amount of your insurance coverage.

● Should your property loss be caused by someone else's negligence, the insurer has the right to sue the negligent third party for recovery of the amount that the insurer has paid to you under the insurance policy. This is the insurer's right of subrogation. Generally, if you ask for this right to be waived, the insurer will comply. You would want this right to be waived if the property you owned were leased out to someone else.

● If a building is under construction you may insure it for fire, lighting, extended coverage, vandalism, and malicious mischief.

Fire Loss Prevention

Nothing can shut you down faster than a fire. Use the following guidelines to prevent fires and help you cut the down the damage a fire can cause, should one occur:

- Have a fire extinguisher accessible and ready for use.

- Instruct employees on how to use the fire extinguisher.

- Have fire and smoke alarms. Check them periodically to make sure that the batteries are not run down, and they are in working order.

- Have No Smoking signs. You do not want your samples and displays to reek of smoke, anyway.

- Check all electrical outlets to make sure they are in working order.

Liability Coverage

Included in your automobile and home owner's insurance policies is liability insurance to help cover legal fees and judgments against you. If you should lose your case in court and your insurance is not enough to cover the liabilities of the case, then your personal assets and income are in jeopardy. Your liability coverage only covers up to the limit of the liability policy. Any additional damages beyond that point become your responsibility. Raise your limits on your policies (relatively inexpensively) to give yourself enough coverage.

Your home owner policy will probably not cover a business run out of your home. Have a separate policy written to cover the business or have an umbrella policy or excess liability policy added to your home owner's policy to cover you in everything. An umbrella policy will take over where your auto and home policies end.

- Insure yourself for umbrella or blanket liability coverage for $1 million or more for adequate coverage. Should you get sued and lose, it covers personal liability up to your allotted limit. You will need to keep your auto policy in the upper limits and have an adequate home owner's or renter's policy. Umbrella or blanket coverage gives you coverage where the other two policies stop. This type of coverage for $1 million is only around $100 per year. Don't forget to factor in the extra costs for high auto insurance costs.

- Most liability policies require you to notify the insurer immediately after incidents that could possibly cause a future claim. Even if the incident seems relatively small, this is a requirement by insurance companies.

- Today, most liability insurance policies cover personal injury in addition to bodily injury.

- Personal injuries include libel, slander, etc.

- Under certain conditions, your business may be subject to damage claims from trespassers on your property.

- Even if you have exercised reasonable care, you may be legally liable for damages.

- Should a suit against you turn out to be frivolous or fraudulent, the liability insurer pays court costs, legal fees, and interest on judgments, in addition to liability judgments.

- You may be liable for the acts of others under contracts you have signed with them. This liability is insurable.

- It is possible to be held liable for fire loss to property of others in your care. This property will normally not be covered by your fire or general liability insurance. Cover this risk by fire legal liability insurance or through subrogation waivers from insurers of owners of the property.

- Check insurance coverage regarding your liability circumstances when working on or installing design jobs.

Product liability insurance:

Product liability insurance is an important insurance to have to protect you against lawsuits by consumers who have been injured while using your product. The legal rule of product liability is, "Defective product plus injury arising from customary or foreseen use equals maker or seller pays."

You can offer yourself *some* protection by including instructions on the proper use of your products (have the customer sign a copy of instructions for your records).

Product liability insurance prices will vary from state to state, and depend on your annual gross sales, the number of products you sell or expect to sell, and the possible risks associated with the products (e.g. drapery cords). The insurance company will take a close look at your products. If your gross sales are small and your line is limited, you may find an affordable policy. You will need high limits of coverage. Have the policy written so that the limits apply on a "per claim" basis instead of a "per occupance" basis. Another consideration is to incorporate your business for the liability protection.

Commercial general liability:

This insurance package includes premises operations, products and completed operations, advertising injury, personal injury, host liquor, employees as additional insurers, broad contractual liability, broad form property damage, fire legal liability, incidental malpractice, reasonable force for protection, nonowned watercraft, and medical payments. The package is subject to limits allotted by the insurance company on aggregate limits, products and completed operations, professional limits, personal and advertising injury limits, each occupance limits, fire damage limits (any one fire), and medical expense limits (any one person).

Product Liability Prevention

Product liability suits are a businessperson's nightmare. This is an extremely good argument for incorporation of your business. Although you may not have manufactured the product, you will be named along with the manufacturer in the lawsuit, should one arise. If it is set up right and the corporation rules and regulations are followed, incorporation will limit your person liability to the corporation. If you do incorporate, sign documents in corporate capacity (corporation name). Do not sign personally for anything. Use the following guidelines to limit product liability suits against your company:

- Use quality controls. If the product is defective, don't install it or sell it. Return it to the manufacturer or sell it "as is, with all faults."

- All customers should be supplied with adequate instructions on product or packaging of products. Have installers demonstrate and hand the customer the product instructions on any limitations. Have all customers sign a statement that they received instructions for the product.

- Use disclaimers on contracts and sales agreements.

- Write warnings about the product in contracts and sales agreements if there are any ways to misuse the product that the customer should be aware of.

- Discuss with your business attorney ways to limit your liability.

Automobile Insurance

- If an employee or subcontractor uses a vehicle on your behalf, you may be legally liable even though you are not the owner of the vehicle.

- If you own five or more vehicles under one name and operate them as a fleet for business purposes, you can generally be insured under a lower cost fleet policy against both material damage to your vehicle and liability to others for property damage or personal injury.

- To reduce the amount of your insurance premiums, take a deductible of $250 or $500.

- Automobile medical payments insurance pays for medical claims incurred from automobile accidents, regardless of who was at fault.

- Most states require liability insurance or require you to post a surety bond of financial responsibility should you be involved in an accident.

- Purchase uninsured motorist coverage to cover your own bodily injury claims for accidents you could become involved in with uninsured motorists.

- Personal property (including tools, samples, etc., for work) are not covered in vehicles under your automobile policy.

Worker's Compensation

Worker's Compensation is a governmental regulation, but it is also an insurance requirement: it is listed here so that it doesn't get overlooked or forgotten.

If you employ workers, your state will require you to have worker's compensation insurance to protect them. The amount of the premium will depend on how many employees you have and what type of work they do for you. Worker's compensation insurance is available through insurance brokers or by contacting your state's administering agent for worker's compensation insurance (state fund). Should you purchase the insurance through your state, you will probably pay the same rates and receive literally no service. You may receive dividends through a private supplier. Check before buying. **Federal and common law require that an employer:**

- Provide employees a safe place to work.

- Hire competent fellow employees.

- Provide safe tools for work.

- Warn employees of existing danger.

Should an employer fail to provide the above, the employer is liable for damage suits brought by an employee and possible fines or prosecution.

State law determines the level or type of benefits payable under worker's compensation policies.

Not all employees are covered by worker's compensation laws. Exceptions are determined by state law and therefore vary from state to state.

Almost all states require you to cover your workers under worker's compensation.

Save money on your worker's compensation insurance by classifying your workers properly. Reduce your premium costs by reducing workers' accident rates below the average. This is done by using safety and loss-prevention measures.

Rates for worker's compensation insurance vary from 0.1 percent of payroll for "safe" occupations to around 25 percent or more of the payroll for hazardous occupations.

Ways to cut costs with worker's compensation insurance (Check your state laws regarding worker's compensation insurance:

- Shop around for the best insurance carrier. Don't just compare pricing, compare history of claim processing and service. Regularly review your coverage with your insurance broker and make necessary changes.

- Report regular hours worked. Don't inflate the hours and the premium by adding in overtime.

- Have your company pay for the small claims or pay toward the claim. Check with your state for its laws on worker's compensation. If you pay the small claims or pay a portion of the claim, you are reducing the claimed amount. Even if you pay the small claims out of pocket, all accidents must be reported to the insurance company, immediately. To avoid doing so will subject your company to extreme fines and penalties. What appears to be a small accident may actually grow into a severe health condition for the employee later.

- Self insure your company. In most states you are allowed to self insure or join or form an association of small companies that pool their capital. Consider these avenues once your company pays out more than $8,000 a year in worker's compensation insurance costs.

- Read all paperwork you receive related to your worker's compensation insurance. As with any business, many errors will be spotted (errors raise your insurance premiums) if you only review the paperwork. Have the errors immediately corrected.

- Check to see if you have classified your employees correctly. Ask your insurance broker for a copy of the class code book that describes each employee classification.

Employee Accident Prevention

As a business owner who has to pay for worker's compensation insurance and who will probably pay for small accidents out of pocket, you'll find it pays to take some necessary steps to do what you can to reduce employee accidents. Use the following guidelines to control the amount of accidents that occur on the job:

- Use trained personnel.

- Have exits properly marked and unlocked (or easy to unlock) from the inside.

- Keep work areas clear of debris and boxes.

- Use proper ventilation. Have air conditioning and heating filters changed regularly.

- Regularly maintain equipment and keep maintenance records.

- Have first aid supplies on hand and easily accessible. Have key employees trained in CPR.

- Have emergency telephone numbers mounted on telephones and in your outside windows.

Bonding

Bonding is another type of insurance to assure your customers that your company is trustworthy, reliable, and that your employees are protected against all types of losses while in customer's homes. Bonding is available thorough insurance brokers; bonding companies are listed in the yellow pages.

Other Insurance Coverage

While not essential, other business insurances will add to the security of your business. These are business interruption insurance, crime insurance, glass insurance, and rent insurance. Check with your insurance agent for other needed coverage. It is easy to become "insurance poor" if you add coverage for all insurance available to protect you and your business.

Business Interruption Insurance:
In the event a fire or other peril shut down your business, you may want to have insurance to cover salaries, taxes, rent, interest, depreciation, and utilities in addition to lost profits.

Some policies will also let you collect in the event your suppliers are shut down by a peril. This type of insurance also provides payment for amounts you spend to hasten the reopening of your business or other incurred expenses even if your business is simply disrupted after a fire or other insured peril. Make sure you buy this insurance in *adequate* amounts should a disaster close you down.

If your policy is correctly endorsed, you can get business interruption insurance if your operations are suspended because of failure or interruption of the supply of power, light, heat, gas, or water furnished by a public utility company.

Crime Insurance:

- Crime or burglary insurance will exclude property such as accounts and manuscripts.

- The insurance company will not pay a claim for crime insurance unless they see visible evidence of a break-in.

- Crime insurance can be written to cover inventoried merchandise and damage incurred during the course of the burglary in addition to money in a safe on the premises.

- Robbery insurance protects you from loss of property, money, and securities by force, trickery, or threat of violence on or off your premises.

- Comprehensive crime policies written just for small business owners are available.

- Comprehensive policies cover other types of loss by theft, destruction, and disappearance of money and securities, in addition to burglary and robbery. It will also cover thefts by your employees.

- If your business is located in a higher risk area and you are unable to obtain insurance without paying excessive rates, you may be able to get help through the federal crime insurance plan. Your insurance agent or state insurance commissioner has the information on how to go about getting insurance through this plan.

Glass Insurance:

Glass insurance policies are available to replace glass that may be at risk such as plate-glass windows, glass signs, motion picture screens, glass brick, glass doors, showcases, counter tops, and insulated glass panels.

The glass insurance policy will not only cover the glass itself, but the lettering and other ornamentation, and any boarding up of the windows after the glass has been broken out.

Even if you do have a claim for broken glass, full coverage will resume without any additional premium for the period covered.

Rent Insurance:

Rent insurance is available to pay your rent if the property you lease becomes unusable because of fire or other insured perils and your lease demands continued rent payments even in this situation.

"Key-Man" Insurance:

Should a small business lose a key employee by death or serious illness, whether this important person is a partner or a vital employee, the company will probably suffer severely. Insure your key employee with life insurance and disability insurance, called "key-man" insurance paid by your company.

- Proceeds of a "key-man" policy are not subject to income tax, but premiums are not a deductible business expense.

- Cash values of key-man insurance, which accumulates as an asset of the business, can be borrowed against and the interest and dividends are not subject to income tax as long as the policy remains in force.

Part 16

More Government Regulation

Immigration Reform and Control Act of 1986

With the passage of the Immigration Reform and Control Act of 1986, it is unlawful to hire undocumented workers who do not possess the correct permit for employment. All employees hired after November 1986 are required to furnish you with identification and work permit information. Forms are available from the U.S. Department of Justice. Take a photocopy of your employee's drivers license for your records to prove identification.

OSHA

OSHA is the U.S. Labor Department's Occupational Safety and Health Administration. OSHA is responsible for helping make work premises safe and healthy for employees. For complete information contact the Department of Labor for its two handbooks, *All About OSHA* and *OSHA Handbook for Small Businesses*.

Fictitious Business Statement

Fictitious name statements are required to be filed with the county by *almost* everyone starting a business (check requirements in your state).

Filing a fictitious name is a requirement if your company's name does not include your last name, or if it does, also includes the word "company," "corporation," "limited," "brothers," "and sons," or other words that suggest multiple owners of the business. If the name is a name such as Smith's Antique Shop, the name does not suggest that there may be additional owners of the business so filing of a fictitious name statement is not required.

Fictitious name statements need to be filed within forty days of start of business. The purpose of filing a fictitious name statement is to make a public record of the individual members of businesses for the interests of those who transact business with them. Statements need to be renewed every five years from December 31 of the year that you initially filed. The name statement also expires forty days after any change in the facts of the statement; the exception is a change in the residence address of an individual, general partner, or trustee.

A person transacting business under a fictitious name that hasn't been filed with the county clerk has no legal recourse to collect on an account or contract in the fictitious business name, until the fictitious name statement has been executed, filed, and published. Failure to file a fictitious name statement simply extends the pending lawsuit. A business may enter into binding and enforceable contracts and transactions under the fictitious name, even though the statement has not yet been filed and published. The one prohibition is against preserving legal actions upon the contracts and transactions.

The filing of a fictitious name statement gives the registrant the exclusive right to use the fictitious name statement and disallows the use of another confusingly similar trade name by another party, as a trade name, in the county of filing. The registrant must be the first to file the fictitious name in the county and must actually engage in business or trade using that fictitious business name, or a confusingly similar name, in such county.

Procedure for filing:

A fictitious name statement must be filed with the county clerk's office where the registrant has his or her place of principal business.

Before filing your fictitious name statement, you must check the availability of the desired name by doing a name check. This is done by looking up the name on the microfiche and recent computer printouts at your local county courthouse.

Registration of a fictitious name statement will not guarantee exclusive use of your fictitious name statement.

Within thirty days of filing you must publish the fictitious name statement in an area newspaper that publishes business name statements. The name statement has to appear once a week for four successive weeks. An affidavit of publication must be filed with the county clerk within thirty days of the publication.

After you file the statement, you will probably be contacted by several newspapers whose primary revenues come from publishing business name statements. Take the lowest bid, but make sure that the newspaper you select is an "adjudicated newspaper" and will send an affidavit of publication of the published name statement to the county clerk for verification. The county courthouse has a list of adjudicated newspapers available for your information.

Filing a fictitious name statement will generally cost $10 plus $2 for each additional name (owners). Since your county cashier will only accept cash, come prepared with the correct amount of money.

Should you abandon your fictitious name statement at a later date, the fee at the county courthouse will run $5.

Resale Permits

You will need a resale permit (seller's permit) when you start your business. Apply to your State Board of Equalization for the permit.

The owner, partner, or corporate officer of your business must apply for the resale permit with the driver's license numbers, social security numbers, and home addresses of all owners, partners, and corporate officers of the business. Be prepared to also supply the names and addresses of three business references.

Resale permits are free, but you may be required to supply a security deposit. Depending on your projected sales (your guess), the State Board of Equalization will determine how often you need to file a statement and pay all collected sales tax that is due.

The State Board of Equalization will send you a return form about 10 days before the date your return is due. In the event that you do not receive your filing form when it is due from the board, mail all sales tax due with your account number, address, filing period, and a letter explaining that you did not receive your filing form.

Contractor's Licenses

Most states will require most of your installations and construction work for design jobs to be completed by a licensed contractor. A business owner may decide to become a general contractor and receive the necessary license. Usually, designers simply hire licensed subcontractors to do the work.

If a designer hires an unlicensed contractor when a licensed contractor was required by the state, the client *may not* be required (legally) to compensate the designer for the work. The designer may also be fined and arrested. Check your state statutes for requirements for licensed contractors.

Deceptive Advertising

Under federal and most states laws, an advertisement is unlawful if it tends to mislead or deceive. This is true even if the ad doesn't actually fool anyone. It also doesn't matter what your actual intentions were, either. If your ad is deceptive, you will face legal problems, even if your intentions were the best. What is judged is the overall impression you establish with the advertisement, not the detailed sincerity of the individual portions.

Through the years, the Federal Trade Commission (FTC) has taken action against many businesses allegedly involved in false and deceptive advertising. If the FTC is convinced that an advertisement violates the law (the advertisement is unfair or deceptive), it generally makes an informal attempt to get the violator to voluntarily comply. If this fails, the FTC will probably issue a cease-and-desist order. If the business still doesn't comply, the FTC levies a fine of $5,000 per violation. Each day that the order is ignored constitutes a separate violation of $5,000. The FTC may instead choose to bring a civil lawsuit on behalf of people who have been harmed, and seek a court order or injunction to stop the advertisement in question while the investigation continues. The offending advertiser is then required to run corrective ads stating that its earlier ads were deceptive (a great way to quickly dissolve any credibility a company has).

Customers also have the prerogative to sue advertisers under most states' consumer protection laws. Suits are generally brought in small claims court for refunds or the customer may be joined in a class action suit with other parties and sue in another court.

Recently, the FTC has been particularly concerned about deceptive advertising and "bait-and-switch" advertising. Bait-and-switch advertising involves advertising a product at an especially tempting price to get the customer to come in the store. This is the "bait." Once the customer is there, he or she is then "switched" to a more expensive product due to the "bait" being sold out or by telling the customer that the "bait" is an inferior product. An advertiser who resists showing the advertised item to the customer or who has inadequate quantities of the advertised item available is engaging in unfair trade practice in violation of Section 5 of the FTC Act.

Deceptive Pricing

The two deceptive pricing applications that are likely to get your business into trouble are: 1.) making incorrect price comparisons with your competition or with your own "regular" prices or 2.) offering something that is supposedly "free" when you are actually charging for it.

Offering a sale price from a regular retail price is a common sales method. This is not a problem, unless the sales price is the actual, bona fide price at which you always offer the item. If this is the case, it is misleading and you are in violation of the law.

Be very careful in purchasing merchandise especially for a sale and creating a fictional regular price or one that you offered the merchandise at for only a couple of days. This is a common practice with seconds or discontinued items.

If you compare your price with a competitor's price in an advertisement, be very sure that:

● The competitor is selling the exact same product.

● The competitor/competitors have sold enough of that exact item in your area at their higher price so that what you are offering is a verifiable discounted price. Be sure that the example of the competitor's higher price for the questionable item is not an isolated or unrepresentative price for the item.

For "free" items or services, you may offer gifts only if there are no strings attached. If you raise another price to be able to include the "free" item, the price is not free. If you usually throw in delivery or other service as part of the package with the purchase of the item, but are now not giving that service because you are giving a "free" item, than the item is not considered free.

Part 17

Legal Factors

Disclaimer:
Use the following information as a guideline, only. I am not an attorney, nor has this section been written by an attorney. I am not attempting to give you *any* legal advice. Use the following information as guidelines for what is *probably* necessary. Seek a business attorney's advice for your company's individual needs, buy legal books on the laws in your state on the various following subjects (written by attorneys), and research material at your local law libraries for absolute information on any given subject. Neither Touch of Design nor I will accept responsibility for any misinformation or any misconstrued information, herein. The information in this section is simply an *approximate* overview of what to expect.

How to Prevent Lawsuits

Today, unfortunately, you cannot be too careful with the way you do business with customers. Be very careful and watchful of what your decorators promise with delivery dates, product quality, etc. Lawsuits over false promises are becoming popular now, whether it is a commercial job or a residential job. Designers are now being charged with fraud and misrepresentation with the intention to deceit. These lawsuits stem from oral and written promises and deceptive advertisements and sales pieces handed out to customers when interest is expressed in a certain product.

To be on the safe side of the law, have an attorney review brochures and advertisements that you or anyone connected with your business design firm will be distributing. If a customer sues because an item is of inferior quality, you may be joined in the lawsuit due to your supplying fraudulent verbal information and handing out brochures with false information.

Because of the need to be extremely careful about product quality, sell top-quality merchandise and be realistic about product quality. Use the words *approximately, about, around, roughly, almost* and *nearly*, very freely. Include them in almost everything you promise. Cover yourself. "The window treatments should be completed and ready to be installed in approximately four weeks. We will keep you informed of their progress." If you do not make it a practice to be realistic about what you promise customers, they may hold you to everything you say and provide them in writing, including sales contracts and written sales pieces.

If you are not *extremely* specific in writing about what you will and will not provide and take very accurate notes and document everything, every time you meet with your customer, you are taking a very real chance of being sued. Earlier, years back, interior designers tended to feel they had more leeway in this area. Today, realize you must write everything down and do not leave anything to chance. If you do, and your customer decides he or she isn't happy about something or with you, look out.

You are Being Sued!

After you start doing well with your business the situation may come up where someone files a lawsuit against you or you need to file a lawsuit against someone else. Most people fear a lawsuit or having to bring one against someone. This section of the book is an overview of what occurs when a lawsuit if filed. The person bringing the lawsuit against another is called a *plaintiff*. The person having the suit brought against him or her is called the *defendant*.

- The plaintiff must have a notice *(summons)* and a *complaint* served upon the defendant (the one being sued), saying he or she is being sued. The summons gives information about the issues of the case.

  - The *summons* may be served on the defendant by a third party such a marshall or process server. The summons gives the date the defendant must appear in court to defend his or her position regarding the issues of the case.

  - The *complaint* reviews the facts of the case, the laws that are relevant to the matter, and financial relief sought in court.

- An *answer* to the plaintiff's allegations is prepared by the defendant and submitted back to the courts. The answer admits, denies, or pleads ignorance to the allegations brought by the plaintiff. At this point the defendant may present to the plaintiff an *affirmative defense argument.*

- *Discovery* is the next level of the lawsuit. Both parties contemplate the evidence to be presented by the other party. Included in the *discovery* stage are depositions or written interrogatories, witness's statements, and any physical evidence.

- Most cases end right here after discovery with a *summary judgment.*

- If the case is not dismissed, it is placed on the court's calendar for trial. *Fast track* (currently becoming very popular) is the court system that is instituted and in use in many areas to get the trial over with within eighteen months. At the end of the trial, the court decides on the merits of the case and awards or denies damages.

Small Claims Court:

Small claims court handles minor lawsuits up to $5,000 in California. You may seek a lawyer's advice, but the lawyer may not accompany you into small claims court to represent you in California and other states. If you are sued, bring all evidence you have (especially written evidence) to defend yourself. See the section on collection problems for more information about presenting your case in Small Claims Court.

Municipal Courts:

Guilt must be *proved beyond a shadow of a doubt* in criminal cases while civil lawsuits need only show a *preponderance of evidence* to find the defendant guilty. Because attorney costs will eat up awards in smaller lawsuits, consider having the lawsuit or dispute *mediated* or attempt to work it out among each other. Mediation or arbitration are less expensive alternatives to running up a huge bill with an attorney. Both mediation and arbitration processes are both quick (usually only three to six weeks) and informal. Mediation is a cooperative effort by both the plaintiff and the defendant to work out the problem rather than declare one the winner and one the loser. Arbitration is the most frequently used method of the two.

How to Find an Attorney

- Go to a law library or a large public library and find the *Martindale Hubbell Law Directory.* Included in this resource is a brief description of lawyers with the areas of law that they specialize in. Realize that the information given was probably written by the attorney and is an advertisement for the attorney.

- Call the bar association in your area for the number to its lawyer referral service. Call the service and ask for the name of an attorney that specializes in the type of case that you have. Bar associations do not charge attorneys for the referrals, they do not recommend attorneys, nor do they have information on the attorney's background. They will give you only one attorney's name at a time, with two referrals the limit. There are other privately run lawyer referral services that attorneys pay to belong to and get recommendations from.

- Talk to other business people that may have had a similar problem. Be sure that if you are asking for a name of an attorney, consider the credibility of the source providing it.

- Ask another attorney or one you use for other matters, who would be a good choice for the particular problem. You should be able to get a good referral this way.

- Ask a law school professor for his or her recommendation.

Attorney Consultations

Have a consultation with all attorneys that specialize in your type of case. If an attorney doesn't have a great deal of knowledge in your particular area of concern, you will have to pay much more in fees for the time required to research the particular area. Go to an attorney who already has the knowledge and experience.

- Be sure that the attorney you are considering is attentive and interested in your case.

- Do you feel comfortable working with this person? Does this person intimidate you or make you feel inferior? Can you readily talk with this person? Make sure the attorney you select outlines the options available to you.

- Can you understand what the attorney is telling you? Is the language used clear and concise? Have the attorney throw out the legalese and talk to you in plain English.

- Realize that though one attorney may have lower fees, he or she may not be the best answer for you. If the attorney don't do a good job for you, he or she isn't worth the money.

- The attorney should not guarantee you huge winnings. He or she may be trying to convince you to take them on as the attorney of record. The only promise made is that he or she will try his or her best.

- If the case appears destined for court, does the attorney have previous trial experience?

- Can the attorney afford to take on the case? He or she will be fronting all necessary expenses during the time the case takes to go to trial.

- If you are unhappy with the attorney you select, speak up and say so. The attorney should attempt to resolve the problem areas with you. If the attorney doesn't or won't, get another one. Your new attorney will notify the former one that he or she is now representing you.

The Ways to Resolve a Legal Dispute

A customer whose problem you resolve is not likely to complain to any legal agency or board with power to oversee your business. If you have ever had to cope with any type of investigation, then you know that although the complaint may be unfounded, the investigative process is time consuming, worrisome, and if you have had to call in an attorney, expensive. Here are the ways legal problems and complaints may be resolved:

- **Structured negotiations** between both parties with legal counsel. Least expensive method.

- **Mediation** before a nonbiased third party with counsel present. Any decisions are nonbinding.

- **Post-lawsuit mediation.** Complaint is filed with the courts. Have counsel present. Nonbinding decision.

- **Mini trial (mock trial).** Review of the case issues before a judge who is usually retired or sometimes other legal counsel. The decision is nonbinding.

- **Arbitration.** Both parties agree to accept the finding of the arbitrator. During the arbitration, legal issues are examined. The decision is binding.

- **Court trial.** Appearance in court before a judge with or without a jury.

Ways to Cut Down Legal Costs

There are ways to trim down the legal costs. The following lists ways for you to monitor the legal expenses:

- Discuss fees at the onset of meeting with a attorney. Realize that fees are negotiable. Most attorneys you will be working with are in business for themselves.

- Do not proceed with the discussion of what legal matter you need help with, until you arrive at a mutually agreeable fee schedule. Some attorneys will give you an free initial consultation. Determine over the phone before your appointment if the initial consultation is free, or how much is the charge for the initial visit.

The following is the way that attorneys charge for their time:

- **Flat fees.** Based on the task or project requirements. If the task or project takes less or more time for the attorney, you pay what you initially agreed to pay.

- **By the hour.** The attorney charges you his or her hourly fee to do the task or project. Hourly rates vary with the attorney's expertise, experience, and the going rate for the specialty. Hourly rates for attorneys presently range from a modest $100 per hour to more than $300 per hour.

- **Contingency fee.** The attorney agrees to take a percentage of the recovery of the settlement either through negotiations with the other party or through a trial. If the attorney is unable to recover any settlement, you will not be charged for the attorney's time. You will still have to pay any and all expenses incurred.

- All attorneys demand reimbursement for out-of-pocket expenses such as filing fees, long distance telephone calls, fax expenses, copy expenses, transcript of testimony (depositions), etc., in addition to their flat fee, hourly fee, or contingency fees.

- Shop around and select the most favorable attorney and method of payment for the task you need help with. If the case seems to be straight forward and you are dealing with a seasoned attorney in the same area of expertise, you will get off less-expensively by paying by the hour. The attorney will know what to do without any undue time spent on research (at your expense). Do not give up a large percentage of your recovery of a simple case that you know the attorney will need to work only a few hours on.

- If you know that you will be seeing the attorney repeatedly during the year, establish that fact with the attorney when you discuss payment. If the attorney realizes that you are coming back, he or she is probably going to give you a more favorable rate in order to count on your continued business.

- Use a collection agency rather than an attorney to collect your delinquent accounts. Otherwise, use an attorney that is fresh out of law school and eager to do collections for you at an affordable percentage.

- If you are having an attorney help you with setting up contracts that you need for use with your business, have the attorney design contracts that you may reuse — forms where you may fill in the blanks with appropriate legalese. With most situations they will work fine — with special cases, speak with your attorney.

- Bring all necessary records to the initial meeting with your attorney. Don't wait to be asked for them — just bring everything you think may pertain to the matter. Ask what the attorney would like you to bring when you make the initial appointment.

- It is preferable to settle a case out of court when you can. If you get stuck on fighting for the "principle of the thing," it may cost you far more money in expenses and fees than if you would have taken the initially offered settlement to end the fight. Some minor matters may be settled on your own without the aid of an attorney. Law libraries are available for the public to use everywhere. Use them.

- Use class action suits to get others to share the attorney expenses with you when appropriate. The attorney stands to make much more in percentage cases when other victims are involved. On hourly rates or flat fee cases, you stand to cut your legal fees. Be sure that there is not a conflict of interest between the attorney representing any clients you bring into the lawsuit or other matters.

- Ask the attorney how he or she charges for phone calls with you. What fractional cut-off point per hour is used. For example, if you make a five-minute call to the attorney, are you charged for fifteen minutes, because fifteen minutes is their minimum charge?

- Let the attorney know that you expect an itemized statement of costs and charges each month. You will know what was or wasn't done on your case or project, and you hold the attorney to strict accounting of the time spent. If there is an entry on the statement you don't understand, call and ask for an explanation.

- Because many attorneys are well off financially, they may not be as aware or concerned with how your money is being spent. If you think of ways you can cut costs and are willing to do some research, etc., speak up. Let them know that money is scarce and needs to be tightly controlled.

- If you come across pertinent articles, make copies and highlight the points you want your attorney to see (you can research magazines on the computer at the public library). You are saving valuable research time on new developments in that area. Many attorneys are spread so thin into various areas, they are not keeping up on new developments like they should be.

- If the case is going to take some time, ask to be kept advised of the progress and new developments with periodic progress reports. In each report, have the attorney give you an approximate idea of how much more money will be required to resolve or complete the matter at hand. You may decide to go ahead and settle the case or find another way to finalize the case quickly, rather than litigating the matter in court.

- Speak with your attorney during normal business hours. Some attorneys advertise that they work during the evening and on weekends by appointment. Do they charge extra for these time slots? Some certainly do. Also try to meet your attorney in his or her office rather than in a more costly visit to at your business.

- Consult with your attorney about several legal matters at the same meeting or over the phone during the same phone call.

- Stick to the legal matters at hand and make little small talk if you are being charged by the hour. Avoid an attorney who gets easily sidetracked and won't stick to the legal problems that you need to work on — you are being charged for on an hourly rate.

- Consider handling some matters yourself. If you can put together your own business, you can do some legal work yourself. Take customers that owe you or that you have disputes with under $2,500 to small claims courts. Neither the plaintiff nor the defendant can have an attorney represent them in small claims court.

- When working with an attorney on a case, come right out and ask what you can do to help expedite things. You can make less-expensive trips to the court house to file documents, pick up certified copies of documents, etc.

- Don't change attorneys frequently. Find one that you can use and work with for most areas that you require and stick with that one. He or she will have a clear idea of where you are coming from, what you expect, and how to work with you.

Ask around to other business owners to find out what attorney they use and are happy with. Call around to determine fees and methods of charging, before making an appointment. If you know what the going rate and usual method of payment for a procedure is, you will feel better when you meet with the attorney to work out the details. Determine what expertise level you are working with before you make a commitment to work with a particular attorney. If the attorney is new to the area that you are concerned with and is going to have to research at your expense (hours of time lost here) — it is less-expensive to pay another attorney twice as much per hour if they know how to quickly proceed on the problem or matter.

Copyrights, Patents, Trademarks, and Trade Secrets

As a designer, you may choose to protect your drawings, illustrations, sketches, floor plans, design ideas, sample boards, written works, inventions, company name, and logo against copying or duplication (infringement) from others. You protect ideas and written works by filing copyrights, patents, and trademarks, which are overseen by the U.S. Congress.

You do have some protection even if you never register a copyright for any of your work. The minute you write or draw something it becomes your **copyright**. You can protect your work somewhat by spelling out the word "copyright," or using the copyright symbol, the year and followed by your name on all of your work — copyright (or©) 1993 Linda M. Ramsay. In order to file a copyright suit against another party, you must register your copyright. It is costly to copyright everything. If you see a suit or a problem pending, register a copyright.

Should you decide to have some of your work published, register your copyright on the work *three months after publication* for maximum copyright protection. If you do so you can receive additional statutory damages up to $50,000 plus payment of attorney fees and legal costs of the lawsuit.

If you do work while employed by someone else's company, you are under the copyright statute of *"work for hire."* The employer will be considered the author of the work and will own the copyright unless you have legally arranged otherwise.

A copyright is protected by the Copyright Office in the U.S. Library of Congress. Use a copyright to protect written works and design works. Copyrights are given as protection for writers, artists, and composers. A copyright is a legally protected, exclusive right to sell, publish, or reproduce artistic, musical, or literary works for the life of the author plus fifty years. An infringement can result in an infringement action in federal court, with injunctive relief and damages being awarded to the holder of the copyright.

Ideas, plans, methods, systems, procedures, or discoveries are not copyrightable, but the expression and phraseology in written form is. You cannot stop others from using your basic business idea.

To register serials, periodicals, newspapers, magazines, bulletins, newsletters, annuals, journals, and proceedings of societies use form SE. Each SE copyright registration cost $10 (all registration prices are of mid — 1993).

To register nondramatic literary works, books, directories, and other work written in words, such as how-to instructions, use copyright form TX. Each TX copyright registration cost $20.

To register works of the visual arts, which applies to pictorial and graphic works including photographs, charts, technical drawings, diagrams, and models, use form VA. Each VA copyright registration cost $20.

For more information on filing forms, contact the Copyright Office, Library of Congress, Washington, D.C., 20559. Enclose a stamped, self-addressed envelope.

A **patent** is a governmental grant of monopoly power given to inventors to make, use, or otherwise enjoy the fruits of their inventions, provided the invention is new, useful, and not obvious to one of ordinary skill in the same field. Use a patent to protect custom product ideas and designs. Patents grant the inventor an exclusive right to sell, use, and make the product for seventeen years from its issue date. If anyone violates this exclusive right, the patent holder has the right to file an infringement suit. Should the court uphold the patent, the infringer will be enjoined from further production and will be liable for damages to the holder of the patent.

Registration of patents is a very complicated and expensive process. Due to the patent offices poor filing system and antiquated office procedures, many patents have been granted and then invalidated at a later date. It's been said that up to 20 percent of the patent files are "missing" and therefore anyone attempting to file a patent can never be sure if he or she is the owner of the patent or not. A patent only gives you the right to file a court action. You still must prove your case in court.

For more information on filing a patent, cost of filing fees, filing forms, and procedure, contact the Commissioner of Patents and Trademarks, Washington, D.C., 20231, (703) 557-INFO. Enclose a stamped, self-addressed envelope for information requested.

A **trademark** is any mark, word, letter, number, design, symbol, picture, or combination thereof any form adopted and used by a person to identify a particular brand name or product that is not a common or generic name for the goods nor is descriptive of the goods. Copying the trademark of a competitor or using a symbol deceptively similar to that of a competitor is a violation of the Lanham Act of 1946, and the violator is subject to an injunction and the imposition of damages. Protection from infringement upon a trademark is managed by the common-law action for unfair competition.

For businesses that will only be operating within their state, state registration offers protection within the boundaries of the state and is usually less expensive and a simpler process.

Filing a trademark federally currently costs $175 for each class the trademark is to be registered in. Filing only in your state will vary with the state, check with your secretary of state.

Before registering a mark, a search should be made to determine if anyone else is using the same mark on similar products. You can decide to do the search yourself, as best as you can, at the largest library in your county that carries federal copyright records (or state if you are only filing with the state). Your county library will only have records of approved trademarks, and you won't know about pending applications. The Commissioner of Patents and Trademarks office is months behind in processing applications. Unless you travel to the search library at Crystal Plaza 2, 2nd Floor, 2011 Jefferson Davis Highway, Arlington, VA 22022, and search all available records, you can only be partially sure that the mark desired is available.

You can also hire a trademark attorney that probably has the copyright database via modem on computer to search records, or you can hire a company such as Government Liaison Services, Inc., 3030 Clarendon Blvd., Ste 209, P.O. Box 10648, Arlington, VA 22210, (703) 524-8200, to do the search for you. Depending on the intensity of the search, the fee will vary between $100 and $200 If it is determined that the mark or a similar mark is already taken, you are out the money for the search and must pay another search fee for the next mark you attempt to search. If you do not do a search and it is determined that someone else is using the same mark or a similar mark, you will have wasted the $175 filing fee.

To do your own search through your county library is a shot in the dark, but if you are correct that the desired mark is available, you will have saved quite a bit of money in attorney's fees and repeated search fees through private companies. If you don't mind risking the $175 filing fee after you are reasonably sure that your mark is available, do it. I did, and I was correct. The desired mark was available, I registered it myself, and I came out at least $1,800 ahead! The worst case scenario was that I would have picked a mark that was taken, lost $175, and my time, and had to start over with another mark.

For more information, cost of filing fees, and filing forms contact the Commissioner of Patents and Trademarks, Washington, D.C., 20231, (703) 557-INFO. Enclose a stamped, self-addressed envelope for information requested.

A **trade secret** is a type of valuable business information that a business keeps secret. The recipe for Coca Cola is a closely guarded trade secret, for example. Unfortunately trade secrets are not legally protectable except in the case of fraud or theft.

For any of the above registrations, buy books and review them on the subject. For a list of self-help law books that will guide you through many processes including copyright, patent, and trademark, call or write Spinx International, INC., P.O. Box 2005, Clearwater, FL 34617, (813) 587-0999 or (800) 226-5291.

Government and Legal Checklist

Before starting a business, you will need to consider various laws that will affect you if you do not comply with them. The additional list of items is necessary information for your new business:

- What licenses and permits are required for interior design firms in your area?

- Is the location zoned for having a business? Can you get a variance if not zoned in your favor?

- What business laws do you need to comply with?

- Has your attorney informed you of your responsibilities under federal and state laws and local ordinances?

- Have you registered your fictitious business name at the county clerk's office? If the name for your business is different than your legal name, it is necessary to register the name and pay the fee for registration.

- If you are not a sole proprietor and do not have a social security number or have employees, file an application for an employer tax identification number.

- File an application for a sales tax identification number (resale number), obtainable at the Board of Equalization. If you are selling products, you must tax your customers. If you are purchasing products for resale within your same state, that are subject to sales tax, you must fill out this form.

- If you have employees, you must file a application for a state unemployment insurance number. Company owners are not considered employees.

- If you have employees, you must file an application for worker's compensation insurance numbers and state disability insurance.

- Have you obtained employee compensation records, W-4 forms, withholding exemption certificates, and applications for employment?

- Have you applied for other licenses required by federal, state and local law?

- If you are a partnership, have you drawn up partnership agreements that are favorable to all partners? Have you made copies of the agreement for all partners?

- For corporations, have you incorporated the company yet? Do all members of the corporation have copies of the corporate kit with stock certificates, seal, and articles of incorporation?

- Have you obtained copies of purchase agreements with the suppliers you will be using?

- Has your attorney made up your business contract (sales agreement) for your customers to sign?

- Have you made a list of the company's property, serial numbers, and noted the property value of other items used in the business?

- Do you have life insurance policies for each partner and officers?

- Do you have liability insurance for the business and the premises?

Part 18

Contracts and Door-to-Door Home Solicitation Agreements

Law of Sales

The Uniform Commercial Code (UCC) governs the law of sales, including warranties. As a businessperson in business to sell goods, you should become familiar with the UCC. Any quality business law book will include a copy of the code. Since space is limited here, only a brief overview of the law of sales as it pertains to the sale of goods is presented. Take a comprehensive business law course at your local community college or state university; a business law textbook will provide some insight into laws regarding sales and contracts.

According to the UCC, a **contract** is a promise, for the *breach* of which the law supplies a *remedy*, or the *performance* of which the law recognizes as an obligation; a transaction between two or more individuals, where each has mutual rights to demand performance of what is promised. **A legally valid contract** (that is one that has legal remedies) **must contain certain legal elements to be enforceable. There must be:**

- **An offer.**
- **Acceptance of the offer.** All parties consent to the terms of the contract.
- **Consideration** (something of value given in return for performance or promise of performance).
- **Contractual capacity.** All parties must have the ability to perform legally valid acts.
- **The object of the contract must be legal.**
- **The contract must be in writing.** The statute of frauds provides that any contract over $500 must be in writing.

Common contract terms:

A **unilateral contract** is a contract where only one of the parties makes a promise. A unilateral contract may be a promise for an act or an act for a promise.

A **bilateral contract** is a contract where both the contracting parties make promises. A promise to sell and deliver goods given in exchange for a promise to pay the agreed purchase price at a future date is a bilateral contract or a promise for a promise.

A contract becomes **executed** or terminates when all of the parties to the contract have fulfilled all of their legal obligations created by the contract. Until all legal obligations have been fulfilled, the contract is executory. If one of the parties has partially fulfilled his obligations under the contract, the contract is referred to as a partially executed contract. Within contract law there are **three types of performance: complete or satisfactory, substantial performance, and material breach.**

An **express contract** is one in which the promise or promises are stated or declared in words. These words may be spoken or in writing.

An **implied contract** is one in which the promises or promises are not stated in direct words but are gathered by necessary implication or deduction from the circumstances, the general language, or the conduct of the parties.

A **warranty** is the assumption by the seller of goods of the responsibility for the quality, character, and suitability of goods sold. A warranty may result from representations made by the seller, or it may be imposed on the seller by operation of law.

To expressly warrant goods (**an express warranty**), you need not use the words "warranty" or "guarantee." Any recommendation of fact or promise, any description of the goods, or a sample or model of the goods used as a basis of the contract is an express warranty. An endorsement simply of the value of the goods or a statement claiming to be simply the seller's opinion or recommendation of the goods does not create an express warranty.

A **warranty of title** is different from other warranties because it protects the buyer in his ownership of the goods he has purchased. Other warranties cover the quality of the goods sold. Unless the buyer knows that the seller does not have title to the goods (they have to be ordered) but is selling in an official capacity and professes to sell only such title as a third person, a warranty of title attaches to the sale.

An **implied warranty of merchantability** attaches to a sale made by a merchant dealing in goods of the kind sold. Goods to be merchantable must be at least such as to: pass in the trade under the contract description, be of fair average quality within the description, are fit for the ordinary purpose for which such goods are used; be comparable in quality to other like goods; goods must be packaged and labeled; and goods must correspond to the descriptions made on the labels or packaging. Interior design firms will generally be named in any lawsuit along with the manufacturer of the goods should the product fail, break, or harm a person or his or her property.

An **implied warranty of fitness** for a particular purpose is based on the seller's having reason to know the particular purpose for which the buyer wishes the goods and the buyer's reliance on the seller's skill and judgment in selecting the goods suitable for his or her purpose. The warranty can be excluded or modified. If the goods are defective, unbeknownst to the seller, the seller is still liable for the warrant of merchantability.

To exclude or modify an implied warranty of merchantability, merchantability must be mentioned and be written conspicuously. Implied warranties are excluded by wording such as "as is" or "with all faults."

Goods you carry and recommend must meet minimum standards of materials and workmanship, and be able to be used for their intended use. Failure to honor a warranty is a breach of contract duty and the client has the right to sue the merchant.

Contracts or Sales Agreements

When starting a business, you should work with a business attorney and a CPA for your protection. Seek help with drafting your business contracts and the statement of your business's terms and conditions. The statute of frauds stipulates that any sale of goods over $500 must be in writing to be enforceable. Should a client refuse delivery or refuse to pay for ordered goods, this provision allows you to take the client to court in an attempt to recover monies owed.

Have all corporate contracts reviewed ahead of agreeing to jobs. Determine whether you really can perform under the terms supplied you.

All sales of goods and services, regardless of their dollar amount, *should* be in writing. Anytime the customer adds more items or adds on additional rooms after the initial contract is signed, be *sure* to write another separate or add-on contract to include the additional charges. Never allow anything to be ordered without a signed sales agreement.

The sales agreement binds the designer or decorator to sell the goods/services at the prices quoted and binds the customer to pay the prices agreed. All terms and conditions of the agreement must be stated within the sales agreement or contract. The customer signs that he agrees to the terms and conditions stated within the agreement or contract.

One positive aspect about becoming an ASID member is the availability of the use of ASID contracts. They have been prepared by highly qualified attorneys and cover practically anything that can arise in the course of an interior design project. They protect you from being taken advantage of by customers. Unfortunately, because these contracts are lengthy and thorough, they tend to be intimidating to customers. You may wish to use them as outlines and adapt them for use in writing your own contracts.

Once you agree with your customer and have closed the sale, you need to put every detail in writing. Under no circumstances should you start the job without a signed sales agreement with a deposit. If the sales agreement is unsigned and you have no deposit, your customer can easily back out of the job, after you have incurred costs and time. Insist that a signed sales agreement and deposit are your policy and you cannot proceed without either one of them. **Note:** photocopy any check given you by your customer and add the check to your customer's file — you have accurate information on their bank and account number if there should be collection problems later.

What to include in contracts and sales agreements:

- Have a print shop or desktop publishing business create a sales agreement for your company, complete with your logo and information. Stationery and office supply stores also offer required pre-printed business forms on which you can imprint your logo and address. You want to appear very professional and this is one way of doing it. You should outline what you want included in the contract and seek an attorney's advice to fine tune the sales agreement, making it legally binding.

- Customer's name, home address, home phone number, work phone number, and address where products and services are to be installed.

- It is very important to begin every sales agreement description with the words *"customer has selected."* Take the time to read and review with your customer *every detail* of the job listed on the sales agreement before he signs it. You will find *many* small errors here that may not be found before the item is fabricated (the customer got mixed up and thought you said you were making it a pair, not a panel; he thought he agreed to another color, etc.). After a careful review, have the customer sign the sales agreement. Carefulness shows your customer that you do care enough to take the time on each detail, that you do not want *any* mistakes, and that you care how the job is going to come out.

- **State exactly what you are going to do for the customer.** Provide a **complete** description of the items ordered and to be fabricated. You cannot be too precise here. Describe precisely the services and products — e.g., pairs, panels, mounted on new hardware, mounted on old hardware, whether you are having the installer remove the old hardware, whether the items are to be lined; if so, what type of lining, general placement of window treatment items; five inches above the window or up to the ceiling, color, fabric name, fabric number, lined or unlined, sizes agreed upon, pairs or panels, floor length, sill length, apron length, straight hang, tied back, rod pocket shirred, pleated, use of new or existing rods, any existing rod removal, reinstall on old hardware, etc. For commercial projects, state the square footage of the area that you are to work on. Later, they can't come back and say you were suppose to include this other area also.

  You may think that this is extreme. **You cannot overdo your description of items and services that you are to provide.** You may think it is extreme until a customer says, "I didn't want that drapery sill length, I wanted it to the floor." Since you weren't specific on documenting the size on the contract, even though it was discussed, and didn't make a note on the work sheet that the customer knows the drapery is sill length, *you will remake the drapery at your expense.* Once it happens a couple of times, you will remember to be very specific. Sometimes the delivery takes forever and you are also not sure what the customer ordered — after all, that was thirty customers ago! Other times, customers will get items installed that they just don't care for, even though they helped pick them. They look at their sales agreement and see how nonspecific it is and say, "you picked that color, style, length, and trim. I *didn't,* and I don't care for them, and I don't want them." Nothing teaches us better than the pain of paying to redo things out of our own pocket.

  If you use complete descriptions, then later, if the customer says, "I didn't agree to that," you can pull out your sales agreement and say "yes you did, I reviewed this with you verbally, and it is also here in writing. Here is your signature."

  Complete descriptions *do* take longer to write, but they are your insurance policy for the design job. A description should include:

- **Who is to procure the purchases.** If your firm is outlaying the cash, what collateral is to be provided? A lien against the property?

- **State exactly what the job includes.** Will you be providing everything or only specific items? How many rooms are included? Which rooms?

- **What is expected of the customer.** What is the customer to provide?

- **How you are going to complete the job.** Will it be subcontracted out? What areas will you be responsible for? Which areas will you not be responsible for? Be very specific about what you are providing and what other subcontractors are providing.

- **How changes with the job will be handled, how much the changes will cost, and how the changes will affect the time frame of the job.** Include a disclaimer, denying any responsibility for changes authorized by anyone else connected to the job.

- Include a statement that should the client cancel the order after the goods have been shipped, there will be a restocking charge for cancellations for _____ (state anywhere from 20 percent to 50 percent for the restocking charge). Always wait the three days *before* ordering any goods *unless*, *"customer waives the right to his or her three-day cancellation, truth-in-lending waiting period." Write* the statement on the contract if this is the case.

- A statement that you and your subcontractors must have ready and easy access to the job site to accomplish all related work.

- Original price of the item, and the sale price (if any) paid by your customer should be noted. Draw a line through the original price and write 30 percent off sale and the new sale price next to the original price.

- Charges for extra services and any other expenses incurred while completing the job. Note how you will be reimbursed.

- **Installation charges.** Note the installation charge next to the sales price. You will be adding all installation charges together and will note them after the subtotal where tax has been added. All installation charges are nontaxable.

- **The order of the phases of the job. What are the phases?**

- **Approximate delivery date of the entire job.** Note: if all items will not be completed in approximately the same time frame, break up the job into parts and write them up on several sales agreement. You do not want a slight delay for one item to hold up the whole job and payment.

  By breaking up the job on various sales agreements and taking several deposits (can be one check, that totals the deposits on all of the sales checks), you will ensure that you get paid for the bulk of the items installed at all times. If all items are listed on the same sales check, and one tieback is missing, this one small item can prevent you from collecting the balance due on the entire job.

  Include a clause covering you for things out of *your* control — acts of war, natural disasters, strikes, etc.

- By law **you must list the fiber content** of all fabric items. Later the client is able to refer back to the fiber content listed on the sales agreement for fabric cleaning. You should also stamp your sales agreements with the words **Dry Clean Only!** You are releasing your responsibility to the customer when she washes the item and comes back to you to complain that the item now looks terrible.

- Indicate whether or not the fabric has been stain protected.

- For upholstered furniture: indicate whether or not arm covers are included. Include type of cushion included.

- For wood finishes: indicate type of wood finishes.

- Always include a clause in your bids, *"the price is subject to change due to price increases of manufacturers and wholesalers."* Use this as a reason to effectively close the sale. The customer needs to make a decision and act on the contract immediately, to avoid a price increase.

- A written statement that a client's verbal agreement is legitimate if the selling party delivers the purchaser (either with a certified letter or in person) a signed confirmation outlining the details of the contract. The purchaser has seven business days to respond in writing to any conditions of the offer she is not in accordance with. If the purchasing party fails to respond within the seven business days, the agreement becomes a valid sales agreement (contract).

- **A disclaimer.** A disclaimer limiting your liability and conditions for which you are not responsible causing problems or delays that should arise due to nature, strikes, transportation problems, or the accomplishment, quality, or prompt completion of work by other people.

- **Method of payment.** What type of down payment do you require? How is the balance to be paid for? When? Is the job is to be paid via a COD, Visa, Mastercard, or is the client to be billed for goods and services rendered. The amount of the down payment is also noted. Always take a down payment or retainer of one-third to one-half of the total. Also state whether your compensation is to be on an hourly basis, on a total cost basis, or on a percentage of the total job.

    Include a statement that if the fee schedule isn't met in a timely matter, the contract becomes void and all costs and fees incurred to that point become immediately due and payable. If charges are to be placed on a credit card, note type of card (Visa, Mastercard), card number, and expiration date.

    There are different ways to bill. You can bill upon the completion of the sales agreement, or bill as each item is delivered and installed. However you decide to bill, for legal and collection reasons, state how you are going to bill on the sales agreement in this manner, *"Goods and services are billed upon delivery or when services rendered. Payment for goods and services are due ten days after receipt of the invoice."* Or, *"Goods and services are billed upon completion of each sales agreement. Payment is due within ten days of receipt of the invoice."*

- Retain all publishing and photographic rights of any written works.

- **Designate who is the owner of the job specifications and drawings.** Should something go wrong with someone else using the specifications or drawings, you may be sued. Considering copyrighting your drawings and written specifications for your protection. Always retain the rights to use any of your drawings, ideas, designs, and specifications at a later date. If you come up with a great design idea or window treatment, you will want to adapt the idea for other customers, or even consider publishing your ideas for use by others. Remain in control.

- **For jobs requiring special certificates and guarantees,** have the manufacturer or supplier prepare them and send them directly to the customer. Let them have the responsibility to supply these *personally* to the customer.

- A *stop-work clause* should the client not make their payments for the job as agreed.

- **A termination clause:** This agreement will terminate with the written notice given by either the buyer or the seller as long as seven business days notice are given. Should the buyer terminate this agreement, all monies for work and expenses incurred through the seven business day termination period are due and payable. Any amount of down payment or retainer remaining after buyer terminates work and expenses have been paid shall be returned to the buyer from the seller.

- *A note stamped on the face of the sales agreement that cancellation of this job after the truth-in-lending, three-day-cancellation period will result in forfeiture of the deposit.*

    You may not want to be completely hard nosed here. If the customer cancels with a legitimate reason — job transfer, the orderer dies, etc. — you may want to deduct only the exact costs you have actually incurred up to the cancellation of the order. Deduct the fabrication costs up to that point, the fabric restocking fees, the installer remeasures, etc. It is up to you.

    When you have the note stamped on the face of the sales agreement, you will vastly cut down on your cancellations. Even if some event does occur in the buyer's life, she may just as soon go ahead with the job, rather than lose one third to one half of her money.

- For items where labor or delivery are not built into the package price, do not charge a customer sales tax on labor or delivery.

- A thank-you and welcoming statement to the buyer for her business. Also make a statement that while you and your subcontractors will do their best to keep noise, dust, and early morning working hours down to a minimum, some disruption of regular living can not be prevented and should be expected.

- Date, designer's signature, customer's signature.

Note: calling a sales contract a sales agreement is less intimidating to your customers. No one likes to sign contracts. Keep *all* language (including legal) and descriptions outlined in the sales agreement easy to read and understand.

Note: for commercial projects, make sure to get the billing address in addition to the address of the job site.

Door-to-Door Home Solicitation Agreements

Due to federal law, consumers are able to cancel contracts for $25 or more within three business days of signing, if the contract was signed *away* from a seller's regular place of business. Initially, this rule was brought about to guard homebound, inexperienced consumers from fast-talking salespeople.

Federal law provides that consumers must receive and *sign* a home solicitation sales agreement or sales contract that states the customer's right to cancel the contract within three days.

The home solicitation or sales contract must state the following (include either separately or on the sales contract):

BUYER'S RIGHT TO CANCEL

You, the buyer, may cancel this transaction at any time before midnight of the third business day after the date of this transaction. See the attached notice of cancellation form for an explanation of this right. Next, the home solicitation must be signed and dated by both parties — the buyer and the seller.

NOTICE OF CANCELLATION

You may cancel this transaction, without any penalty or obligation, within three *business days* from the above date.

If you cancel, any property traded in, any payments made by you under the contract or sale, and any negotiable instrument executed by you will returned within ten days following the mailing, delivery, or telegraphing of your cancellation notice to the seller, and any security interest arising out of the transaction will be canceled.

If you cancel, you must make available to the seller at your residence, in substantially as good condition as when received, any goods delivered to you under this contract or sale; or you may, if you wish, comply with the instructions of the seller regarding the return shipment of the goods at the seller's expense and risk.

If you do make the goods available to the seller and the seller does not pick them up within twenty days of the date of your notice of cancellation, you may retain or dispose of the goods without any further obligation. If you fail to make the goods available to the seller, or if you agree to return the goods to the seller and fail to do so, then you remain liable for performance of all obligations under the contract.

To cancel this transaction, mail or deliver a signed and dated copy of this cancellation notice or any other written notice, or send a telegram, to (name of seller), at (address of seller's place of business) NOT LATER THAN MIDNIGHT OF (date). I hereby cancel this transaction (date), (buyers's signature).

The seller must give the buyer a signed copy of the above statement. If the buyer is not given a form, she can request that the seller send one. Her right to cancel is then extended until she receives the form in the mail.

If the seller wants to cancel her transaction, she can call you and tell you. She must also return the notice of cancellation to the seller's place of business either in person, by certified mail, or by fax.

After receiving the cancellation notice, the seller must refund the money within ten days. Any merchandise must be picked up or reimbursed for the shipment back to the seller's place of business within twenty days. If the seller doesn't arrange to get the merchandise back, the buyer is allowed to keep the merchandise.

Door-to-door home solicitation sales agreements can easily put a damper on business. After consuming hours of your time, the customer gets buyer's remorse and has the right to cancel. You will get many cancellations this way. If you do not use these agreements, you are taking a chance of being audited. If a certain percentage of your customer folders do not contain these agreements, you are fined accordingly. Since they are mandatory, you should always wait until the three-day cooling off period is up before proceeding to do any paperwork or placing any orders for items.

Part 19

Collection Problems

Credit Checks

Make it a habit to do credit checks on prospective employees and customers for jobs over certain dollar amounts (decide the dollar amount with your CPA), whether a commercial job or a residential job. While a credit check will not guarantee that you will be paid for the job, it will offer some assurance that you probably will be paid.

The Fair Credit Reporting Act of 1970 requires credit agencies to share their data only with those who have a legitimate business need for the information. That includes both businesses and employers.

If you do credit checks on customers, it will make your life less stressful. Credit checks can be done at a variety of places, including Office Depot, banks for a nominal fee, or credit checking services. If you think you are going to do credit checks frequently, sign up with a credit checking service. To receive a TRW credit report on a customer, call (900) 884-4TRW. You'll pay for the cost of the 900 number phone charge plus $28. Other credit reporting agencies are located in the yellow pages of the phone book. Dun and Bradstreet, P.O. Box 3MV, Allentown, PA 18105-9959, is the credit agency to check with for your commercial (corporate) clients. *CBI/Equifax, Trans Union,* and *TRW* are all in the business of gathering and selling information about a person's credit history.

Credit bureaus track bill-paying habits, income, creditors, mortgages, lawsuits, and also note which companies have asked to see a credit rating for job screening. Because of this, current employers are able to check and see if an employee is applying for other jobs.

Information available in credit reports includes employment, residential, debt, and spending history collected by credit bureaus. Negative information can remain on file for seven years and bankruptcies remain on file for ten years. Incorrect, ambiguous, erroneous, and outdated information has been known to surface in credit reports. Always let your customer know what was reported, as they might be able to easily correct the problem, thus allowing you to proceed with the job.

If your customer insists that there is an error in her file, she should insist the credit bureau remove the incorrect information. Direct her to put their request in writing. Have her send copies of your letter to the credit department and the customer service department, vice-president of marketing, and president or CEO of the creditor who reported the erroneous information. If the incorrect information was reported by a collection agency, send the collection agency a letter also.

If this doesn't work, your customer has the right to make a one-hundred word statement disputing the negative information. This statement is placed in her file. Unfortunately, credit bureaus are allowed to summarize statements, and most summarize them to a few meaningless words. Most creditors who request reports will not *even receive* a copy of the summarized statement.

Customers can call the *Consumer Credit Counseling Service* in their area or call the computer-run toll free line (800) 388-CCCS for the number of their local office to help clear up credit problems.

What to do About Bad Checks

Most people do not purposely write bad checks. It costs too much in NSF (nonsufficient funds) bank charges and penalties charged by the retailers. If the check is charged back against your account when you are using the money to pay your bills, it can be a real headache. If you do receive bad checks, there are legal remedies for you.

For customers that come into your store and make purchases that they take with them (as with accessories) that they pay for with a check, ask for their driver's license. Compare the picture against the person standing in front of you. Write down the driver's license number of the person across the top of the check. Some states allow you to ask for a credit card for a backup. If your state does, record the type of credit card, the credit card number, and expiration date.

Watch out for checks with illegible signatures, without a sequence number, or without a printed address. Checks with sequence numbers under 300 are more likely to bounce than those with higher numbers. If you receive a check that is suspicious, call the bank that issued the check and inquire if there are sufficient funds in the account to cover the check.

State laws concerning recovery of bad check charges vary from state to state. Check your state statues before proceeding. In California, merchants and business owners may recover bad check losses plus punitive damages in civil cases where the bad check writer fails to show good faith. Criminal statues require that the bad check writer must have *knowingly* written a bad check. Civil statues allow recovery only upon proof of the writer's failure to make good after being notified of the problem. Should you receive a notice from your bank showing that a check deposited has been dishonored, follow this procedure:

- Wait a few days and either redeposit the check or call the bank to see if there is enough money in the account for the check to clear.

- Notify the writer of the check about the bounced check in person, by phone, or by mail. Inform this person that the check she wrote has been dishonored and returned by the bank. **Request immediate payment.**

- If you do not get payment or payment arrangements as requested from the source of the bad check, you may need to begin legal proceedings for collection of damages. **Mail a "demand letter" by certified mail, return receipt requested.** If you should go to court, be sure to take the postal receipt.

- If you still do not receive payment thirty days after the demand letter went out, **file a claim in small claims** (check your state's dollar limits for small claims court) **or municipal court.** You are able to recover the cost of the filing fee for the case to be taken to court if you win the case. Review the section in this book on small claims court.

- You will receive notice from the court regarding the date and time for you to appear in court. **Come prepared to present all documents relating to the case. Include the bad check, the bank notice, notes about conversations held between you and the bad check writer, copies of any correspondence between both parties, and a copy and receipt of mailing of the "demand letter." If you were not the one who took the bad check, for identifying purposes, bring the person who did, as a witness.**

- **If the court rules in your favor, you can collect the amount of the bad check, court costs, plus three times the amount of the face value of the check up to a maximum amount of $500 in punitive damages.** The judgment may be collected against assets for a period of ten years after the date of the decision.

- **For criminal intentions:** In the case of criminal intentions or habitual violations, criminal charges may also be appropriate. Criminal charges are prosecuted in the criminal courts with fines and/or jail sentences.

Declined Bank or Merchant Account Applications

After submitting a bank application for a loan or a merchant account you may be told that your application has been denied. You may have paid a bank application fee, and don't relish the thought of paying another application fee elsewhere. The finance company or the bank should have pre-qualified you before even taking your application fee. Call and ask why you have been denied. By law, you have to be given a reason for the refusal for the credit. These are some of the more common reasons that are easily remedied:

- You may not have provided sufficient information.

- The bank or lending institution may be out of funds at the present time.

- One of your suppliers or creditors may have given a negative report about your credit. Your credit profile doesn't meet their criteria.

- The bank or lending institution does not fund your type of business venture.

- The loan has not been secured adequately to protect the lender's interest.

If given "no" for an answer, ask what the problem is. Then ask what can be done to remedy the situation. Many loan proposals can be modified to meet the bank's requirements. Ask for advice from the lender on how your proposal may be improved. Ask his or her reaction to the proposal and how he or she would improve it for the presentation. Take his or her advice. The financial data provided may not be expressed in such a way as to enhance your business's profile, rather the information may take away from the business's image.

Declined Credit Cards

Whenever you take an order that is to be applied to a credit card, follow this procedure:

- Ask what type of card it is. Make sure you handle that particular credit card. Standard cards include Visa, Mastercard, American Express, Diner's Club, and Discover cards.

- Ask for the name on the credit card.

- Ask for customer's, address, and telephone number.

- Ask for the expiration date on the card.

- Repeat the information to the customer to make sure that you have written down the numbers correctly.

Many times you will attempt to enter a credit card number and it will come up declined. Try to enter the number again, calling the customer and telling him that his card was declined. This may or may not be true. Simply tell him that for some reason your terminal is rejecting the card, probably due to the fact that *you* didn't write the information down correctly or transposed a couple numbers. Review the information again with the customer. If his information matches your information, ask for the issuing bank's name and phone number. Or call the issuing credit card agency.

This information is found on credit card bills. Call the number and ask why the card won't go through. They won't provide you any information other than it should have gone through, try again, let me help you, or that the card is declined. Report back to your customer and tell him what they told you. He may need to pick up the phone, call the bank or the issuing credit card agency and correct the problem. After the problem is corrected you will probably be able to proceed.

Another alternative when a sale has been declined is to break the sale amount into two sales, get an approval for one half of the total sale, wait a day and get an approval for the other half.

If the second one half won't go through the next day, let the customer know that you did receive approval for the first one half, but not for the second (they are at their card limit). Request payment for the rest of the amount. If you have requested 100 percent pre-payment for ordered goods, do not proceed with the order until the customer pays you in full, either with another credit card or by cash or check.

If the rejected credit card's amount is the balance money for an order you are attempting to collect, and the customer ignores your telephone call or letter asking him to pay the balance of his account, send a polite, but firm, "final demand" letter requesting immediate full payment.

The use of a credit card that is no longer valid or is up to its limit is fraud and the customer can be prosecuted for the offense.

Accounts Receivable Collection Problems

Although you should always try to get the customer to pay for the job as it is completed (separate sales agreements for small groups of items), sometimes you will run into problems where one item is missing, has to be reworked or remade, and the installer is unable to collect payment on the trip out to the home. After the item (which is holding up the bill) is finally ready to be installed, you may run into trouble with the customer allowing you to come out and complete the job and settle the bill.

Another difficult area is charging the balance of the job to cards such as Visa or Mastercard. Although the cards had enough funds when the customer placed the order, they may not have enough available when the order is completed.

What should you do when a moderate amount of time has passed and you have not collected payment from a customer? Attempt to collect the bill. Review the *Bad Debt Collection* section below.

Bad Debt Collections

As with any businessperson, an interior designer will occasionally have a customer's check bounce due to insufficient funds. The customer may have accidentally overdrawn her account. Since you are able to redeposit a check only one time, it is best to call the customer, tell her about the returned check, and ask her if there will be funds in the account to cover the check when you redeposit it.

Should the check fail to clear a second time, type a letter on your business stationery to the delinquent customer telling her that you will be notifying an attorney to handle the collection of funds if you do not receive payment by a specified time.

You may or may not have a business attorney lined up to help you on matters of this type. Your customer won't know if you do or don't.

Save the bad check as proof of your customer's indebtedness to you. If you feel that your customer is really trying to take advantage of you (and probably others), send a copy of the check (front and back) with dates that you attempted to deposit the check, any other notes about contacts you have made with the customer attempting collection, and copies of correspondence with the customer regarding the bad check to your district attorney's office and to your local police department. It is against the law to write bad checks.

Some banks will attempt to make collection on checks with insufficient funds for you. They may or may not have a small charge for providing this service. The bank will send the check back to the bank of origination with instructions to pay you as soon as enough funds have been deposited in the offending account. If the customer doesn't make any deposits within her allotted time period (generally one month), the bank will be unable to help you.

Join forces with your business attorney and write a letter to the debtor (on the attorney's stationery) covering the following points:

- This law firm has been retained to collect the money owed to your firm.

- The law firm hopes the matter can be settled by the payment of the money, thus avoiding litigation and extra expenses to the debtor.

- To avoid having a lawsuit filed and extra expenses incurred, pay the specified amount immediately.

- Give directions on how to go about paying the money owed: where to send the money, whom to write the check, etc.

- Close with the statement that your interior design firm has always tried to work with its customers in a reasonable manner, but that you must collect all money owed immediately.

Step one:
Begin your collection efforts by sending your customer reminder of an outstanding balance with your company.

In your first letter, do not show anger or act accusatory. You are simply reminding them to pay you. Ask them to send you a check today, and enclose a stamped, self-addressed envelope for ease of payment.

Consider offering them a slight discount if they will pay you within the next ten days. Or let them know in your letter that bills thirty days past due incur interest at a rate of 1.5 percent - 2.5 percent per month on their unpaid balance.

Realize that a customer who owes you money will not be calling you to do more work, so do not worry about offending her. Your objective is simple: collect all money that is due you as quickly as possible. If the customer still does not come through and pay within a reasonable time you must now proceed to the next step.

Step 2:

The customer is either unwilling to pay you, or is unable to pay you. Write another letter, this time a bit stronger, to the offending customer. Simply state that if you do not receive collection of the unpaid balance within the next two weeks, you will start legal proceedings to collect payment and will be taking them to court. This stronger letter should be sent by certified mail, with a return receipt.

Step 3:

If you still do not hear from your customer, you must hire a collection agency or attorney to pursue the unpaid bill, or file the case in small claims court. The more verification of the sale and ordered merchandise, the better. Show signed sales agreements, photocopies of the deposit checks, and original work sheets and purchase orders for the items ordered. Always photocopy the original deposit checks given to you to start the order. The check shows the customer's intent, and gives you vital bank information that will expedite your collection efforts, after the court awards you the monies owed by the customer.

Illegal Collection Practices

The federal government and some states have laws that protect consumers against particular types of harassment and deceptive bill collection procedures.

It is a violation of the Federal Trade Commission Act for a creditor to use any deceptive means to collect debts or to obtain information about debtors. You may not attempt to find out information through the use of forms, letters, or questionnaires for the purpose of making a bad debt collection, unless you reveal to the consumer the purpose of the forms, letters, or questionnaires.

The United States Congress enacted the Fair Debt Collection Act in 1977. The Fair Debt Collection Act makes it a federal offense to threaten consumers with violence, use obscene language, or call consumers by telephone at inconvenient times or places (such as work) in an attempt to make a collection on a bad debt. You also may not pretend to be an attorney (writing your own letter on an attorney's stationery or misrepresent yourself as an attorney), obtain information under false pretenses, or make collections of more money than is actually owed. The following is a list of prohibited debt collection practices. **Debt collectors may not:**

- Make threats of violence or harm to the debtor, debtor's property, or reputation.

- Call people acquainted with the debtor without identifying themselves.

- Make repeated, annoying telephone calls.

- Advertise the debt where others may see it.

- Publish a list of debtors who refuse to pay their debts (except to credit bureaus).

- Use obscene or profane language.

- Make false statements when attempting to collect a debt.

- Falsely represent themselves as an attorney or government representative.

- Imply that the debtor has committed a crime.

- Debt collectors may not falsely represent themselves as owning or working for a credit bureau if they do not.

- Misstate the amount of the actual debt.

- Suggest to the debtor that papers sent through the mail *are* legal forms if they are not.

- Suggest to the debtor that papers sent through the mail are *not* legal forms, when they actually are.

- Make statements to the debtor that if they don't pay the debt they will be arrested.

- Make statements that property or wages will be seized, garnished, attached, or sold unless the debt collector intends to do so.

- Make statements that illegal action will be taken against the debtor.

- Provide false information about debtors to anyone.

- Make a deposit of a post-dated check before the date of the check.

- Require a debtor to accept collect calls or pay for telegrams.

- Threaten to take property illegally.

- Contact a debtor by postcard.

- Place anything on an exterior of a debt-collection envelope other than a name and return address. If the name with the return address is the name of a collection agency, the name cannot be used, as this might reveal that the debt collector is attempting a collection.

Within five days after a person is notified that he owes money, the debt collector must send a written notice telling the debtor the amount of money owed, to whom it is owed, and what the debtor should do if he feels he does not owe the money.

Should a debtor notify the debt collector in writing (within thirty days) that he does not owe the debt, the debt collector may not continue to contact the debtor. If proof of the debt is presented by the debt collector that indeed the debtor does owe the money (signed sales checks, copy of bills), collection activities by the debt collector may resume.

In some states it is illegal to inform a debtor's relatives, employer, or other close associates about a debt in order to obtain payment. The laws have been formed to prevent unfair collection practices and to protect debtors from embarrassment and invasion of privacy.

A consumer can stop a debt collector from contacting him by simply writing them a letter and telling them to *stop* contacting him. After receipt of the letter, the debt collector may only correspond to the consumer one more time — to tell the consumer that they have received the letter and there will be no further contact. The debt collector is allowed to notify the debtor that some specific action will be taken, but *only* if the debt collector or the creditor intends to take the specified action.

The debt collector may contact the debtor's attorney about the debt if the debtor has an attorney. If the debtor doesn't have an attorney, the debt collector can contact friends, relatives, and acquaintances to attempt to find out where the debtor lives and works. Usually collectors are not allowed to tell anyone besides the debtor's attorney that the debtor owes money. And debt collectors are usually prohibited from contacting any person for any information more than *one* time.

Should the debt collector break the law, the debt collector may be sued in a state or federal court within one year from the date that the law was violated. Should the debtor win, he may recover money for the damage he suffered. Court costs and attorney's fees may also be recovered.

Many states also have their own debt collection laws. Check with your state attorney general's office to determine your rights under state laws.

Collection Letters

When an account is net thirty days, ideally, on the thirty-fifth day your customer should be notified by mail or telephone that their account is past due. When writing collection letters follow these collection tips:

- If you notify your customer by mail, start with regular mail and then progress to return receipt requested certified mail on subsequent late notices.

- For commercial accounts, address the collection letter to the owner or CEO of the company. Make it clear that you are talking to him or her.

- With your first notice to the customer that the account is past due, you should try to courteously and diplomatically work with the customer, while attempting to preserve the business relationship. Keep the doors open for future sales from the customer. This may only be a temporary financial condition.

- Remind the customer that he promised to pay for the goods and services. Let him feel that his integrity is at stake.

- Create a sense of urgency. Demand that the money is due and payable, **now.**

- The letter should sound and feel sincere to the debtor, and project that you only wish them the best.

Collection Agencies

Another alternative to bad debt collection is collection agencies. Collection agencies may or may not be successful in making the collections for you. They will *legally harass* the customer about the money owed. Collection agencies will keep 30 percent to 40 percent of the money they collect for you.

Higher quality collection agencies generally belong to the American Collector's Association. Should your customer reside out of state, and you decorated her vacation home in your state, the association will network and pass the information to a collection agency in the debtor's local area. Since your local agency will be working with another collection agency out of state, their fee for successful collections will generally run about 50 percent of the money collected.

Small Claims Court

Small claims court is the lowest trial court of record and is consumer oriented. In California (check with the small claims court in your state), attorneys are not allowed to appear in this court on behalf of a client. Only the parties that are involved in the action are allowed to appear. Other states allow attorneys to appear, but they are not required to present a claim.

Generally small claims cases are heard before a judge. Some states allow you to request a jury trial if the party bringing the action makes a deposit of a specific amount of money.

States vary on their limits that may be disputed in small claims court. California's limit is now up to $5,000. Anyone may file a claim in small claims courts for a small fee ($16 in California). The party bringing the suit is the plaintiff. Although you may win your case, it is still up to you to collect.

In California, the plaintiff is not allowed to appeal the court's decision if he loses, unless he is ordered to pay as a result of a counterclaim filed by the defendant. Other states allow either party to appeal a small claims court decision. Find out about your state by checking your states statutes and check local court rules to determine if you are eligible to appeal and the rules regarding an appeal in your state. Appeals from small claim courts are normally taken to the highest court in the county or district.

Filing a small claims court action:

- Find out the legal name and address of the person or persons you are suing. Do not use a post office box for the address. Using the correct address helps you to establish the correct jurisdiction where the case should be filed.

- Forms for a small claim's court action are available from the clerk at the local small claims court in your area. Normally, small claims court is part of the county or district court.

- Fill out the forms, present them to the clerk, and pay the filing fee.

- A subpoena or order must be served on the defendant. Some jurisdictions allow you to have someone not involved in the suit, and over twenty-one years old, serve the subpoena. The subpoena will contain the date of the trial.

How to Present a Convincing Case in Small Claims Court

Research the law:

Research basic law regarding your case. Law libraries are open to the public free of charge. Law libraries have card catalogues and knowledgeable librarians to direct you to the information you need. Public libraries also have information for your use.

Book stores carry basic law information books, and law book stores are where attorneys shop for their law information. Find out what type of evidence you will need to show the judge to convince her that you are right. Look in the bibliography sections in related material to find other legal source material on the subject. *Books in Print Subject Guide* (at the library or book store) can give you order information on other books with related material.

Get all the facts straight:

List everything that happened regarding the case in chronological order. Make a complete outline of everything you want to cover in court. Remember, unless you are well-versed in going to court, you will probably be slightly nervous and may forget to call certain points to the judge's attention. Write everything down. Discuss each point in the correct order by referring to your outline when you speak to the judge.

When discussing your case, bring up only *relevant* facts that concern the liability of the case. It doesn't matter how you felt, or what others said or did.

Present proof:

Back up the facts with proof. The judge wants to see concrete proof, not just hear a story about what happened. Present evidence of signed receipts, sales checks, documentation, and witnesses.

Witnesses will probably not be expected to testify at length, but should be available if the judge wants to ask a few questions about the problem. If your witnesses are not available to come to court, have them sign sworn statements (signed in front of a notary public) or write a letter stating the facts they have knowledge about or that are pertinent to your case.

If you are unable to collect all pertinent evidence to present your case by the specified court date, you may be able to reschedule your date if you let the judge know why you need more time. Call the court as soon as you realize you need another court date.

Justify amount sought:

Present evidence to the judge to justify the amount of money sought through small claims court. Make an itemized list and have all supporting signed sales checks and receipts to prove that the amount you are requesting *really is* the amount you are owed.

Rehearse the presentation:

Before presenting your case in court, rehearse what you are going to say. Organize all sales checks, receipts, photographs, letters, and other pertinent documentation. Place the documents in order and number them Exhibit A, Exhibit B, etc.

While the defendant is presenting her case, resist the urge to jump in and say something. You will get your turn at the end. Don't argue with the defendant in front of the judge, whom you should treat with respect.

Collection of Money Awards

Although you may be lucky and win your lawsuit, collection of money awards is another matter. Court judgments are good for anywhere from three to twenty years (it varies from state to state) and can be periodically renewed. While the debtor drags his feet in payment of the judgment, the judgment collects interest — usually 10 percent to 12 percent annually. Even if the debtor does not currently have any assets, someday he may.

Realize that a debtor is also protected legally from harassment and public embarrassment by creditors. Therefore, *do not threaten, harass, humiliate, or intimidate.* If you do, you are setting yourself up for a lawsuit. Do not discuss the debtor with anyone, other than a credit agency or court personnel. If you talk to a credit agency, stick to the basic facts. Use the following guidelines in the order given in attempting to recover money awarded you by the court.

- Ask the defendant for the awarded money in a polite manner.

- Place the debtor on a payment plan.

- If you (plaintiff) are having difficulty collecting the awarded money from the defendant, ask the court clerk for assistance regarding the collection. Bank accounts, business income, and a portion of the debtor's wages can be attached to satisfy court judgments. Other areas to recover money from are royalties, money owed to the debtor by others, personal property, extra vehicles, or real estate. Real estate can be a very effective way to collect if you file a lien against the debtor's property. When the debtor wants to sell or refinance the property, he or she must satisfy the lien placed against the property before the title is cleared.

  You cannot seize or force a sale on a debtor's automobile that he depends on to get to work or with tools that he needs to perform work. You cannot seize more than 25 percent of the debtor's wages, his food, clothing, and other necessities.

- If attempting to recover the money from a bank account (you will pay a fee whether you are successful or not), time the collection effort *right after* the first payday of the month when the debtor will have probably deposited his paycheck, and before other creditors attempt to collect from the account.

- Make constructive suggestions to the debtor on ways to pay you. I.e., credit card advances, money set aside for vacations, IRAs, education funds, loans from relatives, or even a garage sale.

- If the debtor has only a portion of the money owed, consider accepting less money to get the problem quickly resolved. True, you may collect the whole amount years later, but you will have the problem on your mind and might never collect any of the money.

- Turn the matter over to a credit reporting agency. A judgment against a person that hasn't been satisfied is a negative on a credit report.

- Attempt to keep track of the debtor. If you do, then you'll know what assets to go after and when.

- Look in the yellow pages for a computer data base search company to search for assets held by your debtor. They can tell you where the debtor lives, what real estate he owns, businesses owned, or about other owned personal property.

- Although the debtor may have declared bankruptcy or died, file a claim against the estate and recover all or part of your judgment.

- Don't spend too much more of your money and time trying to collect from a deadbeat.

- Turn over the collection of the judgement to a collection agency or attorney. And realize that if you do, you will forfeit one-third to one-half of the collected amounts.

Part 20

The Selling Process

Interior design businesses are sales businesses. To have a successful interior design business you must have designers and decorators that are capable of closing the sale. If you or your employees can't close sales with prospective buyers, then design ideas, money and time spent marketing, planning and estimating jobs, and wining and dining the customer will not be paid for.

There are several ways that a designer must sell. First of all, she must be able to "sell" herself and her company to the customer. Next, the designer must sell her ideas and solutions. Finally, the designer must sell the products.

To be successful with selling, and to make it much easier to make sales, the designer *needs* to believe that she works for the best firm, and to provide superior service and a superior line of products. The designer should carefully listen to what the customer is saying. The customer is telling you what she thinks she wants. If what she wants is feasible for the particular design situation, *give it to her*. If you try to force her to accept your ideas, the customer will not be satisfied and will not give you the sale.

The next step in successful selling is to have an enthusiastic, positive attitude. Show the customer that you are interested in her design problems and are eager to offer assistance in solving the problem.

Realize that some customers come to you to help them make decisions. Some people do not have confidence with making design decisions. They may think they know what they want, but need *you* to confirm that their selections or ideas are sound ones.

In our book, *Secrets of Success for Today's Interior Designers and Decorators*, the section *Customer Psychology, Steps to a Sale, to Servicing Your Customer*, is comprehensive and highly recommended and will take you completely through the interior design selling process. This section contains very revealing questions to ask; when answered, they will give you information and direction on which way to go with products and planning of the job.

When the needs of the customer are revealed through listening and careful questioning, the designer's job becomes much easier. The designer is *then* able to discuss the assorted features, advantages, and benefits of the various treatments and products. This is also covered in *Secrets of Success for Today's Interior Designers and Decorators*. Once features, advantages, and benefits are correctly applied to the products and design ideas, the sale is easily and quickly closed, and the design job started.

The Prospect's Interest in Your Products and/or Services

The prospect's interest may be immediate and strong. She may *need* your products and/or service, she has the money, and is ready to buy. She may just want to investigate to see what you and your company have to offer, and find out pricing for the products/services. The prospective buyer may want to get verbal and written information from you about the various products/services she needs.

The prospective buyer's initial interest may be created in a variety of ways. The predominant method to gain a prospect's interest is through a well-known favorable reputation in the decorating field.

The other predominant method is through direct marketing. Direct marketing is marketing with the use of printed advertisements and/or direct mail. High-visibility public relations is another direct marketing technique. Give seminars, write articles, and send press releases to the media. People will automatically seek you out, as you are now the perceived expert in the field. Prospective customers will ask for you to send printed material about your services, products, and company. Have a well-planned company brochure and packet of information available for these inquiries. Tailor the packet to the individual customer. Answer questions that the prospect asks.

Lead Rotation

For studios that have more than one designer or decorator it is important to establish lead rotation rules. If you don't, you will be called in to referee many needless arguments among your personnel. It is imperative that once the rules are set down that everyone follow them. If they do, lead distribution tends to balance out.

All leads should be logged in, and the source of the lead noted. Advertising methods that generate the most leads need to be capitalized on and repeated until they no longer work. Keeping records of logged in leads will be the only way to determine if advertising methods are working. Take lead counts, and track how your decorators are doing with their closing ratio (how many leads they are taking as appointments versus how many sales they are making).

Walk-in leads for decorators that are on scheduled floor time:

The decorator with scheduled floor time who is on the floor gets all prospect leads that walk in during his floor time. If the decorator is on a lunch break or is on the phone, he *still* gets the lead even if another decorator waits on the customer.

If the scheduled decorator is not on floor time for any other reason when he is scheduled, the decorator losses the right to the lead. The lead is rotated on the rotation list to the next available decorator. Should another decorator (not scheduled) be present when the customer walks in and waits on the customer, the decorator who is present takes the lead.

Phone-in leads:

The studio coordinator should always try to answer the phone and work with prospective incoming leads. Every phone-in lead should be logged in and written up on a referral slip. Some studios like to rotate phone-in leads down the list of decorators. To keep everyone honest, it is best to log in the leads, fill out a referral slip, and give the lead to the decorator on duty. The decorator may then pre-qualify the customer and discuss the in-home appointment. If everyone rotates their floor time every week, everyone gets some of the better lead days and everyone gets some of the lousy lead days. This method shows no favoritism by the studio coordinator, who otherwise may hand out more leads to her preferred decorator. For all leads that come in, the studio assistant should take the client's name, address, and phone number. If the studio coordinator is on a break or out of the studio, the decorator on duty should handle the calls and set up the leads for themselves.

Personal leads:

Any lead generated by a decorator, whether the decorator spoke to the customer previously, whether the customer was a referral by another customer, or whether it is an old customer, is the property of the generating decorator. The customer *must* ask for that decorator by name. In cases where the customer can't remember the name of the decorator, she must try to describe the decorator. All of the decorator's names should be recited to the customer by the studio coordinator, and if that fails, pictures of all decorators should be shown to the customer. Old orders should also be looked up, in an attempt to find out who was the previous decorator. Practice these methods to maintain harmony in the studio. Everyone must practice the same methods so that everyone works the same way.

If it appears that a decorator on duty does not attempt to clarify *who* was the original decorator when the customer indicates there was a previous decorator, the customer should be diplomatically called by the original decorator and asked if the decorator attempted to trace the original decorator. Once this happens to the offending decorator who gets double checked, he or she *won't* do it again.

Outside source referrals:

Any lead generated from an outside source not due to an individual decorator's efforts should be rotated on a separate log sheet for the next available decorator in the order the leads come in. Use the same log sheets for all rotation leads.

Decorators on vacation:

If the vacation is a short one (three days), keep the decorator on rotation. If the vacation is longer, take the decorator out of rotation, putting the decorator back on rotation three days before she is due back at work. The object of making sales is to get to the customer as soon as possible, not to put the customer off for a week or more.

Decorators present when leads come in and no one is scheduled for floor time:

Any decorator present when a customer walks in or phones in, when another decorator is not scheduled to be on the floor, receives the lead. This is an incentive for decorators to put in as much floor time as possible. It is important for you as a business owner to have qualified decorators available to help customers whenever possible. Encouraging decorators to work floor time also helps free up the studio coordinator for other duties. Realize that a decorator working on commission is going to try harder than an assistant who is not on commission. This is a good argument for putting the coordinator on commission, also.

Rotation leads:

Every attempt should be made to set up rotation leads with the decorator whose turn it is. If you *must* skip a decorator to accommodate a customer's schedule or to accommodate a decorator's day off, then skip to the next decorator. When the next lead comes in, go back to the skipped decorator and give her the next lead. If at all possible, all leads should go to the decorator whose turn it is. When the leads are skipped around among decorators, there is potential for a studio coordinator to give one decorator a great lead because it is her favorite decorator and say she couldn't fit it into the schedule. Have the decorator whose true turn it is, call the customer to set up the appointment if it appears that the customer can't be fit into the schedule. Let the decorator whose turn it is make the decision to give the lead to the next decorator.

Personal leads for decorators that no longer are employed with the company:

If a customer walks in or phones in requesting a decorator who no longer works for the company, the decorator on duty should take the lead. If there isn't a decorator on floor time, the lead should be rotated.

Two or more decorators present for free floor time:

If two or more decorators show up for free floor time, the one who gets there first gets the first walk-in or call-in lead. The leads are then rotated back and forth among all decorators in attendance.

Canceled rotation leads:

The decorator or studio coordinator should make an attempt to reset the lead at a later date. If the customer will not reset the appointment, then the lead should be removed from the rotation sheet (white it out) and the next lead should be filled in the canceled position for the decorator who lost the lead. This is a business where customers frequently have second thoughts and cancel their appointments. Sometimes the customer will remember to ask for the decorator she initially canceled with, when she calls back to reset the appointment. More than likely, she won't. If you do not put the decorator back into rotation, the decorator will be unhappy, feel unfairly treated, and may have a run of cancellations that are not her fault.

The Initial Telephone Call From Prospective Customers

During the initial telephone call with your prospective customer, work with the customer and attempt to establish the following:

- Pre-qualify the customer.

- Relay to the customer what you feel you have to offer him or her.

- Try to find out what the customer is really interested in.

- Get the customer to come in and work with a decorator in the studio.

How to Pre-Qualify Customers

You need to be able to get to the heart of the matter and find out which prospects are qualified to purchase from you and which are not. Pre-qualifying will allow you to spend time with true prospective buyers and eliminate time spent with unqualified wishful thinkers.

Who is a qualified buyer? A person who is likely to buy from you, able to buy from you, and a person who will benefit from your offered products and services.

During your first encounter with the customer, you need to determine if the prospect is a qualified buyer and worth you spending your time with that customer. Pre-qualification of a customer is done by asking simple, to-the-point questions.

Consider enclosing a questionnaire to be filled out by your prospect with the initial information packet you send out or qualify the customer when he or she calls in wanting to set up an appointment.

- *How soon does the customer need this job completed?* Is he flexible on the time frame? Can you meet these expectations?

- *Does the customer have an immediate need for the item?* Don't set up an appointment until he is close to the time frame for the needed job. The customer may completely change his mind about what he wants to buy by the time he is ready to buy, and you will have to start completely over — thus wasting *hours* of your valuable time. Give them ballpark estimates, send them information, and put them on your mailing list for future sales.

    The customer with an immediate need is your most valuable customer. Come right out and ask if he or she is planning on making an *immediate decision* about placing an order for the proposed products and services. If the need is not immediate (try to pin him down on about *when* he will be ready to purchase), but sometime in the future, notify the customer when you have a sale on the proposed fabric or item in the near future.

- *Does the customer have the money or credit to go through with the purchase?* Or in the case of a commercial job, *does the customer have the authority to authorize and get the job started?* A prime prospect is someone who has the money and the means to go ahead with the purchase of the proposed items.

At the risk of turning off your customer, you need to give him an estimate early on. Does he have a realistic idea of what interior items cost? Can he afford your quality and price? If you wait to discuss until after romancing your customer with the value and prestige of owning the proposed items, while showing numerous samples to get down to the actual bid on the job, you will have already spent some time working with a customer who you have not yet determined is capable of buying your products and services. Spend your valuable time with customers that have the potential and means to buy from you, period.

Beware of the customer whose first question is what is your price on a particular product or service. This person is obviously shopping price, and only cares about going with the lowest bidder. He will not even care to hear about your fabulous quality and service, until he has received poor quality and service when he buys elsewhere.

Separate the buyers from the shoppers by giving quick estimates of your prices on your products and services. If you are going to sell primarily services to this customer, then quote him your hourly rate and ask for a large retainer to get the job started — $1,000 or more.

If the customer is really serious, he will start asking you questions, trying to learn what he will be receiving for the proposed fee. A customer who is not really interested will tell you that he will get back to you, or he will be contacting you, or will think that your quoted amount is very high, or that he will put the check in the mail, etc.

If the potential customer or business is one that you know about, or really want to do business with, and you feel that they are qualified, go ahead and spend the time romancing them into the sale, taking a chance that they may or may not buy when you finally arrive at a proposed bid.

Does the prospective customer have the authority to go ahead, sign the contract, and give you the deposit? If not, then you need to set up a time to make your presentation when the decision maker will also be in attendance. Most spouses will not make a decision without involving the other spouse. You will make your lengthy presentation to the wife (usually) and then have to present it later to the husband. Make an appointment when both may be present. Come right out and ask at the time you set the appointment, if they both need to be present to make the decision to go ahead. You run the risk of offending very independent people, but your time is valuable. You cannot afford to make extra trips, and waste time presenting the proposed job to the other party.

If you are dealing with a company, where the purchasing agent or person who is requesting information is not the sole person involved in making the decision to go ahead with the purchase, give him or her a preliminary idea of the amount of money to do the job and then set up a time to go ahead and make a presentation with all who are involved in the decision-making process.

- *Can you work easily with the prospective customer's personality?* You will have to be able to get along reasonably well and work with this customer for the months to come. Not only will you have to work repeatedly with the customer on checking on the order, through installation, but you will be servicing the customer on the ordered products for at least the next year. You will not simply be selling them a product and dropping them. If you do not feel that you can get along with the prospective customer, do not take his or her order. Review the section on *How to Get Rid of a Customer Who You Don't Want to do Business With.*

- *Can you really help this customer?* Do you have the required goods and services for your prospect? If you really cannot help your customer with your goods and services or you don't have access to required goods and services, you will never satisfy your customer. You may be able to talk him or her into buying what you do have, but you will also repeatedly get phone calls from an unhappy customer. In the end you will not get repeat sales from the customer (plus not gain referrals) and will probably end up canceling the order after it is installed. You will be left with un-resalable goods. Through your networking efforts, find another supplier to refer this customer to and forget about trying to sell them goods that won't take care of their wants and needs.

How to Follow Up On Sales Leads

When you attract customers through advertising and referrals, you need to have a sales plan already in place.

- If the customer appears to *only* want more information, tailor your cover letter and information packet to the customer and promptly send it out.

- If the customer sounds serious, try to set them up with an in-store appointment with a decorator. The idea here is to make the customer commit to meeting the decorator in the studio so he or she may determine what the customer is interested in. The decorator then has the opportunity to qualify the customer by giving him an idea of pricing.

- For commercial customers, set up an appointment to go out to the job site. Get a general idea over the phone as to the needs of the company, so that the presentation and samples may be tailored to their requirements.

- For more sophisticated customers who seem to have a handle on what decorating items cost, go ahead and set an appointment to go to their home. Pre-qualify them over the phone and ask if they would like a preliminary idea of pricing based on their perceived measurements of the item. Pick a midrange fabric or material and tell the customer that this is an *average* fabric before quoting a price.

Some customers just want you to come out and won't cooperate in providing you with measurements. They may be shopping around trying to get as many decorators as they can to come out, to compare prices and possibly use their ideas. They don't mind wasting your decorator's time. Explain to the customer that since your decorators are very busy, your company policy is to let the customer know *about* what he or she will be spending to have a particular item custom made. If this sounds good to the customer, then you are happy to send a decorator for an in-home appointment. If he or she seems surprised at the price, explain that your prices are extremely competitive and you are a fine company.

You are bullet-proofing the visit by the use of this technique. The customer will probably still want to proceed, and you have already given her an idea of the price. Now the shock will set in and then dissipate. If she really wants the item and has the means to pay for it, she will still make the purchase. She will shop around first though. Instead of shocking her at home and having her put off the decorator while she gets used to the price, she will call around and find out that this is the going rate. Send the client a cover letter and information packet outlining all of your best points. Have your coordinator set up an appointment in another week or so, after the customer has absorbed the price and has justified it in her mind.

Your decorators should be in the store following up on orders, keeping their existing customers happy, writing letters to past customers, and making other marketing efforts instead of running out to unqualified customers' homes that had no idea what decorating purchases cost.

Rid of Customers You Don't Want to Work With

You will occasionally run into a customer that for one reason or another you just don't want to take a chance with. This person may have a difficult personality, be hard to get along with, have a bad reputation around town, have just canceled a job with another company that you cannot see the faults with, etc. You need to gracefully encourage this customer to go elsewhere.

The best technique is to give them an exorbitant price on the project. Pad the price for any and all problems that *can and will* come up. If you do get the job, you are covered and compensated for the irritation of having to endure the project with a demanding customer.

Follow Up on the Prospect's Initial Interest

Follow up on the initial interest expressed by the prospect by either meeting with her in person or by speaking on the telephone. The next step is to have an initial consultation in the home.

The reason you need to follow up is to help the very interested prospect become a customer and to eliminate prospects that showed interest but are not really serious about buying your products and services.

Therefore, you need to qualify the customer. Determine which customer is really interested in making a purchase from you. A qualified customer can afford your products and services, and your company has the ability to supply the needed products and services.

Try to complement your personality with that of your potential customer. If you cannot relate well with the potential customer, the job will be an ordeal, complete with disagreements, frustration, pressure, and tension.

As you determine that some of your prospective customers are not very good prospects due to lack of money, difficult personalities, or you do not offer what they are looking for, find a way to gracefully decline. Tell them you just really don't have what they are looking for, or cannot supply it within their time frame.

Establish Rapport With Your Prospect

Establish rapport with your customer in order to make an effective sale. Customers like to deal with people they feel comfortable with, like, can trust, and that are knowledgeable about their products and applications.

Sometimes you meet people that you just do not feel comfortable with or you just cannot effectively work with. Consider referring them to another designer.

Do not aggravate a customer by acting very egotistical or arrogant, overly confident, as thought you have the sale in the bag or by bragging about what a great designer you are.

Review the companion book *Secrets of Success for Today's Interior Designers and Decorators* to see what qualities customers want in their designers and decorators.

Set a Goal for Each Step of the Selling Process

When you start working with a customer, decide what your goal is during each step of the sales process:

1. When the customer phones or writes in for information, your goals are to pre-qualify the customer and entice the customer to meet with you or a decorator in the studio.

2. When the customer comes into your studio, your goal should be to give him an idea of pricing, get him to narrow down his choices of fabrics or samples, and set up an in-home appointment.

3. During the in-home appointment; your goals are to measure and decide exact styling for the treatments, select the fabrics or samples, write up the contract, get the customers signature and deposit for the order.

Selling to Residential Consumers

Residential customers may feel the need to decorate because they have company coming, they may have purchased a new home without window coverings, their present window treatments or sofa look shabby and worn out, or they want to have a new interior look. In short, only rarely do customers have a need that has to be taken care of *immediately*. Unfortunately for decorators, most consumer needs are not really needs, but wants. They buy because they think their lives will be enhanced with the ownership of a particular item.

This kind of buyer is not sophisticated. She probably doesn't know much about available products and services. And she won't spend much time deciding whether or not to buy from you. You don't need to overwhelm this type of customer with information. If given too much information, they will not be able to make a decision.

The approach to take is to act like you know what you are doing. Project that you are responsible and dependable, and that the price you are asking is fair. Show the prospect that you know which product selection is right for them. The customer needs to feel that you can do the job, before she will make the decision to buy from you. These customers needs to get right to the benefits of the proposed solution (product and services), because they are busy people. Remember this when you design your advertisements and brochures — make the ads easy to scan and read. If you can convince the qualified customer that you are offering the solution, you will usually make the sale.

You will meet up with want-to-be decorators and designers, or other people in related fields who will require more technical information from you. Everyone has someone in their family that is a "*decorator*." There are also a lot of "do-it-yourselfers" out there. They will *literally* use you for your ideas without having serious intentions of buying from you or your company.

Make it clear *what* you are offering customers, and what exactly they will be getting. Clearly spell out the benefits and results that can be expected. If you confuse your prospect with information, she will put off making a decision, possibly indefinitely.

Selling is a multiple-step process. You must generate interest, then secure the appointment, then get the customer to make a commitment and sign the contract, and finally keep the customer satisfied and coming back for future sales.

You cannot skip any of the steps and come up with satisfactory results. You cannot rush your customer into a premature decision to buy. You must take your customer through each step, one at a time. If you do a thorough selling job, you will be rewarded with repeat sales and referrals from satisfied customers.

Should You Charge for the Initial Consultation?

Sales professionals work with customers in fulfilling their wants and needs. Since interior design is a service and a product business, you will need to give some initial time to the prospect to entice him or her to do business with your company. Successful professionals should give a *minimum* of time before they start charging the customer.

Customers will *use* as much of your time as you will give them. Take control of the situation, give them an idea of the price, and if that sounds favorable to the customer, proceed with the sale of products and/or services.

The pre-qualification process must start the minute the phone rings. Discreetly let the customer know that you are happy to work with her if she is going to consider buying from you. Give her an idea of pricing right from the beginning. Let her know you are happy to come out to her home *if* the information you have just provided sounds like what she wants.

If you waste your time running around chasing every so-called lead, you will not have the time to really take care of the customers that buy from you or spend the time seeking out new business. You will get burned out from giving bid after bid to nonbuyers who were actually *just* seeking information, who had an idea that they might redecorate, but had no idea that it cost so much. You will be wasting much of your time, day after day.

Give enough information to the prospective customer to help convince her that you are an expert, can solve her decorating problems, and can take care of her decorating wants and needs. You need a commitment from the customer to hire you to do the job. Don't just give her your design or product ideas that you would use to solve her problems. She will take your solutions to a cheaper source.

You will work daily on running your business and there are only so many hours in a day available for you to get everything accomplished. If you do some of the preliminary work getting the customer interested in working with your company, you will have more time available to keep everything else running smoothly.

If you jump in your car every time a potential customer snaps his or her fingers, you create an image of a company that is not very busy and successful — one that is hungry and desperate for business. If you work on pre-qualifying the customer and let her know that yes, you are available if she is *really* interested in doing business with you and your company, you create a much higher quality image for your company. Let her know that your company is also very competitive on pricing, has an excellent reputation, and is the company to select when the customer has decided to buy.

When you build your company's reputation as the one to select for interior design work, consider charging an hourly rate for all consultations. Credit the hours toward purchases made by your customer. Have your studio coordinator or decorators send out information, give the customer preliminary pricing ideas and then tell the customer that they are happy to come out if the information provided sounds like what the customer wants to do. Let the customer know there is an hourly consultation charge of $40 an hour that is applicable to purchases made. For every $100 ($40 your cost) spent on purchases, deduct $40 in consultation charges. In other words, your time is free when they make purchases. Customers will not use up time in unnecessary, repeat sales calls if they realize that the time is costing them money.

Consider giving customers initial time *free*, if they will bring measurements into the studio. The decorator can then qualify and work with the customer without scaring him or her away. Any subsequent visits then should be charged against purchases made.

Crediting the consultation fee against purchases will ensure that the residential customer will go ahead with the order. Customers will see that your company places a higher value on its services than other companies place on theirs. Review the pricing section of this book on the various ways to charge for products and services.

The Initial Consultation — Establishing Wants and Needs

The main purpose of the first consultation is to convince the prospective customer to buy your products and services. At the end of the sales call, you want the customer to feel as if he is obligated and committed to buying your products and services to solve his design wants, needs, and problems.

Do not make the customer feel that you are making the in-home sales call to sell him something. Instead, strive to make the customer feel that you are a valuable, highly trained consultant in your field, happy to come out to visit your customer to help him solve his design problem. The customer should feel that your visit is *valuable* for the service provided in addition to the products that you sell.

Even if your in-home visit is merely an estimate of the cost to purchase one thing, the estimate was provided and estimated by *you*, an expert in your field. The prospective customer will be able to compare your estimate against other estimates they may have gotten to see if the others are accurate and fall within the same pricing guidelines.

As a designer, you will want to give some design tips to the customer while on the in-home visit. It is not that you want to give your ideas away to a client that may or may not use your services, but you want to convince the customer that you are an *expert*. These ideas may or may not be used by the customer, even if you do not get the job.

Since a consultation at the home costs you lots of money in time spent — time you might have spent elsewhere making a sale if the in-home consultation doesn't turn into a sale — many companies are wisely starting to charge for this service. They charge a minimum service call fee that may be applied to the purchased products and services.

If you do not charge for the in-home visit, stress in all your advertising that your company offers a *"free, no obligation in-home consultation."* This in-home consultation is very valuable to a customer, and if yours is a *free* consultation, this is one of your main selling points.

Listen to Your Customer

When making a presentation to your prospective customer, realize that he only cares about his perceived decorating wants, needs, desires, problems, interests, concerns, aspirations, and dreams. Do not memorize a dissertation or speech to make for your presentation. Tailor the presentation to the customer's wants and needs. *Show* how the features of the proposed products and services *fill* the customer's wants and needs, and *solve* their problems. A professional designer or decorator must tailor and plan her presentation for the customer after hearing where the customer is coming from in these areas.

Remember that you are not on the in-home appointment to *hard-sell* the customer. You are attempting to meet their wants and needs. When you make a customer feel that this is what you are doing, you do not need to hard-sell them. If you don't take care of his *expressed* needs, you will not get the order. If you give him something else, he may buy it now, will cancel it later, or will constantly let you know that he is unhappy. You *will* end up removing the items and canceling the order later.

In order to discover and solve these wants and needs for your customer, you need to actively **listen** to your customer. Let the customer speak about 60 percent to your 40 percent of the time.

Start by *really listening* to what the customer is expressing to you. Give your customer your full attention. Take notes on everything the customer is discussing with you. Quickly write down questions that come to mind as your customer is talking to you. Write down future purchases that the customer is considering, and remember to mail out information to him when these items go on sale.

Respond to your customer while he is speaking to show you are interested in providing the ideal solution to his problem. Try rephrasing the prospect's statement as a question, and repeat the question back to the customer. So you are looking for a fabric that is semi-sheer, printed in these colors, with an off-white background?

When the customer gives you a positive response (the only response possible, as you are repeating the statement they just made to you), this puts the customer psychologically in a positive frame of mind when you go for the close later.

Attempt to offer even stronger questions. So if we can deliver by such and such, you will be interested in going ahead with the order, right?

Show positive body language when working with your customer. *Leaning forward slightly* shows that you are interested in what he is saying. Do this while looking him in their eye. *Leaning back* with no eye contact gives the customer the idea that you are not paying attention and not considering his needs.

Note taking shows the customer that you *are* concerned, are actively listening to him, and *do* want to tailor the interior to his wants and needs. Always take notes on everything that is discussed. Your customer may veto ideas and proposals that you present. Later when you go along with what he has selected and he is not happy, you can pull out your original notes and remind him that you discussed other options, but he vetoed them and opted to go with his idea.

Notes keep you covered. They are the documentation of your sales calls. You cannot afford to replace and redo things at your customer's whims. If your idea was bad, you should redo the job. If your customer opts for his ideas against your suggestions, you should never consider redoing the job. You are sorry, but you have documentation showing that the area was discussed at length.

Ask Questions

You need to ask the right questions to determine your client's needs. Questions will help you to determine your prospect's requirements and needs so you may tailor your services and help select the correct products for his or her wants and needs.

What do they really need to correct their problems? Customers do not want to listen to you talk about anything but their problems and the way to solve them.

Get right to the point on the reason why the customer has asked you to come out. *"How can I be of help?"*
Each question you ask should to help clarify the customer's wants and needs. You want to quickly get to the subject at hand so you are able to review the available options.

Act like an expert that can solve their problems when you go to the initial in-home consultation. *Show* your prospect that you *do* know the answer, you *do* know how to proceed, but that the information is valuable and you are happy to share it with him *if* he will hire you to do the job. Demonstrate your abilities. Tell the customer that "yes, I can solve that problem. When we get further into the design process, I will give you ideas on the various ways we can eliminate the problem, or take care of your needs." This type of answer tells your customer that you are an expert and *know* how to solve the problem. He now has to make a commitment to hire you, before you will *give* the answer.

Get Your Customer's Attention

In order to close the sale, and to keep from repeating the same information, make sure that the customer is absorbing the information that you are providing her.

- *Grab the customer's attention by asking a question.* A question will stimulate her interest and arouse her curiosity. Make sure the question is relative to the prospect's personal interests regarding the product or service.

- Use an opening remark that can lead to other remarks.

- Make sure that the prospective customer is comfortable.

- Attempt to research your customer before your appointment, so that you know who she is and what is probably important to her. The more you know about the customer, the better are your chances of making a sale because you are more on track with the correct approach to take.

- Put something tangible in your prospect's hands to look at while speaking to them. This may be a photo album of other jobs, pamphlets of information, or a demonstration and examination of studio displays. If you do, the information you are providing will make a better impression.

- Speak the customer's language. Use terms and vocabulary that are easy for the customer to understand. If you don't, you will have to repeat yourself using clearer terminology when the customer doesn't understand what you mean.

- Do not sound like a broken record. If you are repeating the same information, say it another way each time.

- Don't talk down to the customer. Don't assume that she doesn't know anything about the product you are reviewing. She may already have been shopping all over town, and may have heavily researched the product before coming to see you.

What to Discuss During the Initial Consultation

(This area is covered thoroughly in *Secrets of Success for Today's Interior Designers and Decorators*.)

Lifestyle:
- *All* about the family that resides there.

- Type of entertaining.

- Hobbies, entertainment requirements.

- Color, style, and design desires.

- Any furnishings and accessories to be reused, including antiques and art work.

- Health problems. (e.g., allergies)

- Budget for the design job.

- Time available to complete the job.

Tailor Your Presentation to Fit Your Prospect's Wants and Needs

Select samples and products to show your prospective customer that will work to meet her wants and needs. If she expresses interest in a particular product during the preliminary interview, show the samples for the products, even though you feel they won't work. During the in-home consultation, show the customer why these products are inappropriate to fill her needs. Then show her another alternative.

Plan and prepare your presentation for your prospect in advance of the meeting for an effective exhibition. After you repeatedly present the same products, you will become very polished in your presentation. Remember that the products and services must still be tailored to the individual customer's wants and needs. Anticipate any objections and questions that will be raised by your customer. You cannot be sure what direction your presentation may take. You may start out thinking that *this* is the correct product and course of action to take; by the time you leave you may have switched to a completely different product and solution.

Anticipate customer objections to your various products. Prepare answers to these objections that can turn a negative question to a positive answer. The more calls you go on, the more you will face answer similar questions. And the better you will be at turning them around into an opportunity to express a positive answer. Be prepared for negative feedback from the customer. Think of this as an opportunity to affirmatively answer objections.

You need to be able to be flexible with your presentation. Every customer has a different personality, and will take a different look at your presentation. Their wants and needs will always be a little bit different than someone elses. This is what makes the job interesting — and keeps it interesting.

If the prospective customer *really* wants what they want, you had better give it to them. They probably will never come back and complain about the color or design they selected. They got what they thought they wanted. If you do not give it to them, someone else will. If you talk them into accepting your ideas, when they are your ideas and not what they really want, they will cancel the job on you, either before their three day (Truth and Lending law) recision period is up, or after the job goes in and they again affirm to you that "*that isn't what I really wanted.*"

If you insist on not listening to your prospects, will not work with their ideas, and will not tailor your presentation to understanding their wants and needs, you will not be hired and will sell far fewer jobs than the sales professional that is willing to adapt themselves to what their customer really wants.

Presentations

You are frequently required to give presentations to obtain design jobs. The prospective customer may be interviewing several designers and wants to see which one has ideas that she can relate to, or this may be the first time you have worked with the customer and she wants to see what you have to offer and find out *why* she should select your company over another. Normally, presentations are given to commercial customers. If you are regularly going to make commercial presentations, consider spending the money and the time to have an audio-visual slide presentation created about your company. It is relatively inexpensive, considering the impact.

Preparing for the presentation:
Before planning and presenting a design job, you need to find out several things:

- What are the wants and needs of the customer.

- What does the customer *want* to know. If she has asked you questions that you have not yet answered; now is the time to provide the answers and information.

- Any special requirements for the particular job.

- To whom you will be making the presentation. Usually you will make the presentation to the key person in charge of deciding who will get the job, and who is also in charge of approving the design ideas.

- How many people will be in attendance.

- Who from your firm will be making the presentation.

- If you are making the presentation, who will accompany you from your firm to offer support.

- Where will the presentation be made. Generally, the best place to make a presentation is in your nicely designed studio, where all of your support materials are available. You will be able to stay in control of the situation should any distracting arise.

  If you must make your presentation at the customer's home or office, do it in the dining room. With a commercial job, ask for a separate, quiet room with a table and enough chairs to accommodate all of those in attendance.

- Determine what information can you provide to the customer about your company.

- Decide which references would be pertinent to this particular prospect and compile a list for the customer.

- Find out how much time will be allotted for you to make the presentation. Plan it to run for the allotted amount of time.

Making the Presentation:
The goal in making a presentation is to get the customer to decides on her selections, sign the sales contract, and give you a deposit to start the order. The least that you should be satisfied with at the end of the presentation is a firm commitment stating, *"we will go ahead with the order."*

To effectively make a sale, you need to believe in your products and services. You need to be very enthusiastic throughout all dealings with a customer. Let her feel that she is getting a good value. If you act bored, indifferent or burned out, you will probably not get the sale. If you don't project excitement about the job, you cannot expect your customer to get excited and go ahead with the job.

You project enthusiasm to your customer through your body language, voice, personality, eye contact, attitude, mannerisms, and in the way you make your presentation. **These are the rules to follow for presentations:**

- While having your presentation meeting, tell your client what your weak points are before he or she notices them. Doing this will give you credibility when you point out your strong points.

- Project your voice loud enough so that everyone can hear you.

- Wait until the end of the presentation to hand out any information. If you hand out the information at the beginning of the presentation, your customers and their support staff will read the information while you speak. You will have to repeat the same information because you will not have everyone's undivided attention.

- At the end of the presentation, review all of the main points you want to emphasize.

- After your review, ask if there are any questions.

- This is the time to satisfy final objections. When this is done, ask for the sale.

- Thank and shake hands with all in attendance. Invite them to call you if they have a question or want more information.

- Follow up the presentation with a thank-you note and a three-page letter summarizing the reasons the customer should select your firm. Restate all positive points in doing business with your company at this time. Let the customer know that you really want the job and want to continue working with the company in the future. Also send a note to all key personnel who were at the presentation.

Try to Sell the Total Package

Offer a complete package price for doing the whole job. Customers want to know in advance what the price is for the whole job. They would prefer to do the whole job, rather than piece by piece or hour by hour. Customers understandably get nervous when billed by an hourly rate or piece by piece. They may feel that you will add in extra unneeded hours or have no idea of how many hours to expect. Give the customer a complete price for the whole project and let them opt not to do all of it at once.

When you give customers a complete package price for the whole job, you also outline for them what is included in the price. They automatically feel that they are getting more for their money than when presented the job hour by hour or piece by piece. They know what is coming and what they are getting. Your hourly rate may seem high to the customer, who may decide against the job.

More Presentation Techniques to Ensure That You Get the Job

Key ideas to ensure that you get the job:
- *Act as if you already have the job.* Act as if you are only there to take measurements and make final selections.

- *Don't talk too much.* Ask the necessary questions to arrive at appropriate solutions. Sit back, listen, and let your customer talk. You will learn a lot by listening and will find out which way to let your presentation go. When you do speak, speak slowly and briefly. You do want to be friendly and bond with the customer, but talking too much can cause you to lose the sale.

- *After listening to your customer, make her fully aware that you are the person to help her do the job.* Give the customer only enough information about you to help ensure that she will select you for the job. You don't need to review your whole life story and employment history to get her confidence.

- *Don't relate any negative thoughts or stories to your prospective customer.* Review only the positive events.

- *Customers only want to work with successful people.* Even if you are new to this business, you need to appear successful to your potential customers.

- *Always ask for the order.* If the customer objects to going ahead with the order, *insist* on doing a smaller part of the project to show that you will deliver quality service and quality products. Then when she is satisfied that you will deliver as promised, she can go ahead and let you do the rest of the job.

- *Leave as soon as you can after getting the order.* Even if you are not that busy, appear extremely busy and act as if you must get going. This is important, since you probably just quoted this customer a high hourly rate.

Don't Overwhelm Your Customer With Too Many Selections

Cut down your presentation to only a few correct selections. Too many choices will overwhelm your customer and prevent him from not coming to a decision that day — or ever. Too many selections cause confusion for customers, who then shop the competition to help determine the correct action to take. If the competition has a lower price, they often get the job. They often come right out and ask the customer what price he was quoted for the identical item, and purposely undercut it.

Narrow down the selections from solid to patterned fabrics, textured to plain fabrics, medium to lightweight fabrics, etc. Get the customer in the right fabric family before you even start bringing in samples.

Customers want you to help them make the selections; that is partly why they are willing to pay you for your services. They want to make informed, educated decisions.

Be Realistic in What You Promise

One of your main objectives is to get your customer to return with a repeat sale. Be realistic and truthful in what you are promising your customer in order to achieve this.

Present your company, your products, delivery time, and quality in a positive manner without overstating anything. *Dwell* on the positive points, but do *mention* the negative points. The customer must make an informed decision. You do not want to be accused of not telling her something, or not being truthful. If you go ahead and say that the fabric may be on back order for several weeks, or that the delivery is really eight weeks, not six, the customer will not like hearing it, but chances are she will accept it. Later, when you actually deliver the item in eight weeks, you will have a customer that is going to tell you, "you said six weeks for the delivery." You run the risk of upsetting them to the point of canceling the order or at the least the possibility of having to make a price adjustment to save the order. Be truthful in the beginning.

Conquering Fear of Selling

Selling can be learned. If you or your employees don't consider yourself salespeople, you may fear making that first sales call on potential customers. Analyze what it is you are fearing. Why do you feel this way? You may have a lifetime disdain for aggressive salespeople. You may feel that salespeople want to make a sale at any cost to the customer. And that they don't care what their customers buy, or what untruths they tell the customer — as long as they make that sale.

There are many unprofessional salespeople out there. Many have questionable ethics, are dishonest, and have given salespeople a bad name in general. Professional salespeople who care about their customers, do care what their customers buy and what promises they make to their customers, while attempting to make that sale. They are ethical and want to provide their customers with quality products, the right products for the customer's situation, and also strive to deliver the goods in a timely manner.

If you believe in the quality of the products and services you are selling, and want to work with your customers in an honest manner, making the sale is relatively easy.

If you are a beginner at making sales calls or are working with a beginner, follow these basic rules to get comfortable with the selling process:

- Read all available information about the line of products and services you will be selling. Carry samples, brochures, and pictures of the products to show your customers while on a sales call.

- Dress in a professional manner. You are representing your company. Your customer may have never been to your studio and this is the first glimpse the customer has of your company. The image you will project will leave a lasting impression.

- Use the first sales calls to practice basic selling skills. You may or may not make the first couple of sales; the idea here is to get comfortable with making sales calls.

- Be warm, friendly, and willing to work with customers on their decorating projects. If you promise to get back to them with more information, you will be sure do it.

- Be brief and get to the point of the visit. Attempt to establish rapport with the potential customer, but do not put on heavy pressure while making a sale.

- Obtain enough information from your customer to make correct decisions on appropriate products for their situation.

- Provide your customer with enough information to convince her that the products are what she needs for her situation.

- Leave your customer with brochures about the products. Jot down all pertinent points that will help your customer come to a decision. Do not rely on the customer to remember these points later. You will probably not be the only one to give an estimate. She needs to be able to make realistic comparisons.

- Thank the prospective customer for her time and for allowing you to make your presentation.

- Follow up on the sales call. Write your prospective customer a short note thanking her for allowing you to make your presentation and encouraging her to call you if she has any more questions. By doing this, you are keeping your name and your company's name current in their minds.

- Add the prospective customer to your mailing list, whether or not you make the sale. She may not buy from you this time, and may buy from another company that doesn't provide the service you provide. She may be embarrassed and sorry she didn't buy from you. By keeping her on your mailing list, and periodically mailing letters, newsletters, sale sheets, etc., to her, you are inviting her to do business with you later.

Handling Customer Objections

Objections are the reasons given to you by prospective customers about why they are not ready to buy from you.

- Objections are the obstacles that you must *overcome* to make the sale.

- You must thoroughly *answer* to the customer's satisfaction any objection raised.

- Objections are raised by prospective customers *to avoid* making decisions or commitments to buy from you. They are not raised because the customer doesn't want the product or service.

- Objections raised regarding the services you provide may be an indication that this isn't a good potential customer for you.

Listen carefully to any and all objections raised by your customer. What is she *really* saying? *How* is the customer saying it? What is the customer's attitude? Depending on the objection and the way it is *expressed, this will* tell you whether you should pursue this sale and whether or not this customer is one you *should* work with. Once you satisfy your customer's objections, she should be ready to buy from you.

The Different Types of Objections

Objections fall into the different categories as outlined below.

Objections that send warning signs about working with the customer:
Some objections hit you as warning signs. The way they are stated may send you signals to drop this customer now! He or she is trouble and may be potentially disastrous. The customer that will send this type of message is usually hard to get along with, has a difficult or unpleasant personality, has had "problems" with other companies, or has ordered the job elsewhere, had it installed, didn't like it, and canceled the job.

Trust your instincts. Listen to the message the customer is expressing and run away as fast as you can! Unfortunately, you probably need the job. You may be +headed for an expensive mistake! You will end up regretting your decision to go ahead with the job. The job will not go in smoothly, the customer will be extremely difficult to work with, and in the end, you may end up taking the whole job back. Can you afford this? Walk away before you have invested anything more than a bit of your time.

Look at your customer's body language as she is talking to you. Notice the tone and manner in which your customer is speaking to you. Watch the customer's body language. Do you want to work with this customer?

Legitimate objections:

A legitimate objection is one where the customer needs more information. You have left out a few things, or passed over some information too quickly to satisfy your customer. Listen to the question or objection and answer it as thoroughly as you can.

Does the customer want to get very technical? Then get very technical. Use caution here; too much information will overwhelm the customer into making *no* decision.

Determine how strong the objection *really* is. How will the customer benefit by making the purchase from your company? If she will not benefit, you should not proceed with the sale. You will end up with an unhappy customer. Realize that her objections are legitimate. Be honest. This customer may still come back to you later for items that you can provide her. You cannot meet everyone's needs, all of the time.

Arbitrary objections:

Arbitrary objections are those that prevent you from closing the sale. This objection is based on a prospective customer's opinions and misinterpretations, rather than on reality, and is not a legitimate reason for not completing the order. To make a sale, you must remove these objections by giving the prospect more information that convinces her that your products and services fulfill her requirements.

These objections are raised to avoid making a purchase. They are not usually the real reason why the customer is stalling the order. These are excuses a prospect raises to keep from going ahead with the sale. The customer may not be able to make decisions.

This type of objection is also raised to mask the real reason why the customer is not ready to go ahead with the order. If you feel that the customer may be trying to cover up the real reason for not going ahead with the order, come right out and ask if the objection she has made is the real reason she is hesitating. The customer will usually tell you. Other customers will stick to their arbitrary objections and never reveal what is really bothering them.

Other customers may feel they have a legitimate reason for their hesitation. Something new may have arrived that the customer perceives is a better product to fill her needs. You and your company may not carry that product yet and the customer may feel that she needs to check it out before making a decision.

If faced with an arbitrary objection:

- Keep a positive attitude.

- Project a friendly, helpful attitude toward satisfying your customer's objections.

- Do not make your prospect feel stupid or ignorant for voicing her concerns.

- Realize the objection is raised because the customer doesn't have enough information to come to a decision at this point. You need to provide your customer with more information, so that she may come to a decision.

- Never tell your customer that she is "wrong or incorrect." You will put the customer on the defensive, make her angry, and lose the sale with that approach.

- When an arbitrary objection is raised, repeat it to the customer in her own words. Do this to show the customer that you are listening to her concerns. Now give the customer your perspective on the problem.

- Persuade the customer that the advantages of letting you do the job outweigh any objections that she has. This is done by answering the objection thoroughly, and then changing the subject from the objection to a very positive reason why the customer should give you the job.

Typical Customer Objections

(Our book *Secrets of Success for Today's Interior Designers and Decorators* includes six pages of common objections and the way to answer.)

Objection: *"Your price is higher than (the competitor)."*

Answers: *"Our price may be slightly higher. Our quality and service are exceptional quality."*

"Have you compared exactly the same fabric, construction quality, and service? How can you be sure that they are the same quality? The two products may look similar, but if you want lasting quality, ours is a superior product."

"Are you sure that they added in sales tax, installation, etc., in their quoted price?"

Objection: *"We can't fit it into our budget allocation."*

Answers: *"How much do you have available to spend for the project? Let's see what we can do with the amount you have available.* The customer or company may need to start with only a portion of the job or may need to select less-expensive alternatives. After they see the difference in their interior with only a small part of the job completed, they will probably be very motivated to work on completing the job as planned. They may use creative efforts in coming up with the money.

   Give the customer or company the quality and service that they can afford. If they want a top-quality job with top-quality service and products, they will have to pay a top-quality price for it. Give them the *amount* of your time and quality of products that they are able to pay for. This objection may be a ploy to get you to drop your price. If you can shave it slightly, then do it.

Objection: *I can buy this less expensively from (the competitor)."*

Answer: *"How can you be sure that you were shown the same high-quality product?"* Products may appear the same, but quality varies widely. The product I am proposing is top quality.

"Would you prefer that I show you a similar product of lesser quality?" Demonstrate the difference in the qualities by comparing different products.

"Are they really going to give you the service that my company will?" This is the time to pull out testimonials or provide your prospect with jobs to look at, and provide previous customers' names and numbers so they may verify that you do provide quality service.

"Interior design companies may appear the same, but we are not the same. Will they give you the guarantee and the same quality products or services?"

"Does the decorator have my experience and offer innovative ideas? Will they be in business in a few months when you have a problem with the product? Do you feel that they have our reputation for dependability, experience, and trustworthiness? Our reputation, quality of products and services, reliability, and provided guarantees far outweigh a slightly less-expensive price quoted by our competitor."

Your prospect is asking you to justify your price difference to them. Help her decide to buy from you, not the competitor. She probably realizes that yes, the item may be of inferior quality, the company may not have your reputation, and it may not be in business later when she needs a service call. Help clarify the price difference for your prospect so that she can buy from you.

When shopping the features and price, customers start getting the products confused very quickly after examining only a few. They start thinking, *which one is the least expensive?* The least expensive is usually the *least quality,* and they need you to remind them of this fact to get them back on the track of selecting the product that will fill their needs, regardless of the price differential.

"I understand that some customers are primarily interested in price only. Here at (your company) in addition to providing you with higher quality products at very competitive prices, we also strive to provide the best service of any interior design business around. I'm sure you have heard about our reputation, haven't you? If in the future you are interested in working with an excellent company that provides high-quality, excellent service and competitive pricing, please give me a call."

Objection: *"I think I will just do the job myself."*

Answer: *"Yes, you may want to do the wallpapering and accessory buying yourself. Window treatment planning is a difficult thing to do without experience. If we do the planning and measuring for you, the treatments are guaranteed to fit. Why not let us do the more difficult portions of the job to ensure that they will come out to your satisfaction?"*
It is easy for the customer to say that she is going to do the job herself, when faced with a large bill. But, if she isn't experienced, she is not able to do this. Let her do the easier parts, if she likes. Insist on doing the difficult portions.
Let the customer know that if she changes her mind, you are very qualified and willing to go ahead and help. Chances are, when faced with actually doing the job, or after they hit the first snag, she won't get around to it and will call you back for your services.

Objection: *"We'll have to get back to you on this, we don't have time to discuss it now."*

Answer: *"When would be a convenient time to discuss the job with you?"* Call back at the more convenient time. The customer may really be busy and has not had time to digest your information.
This objection may also be used as an excuse to cover up the real reason why she is not ready to buy.

Objection: *"We are not ready to do a project at this time."*

Answer: *"Please consider us for the job when you are ready to do the job."* This objection may come up when you are following up on information you have sent out to a customer. Some prospects are not really prospects at all. They may be interior design students gathering information, people dreaming that they can redecorate, but without the means to do so, competitors, or other interior designers attempting to start their own businesses. Ask them while you have them on the phone if they have any further questions (they also have friends and relatives to refer you to), and if they feel that sometime in the near future they may be interested in your services (this answer tells you if you should keep them on your mailing list).

Objection: *"The project has to be approved by my spouse, boss, or a committee."*

Answer: Always make your presentation when the decision makers can be present. Ask when you are setting up the appointment if the prospective customer is in a position to make a decision about going ahead with the job when you come out. At this point if the prospect is not in the position to make a decision, she will tell you that she needs to get the information and discuss it with the other party. At this point ask to set up the appointment when the other party may be present to receive the information. This is to keep you from making the presentation twice. You may not be able to get the other party to attend your presentation. You are indicating that your time is valuable, and you are inviting the other party to attend the meeting.

Objection: *"We usually do business with (the competitors)."*

Answer: *"How long have you been doing business with them?" "I bet you stopped price comparing their prices after the first time you used them, didn't you? We are also a fine company that does high-quality work and provides exceptional service. We also have very competitive pricing. How about allowing us to bid on your next project, for comparison's sake?"* Now give the prospect some reading material and your card to contemplate giving you a chance to do business with their company in the future. You will probably be called sooner than you think. Remember that companies are made up of employees. When you do a job or work with a company, most of the time you will also end up doing jobs for some of the employees of that company.

Objection: *"We love the window treatments shown us, but you don't carry the carpet we like."*

Answers: *"I would like see the carpet sample to see if we may also order that for you."* You may be able to order the carpet from that or another vendor. Go and see the carpet sample or have the customer bring in a sample. Make sure that it is a suitable selection for your customer's needs.

"How about letting me go ahead and do the window treatments for you? If you will, I will give you an additional $25 discount." Everyone wants to save money where they can. They may object that they don't know if the window treatments will match the carpet. Have the customer borrow the carpet sample (try not to loan them your sample; if the other store sees it, they will try to undercut the price with the customer).

"I have an associate in the carpeting business who I know will give you a competitive price on the carpet you love. Let me help you with the window treatments and set up an appointment with my friend to get together with you." Try to do the portions of the job that you are equipped to do. Then have referral sources available to keep them happy. Have a reciprocal arrangement with the referral source. Or you can work out a split commission amongst yourselves.

Stress that because you are so specialized in the area that you do cover, you are a far superior expert than the company that does a bit of everything. Many generalized companies sell many products and employ inexperienced people.

Stress to the customer that your overhead on your smaller shop or studio is lower, you pass the savings on to the customer in lower prices.

Objection: *"What if we don't like the way the job comes out?"*

Answer: *"We work with you on the selection of the correct products, fabrics, and services that meet your needs. We show you pictures or draw sketches of what the proposed selections will look like for your final approval before we begin the design process.*

"Since the products are custom made to your approved styling and made to fit the measurements of your windows in the fabrics or materials that you confirm, if you decide that you do not like the styling, fabric, or material, the treatments are nonreturnable. The reason for the products' not being returnable is because the chances of another customer coming along wanting that exact styling in those measurements and fabric are not very likely. We are not able to re-sell custom-made products. But everything we sell is guaranteed to fit and perform as indicated to you.

"We use quality fabrics and products, and allow only the highest fabrication standards for everything that we offer. Anything purchased from us has a one-year guarantee to perform to your satisfaction. We strive to keep you happy and coming back for future purchases. Any potential problems that are likely to arise, will usually show up within this time period."

Objection: *"Why do you require a down payment of half to one-third of the total amount of the sale?. I want to pay you when the job is completed."*

Answer: *"Everything that we sell is custom made to fit your measurements, in the style and fabric of your selection. All of the items have a high initial cost to us, and we must ensure that you do not change your mind about going ahead with the purchases after the fabrication process has begun.*

You do have three business days to cancel. If you should cancel after this period, you will lose your down payment."

Objection: *"How long did you say you have been doing this?"*

Answer: Unless you are extremely experienced and have many years in this business, this is a touchy question. You can say something like, *"including my years of college and experience, I have been in this business_____years."*

Many companies employ inexperienced decorators and designers or ones who haven't gone to college and majored in interior design. These companies instead try to get experienced salespeople who can close a sale. So the prospect is under the impression that she has a design professional in her home, when in reality she has a sales professional with *little, if any,* design training and experience.

Try to foresee other objections that your prospect may raise. Practice an answer for each that you can come up with. Objections as shown here, or a variation of them, will be raised depending on the personality of the prospect.

You will be able to overcome the vast majority of the objections. If you don't overcome them, take this as a warning that you probably shouldn't do the job anyway. Concentrate on working with customers that you can work with easily and comfortably.

Working With Difficult Customers

Some customers are difficult from the moment you meet them. Others become difficult when a problem arises. Strive to pre-qualify your customers and work only with those you feel comfortable with when you're just starting out in business. However, you cannot afford to be as choosy about whom you choose to work with.

If you cannot stand to work with the customer's personality style, pass on the job. Here are some common difficult customer situations you will be running into:

- *Your customer may not be happy with the completed job.* Chances are you will have to do some finishing touches on the vast majority of the jobs you do. This is the nature of this business. By all means, if the customer is unhappy and you can make some small addition or correction to the job to make the customer happy, do it at your expense. Most customers will be happy to pay for some extras to have the job completed to their satisfaction.

    This is why taking accurate notes and clearly spelling out on the sales agreement what the customer has agreed to is so important. Cover yourself and agree to make minor changes at your own expense as a *favor* to make your customer happy — not because you are obligated to do so.

    Sometimes living with the job for several days, after the shock of the change has set in, will alleviate your customer's feelings of dislike for the finished job. The job may very well grow on her. She may discover that she basically likes the job except for a few minor details.

    Some fabric items need time to "hang out" for a few days to improve their hanging ability and appearance.

- *Your customer may exhibit rude or offensive behavior.* If the customer acts like this during your initial meetings, decline the job. If this behavior is exhibited later over any small delay or problem, let the customer know that you would not treat her this way and will not tolerate her treating you in this manner. If she persists, finish the portions of the job that are started, have them installed, and cancel the rest of the job.

- *You may do something that is not exactly what the customer thinks you should do.* She may show her anger by complaining to another employee of your company.

- *You and your customer do not agree on how to do the job.*

- *The customer's style and taste differ from yours.* Work with customers that like your style.

- *The customer expects more than she is willing to pay for.*

- *During a stressful situation, either you or the customer may say something that is later regretted by the party who said it.*

- *There is miscommunication between you and your customer.*

- *Your customer wants to change the order after you have already started it.*

- *Although your customer may be nice to work with, she has a difficult spouse, other family member, employees and/or other staff members (in commercial sales) that you also have to work with.* Limit the amount of communication you must have with the difficult family member or employee.

- *Customers that try to use lots of your time, needlessly.* They may be indecisive or need constant reassurance about their selections while awaiting delivery. They either come in or call you daily with more questions and more objections after the job is in the works.
  If the customer persists in using lots of your time, remind her that you do have other clients and are trying to run a business. The job will get done faster if you are allowed to work on it. You must clearly limit the amount of time that they are allowed to take.

- *The prospective customer may be mentally ill, high on drugs, or drunk when you go for the in-home consultation.* By law you cannot contract with a court-diagnosed mentally ill or drug or alcohol incapacitated person. You may want to reschedule the appointment for when they are "feeling better" or just do planning and measuring while you are out there. Insist on the spouse being present when the contract is signed.

- *Despite repeated warnings that payment must be collected at the time of installation, the customer is not prepared to pay it when the installer arrives.* When you have a customer sign a sales agreement that is a COD, tell the customer that the payment is collected the day the installer installs the interior items. Always have the person setting up the appointment for the installation remind the customer, that the amount of $_____ is due upon completion of the installation. When the installer calls the morning to confirm the installation, he should again remind the customer that he is expecting a check. Any hesitancy by the customer should indicate to the person on the phone that this person may need to be rescheduled for installation.
  The installer should not install the items if there is not a check. Many jobs will not be completed on the first visit due to some small problem. If the installer has copies of the sales checks in his hand, he will know what is installed and completed, and what is the price of the item. He *should* try to collect on what is completed to the customer's satisfaction. This is why multiple sales agreements for the job are so important. Insist on collecting as individual sales agreements are completed. These situations must be resolved quickly and as painlessly as possible. Your objective is to satisfy your customer, keep her referring to you, and keep her coming back for repeat sales.

Always part company on good terms, whether or not you or your customer quit the job midway. A disgruntled customer will spread negative news about you to all people that will listen. Let her know that you are available to work with her in the future, if she should change her mind. The disgruntled customer may not be experienced in redecorating and may not realize that delays occur, regardless of *where* she does business. Later, after she is more experienced and has more time to allow you to deliver and perform, she may want to come back.

Closing the Sale

After making your sales presentation and answering all objections, it is now time to close the sale.
In order to close a sale, you need to come right out and *ask for the sale*. Tell the customer that you would like to work with him on this project. To close a sale is, in essence, *to ask for the order*. Closing the sale is mandatory in overcoming any further sales resistance or putting off the buying decision by your customer.

Consumers hate to spend their money, especially during tough economic times. It is easier to think about doing something than to actually do it. You need to call them to action and tell them exactly what the next step is. For example, "I need you to sign this sales agreement and give me a deposit of $_____ to get the job started." By closing the sale or calling them to action, you are showing your prospect what the next step is. Some of the techniques outlined below setup the sale for you to easily step in and close it:

- Realize that the *worst* possible thing that can happen while you are attempting to close a sale is that the prospective buyer will say no.

- "No", usually means *the customer needs more information.*

- A refusal is not an affront that should be taken personally. If the prospect will not let you do the job, do not let his negative response affect you in *any* way.

- Bolster yourself with the attitude that if the prospect refuses to allow you to do the job, the loss is really theirs, not yours.

- Adopt the attitude that you are doing your prospect a favor by doing the job for him. If he cannot see that, that is his problem, not yours. Move on to customers that truly appreciate your expertise.

- *The more time the prospect has invested in working with you, talking with you, visiting your studio, and making trips to see you, the easier it is to get him to commit to buying from you.* This is a contradiction for you because you do not want to invest much time unless you are sure that you are getting the sale. If you can get the prospect comfortable with you, he is more likely to select you rather than one of your competitors to do the job when he is ready. Build a relationship over time. Prospects naturally like to hire the decorator they have already put time and effort into getting to know rather than someone new.

  There is normally a series of small closes leading up to the large final close. Get the customer to agree to suggestions on styling, the placement and measurements of the proposed treatments, and the fabric or material selections. You and the buyer have slowly agreed on each thing, before you have worked out a corresponding price to quote. Quote the price back to the customer, noting that this is the style, fabric, placement, etc., that *he* has selected. After selecting and agreeing to everything, it is difficult for the customer to back down and say no to the final package and price.

  During the selection process for each detail, you and the customer will have to work out the selection until it meets the customer's satisfaction. You will also have to overcome and satisfy each objection as it arises.

- *Act as if you already have the job.* Show by your manner, body language, and tone of voice that you feel that you are going to do *this* job for the customer. Convey confidence to the customer. You are out at the customer's home merely to clear the formalities out of the way of the details of pricing and selections, so you can proceed to do the job. Come right out and tell the prospect that you are the most qualified and knowledgeable to do the job. Tell the customer that you can easily handle the job for them. Ask them to sign the sales contract so you can get started.

  If you act confident that the job is one that you easily can take care of for the customer, he will want you to take the reins and do it for him. Customers want to work with people who know what they are doing and who are interested in solving their problems.

  When you act like you have the job, you remove yourself from having to try to persuade the customer from buying from you. You act as if he already is persuaded and has decided to give you the project, and you are ready to get to work.

- *Fill out the sales contract during the in-home visit before the customer has agreed to make the purchase from you.* If the customer doesn't stop you, you surely have the order. If the customer attempts to stop you, tell him that you are simply getting each and every detail down before any of them get overlooked and the contract is ready for the customer to sign when he is ready to get started on the job.

- *Assure the customer that there is no risk involved in making the purchase from you.* Remove the risk of buying from the customer and place it on yourself. Remind him that any product or service that you provide is guaranteed to perform and function as specified for one year. Strive to make purchasing as painless, easy, and risk-free as possible.

- *Insist on providing the customer with samples of your work.* If your prospect is hesitant about giving you the job, be flexible and insist on doing a small portion to demonstrate your quality and service. This allows your prospect to try you out with little risk.

- *Ask for the order.* Hand the customer the sales agreement, show them where to sign, and ask for a deposit to get the job started. Tell him what the next step is in placing the order.

   If he won't go ahead with the order right then, tell him you will call him back on a certain day — about four days away. Write a note in your appointment book to remind yourself to call —and make sure you make the call. You must follow up. Show the customer you really want his business.

- *Fill out the contract with all the specifics of the order.* Review the specifics and let the customer know that if he will not commit, that all you need is his signature and a deposit to go ahead with the order. Chances are if he doesn't try to stop you from filling out the contract, he will buy right now. If he attempts to stop you, go ahead and tell him you want to get it all down and review everything so that it will save you time later in trying to recreate the bid and you want to make sure everything is clear. The more professional you can appear to your customer, the more unprofessional your competition is going to appear.

- *When the customer is ready to give you the order, finalize the order and get out of there.* Don't give him any time to think about it, to reconsider and change his mind. As it is, with the three-day, right-to-cancel period, many customers feel buyer's remorse and cancel their orders. They may also shop elsewhere and find a better value.

   Don't rush into getting your paperwork done unless your customer is in a hurry for his order and you write on the sales agreement *"the customer waives his right to cancel."* Otherwise you may have fabric cut at the supplier and already enroute to you when the customer changes his mind or cancels.

- *Use a sales technique that the customer is comfortable with.* You need to match the mood and personality of your customer to effectively lead to the close. Most people would prefer to buy from people that are similar to them, rather than from people who are different from them. Be responsive to your buyer's moods and personality and adapt your mood and personality to match your buyer.

Getting the customer to sign on the dotted line and getting a deposit is, in essence, closing the sale. You and the customer have agreed upon the price, selection, time frame, payment terms, etc. Only when you finally have a signed contract and the deposit in your hand or charged to the Visa or Mastercard have you actually made the sale. The customer still has three business days to cancel an in-home transaction. Therefore, you need to keep your customer *sold* on your products and services. You are only paid for services rendered or fabricated items sold to the customer up to the point of the cancellation of the order by the customer. Since the customer may receive goods that were not what he expected, you haven't finalized the sale until the customer is satisfied at the end of the installation.

How to Stay on Target With Deadlines

This is an outline for staying on target with your proposed deadlines:
- If the customer tells you that he *must* have the items by a certain date and you doubt seriously that you can meet that deadline, be honest with your customer and let him go elsewhere to purchase the items if he cannot extend his deadline.

   Anything can and will happen in this business. You cannot afford inflexible customers. If their deadline is not met, they will cancel or threaten to cancel. You may have to offer them an adjustment to keep them from canceling the sale. An unhappy customer is going to spread the news about your being late to all people who will listen.

- Don't take on more jobs than you can comfortably handle and keep up with. You cannot afford to cut your quality of service for any of your customers. All jobs must be tracked regularly. If you overload yourself, you will not do as high quality work.

- Get the paperwork done immediately after the three-day-cancellation period. If you can get the customer to *waive* the cancellation period on the sales contract, do it, and get the paperwork done immediately and on its way to the vendors.

- If you must temporarily work during the evening and on the weekends to stay on schedule, do it.

- Hire a studio coordinator that is very interested in learning about the interior design business to do some of the easier portions of your work for you.

- Always leave some time open daily for the unexpected to come up. In this business, you will have unexpected multiple problems every day.

- List the deadlines for your various jobs on your calendar by your desk. Check the deadlines regularly and track the orders regularly. Stay on top of the situation.

Following Up on Prospects

After giving an in-home bid, an in-studio estimate, or after sending out packets of information to prospective customers, you can vastly increase your sales by following up on the prospect. You should follow up on all bids and estimates within a week. Follow up on sales information mailed within two weeks. Give the prospect a chance to review the information. If the information request resulted from a sales call, it is to your advantage to deliver the information and review it with the customer.

When you call back your prospective customer, do not try to be overly pushy and try to "sell" the customer. Gear your personality and working style to fit with the customer's. Try to bond with the customer and become friends. If the customer seems annoyed, harried, or busy at the time you call, ask her if you should call back at a more convenient time. Don't waste your time or set yourself up for rejection if the prospect clearly doesn't want to talk when you call. You may have just reached her when she is rushing out the door, and she really is interested in talking with you.

If you've called at a good time for the prospect, ask her if she received the information you sent out, or if she has decided about going ahead with the job. If she has more questions, answer them clearly. Provide her with more information to help her buy.

If the prospect did not receive the information in the mail, mail or deliver another packet immediately. Call back in another week to ask if they have any questions.

If the prospect is semi-interested, but for one reason or another is just not ready to go forth with the project right now, add her to your mailing list. Show her that you want to do business with her. Call back in a few months, after she has received several of your mailings. She may not want to be contacted until she is closer to making a buying decision.

If the prospect says she is not interested, try not to show irritation for the time you spent and for the expense of the information you sent out. Perhaps she will call you in the future or send you a referral.

If you should make a follow-up call and find out that the job has been given to another firm, ask the customer what firm was selected and why it was chosen over yours. Ask the customer if your firm will be considered in the future for other projects. Leave the customer with a positive impression and let her know that you will be happy to work with her in the future.

Keep Your Name Current With Customers

Establish a frequent program of mailing newsletters, letters, sale flyers, brochures, holiday cards, and thank-you notes to your customers. A regular friendly phone call is also suggested. Most customers would prefer not to hear from you over the phone, unless they have a pending order.

You want to keep your name current and on your customers' minds. They may hear someone say that they want to redecorate, and your company will come to their mind, because you have worked hard to put it there.

Your best lead is the referral or a past customer. New, fresh leads have to be worked three times as hard, to make the sale.

To really make an impression, you *have to be persistent*. To make the sale you need to contact the prospect six to seven times within one and a half years. How do you go about this?

- Telephone the customer occasionally just to say hello.

- Mail your prospects current sales ads, accompanied by a friendly cover letter from you.

- Whenever you have an article published or a press release printed about your company in a newspaper or magazine, send out reprints of the article with current sale advertisements.

- Send cards at the holidays.

- Send a quarterly newsletter to all past and prospective customers.

Customer service is a very important element of the interior design and decorating business. To be paid in full for the job, to receive referrals from satisfied customers, and to have your customers come back again and again, you must provide services and products that *satisfy* your customers.

Part 21

Trade Sources, Resources, Subcontractors, and Terms of Doing Business

Trade Terms

CBD   Cash before delivery. The order will be processed, but will not be shipped until the payment is received.

CIA   Cash in advance. Means the same as CWO. Orders will not be processed until full payment is received.

COD   Cash on delivery. Payment for the merchandise must be made at the time of delivery. It may be necessary to do this on initial orders when you haven't established credit and want a timely delivery.

CWO   Cash with order. Means the same as CIA Orders will not be processed until full payment is received.

EOM   End of the month. The invoice will be sent out at the end of the month.

FOB   This term means "*freight, or free, on board.*" These initials with the city name immediately following indicate the point to which the seller will pay the freight. If the customer is to pay freight, the notation would read FOB, his city. If the goods are lost or damaged in transit, the person who holds the title of the goods would be the responsible party. Legally, title changes hands at the FOB point.

MOM   Middle of the month. The invoice will be sent out mid month or the fifteenth of the month.

Letter of credit   A bank-issued document guaranteeing the payment of a customer's draft, up to a specified amount for a certain period of time.

Line of credit   A commitment made by a bank, under certain conditions, to loan a certain amount of money for a short period of time. The loan may be on a revolving basis. Lines of credit usually have yearly service charges to keep the funds available, and to pay for the overhead necessary to monitor the account. The bank will regularly review your account and financial ability to repay the loan.

Pro forma   For the first order to a supplier, if no credit is established, to keep the order on schedule it may be necessary to pay the supplier in full or make partial payment before they will ship the merchandise. Once you order several times or they establish your credit rating, they will probably extend you credit.

Terms of sale   2/10/30 is the same as 2%, 10 days, net 30. Either term on your invoice indicates to the buyer that you will receive a 2 percent discount if payment is made within ten days, and full payment is expected within thirty days. Term amounts vary, but are all read the same way. If you do not want to offer a discount, but simply want full payment within a specified period, write Net 10 days or Net 30 days on the invoice.

Trade Sources

Interior design trade sources are the suppliers of the various products and services a designer uses for interior design projects. These sources include manufacturers, tradespeople, distributors, and suppliers.

To be successful as an interior designer, you need to familiarize yourself with the variety of products and services that are available to you and get to know the providers of these goods and services in your regional area. A successful designer must have the ability to coordinate various products, services, and labor sources to work together as a unified entity. Below is an overview of the sources available to you as a designer:

Dealers:

These are furniture retail sources that carry and stock manufacturers' lines of furniture and other interior design products. They usually have on their staff interior decorators to work with customers on making selections.

Distributors (jobbers):

Distributors are the middleman between the designer and the manufacturer. Generally, a designer is not in a position to purchase massive quantities of products, so she must rely on paying a higher price to a distributor to supply many needed products. Along with a distributor comes a higher price — between wholesale and retail for the products.

Individual showrooms:

Smaller, individual showrooms are single showrooms representing a manufacturer's line of products. Individual showrooms generally emulate larger market centers with their pricing, ordering, and admittance policies.

Market centers:

Market centers are groups of trade sources gathered together within a localized area. Market centers are usually open to trade professionals and are off-limits to the general public. Some of the trade sources will allow public access regularly or on certain days.

Marts and design centers:

A mart is a building in which various trade sources lease space to display their products. Each source has its own showroom or shares a showroom with another source. Designers are able to see the products and quality of products that they are selecting for customers. Customers are generally welcome if accompanied by their designer, architect, or a letter from the design firm the customer is working with. To appear professional and to keep your visit under control while getting as much mileage as possible out of showroom visits, always make a preliminary visit to pre-shop the showroom before you take your client.

Designers usually need to acquire a building pass before they are allowed to make purchases. Building passes are available through the leasing office of the mart. Most marts will admit and allow design students with student identification cards to browse.

Generally, displayed merchandise is tagged with the suggested retail price or price code. This is done so customers accompanying designers will see the retail price rather than the wholesale price, thus allowing the designer to hold her profit margins.

The larger marts have periodic shows where manufacturers and suppliers introduce new products for invited interior designers, architects, and other professionals in related fields.

When the general public is allowed free access to a showroom, this is known as an "open showroom" policy. When the showroom is closed to the public, this is know as a "closed showroom" policy, or "to the trade only."

Other interior design firms:

Act like a customer and shop other interior design firms to see what they have available to sell their customers. This is an invaluable way to find out about sources that you may otherwise not discover.

Outside buying services:

Buying services can be an excellent way to go for a design firm. Outside buying services will help keep your overhead down, allow you access to otherwise unavailable lines of products, allow you to purchase at better prices, put you in a better position to compete with firms that have better buying power, supply you with superior quality (through repeated ordering), save you time, provide information and literature, notify you of price increases and changes in the product, answer questions about the product, help you make identical reselections with other suppliers, review your POs to see if all pertinent information is included (thus saving weeks of time in receiving the order), allow you access to many more manufacturers' lines, and allow you to closely compete with firms that have more buying power. In short, for small interior design businesses starting up, they become a buying partner that helps troubleshoot the job for you. At the business end of things, you only need to write one check, rather than many to pay all your accounts.

When opting to work with an outside buying service to purchase goods that are otherwise unavailable to you, be sure to call and check the buying service's references. Find out just how happy other firms are that buy through the service.

Sales representatives (reps):

These are salespeople for various manufacturers and suppliers of interior design products. They may work solely for one manufacturer or may represent several manufacturers and suppliers. They are a wealth of information about the products they represent. They are in the position to quote you prices, supply you with product information and literature, make presentations to your employees about products, supply you with samples and displays, etc.

Reps are an important source of information about your competition and the general temperature of the marketplace. Be very guarded about what you reveal about your business to a rep. Just as they inform you about what is going on with the various firms on their route, they will also discuss your business with other firms. Beware of allowing reps back in your working area to observe the various projects you are working on. Meet with them in your conference room or outer office.

If you are unsure about the suitability of a new product presented to you by a rep, ask for the names of other designers you can call to discuss the pros and cons of the product and application.

Specialty stores:

These are stores offering interior design products that *will* give interior designers a professional trade discount, with the presentation of a business card and resale number. They waive the sales tax and allow you to collect the tax later, from the customer, based on the full retail price of the purchased products.

Subcontractors and other tradespeople (installers):

These are the labor providers for interior design products and services. This category includes installers of window treatments, carpet, all types of flooring, painters, wallpaper hangers, and cabinet makers. Installers usually provide products to complete installations such as drapery hardware, carpet padding, wood for cabinet making, adhesives, etc.

Since installers and tradespeople will make or break you with the quality of the service they provide, be sure to ask for and check references of any subcontractor you opt to work with. To avoid possible lawsuits use only licensed contractors.

Vendors:

Vendors are any interior design suppliers of goods and services. A vendor may be a manufacturer, distributor, installer, or an interior designer or decorator.

Establish Credit

When starting your business, start a good credit relationship with suppliers. Give them with a fact sheet telling them about your company. Let them know your bill payment structure (how frequently you pay your bills), what credit arrangement you want with them, what type of business organization your company is, where you bank, how long you have been in business, what types of jobs you do, etc.

As an established interior designer you will want to work with your suppliers with an open credit account. Open credit accounts allow for prompt shipment of ordered products. To establish an open account, fill out a credit application and supply credit references. If you suspect that you will be ordering from a certain supplier with whom you do not have an open account, fill out an application before ordering and find out how much credit is available and at what terms.

Always attempt to get as much credit at the best terms possible. Try for sixty to ninety days interest free. Ask for two % to five % discounts for prompt payment of invoices. If you don't ask, you may not be offered better terms.

Realize that if you wait to get credit approval at the time the order is placed, the order will be held up until they run your credit report and check your references.

Lyons is the agency that furnishes credit information to suppliers of furniture. If you intend to purchase furniture you will need to establish a good rating through them. Register early; don't wait until you need the credit. Contact Lyons Furniture Mercantile Agency, P.O. Box 3505, Chicago, IL 60654.

Dun and Bradstreet is the other main credit information supplier that all *other* design product suppliers will contact to find out about a company's credit. Contact Dun and Bradstreet, P.O. Box 3MV, Allentown, PA 18105-9959. If you want to check credit on commercial suppliers, tradespeople, or commercial (corporate) clients, Dun and Bradstreet is the credit agency to contact.

If you have a dispute with a supplier it is better to go ahead and pay the invoice and then fight about it. If you don't pay, the supplier can easily turn in a negative report about your company's payment procedures to collection agencies, Lyons or Dun and Bradstreet. It is hard to correct a negative credit rating.

Be sure to run credit checks on your customers when you are extending credit to them. Review the credit checks section in this book under.

Subcontracting

Subcontracting out many services may be a workable way to keep a large portion of your capital free and therefore allow your small business to expand, rather than stagnate due to the majority of capital being tied up. You can subcontract out all interior design labor, services, and deliveries. The following is a list of subcontracting services available to use for your interior design business:

- Credit card processing services
- Warehousing and storage
- Packaging and shipping
- Deliveries
- Invoicing
- Accounting and bookkeeping
- Management of inventory
- Telemarketing
- Marketing and advertising
- Public relations
- Photography
- Labor for all types of installations of products and services
- Direct mail services
- 800-number answering services and order processing

Subcontracting these services is fairly affordable and their use will allow you to reduce the cost of running an independent studio. For *you* to provide them, you will need extra training, employees, and the capital to set up and carry out the individual activities. These services can probably be obtained for less money than you would have to pay out if you set up each of these functions yourself.

Since subcontractors are involved in each of these tasks on a large scale for a multitude of clients they have buying power, which thus allows you to have buying power with suppliers and product lines that otherwise would be unobtainable. Subcontractors are able to provide the services at an affordable price to you, while still making the necessary profit required to run successful businesses.

Prices for the above services will vary from business to business. Some subcontractors will charge you a flat rate, regardless of the expected volume of service required; some have minimum charges for minimum amounts. You pay for each item that exceeds the minimum. Others will charge you a flat rate for service per item or task.

As your business grows, some of the activities that you previously subcontracted out may be more affordable for you to provide later in-house, depending on your volume. Compare the price and add the services when it is less expensive to train employees and add services to your in-house capabilities.

Design Centers and Trade Marts in the USA and Canada

Arizona

Arizona Design Center
3600 East University Dr.
Phoenix, AZ 85034

California

South Coast Design Center at Stonemill
2915 Redhill Ave.
Costa Mesa, CA 92626

Design Center South
23811 Aliso Creek Rd. #151
Laguna Niguel, CA 92677

Los Angeles Home Furnishings Mart/LA Mart
1933 S. Broadway
Los Angeles, CA 90007

Pacific Design Center
8687 Melrose Ave.
Los Angeles, CA 90069

Atrium Design Center
69-930 Hwy. 111
Rancho Mirage, CA 92270

Canyon Creek Design Center of San Diego, Inc.
4010-4330 Morena Blvd.
San Diego, CA 92117

San Diego Design Center
6455 Lusk Blvd.
San Diego, CA 92121

The Design Pavilion at 200 Kansas
200 Kansas St.
San Francisco, CA 94103

The Contract Design Center at Showplace Square
600 Townsend St.
San Francisco, CA 94103

Galleria Design Center
101 Henry Adams St.
San Francisco, CA 94103

Showplace Design Center
2 Henry Adams St.
San Francisco, CA 94103

Showplace Square East
Rhode Island at 15th St.
San Francisco, CA 94103

Showplace Square South
235-299 Kansas St.
San Francisco, CA 94103

Showplace Square West
550 15th St.
San Francisco, CA 94103

The Design Pavilion at 251 Rhode Island
251 Rhode Island
San Francisco, CA 94103

Western Merchandise Mart
1355 Market St.
San Francisco, CA 94103

Colorado

Denver Design Center
595 South Broadway
Denver, CO 80209-4001

Denver Merchandise Mart
451 East 58 Ave.
Denver, CO 80216

Denver Center at the Ice

House
1801 Wynkoop St.
Denver, CO 80202

District of Columbia

Washington Design Center
300 D St., S.W.
Washington, DC 20024

Florida

Design Center of the Americas (DCOTA)
1855 Griffin Rd.
Dania, FL 33004

Miami Decorating & Design District-Plaza 1
3841 N.E. Second Ave.
Miami, FL 33137

Miami Decorating & Design District-Plaza 11
180 N.E. 39 St.
Miami, FL 33137

Miami Decorating & Design District-Plaza 111
3930 N.E. Second Ave.
Miami, FL 33137

Miami Decorating & Design District-Plaza 1V
3901 N.E. Second Ave.
Miami, FL 33137

Miami International Design Center I
4100 N.E. Second Ave.
Miami, FL 33137

Miami International Design Center II

4141 NE Second Ave.
Miami, FL 33137

Georgia

Atlanta Decorative Arts Center (ADAC)
351 Peachtree Hills Ave. N.E.
Atlanta, GA 30305

Atlanta Merchandise Mart
240 Peachtree St. N.W.
Atlanta, GA 30043

Piedmont Center
10 Piedmont Center
Atlanta, GA 030305

Illinois

Merchandise Mart
Merchandise Mart Plaza
Chicago, IL 60654

Massachusetts

Boston Design Center
One Design Center Place
Boston, MA 02210

Michigan

Michigan Design Center
1700 Stutz Dr.
Troy, MI 48084

Minnesota

International Market Square
275 Market St.
Minneapolis, MN 55405

Missouri

Saint Louis Design Center
917 Locust
St. Louis, MO 63101

New York

International Design Center, New York, (IDCNY) Center 1
30-30 Thomson Ave.
Long Island City, NY 11101

International Design Center, New York, (IDCNY) Center 2
30-20 Thomson Ave.
Long Island City, NY 11101

Architects & Designers Bldg.
150 East 58 St./964 Third Ave.
New York, NY 10155

Decoration and Design Building (D + D Building)
979 Third Ave.
New York, NY 10022

Decorative Arts Center
305 East 63 St.
New York, NY 10021

Decorator's Center Building
315 East 62 St.
New York, NY 10021

Fine Arts Building
232 East 59 St.
New York, NY 10022

Interior Design Building
306 East 61 St.
New York, NY 10021

International Showcase
225 Fifth Ave.
New York, NY 10010

Manhattan Art & Antiques Center
1050 Second Ave.
New York, NY 10022

Marketcenter
230 Fifth Ave.
New York, NY 10001

New York Design Center
200 Lexington Ave.
New York, NY 10016

New York Merchandise Mart
41 Madision Ave.
New York, NY 10010

Place Des Antiouaires
125 East 57th St.
New York, NY 10022

North Carolina

Commerce & Design Building
201 West Commerce St.
High Point, NC 27260

Hamilton Wrenn Community of Showrooms
200 North Hamilton St.
High Point, NC 27260

International Home Furnishings Center
210 East Commerce St.
P.O. Box 828
High Point, NC 27261

Market Square
305 W. High St.
High Point, NC 27260

Ohio

Ohio Design Center
23533 Mercantile Rd.
Beachwood, OH 44122

Pendleton Square Design Center
1118 Pendleton St.
Cincinnati, OH 45210

St. Paul's Mart
1117 Pendleton St.
Cincinnati, OH 45210

Oregon

Design Center at Mongomery Park
2701 N.W. Vaughn St.
Portland, OR 97210

Pennsylvania

Marketplace Design Center
2400 Market St.
Philadelphia, PA 19103

Texas

Dallas Design Center
1025 North Stemmons Freeway
Dallas, TX 75201

Dallas Home Furnishings Mart
2000 N. Stemmons Freeway
Dallas, TX 75201

Design District & Contract Design Center
1400 Turtle Creek Blvd.
Dallas, TX 75207

Oak Lawn Design Plaza
1444 Oaklawn Ave.
Dallas, TX 75207

Decorative Center of Houston
5120 Woodway Dr.
Houston, TX 77056

Innova
20 Greenway Plaza
Houston, TX 77046

The Resource Center of Houston
7026 Old Katy Rd.
Houston, TX 77024

Utah

Showplace Square
522 South 400 W.
Salt Lake City, UT 84101

Washington

Design Center Northwest
5701 Sixth Ave. S
Seattle, WA 98108

Lenora Square Professional Design Showrooms
1000 Lenora St.
Seattle, WA 98121

6100 Building
6100 Fourth Ave. South
Seattle, WA 98108

Northwest Home Furnishings Mart
121 Boren Ave., North
Seattle, WA 98109

Canada

Designers Walk
168 Bedford Rd., Ste 303
Toronto, ON, M5R 2K9
Canada

Place Bonaventure Merchandise Mart
P.O. Box 1000
Place Bonaventure
Montreal, QUE H5A 1Ga
Canada

Toronto Design Center
160 Pears Ave.
Toronto, ON M5R 1T2
Canada

Source and Product Considerations

Evaluate these questions before making source or product decisions:
- Is the product line the quality that you want to offer?

- Will you honestly want to recommend the products to your customers?

- Does the quality, function, price, and beauty of the product fill your customer's wants and needs?

- Does the product fill your pricing requirements for making a profit?

- Does the manufacturer offer custom services to customize the product for various applications?

- Is the source willing to provide names of other designers that have used the product? If so, make sure that you call and ask the references if they are satisfied with the *source and the product.*

- How distant is the manufacturer or supplier located? Cost of freight is expensive and must be considered.

Successful Products

To make many product sales, select products whose value to the customer well surpasses the products price. Before determining which products to carry, ask yourself the following product value questions:

- Is the product unique or different?

- What value-laden advantages does the product possess?

- How *critically* does my target market customer need this product?

- Is there a need for the product, presently?

- What emotional factors are involved?

- Will the product generate repeat sales?

Rules for Working with Suppliers and Tradespeople

Professional designers need to monitor the quality of products purchased from various sources. The following are ways to do this.

General rules:
- Stay on top of orders. If you haven't received a confirmation of the order or the item hasn't been shipped within two weeks, follow up on the order by calling, faxing, or writing.

- Make sure that the desired and planned materials are available, and find out what they cost *before you start the job.* Be sure that everything required has arrived and the rest is on the way before proceeding.

- When placing orders, writing POs and work orders, supply as much information as you can. You cannot supply too much information. Be very specific. Do not abbreviate words. They *can and will* be misconstrued to mean *something else.* Whenever possible, include accurate drawings or pictures of what is to be done. You do not need to be an artist. A rough sketch is better than no sketch at all, which leaves everyone to guess what you really want.

- State on all of your POs that your design firm is not responsible for the ordered merchandise until it is received and inspected by a representative of your company. Let the manufacturer handle the headaches of freight claims with the shipper.

Supplier rules:

- Let your supplier know immediately about any defects in the supplied products. Even if your customer hasn't complained or tells you to forget about a minor problem, report all defects to the vendor. If you don't, future orders will also be slightly or equally defective.

- If you can speed up the process for repair of the damaged product, do so. Keep customers happy by getting quality products as quickly as possible. Let the vendor know that you have had to work on their defective product. Freight costs are very expensive.

- Make note on purchase orders: *"Customer is very particular about quality."* Let your customer know that you note this on work orders to help ensure delivery of quality products. If you do not mention your motive for writing this, the customer may see the purchase order when she signs for the product and become offended.

- Ask the supplier how the customer should care for the product. What are the recommended maintenance procedures? Pass on this information to the customer.

- What are the government regulations regarding the product? Are flameproofing certificates readily available? How about any other state-required documentation for use of the product for the desired application? Stay on top of state and federal regulations. Be sure to order certificates at the *same* time and on the same PO when you order the initial fabric. If you don't, you may never get the required state or federal certificate.

- For products that are to be customized at the manufacturer, review with the manufacturer or the rep the specifications of the product before you quote a price to the customer. They will let you know how much more the changes and options will cost. They may also be able to give you tips and ideas on how to customize the product less expensively.

- Tour your suppliers' factories, if possible. Talk to and question the employees who work there. Find out the pros and cons of the products and the appropriate applications.

- Do not order the same product or installation twice. If you have faxed or phoned in an order, do not follow up the order with another identical one, unless you note on the PO or work order that it is a duplicate order confirming the phoned or faxed order. Let the supplier know with the first order that you are going to follow up the order with a mailed in copy.

Tradespeople and installers:

- Ask to see samples of the tradesperson or installer's work. Realize that they will show you their higher quality jobs. If the workmanship isn't good, keep shopping.

- Find out if the tradesperson is willing to do unusual custom work before price quoting the job. You do not want your work orders to be put on the bottom of the stack and suffer endless delays, because the tradesperson just doesn't want to do the job or doesn't have the required equipment or tools. He may not know how to do the job or may not be willing to do anything other than standard jobs.

- There may not be many available tradespeople and installers to work with in rural areas. You may need to supply them with information on how to do a particular process. If they are willing to learn how to do it, give them the chance.

- Limit the amount of suppliers and tradespeople that you use. Let them know that they are your desired supplier or installer for the particular product or application. They will appreciate your business and strive to do a quality job for you. Tradespeople and installers that get used to working with you will be able to sense what you really want when you are in a hurry and are not clear on your work orders. They get to know you and your style of doing things.

- If you are repeatedly not receiving products and installations, replace the supplier and/or the installer. Move on to the next supplier and installer even if the costs are a bit more. You cannot afford the delays or the unhappy customers. You are trying to build a business, not go out of business.

Contractors:

- When shopping for a contractor for a job, let them know that you are shopping around and price is important. They will resist the urge to add in extra profit for the job, if it means that they will risk losing it.

- When you decide which contractor to use, have him or her sign a contract that states the job time schedule and his or her agreement to stay on schedule with the job. Emphasize the importance of meeting the deadline.

- Give the contractor the responsibility of obtaining needed permits for the job. You can spend a day down at city hall obtaining the permits. While it is good experience, contractors are more familiar with obtaining permits for customers.

- Never pay for a job in full before completion. Hold back 25 percent until your final inspection. Making the contractor wait for a portion of the money will ensure that the job is completed with an eye to quality and to the job schedule.

- Inspect any jobs in progress, *regularly*. Emphasize that you are the one to contact for any changes. Do not allow the customer or the contractor to make any changes without conferring with you. You are in charge of keeping the price down, avoiding unnecessary changes, and keeping the job on schedule. Many times contractors change the job without authorization and then have to change it back, costing more money and time. Make it clear with your customer that the contractor will do only what is on the work order.

- Make sure that the contractor knows not to discuss the job with the customer. All conversation should be kept to a minimum. Many times, installers will needlessly call to the customer's attention small problems that are easily fixed and should never be mentioned. They should simply fix the problem or call you. It is your job to discuss changes or problems with the customer, not theirs.

Fabric orders:

- When checking stock on a desired fabric, let the supplier know at that time how much yardage you think you will need. Go ahead and reserve the fabric at the same time. Most fabric suppliers will hold the fabric for you for a period of time, allowing you time to complete the sale and get the fabric ordered.

- Include cut lengths. If you don't, fabric suppliers will hold your order until they get a shipment of the particular fabric. They may have matching cuts of fabric available that will work, if they know what your cut lengths are.

- If you are matching fabric to paint, wait until the fabric comes in or order at least a half yard of fabric to match to the paint. Sample book-size swatches are not large enough to accurately use for matching paint.

- For fabric orders that need to be cross-matched with other fabrics or the same fabric, submit the original PO number and a cutting of the fabric to be matched. Give the supplier something to go on when matching the color. Although they may have attached a sample to your original PO record, don't count on it.

- On fabric drop shipments, most suppliers will attach a cutting of the shipped fabric to your PO Immediately verify, by pulling the original sample book, that the fabric shipped is the correct one — before the workroom cuts the fabric. This is your responsibility. Once the fabric is cut, you are out of luck.

- Make sure that all arriving merchandise is properly side marked with the customer's name and PO number when it arrives. Don't procrastinate until you forget who ordered what before you do this. As items arrive, check their quality and their side mark.

- COM (customer's own material) fabrics also require work orders sent to the workrooms to tell them whose fabrics they are and what they are to do with it. Do not send anything unmarked to the workroom; it will be lost in a sea of fabric.

Accounts payable:

- Always note what purchase orders are being paid for. Keep the bookkeeping simple and straight for both sides by simply making note of the PO numbers.

Returns:

- Make all returns promptly. Let the supplier know why you are returning the item.

Money flow problems:

Do not keep your suppliers waiting to be paid. They will wreck your credit for you. If you can't pay in full, make a partial payment and work with their credit department.

Your Interior Design Library

To quickly find information, catalogues, articles, government regulation, and various types of samples, you need to have a organized area to use as your library. You should to be able to put your hands on samples and information in just a few seconds. With this type of business, it's a constant onslaught of material arriving daily to sift through, toss out, and store. Samples come in all sizes, shapes, and types. There isn't a lot of consistency from one manufacturer to the next. Once you select areas to store the various information and samples, remember to put the items back in the same spot each time.

Streamline the amount of sources you do business with. If in doubt, toss it out! You can quickly waste lots of time finding and cutting out discontinued fabric samples. Excessive samples also quickly fill up shelves and file cabinets with needless, never-to-be-used, and sometimes expensive samples.

For each fabric category have a low, medium, and high price group to choose from. When you give most of your business to only several suppliers, you receive better service from them. And you will easily be able to stay abreast of what is available and what is discontinued.

Keep all like items together. Use shelves for books, wallpaper books, magazines, and catalogues. Use file cabinets for loose-leaf items and thinner catalogues. Use notebooks for price lists, noting whether they are cost prices or retail prices. Store cost price lists in a separate notebook of like items so the customer cannot see them. Notebooks can also be used for thinner catalogues and loose-leaf pages that are frequently used. Use shelves and hooks for carpet samples; hooks for fabric samples; and file cabinets for odd items such as mini-blind samples. Streamline the amount of samples you require and go through them frequently to discard discontinued samples and note their position in the library. If you choose to, you may want to cross-reference and catalogue exactly where each item is stored. This will be very time consuming. Depending on how many people use your library, it may be necessary to do so.

Contact Emerling & Company/CALHOOK™, 574 Weddell Dr. #9, Sunnyvale, CA 94089, (800) 422-4665, for a *free* catalogue of reasonably priced sample-hanging and sample organizational products to help organize your samples.

Purchase the *Apple Chart,* a cross reference of fabric sources for items that you are having difficulty obtaining or for items it is necessary to reselect. Rather than spend more time working with the customer to now "sell" her on another fabric and chance losing the order, just purchase the fabric from another source. The *Apple Chart* is available through Touch of Design. See the order blank in the back of this book.

Interior Design Resources

Resources for interior designers are arranged into four categories.

Backgrounds:
- Window treatments
- All types of wall coverings
- Carpets, area rugs, floor coverings
- Miscellaneous surface coverings

Upholstery:
- Sofas and chairs
- Bedspreads and soft accessories

Case goods:
- Cabinets
- Tables
- All types of occasional units

Accessories:
- Wall accessories and hangings
- Lamps and lighting sources
- Table decorations
- Paintings
- Sculptures
- Antiques

COM (Customer's Own Material):
In some instances it can be difficult to accommodate a customer's own material into your design project. You may not know where she got the fabric or other material, what it is composed of, how it will wear, how much it is worth (should it disappear, or become damaged during the project and your company is deemed liable).

Wall Covering and Fabric Samples

When considering wall covering and fabric samples for your studio, plan carefully for what you need and be careful to not overspend. You can quickly end up with multiples of fabrics of the same types and none of other types, and no more money available to buy the needed samples.

Basic fabric samples lines are usually available at no cost to you. Specialty lines and prints are modestly priced. Here are the guidelines to follow when buying a wide variety of samples:

Wall coverings:
- Contemporary — all types
- Traditional
- Country
- Vinyls — solids and textures
- Miscellaneous

Upholstery weight fabrics:
- Corduroys

- Velvets, velveteens

- Casual solids

- Formal solids

- Leathers, suede looks, and vinyls

- Damask and tapestries — small- and large-scale patterns
- Prints — small- and large-scale patterns

- Woven designs — small- and larger-scale patterns

- Stripes — formal and casual

- Plaids

- Geometrics

- Old-fashioned colors, textures, and satins — to match "old" unworn furnishings that customers refuse to replace.

Window treatment and soft accessory fabrics:
- Satins — antique and shiny (full range of colors, fiber contents, price ranges, weights)

- Moires — plain, patterned, several weights, full range of colors

- Jacquards and damasks — variety of patterns, colors, tone on tones, multicolored effects, shiny to dull

- Satin prints — variety of patterns and colors, contemporary to traditional

- Lightweight velvets, velveteens, suedes

- Multi-purpose solids — shiny and dull, full range of colors, weights, price ranges, fiber contents, weaves, patterns, and stripes

- Casement solids, textures, stripes — variety of weaves, colors

- Casement open weaves — variety of weaves, colors, tone-on-tones, multi-color weaves

- Cotton and cotton blend prints — all types from small to large, country to contemporary

- Old-fashioned colors, textures, and satins — for customers with "old" furniture and wall coverings that they refuse to replace (because they are barely worn) but want to match up to new draperies

Sheers:
- 47"/48" — ninons to batistes with and without texture

- Seamless — all types from ninons to batistes with and without texture, heavier seamless fabrics, bordered effects, laces, patterns, prints

- Laces — all types, wide range of colors, patterns from small to large, contemporary to traditional

- **Solids** — smooth, slubbed, striped, woven in patterns

- **Prints** — all types from contemporary to traditional, small to large, tone-on-tone

- **Textures** — fine to heavier textures

- **Stripes** — wide variety of color, wide to narrow stripes, shiny and dull

- **Novelty sheers** — range of textures, patterns, colors

Linings:
- **Sateens**

- **Roclon**

- **Thermal suede**

- **Blockout**

Quilt patterns:
- **Various bedspread quilting patterns**

Carpet and Floor Covering Samples

Carpet samples:
- **Cut pile** — all weights, pile heights, shiny to dull, wide range of pricing and colors

- **Patterned** — all weights, pile heights, shiny to dull, wide range of pricing and colors

- **Berbers** — variety of patterns, fiber contents, pricing, weight, colors

- **Level loop** — all weights, pile heights, shiny to dull, wide range of pricing and colors

- **Frieze** — all weights, pile heights, shiny to dull, wide range of pricing and colors

- **Old-fashioned colors and textures** — for customers with "old" furniture, wall coverings, draperies, and floor coverings that they refuse to replace (because they are barely worn) but want to match up to new carpet

Floor covering samples:
- **Ceramic tile** — variety of patterns, sheens, pricing, sizes, colors

- **Marble** — variety of patterns, sheens, pricing, types, colors

- **Wood** — variety of styles, colors, finishes, types of wood, pricing, weights

- **Vinyls** — carry several lines. Have at least a sample of the different qualities of the types available, and show the customer the line from the manufacturer's book. They can go elsewhere if necessary to see the sample.

Showroom Arrangement

Create a sales atmosphere by the way you design your showroom space. Customers like clean, well-organized spaces that will help them make easy buying decisions. If you have a clean, organized showroom this projects to the customer that you are a stable company that will probably service them, should something go wrong.

Consider the layout of your showroom. Each product category should have its own clearly defined section in the showroom. Within each category, each product should be merchandised by its type. For example, all antique satin fabrics should be in the same section, all printed fabrics should be another, etc.

Products should be displayed so that the lowest are in front (easy to see) and the center of the showroom and the taller products are against the walls or closer to the walls. Customers will have unobstructed views of all available product categories.

Use your basic design principles when designing the layout of the showroom. Everything should appear symmetrical and balance one another as a whole, and within each product category.

Next determine how the traffic pattern should flow through the space. With large areas, create circular aisles that can lead the client past all of the product categories.

Signs should be displayed uniformly in the same colors, style, and at the same height over each product category area and should identify the product category displayed. The signs should be professionally designed and should be visible from the front entrance to your studio.

Signs for current sales in progress should be displayed in front display windows and in the their department, in addition to being placed on an easel in your front entry way.

It is a good idea to name the item (e.g. verosal shades, pleated drapery, balloon top treatment) and price out displays and products so that clients have a realistic idea of what they are looking at in cost. No one wants to repeatedly ask how much each item is.

Disguise labels by using your company name on samples whenever you can. Do what you can to keep your customer from comparing your prices.

Lighting should be natural or similar to natural, if possible. It doesn't appear very professional to keep hauling the samples to the windows or outside to see colors.

Samples for Sales Calls

Hauling tons of samples in your automobile is never an easy task to organize. There are a few tricks of the trade to help you get organized:

● Only haul samples you show frequently. Take all others only when needed and remove them from your car as soon as possible.

● Start by measuring your car trunk.

● Purchase plastic bins or very sturdy cardboard boxes, available from moving companies, to fit as economically into the allotted space as possible.

● Sort all fabrics and other samples into like categories and piles.

● Place fabric samples standing on end within the cartons to take up the least amount of space and the least amount of time when sorting through them.

● Place boxes in their allotted areas in the trunk. You will soon know by memory where your carton of a certain category should go.

● When you go on a call, sort through the fabrics and pull out the fabric samples.

● After the sales call, while still at the client's job site, quickly sort the samples into their appropriate categories and place them back into their cartons for easy access for the next sales call.

● Go through the samples monthly and remove all discontinued items.

Part 22

Commercial Design Jobs

Commercial businesses need to create an image with their interiors. Most businesses need to attract the public, or promote a comfortable, efficient working environment for their employees. Form follows function with commercial design jobs. The interior has to be functional physically and psychologically as well as aesthetically. Traffic patterns, layouts, color schemes, lighting selections, materials used, workable window coverings, the correct selection of fiber contents, signage, graphic works, art forms, floor covering, and wall covering selections are some of the many factors to be considered.

The designer may be brought in to consult with the architect at the beginning stages for her design input, or may be consulted with only after the windows have been poorly placed, the layout is unfunctional, hard-to-work-with architectural elements are already in place, and a poor color scheme has been selected.

Commercial interior design projects may range in size from a very small retail store to huge projects. Commercial jobs tend to be less personal to management you are negotiating with, and may be very competitive among the companies invited to bid on the job. The management board involved in the decision-making process of who to select for the job may take one company's higher priced ideas and have the lower bidder incorporate them into their plans, not paying anything to the company with the original ideas.

Discussions with the board are usually very formal and impersonal and very detailed. Everything must be recorded clearly in writing and not open to misinterpretations. You must clearly understand *what it is* the company wants, and they must clearly understand what you are suggesting and proposing to do, to solve their design problems or desires.

To reach potential commercial customers, part of your marketing efforts must be directed to the commercial area. Advertise in business magazines, business newspapers, and trade journals. Review the areas of the newspaper where permits are being taken out for remodeling, building, or through the county recorder's office. List brokers also can supply you with up-to-date information on permits at a nominal fee. Network with general contractors and architects, and find out the information first hand, early on.

Communication and professional sales ability are very important in negotiating with commercial clients. You must be very professional, knowledgeable, accommodating, easy to get along with, and easy to work with.

You must be willing to review the job repeatedly, while focusing on the smallest of details, doing the paperwork carefully and accurately, doing the layout boards, and making repeated presentations.

The commercial client must feel that your company is one they can count on to do a quality job and one that will follow up on all aspects of the job, keep proposed delivery dates, make correct and appropriate selections, and a company with a good reputation regarding business practices with other commercial clients.

When a business purchasing agent contacts you for your products and/or services, it is almost always because the business has a need for what you may offer. Normally, a commercial client will get several bids. Your ideas, color scheme, sample selections, fabrics, and styling will be compared with other design professionals asked to bid on the job. You must be able to offer them the right selections at the right price, while winning them over with your personality. They have to *want* to give the job to you and your company. Otherwise, they will love your ideas and selections and give them to another designer with the great personality.

These are sophisticated buyers. They may have definite knowledge about the product that they need to buy. Companies pay the purchasing agent to research the needed item and make sound decisions. They may know more about your competitor's products than you do. These types of consultations need to be prepared carefully, ahead of time. The designer going out on these calls may need to take down the measurements and write down the information, and go back and do research on the required products and the price to charge, before giving the purchasing agent the information and pricing. The purchasing agent will want to get very technical with you on all the details — his or her job is riding on making accurate decisions each time — and he or she is practiced and usually quite good at coming to decisions.

If you are catering to the commercial business market, design and prepare detailed estimates, advertisements, and brochures just for this market, separate from the ones you supply for your average consumer. The purchasing agent will review part of the supplied written material before reaching a decision on purchasing from you and your company.

Almost all proposed purchases to businesses must be reviewed by committees. It is difficult to get committees to agree on anything — especially when it comes to interior design. Everyone has different taste. You need to find out who is *really* in charge of making a decision on the purchase of the proposed goods. If you are not able to do this, realize that the purchasing agent is not really that high up the corporate ladder. She may act like she is going to buy, but whether the executive officer above her gives her the go ahead for the order, is another story. Usually the larger the job, the more people involved, and the harder it will be to come to an agreement about your products and services.

Request that the business considering you for the job supply you with brochures or other information for you to learn more about their company. The fact that you are willing to do this will impress them and show that you are willing to put out extra effort in supplying them with products and services to meet their needs.

Sometimes you will be the only one bidding on a job and making a presentation. The board of directors or business owner will be working with you to focus their desires for the project. Other times you will be one of a few bidding for the same project and presenting design ideas.

Before devoting much time and energy, find out what the company's reputation is with dealing with other businesses, contractors, and architects. If you hear negative comments, pass on the job.

Some commercial clients (and residential clients) may just want to use your ideas and give them to another less-expensive design source. They may be required to get several bids for the job, but already know who they want to do the job. When you are asked to leave behind your design boards and job-related materials (not product written materials), diplomatically tell the client or board that *unless* they are willing to pay you for all costs incurred thus far, you will be unable to leave them behind. Tell them that you will be happy to present them and review them again at a later date when they are closer to a decision.

Try not to be taken advantage of. Teach your client what professionalism and integrity *are*. Always be professional and project a businesslike demeanor with all of your dealings with the client.

If you do not find out the required information listed below at the review, you will probably make two presentations. At the first presentation, you may find out that although they like your ideas, they are not suited to their needs.

The architect may also be negotiating and making bids to the client at the same time. This may hinder you negotiations and cause you to have to make changes as the architect makes changes in his or her plans.

Determine how the client is to be charged for the proposed products and services. The scope of products and services provided and the client's budget are the deciding factors on what to charge. As you gain more experience, you will also develop a basis for charging for fees. Will you be doing the purchasing and be providing the funds?

Estimate how much time is required to complete the various phases of the job. If you know that you are one of *many* to bid on the job, do not go all out in spending a lot of time on the proposed job presentation. A few sketches, with samples and pictures of proposed ideas with a financial projection of cost, are all that is required. If you are the firm selected to do the job, then follow up with sketches, boards, and exact costs for the job. Don't divulge any great original ideas if the client isn't paying you for the presentation. Let them know there *is more*, but unless you are selected for the job or paid for your ideas, you won't be sharing them.

Since you are probably only making a presentation and not finalizing the sales agreement, you may or may not want to proceed and work up a letter of agreement or sales contract. The client may not want to spend more time on the project or presentations. They may be ready the day of the presentation to sign the contract.

If the client projects to you an unreasonable installation date, speak up and say so. Never commit to an unrealistically short installation period. Do not let yourself get talked into signing penalty clauses for late installations. You are at the mercy of trucking companies, vendors, distributors, fabricators, and installers. You may be able to guarantee your end of the job, but not anyone else's. If the client insists on penalty clauses for late installations, the designer should insist on *immediate* signing of the sales agreement. You should still include disclaimers for disasters and failures of contractors or suppliers beyond the designer's control.

Should one supplier slow down your delivery, select from another. Carefully select your sources and fabricators. Will they be able to supply a large quantity of items in a limited period of time?

If the client holds up the order by not promptly signing purchase orders, and then signs and wants immediate delivery, point out to them how they have delayed the job and hold them accountable when they point the finger at you for late deliveries.

Commercial customers are used to paperwork, and expect and prefer very explicit sales agreements of what you are going to do and provide for them. Responsibilities of both parties need to clearly be spelled out. Commercial contracts are the same as residential agreements in content, but also list penalty clauses.

The sales agreement or contract will be reviewed by several people including the company's attorney. Your degree of professionalism and business practices will be obvious to them at this point. Spend time thinking through every detail of the job and clearly covering all the fine points of the job.

Most residential design firms only occasionally get involved in commercial projects. In addition to understanding all aspects of the job, the designer must also understand the proposed budget of the client, how to charge for the job, what other people involved in the job will be paid for their work, etc.

Commercial projects are generally more complicated and usually much larger than residential design jobs, and take a longer period of time to complete. As with residential jobs, if something can go wrong along the way, it will! **These are the necessary steps involved in obtaining commercial jobs, after you have marketed and advertised with the correct media to generate interest in this area:**

Initial meeting with the client or board of directors (determine the following):

- *Who* are the architects and contractors involved in the project and *how* is their working relationship with the commercial client?

- How *soon* does the design project need to be completed? Are they flexible with industry situations that arise?

- What do they *expect* from you and your company?

- Have them give a thorough analysis of what they really *want*. Listen to what they say regarding color preferences, size of areas, how many areas, locations, and orientations.

- What is their *approximate budget* and how much money do they have available to complete the job? You must get an idea of their budget so you know what quality and amount of decorating products and services you can provide. If you don't find out the approximate available budget, you will probably miss the mark with the bid and either bid to simplistic with common materials or will overbid with expensive and higher quality products. Find out what the other competitors will be bidding on and in what price range.

- Show pictures of previous jobs, product samples, and pictures of proposed ideas and design looks. Showing pictures and tossing out ideas will determine if you are on the right track with the customer.

- Determine *who* will procure purchases. Will you be furnishing the decorating elements or will the client do the initial purchasing with their own money? If the client doesn't have a purchasing department or prefers that the design firm do the purchasing, ensure that the company is creditworthy before proceeding.
- Will you be supplying all work orders and specifications for the design project?

- Will you need to provide layout boards? How much shopping will it take you to provide all of the required decorating products?

- Do you have the necessary installers and subcontractors to complete the job? Do you have the extra time necessary to supervise the installations?

- Do you have the storage space to store decorating products as they arrive?

- Get the measurement of the job site and an analysis of the furnishings they are going to keep.

- Determine what representative of the company will you be working with. Do you think you can get along well with that person?

- Make a check of the business's references (provide a credit application) and a credit check of the commercial company. Determine early on if the company is a sound one with a good credit history.

- Decide whether your company can handle the size and scope of the job. You will need to handle large responsibilities, hard work, many hours, and probably need a large cash outlay.

- Is the distance to the job feasible? If it is far away, you will incur extra long-distance telephone charges, travel, and additional time expenses for yourself and job support personnel.

After the initial meeting:

- Acquire and review the architectural plans and blueprints for the design area.

- Discuss the architectural plans with others involved in the project, e.g. architects, contractors, etc.

- Develop a rough space plan and furniture layout.

- Determine availability of the necessary materials and goods that are required.

- Can you finish the job within the allotted time frame?

- Make preliminary selection of samples, color scheme, products, furniture and styling selections, estimate, and job pricing.

- Final determination of all charges for products and services. Prepare a financial overview.

- Preparation of sample and layout boards, renderings, models, slides, pictures of ideas, and other visual props.

- Prepare a written description of the scope of the design project proposed by you and your company.

Design presentation:

- Your design presentation to the company board of directors.

- Financial proposal of *all* projected costs to complete the job. Have an accounting of the budget, show how fees were arrived at, and show all costs for the proposed job.

- The board will probably expect you to leave all of your design boards and other materials behind for their review. If they are covering all of your costs for the proposal and presentation, then *do* leave your materials behind. If they are not paying for your presentation, *do not* leave your materials and design ideas behind to be copied by a less-expensive company. Leave the financial proposal for them to review along with a written overview of what you plan for the project. A written overview will help keep your ideas current in their minds.

After you are selected and approved for the job:

- Wait for the board of directors' approval before your company goes ahead with the job.

- Draw up the sales agreement or contract. For larger jobs, have an attorney review the contract before submitting it to the client or board of directors. Make sure all terms outlined are legal and describe the payment plan. Attempt to procure payment of items before they are delivered or installed (this will not relieve you of any responsibility should a problem arise).

- Design drawings for built-in cabinets and other custom furnishings.

- Selection of accessories, artwork, and extra details.

- Product specifying and purchasing.

- Preparation of work orders to subcontractors, fabricators, and tradespeople.

- Decisions on when the different phases will be installed.

- Job supervision.

- Final details completed.

- Final walk-through with the client.

- Customer service after the job is completed.

While bidding on commercial jobs, you must keep your regular advertising efforts in full force to keep smaller design jobs coming in. If you don't consistently market for the smaller jobs, when the big jobs are completed the money from the high-profit small jobs will stop flowing. Even if you are extremely busy, keep the marketing momentum going.

Bidding on Jobs

Federal, state, and local agencies and many public company are required by law to obtain comparative bids on projects before they make a decision on *who* will do the job for them. Many commercial businesses will also get a number of bids before making their decision on which firm to give the job to.

Nongovernmental agencies will send out invitations to bid to their approved "bid list" or select a group of design firms and vendors to shop for their required products. To qualify for a listing on a bid list, your company needs to be pre-qualified with the ability to do the job. When companies work off of a bid list or select a few design firms to contact, they will tend to pay a higher price than if they open the project up and invite anyone interested to bid on the project.

The object of getting bids is to find the company that will provide "the most for the least." Many products will appear the same to the unfamiliar eye, but be vastly different in quality. Most companies who use the bid process go with the lowest estimate if they can. The danger is, the original design concept and product quality can easily get lost and passed over during the process.

For design firms, bidding is a *very* time consuming and expensive process. Review the commercial section above for the necessary steps to getting a project approved.

Should a rejected bidder feel that they were unjustifiably rejected and another company was awarded the project unfairly, the potential for being called into and named in a lawsuit along with the client is very real.

Bidding Terms

Bid award notification	The method of notifying bidders of their successful or nonsuccessful bids. This is usually done by a letter. The unsuccessful bidders may or may not find out who was the successful bidder or the amount of the successful bid.
Bid bond	The up-front bond (subject to forfeiture if the company doesn't perform) required by the design firm or vendor to guarantee that if they are awarded the project, they will sign the contract. The amount of the bid bond is usually 5 percent to 10 percent of the total project. Bid bonds for the design firm or vendor who receive the contract are held for a period of time after the contract is signed. Unsuccessful bidders quickly receive their bid bonds back.
Bid closing date	Date after which it *is too late* to withdraw a bid.
Bid form	Document usually in a letter form that a firm or vendor summits a proposal or bid on.

Bond forms   Legal documents that are used to bind the design firm or vendor to perform all conditions of the contract as agreed.

Bid opening   The time and date the bids will be opened. Governmental agencies and public companies are required to open the bids in a public area where all bidders can be present. Private companies are not bound by the law to open their bids publicly. You may or may not find out what competitors bid for the same job.

Cash on completion   The method by which governmental agencies may use to pay for smaller jobs. If you won't work with them on cash-on-completion, they may take their business, elsewhere. If the job is large, break it up into small segments (separate sales agreements) and have the agency provide you with purchase orders and numbers to pay you as the job is completed.

Closed bid opening   Opening and comparison of bids by private businesses, not open to the public.

Earnest money   The same as a bid bond. Up-front money from the design firm or vendor they will forfeit if they are awarded the project and do not follow through and sign the contract.

Government contract number   A number pre-approving your firm for work by the government. If you do not have a government contract number, notify the government representative you are working with of this fact when they solicit you to bid. The governmental agency can get a waiver to negotiate with your company. Obtaining a waiver is not difficult and they are familiar with doing it. Governmental agencies and other corporations will provide a purchase order number and purchase order.

Instructions to bidders   Provides all essential information and the required bid format to use to prepare and present a bid. If every bidder prepares and layouts their bids in the same format, pricing is much easier to for the client to compare against other bidders.

Within the instructions to bid will be information on drawings and specifications. Refers to your working drawings and plans, and written specifications for products, materials, and any required construction work.

Invitation to bid   When a governmental agency or public company needs a project completed, an "invitation to bid" is published in newspapers. An invitation to bid describes the products and services desired, the scope of the job, how to proceed if a party is interested in making a bid, and the bid closing and opening dates.

Labor and material payment bond   A bond required by the successful bidder to guarantee that all of the labor and materials they have contracted for will be paid in the event the bidder awarded the contract defaults.

Performance bond   The successful bidder must guarantee that they will perform the contract as agreed. In order to do this, a bond (may be as high as 100 percent of the contract value) is purchased from a surety company for a small percentage of the required amount. This is another expense the design firm must consider when placing the bid. The bond is returned after the contract is executed.

Request for bid or quote   Also known as "request for proposal." Forms used by governmental agencies to request bids for their projects.

Request for proposals   Also known as "request for bid or quote." Forms used by governmental agencies to request bids for their projects.

Security bond   If this type of bond is required, security bond facts are usually stated initially in the invitation to bid. If the security bond is sizeable and must be held for a lengthy period of time, you may not be in a financial position to participate in the bidding process.

Part 23

Paperwork, Order Expediting, Shipping, and Installation

The interior design business requires a large amount of paperwork. The efforts you make in selling a customer on a design job are only as good as what you record on the contract or sales agreements, purchase orders or work orders. If you rush and *forget* to record vital information, you will pay for it when you remake the item or with angry customers facing job delays. Paperwork is your means of communication with customers, suppliers and vendors, and installers. Suppliers, vendors, fabricators and installers *all* have to determine what you want. If you are unclear on your paperwork and if they don't call you, they will *guess* — sometimes incorrectly, at your expense. If you delay the order, the customer won't be back. And you lose any possible referrals you might have gotten from a happy customer. Do the paperwork correctly right from the start.

Always be prompt in handing paperwork. The longer you delay, the longer the job is going to take to complete. It is a good idea to wait the three-day, right-to-cancel period before going ahead and completing the paperwork, as many customers exercise their right to cancel. See the section in this book on door-to-door home solicitation agreements for more information.

Use a pen and press hard when writing out specs. Include pictures or rough illustrations of what you are requesting for fabricators and installers.

Note: if your studio coordinator has nothing else to do, have him or her write out as much information on your paperwork as possible. *You* must fill in the vital information on the specs. But he or she should be able to record repetitive information such as name, address, etc. Doing this will save you *lots* of time.

Purchase Orders

Purchase orders are used to order all merchandise from vendors, suppliers, distributors, manufacturers, and other tradespeople. Purchase orders (or POs) are also your written record of what has been ordered, what has been received, and what has been installed or delivered at the job site. Once the goods have been installed and signed off by the customer (installed or delivered in satisfactory condition), your firm may then bill the customer for the goods. The PO should be used to compare the price you were charged by the vendor, against the price you were quoted or took from the price list. Look for discrepancies and mistakes.

Design your purchase orders so they contain categories for all pertinent information required to expedite correct delivery of the ordered merchandise. Most suppliers will not usually fill the order until they receive a *written* purchase order by mail or fax. While they do make a note of telephone orders, they know that duplication easily happens when a written PO arrives for the phone order.

Multiple items for the same manufacturer and the *same customer* should be included on the same purchase order. All customers must have separate POs for job tracking. For items of multiple fabrics with various cut lengths, different drop shipping destinations, or specialized instructions, use separate POs to avoid *needless confusion and problems*.

Always order an extra yard of fabric and a foot or two extra carpet or flooring for problems that may arise. It is hard to get an exact match should you need it a couple of months later. If the installers or the workroom don't use the extra yardage, give it to the customer for possible future mishaps or accidents. **Smaller firms will need the POs designed with three copies, which are distributed in this way:**

● **Copy one** is mailed to the vendor or manufacturer.

- **Copy two** is placed in numerical order in the open order file. By placing POs in order, you can easily see which ones are straggling behind.

- **Copy three** is stapled to the corresponding work order and placed in the client's file.

  Larger firms usually need the POs designed with two additional copies, which are distributed in this way:

- **Copy four** is sent to the warehouse to show what is going to be shipped, received, and an approximate ship date. The warehouse is able to prepare for the shipment and has paperwork to compare to the shipper's when the goods arrive. They can also use their copy for the customer to sign off for deliveries.

- **Copy five** is given to the installer, who can make sure he has all necessary hardware and supplies that he needs to provide to complete the job.

The top of the PO:
- Your firm's logo, name, billing address, delivery address, and telephone number.

- A numbering system for the POs. Use them in numerical order to maintain control over what has been ordered. Make a note for POs that have been ruined or rewritten.

- A space for the supplier's name and address.

- A space for the "ship to" address. This may be your shipping address, the job site, or a drop-ship address.

- Additional shipping information — for writing in required dates, who is responsible for payment of the shipping charges, desired shipper, hold-until dates, etc.

- Side mark or "tag" information. This includes customer's name and work order number.

The body of the PO:
- Quantity of the items ordered.

- Inventory number and/or name of the goods. Include the color number and name if applicable.

- Description of the goods ordered. Write the description as it is written on the sample, in the price sheets, or in the manufacturer's catalogue.

- An indication whether fabrics can be railroaded (fabric goods fabricated crosswise rather than vertically).

- What are the cut lengths of the fabric (the manufacturer may have some matching lengths they can work around to quickly supply you the order).

- Net or cost price of the goods. Compare this price against what you are billed from the vendor later.

- Additional information: include a couple of lines for additional information you would like to include. Note what cut lengths are in case of fabric, request an acknowledgement to verify receipt of the order with an expected ship date.

- Signature of who the PO was prepared by.

Note: if possible, attach a photocopy of the item (in the case of fabrics, a swatch) to be ordered to your store copy of the PO. Deliveries take time and clients forget what they have ordered.

Work Orders

Always use the correct work order for the item to be ordered. Have work orders made up or get them from the fabricator doing the work. If you are making a bedspread, use a bedspread work order. If you are ordering drapes for fabrication, use a drapery work order. And so on.

Mail work orders to fabricators and labor suppliers the same date you mail the PO. They also need to plan ahead and know what they are to supply in the future. If you have *any* questions about a term, on how to plan or measure for *anything* listed below, refer to: *Secrets of Success for Today's Interior Designers and Decorators.*

- On work orders you record *exactly* how the item is to be fabricated. Record what the customer wants.

- Use a separate work order for each labor supplier. The installer gets a copy of the work order for the goods he or she is to install, so don't make a separate copy, unless it is a service request for goods already installed that need extra work. If drapery is being fabricated at one workroom, and the blinds for the same room are being fabricated at the blinds supplier, always place different sources on different work orders.

- If the same labor supplier or fabricator will be working on several unlike items (different in material or fabric), always place these on separate work orders. Otherwise, you run the definite risk of getting the items switched or reversed and made up in the wrong fabric or application and size. It does take longer to write them separately, but its worth it to avoid the problems and costs you will incur if they get mixed up.

- Workrooms usually supply buckram, drapery hooks, cording, weights, and webbing.

Information to include in all work orders:
- Designer or decorator's name.

- Customer's name, address, and phone numbers.

- Cross-reference all other purchase order numbers or work orders involved with a specific work order for the item being fabricated. This does not mean unlike items in the same room. Other items that need to be cross-referenced are those made of the same fabric, or items that require several applications. For example, say you are having fabric quilted at one vendor and shipped to the workroom for fabrication. You have also ordered trim for the bedspread from another source that is to be drop shipped to the workroom. You would include the work order number to have the fabric quilted and the source, the PO number to purchase the fabric and the source, and the PO number for the trim and the source.

- Your company name, address, and phone number.

- Sales agreement number.

- Sale date.

- Approximate promised delivery date or installation date.

- Purchase order number and source.

- Labor costs.

- Quantity.

- Fabric or material name and number and color name and number.

- Pattern repeat size.

- Number of yards ordered, if applicable.

- Selling price per yard, if applicable.

- Total selling price of fabricated item.

- Freight costs.

- Room that the items go in.

- Special instructions. Be specific.

- Map page number, grid letter, and number of the applicable Thomas Bros. map to help your installer find the location. Include nearest large cross streets.

Drapery:

- Lining source, type, color, number, selling price per yard, and total selling price.

- Number of design, if the workroom has supplied you with a group of pictures of numbered styles.

- Number of pairs or panels.

- Measurements for offset pair.

- Center open or one-way-right or one-way-left pull (C,R,L).

- Number of widths. Fullness desired.

- Note if you want balance pleating.

- If you want a different size than standard four-inch hems and headers, say so.

- Finished widths of draperies including overlaps and returns. Find out how the workroom you are using for fabrication wants this written out. Some fabricators like a complete bracket-to-bracket measurement with the overlaps and returns included, while others prefer the face width +6, +12, +16, etc. When you write them out separately, it is easy for the workroom to spot a mistake. They tend to notice that you said the returns were 3 ½", but are adding +16. They call and ask, catching a mistake before it occurs, saving everyone time and money.

- Cut length.

- Finished length.

- Return allowance (sides of drapery that return back to the wall).

- Lined or unlined. Type and source of lining, color, workroom to supply or PO for ordered goods, yardage ordered.

- Type of style: ruffled, cafe, pinch pleated, rod pocket (RP), rod pocket top and bottom (RTB), shirred (2,3,4 cord).

- Rod pocket size (depth).

- Header size (depth).

- Hook set or tab size.

- Flat or fan fold the finished drapery.

- Trim type, placement, source, number, color, yards ordered or to be fabricated. If the trim is to be fabricated out of fabric, note the PO number.

- Total selling price of fabricated drapery, without hardware, and installation.

- Cost price of the drapery.

- Tieback quantity, size and width, style, fabric, trim information, PO and source if the fabric is different from the drapery, and method of mounting.

Top treatments (can be placed on the drapery work order if the top treatment is made of the *same* fabric as the drapery):

- *Inside* measurements for cornices and hard-boxed mounted treatments. Allow for sufficient clearance over the bracket-to-bracket hardware measurement — usually one-inch clearance on each side, to clear the hardware.

- Bracket-to-bracket width. **Make a note** if this is a wall-to-wall (exact), not-to-exceed measurement.

- Face depth of the top treatment.

- Short length.

- Long length.

- Trim type, placement, source, trim number, color, yards ordered or to be fabricated. If the trim is to be fabricated out of fabric, note the fabric PO number.

- Number of yards of face goods ordered.

- Note if the item should be railroaded or not railroaded.

- Lined or unlined. Type and source of lining, color, workroom to supply or PO for ordered goods, yardage ordered.

- What is the top treatment to be mounted on? Who is to supply boards and hardware? Workroom, installer, or PO source and number. Record information here and also list under installation.

- Labor charge for fabrication.

- Selling price of the top treatment.

- Cost price of the top treatment.

Installation section (list out in same order and number the same as all items listed above. The installer will know which item the information corresponds to):

- Hardware quantity, number, color, selling price, and cost price. **Note** if the installer is to supply the hardware or who the source is and PO number.

- Installation selling price and cost price, item by item.

- **Special instructions:** Tell the installer what he is going to do. Spell it out. If there is existing hardware to remove, tell him so he can allow time to do it. Let him know if he is restringing hardware, has missing parts from existing treatments, the placement of treatment, etc.

- If the customer has refused to replace existing hardware and you are not sure if the existing hardware is reusable, have the installer bring out replacement hardware and a sales slip for the customer to sign with the hardware prices already filled in.

- Number of supports required. One support for every four feet is the rule of thumb.

- Make a note if the installation will be tile or concrete so the installer brings necessary tools (drill bits).

- Any tieback holders or special tieback hardware.

Hard window treatments:

- Inside or outside bracket width measurement (IB or OB). Note if an allowance has or has not been taken.

- Inside or outside length measurement.

- Type of fabric, material, color name, and finish.

- Valance, if desired.

- Special head rails, if desired.

- Placement. Where is it to be mounted. How far up, over, extensions. Hangs to sill, apron, floor, etc.

- Projection.

- Ladder and cord colors.

- Striped or duotone.

- Cord lift (right or left).

- Wand side — tilt (right or left).

- Wand or cord length.

- Hold-down brackets or chain.

- One-way pull to right or left or center open (C, R, L).

- Any inserts in head rails.

- Selling price.

- Cost price.

- Specify any nonstandard fabrics, fabrics to be inserted, and their source and PO number.

Client's Folder

Create a client folder for each customer you place orders for. The folder provides all information and specifics about the job. Information in the folder includes all work sheets, contract or sales agreement, all POs, work orders, pictures, and samples.

On the exterior of the folder, keep an accounting record of the job, job tracking, and correspondence information. By keeping this information, you always know what is owed on the job, what has been paid, what items are overdue, what items have been received, any problems, and what has been discussed with the customer.

Design and print folders with the following information across the top of the folder:
- Customer's name, address, home telephone number, work telephone number, sale date, decorator's name, and total selling price.

Across the front of the folder in a column format, in this order:
- Date, purchase order number, supplier, item, receiving date, selling price of the item, cost of item, freight costs, work order number, labor vendor for work order, labor completion date, labor selling price, labor cost, installer, installation date, installation selling price, installation cost, price adjustments (due to problems that arise, to keep customer from canceling), sales tax, balance of account, payment received, and date of payment.

   Take the above information and transfer it to a **purchase journal**. A sales journal is a journal record made up for each vendor of goods or services. As you list information, such as payments received for accounts receivable, and list new items ordered, cross-reference the information to the purchase journal. Keep the purchase journal and the client's folder up to date. Refer to the section in this book on purchase journals.

- **Across the bottom of the front of the folder in column format:** total line for columns with costs and selling prices. You will have totals on all costs, individual selling prices, adjustments, total job selling price, sales tax, amount received from the customer, and amount owed by the customer.

- **Across the back of the body of the folder:** take notes in chronological order by date on customer conversations, problems that arise, solutions to problems, order tracking, any adjustments given, etc.

Order Expediting

The order expeditor may be your studio coordinator, assistant designer, business manager, installations manager, or all of the above. Order expediting is *immediate* following through on purchase orders (POs's) and work orders to ensure that they are completed on schedule. A master sheet (use the back of the client's folder) should be attached to the exterior of the client's file. The master sheet tracks the job; specific progress, problems, and conversations with clients are noted by date on the master sheet.

An order expeditor's job doesn't start until the purchase orders and work orders have been sent to their appropriate destinations. After a PO is sent to its target destination, an *acknowledgement* is sent from the manufacturer or distributor, acknowledging that they have received a PO for the ordered merchandise.

The expeditor compares the information or description on the acknowledgement against the PO in the open order file to ensure that everyone is on the same track with the exact description of the merchandise, quantity, pricing, shipping destination, and the side-mark information. If an item or fabric has been discontinued, you will find out at this point. Any misinformation or discrepancies should immediately be called to the attention of the supplier.

The acknowledgement contains an expected shipping date for the merchandise and method and payment of shipping. The expeditor checks the expected delivery date against the customer's expected delivery date and makes a note if it appears to be running on schedule. The expeditor also examines the method for shipping payment. No one wants her customers to have payment demanded when the design company should be billed. The design firm then bills the client for the shipping.

In the likely event there is a hold up later at the manufacturer or distributor, or if an item has been discontinued, the designer should be immediately informed. The designer will have to decide about re-selecting another similar or identical item from another source. Always keep customers *honestly* apprised at all times of the progress of their orders. Should there be a delay, immediately inform the client. The client may choose to wait for the delayed merchandise, or may choose to re-select.

In the case of re-selecting fabrics, the designer should go immediately to the "*Apple Chart*" and *probably* find another supplier of the same fabric. If this is possible, the client does not need to be informed of a delay, thus posing the very real threat they may cancel their order.

When a re-selection has to be made, inform *everyone* to whom you have sent a copy of the original PO. This includes drop shippers, warehouses, and installers. Send them a corrected copy and state this PO supersedes PO # ___. If you do not inform them, they will be waiting for the original PO to arrive, and will not know what the second PO merchandise is for when it arrives. Fabric can sit in a workroom for months before anyone finds out what to do with it.

Expediters work closely with trucking companies to track shipments from the manufacturer or distributor's factory that are slow in arriving at their destination. At times, the expeditor may have to coordinate quick deliveries of required items. Since the expeditor works closely with orders and shippers, the expeditor should also handle shipping claims and returns with manufacturers. If you use a warehousing service, they should handle freight claims for your company as part of their service.

Freight and Shipping

Generally shipping or freight is handled by the manufacturing company or distributor that you purchased your goods from. Most manufacturers have their own trucks for use for large orders and hire independent trucking companies to ship the smaller orders. On most price lists you will see the term "FOB factory" or "FOB destination." **FOB factory** means free on board from the factory. **FOB destination** means free on board to the destination. In other words, the manufacturer is spelling out his liability and responsibility for the shipped goods.

In the case of FOB factory, the purchaser of the goods is responsible and subsequently *owns* the goods when the goods are loaded into the truck from the manufacturing facility. What this means, is that the designer pays for all transportation costs and accepts the risk of shipping the goods to the design firm.

With FOB destination, the manufacturer is responsible (and still owns the goods until they reach their intended destination) for the risk of transporting the goods to the design firm and is also responsible for payment for the shipping.

Another common term is **FOB factory, freight prepaid**. This term means that the manufacturer is responsible for payment of the freight or shipping, but the purchaser becomes the owner and is responsible for the risk once the goods are loaded in the truck. Rules and regulations and corresponding terms are fully outlined in the Uniform Commercial Code.

A designer should always know how much the shipping will cost before she places an order. Excessive shipping for long distances and heavy weight can quickly eat up any profits. Many design firms also add a small surcharge to the customer's shipping bill to handle paperwork processing. You must recover your costs.

Always state on your PO when you want large items shipped. If you let manufacturers and distributors know when you need the item (even beyond their normal delivery schedule, this may or may not incur an extra warehousing fee from the manufacturer), they will wait and ship it to you when it is more convenient for you to accept delivery. If items are shipped early to their site installation or delivery, you have to provide a storage facility to store them in until they are required.

The supplier or vendor provides a *bill of lading* to the shipper. The bill of lading is a form that lists the contents or the quantity of the shipment. It is imperative that the person in charge of accepting shipments count the pieces that arrive against the shipper's bill of lading. If there are discrepancies in the amount, or *apparent* damaged goods, the discrepancy or the damage should be noted right on the bill of lading, *before* the shipper is allowed to leave the delivery site. Noting discrepancies and damages on the bill of lading ensures your success in recovery of your claim. It is advised to keep a camera ready for instances when damaged goods arrive. Snap the picture in the presence of the truck driver and turn the pictures in *when* you file the report with the shipping company.

A packing list is normally found in a plastic envelope attached to the exterior of one of the items in the shipment. The packing list details the contents and quantity of the shipment. The packing list should always be checked against the items removed from the truck, and compared against the quantity of the goods on the bill of lading. Any difference between the packing list and the bill of lading should be noted on the bill of lading.

Within days of a shipment's arrival you will be invoiced for the shipment of the goods by the trucking company (if the design company is paying the freight bill).

It is convenient to have large heavy items dropped shipped at the installation site, if possible. While trucking companies may or may not charge you extra for deliveries to residential sites, it probably will still be less expensive than having the goods delivered to your studio, housing the merchandise, and then paying for another smaller delivery truck to deliver the goods to the installation site. Unfortunately, a representative of your firm will be forced to wait at the site for the truck to inspect the goods when they arrive. If a representative is not there when damaged goods arrive, your design firm may have to pay to have the goods repaired or replaced without reimbursement. If a representative is present, the damage is immediately noted, and you are protected.

Goods must be immediately inspected upon their arrival. Any damaged exterior cartons or material protecting the goods should be noticed and removed while the shipper is still at the delivery site. If possible, even undamaged exterior cartons and materials should be removed to note any hidden damage or damage not evident from the exterior packaging. Show the damage to the truck driver and make sure it is noted on the bill of lading. Keep the cartons that the damaged item was shipped in. If the damage is extreme, refuse the item and let the trucking company handle the problem. Do not wait and attempt to return the item later to the supplier. The supplier will not readily allow you to return the item after it has been accepted by your firm. You will need to go through a lengthy process, depending on the supplier or manufacturer, of writing them and requesting the return of damaged or incorrect merchandise.

Many suppliers will handle freight claims for you. Select these suppliers for your sources and get rid of some very large headaches. If you use a warehouse to receive your merchandise for you, select one that uses proper procedures for receiving, inspections, and knows how to properly document and file claims for damaged freight.

If you notice *after* the shipper has left the delivery site that you have damaged merchandise, immediately call the shipping company and file a report. The quicker you report the damage, the more likely your recovery for the damages. Make sure that you receive a copy of the shipper's report when they come out to examine the damaged item. For *slightly* damaged items you may feel you just cannot afford the time and the inconvenience of the claim process and have the items repaired yourself. If you reorder damaged merchandise, chances are you will not receive new replacement merchandise for months.

When filing a claim with a shipping company, provide:
- Bill of lading with notations of discrepancies and damage.

- Invoice from the supplier or vendor.

- Photographs of the damage to the item.

- Shipping invoice (should be paid in the interim).

- Inspection report from the shipping carrier.

- Any repairs you have had done and their bills (which you should pay in the interim).

- Any additional costs incurred due to the damaged item such as another shipment of the same item.

Deliveries and Installations

Since it costs you money to deliver or install goods, you must recover your costs from the customer. Even if your design firm has its own truck and crew of installers, the overhead for having them is enormous. You should charge for deliveries with a flat rate to local surrounding areas, or by the hour, or charge an hourly delivery rate, or a door-to-door hourly delivery charge.

When selling very large furniture, or long top treatments, always consider how you are going to deliver the goods and how you will get large items into the house or building. A very large, expensive truck may be necessary. With top treatments, it may be better to select a design that can be fabricated in pieces, assembled, and mounted on boards at the job site.

To save costs on delivery, installations, and billing, coordinate the job so that most of the goods or all of the goods can be delivered and installed at the same time.

Upon delivery, all goods again need to be inspected for damage and their operation demonstrated, if any. Any packaging, cartons, paper, etc., should be immediately removed by the delivery person from the delivery/installation site. All items should be dusted and prepared for viewing by the customer. There are companies available to do minor touch-ups to furniture finishes. Have them come before the customer sees the problem and complains.

As merchandise is received at the customer's site, the merchandise must be signed for by the customer and accounted for. Have the customer sign a copy of the original PO that the merchandise was ordered from. The designer, the truck driver, or the installer can supply a copy to the customer for his or her signature. Make any notes about missing or damaged items right on the PO.

Preassemble anything that can be. You do not want your installers to appear as if they don't know what they are doing. Before arriving at the job site find out how items fit together and what extra parts are needed. For assembled furniture or systems, installation drawings must be supplied to the installer to ensure proper layout and assembly. If the designer is extremely thorough with his or her paperwork, work orders and drawings, especially, and has worked with the installers a number of times, she will probably not be needed at the installation site during the installation. Review *Secrets of Success for Today's Interior Designers and Decorators* for a thorough overview of installations and installers.

Always preview jobs with installers and subcontractors ahead of the installation date or scheduled work to start. Plan ahead for required tools, hardware, and supplies and do any needed research on how to proceed with the job. They may have suggestions for you about how to do the job better and less expensively.

Installers and contractors should always carry on their trucks supplies and equipment to quickly take care of problems that will arise to avoid needless trips and trip charges. All deliverers, installers, and subcontractors must clean and prepare every item they install for the customer's viewing.

Installers should supply you with work orders and POs that were completed the day before. Any further service (incurring extra charges) or additional requests by the customer should be recorded on the work order.

For commercial projects, always inform the building administrator when you will be making major installations or doing major construction. They can help coordinate preparations for keeping employees and visitors out of your way for the required work days.

The day before major installations are planned, check the job site to make sure that it is ready for the installation. You do not want paid workers standing by idly, while the site is readied for the installation.

If at all possible, keep your clients away from the job site during installations. They will slow down the job. Any small problems that arise cannot be hidden or corrected quickly without them knowing about them. Tell them you want them to be surprised and excited by the transformation, and that if they are there during the process, the transformation will lose some of its impact.

Provide all available information on maintenance of new items to the client. Use the manufacturer's recommended tips and suggestions. Any manuals or other information sent with the merchandise should always be left with the client.

Walk-Through

After all installations and deliveries are complete, it is time for the designer to do a walk-through with his or her customer. This the final inspection to make sure that everything specified has been delivered and installed to the design firm's and the customer's satisfaction. This is also an opportune time for the designer to bring other needed design items to the customer's attention. In other words, it's a great time to add on more sales!

Most jobs will require some service after the job is completed. That is the nature of this business. It is a rare occasion when everything will go in perfectly and in the way the customer perceived that it would. Bring some service request forms with you and record what needs to be done to complete the job. The job should not be released for final billing until everything is completed.

Part 24

Customer Service

Quality Sales and Customer Service

Customers are the lifeblood of your business. To grow and stay in business, you need a constant stream of both new customers and repeat customers. You also need to keep your regular (former) customers excited and enthused enough about your business to recommend you to others. To build a loyal customer following, you need to do more than what is required by law. While knowledge about your legal rights and your customers' rights are very important, your main goals should be to build a happy, solid following of customers who won't want to go anywhere else with their business.

After you establish a friendly relationship with a customer, have demonstrated your integrity and your dedication to the quality of your products and services, and have won your customers over to your company, the next sale is easy.

When businesses provide quality customer service, they tend to build a good customer base. Don't lose sight of the fact that people are *individuals with feelings*. People want to be liked, and want to feel that they are valued and respected as a customer. They want to make their purchases from a sales professional whom they trust to do a quality job.

Provide the service that your customer wants. Customers prefer to do business with a warmer person that they can quickly develop rapport with, rather than with a cold, seemingly unfeeling person who may be an expert in the field. If you can get your customer to feel comfortable with you, it is much easier to make that sale. Below are some tips on building rapport with your customer:

- Love the products and services that you provide. When you do, your enthusiasm is contagious to your customers and to your employees.

- Hire capable people. Train all of your employees in all aspects of the business. Make sure that all employees are very capable people. Make your employees want to stay with you by being passionate about your firm, its customers, and the line of products you carry. Give them a bit of freedom to experiment with their own ideas about taking care of customers.

- Listen to everyone. Listen to your customers, competitors, suppliers and employees *all* of the time.

- Track your sales and advertising efforts. Evaluate the amount of sales you have and what your needs are for your goals for the month and the year. Post results constantly for your employees to see where they and the company are in gross sales at regular intervals. Track your advertising efforts. Find out how the customer learned about you. Repeat what works for you and cancel what doesn't.

- Ask your employees for ideas and suggestions. Continuously solicit ideas for improvement from everyone, and attempt to implement them immediately. It is rewarding to make a suggestion and see it put into practice. By attempting to use the idea, you are guaranteeing that ideas and suggestions will keep flowing to you.

- Shop your competition. If you are well known and easily recognizable, then have friends and relatives do it for you. Have these same friends and relatives shop your salespeople also. Then compare notes on the experience with your competitors and with your business. If you let your employees know from the onset that this is what you do, it will keep them on their toes. They won't know if the client they are working with is your Aunt Mary.

- Call several clients weekly. Call customers yourself to find out how they felt about working with your company and your decorator. Was it a positive experience? Do they like what they received? Does the product take care of the initial problem? Were they treated well? Will they come back again in the future for more purchases? Do they have any suggestions on how the experience could have been better?

- Identify and match the communication style of your customers. If they want to talk about everything under the sun before getting around to the subject at hand, flow with it. Match the customer's style. Is the customer a right-to-the-point, no-nonsense, in-a-hurry, business type?

   In sales, you will run into a variety of personalities daily. For long-term relationships, you must tailor your personality to the customer's and make the customer feel comfortable with you. You want that customer to feel right at home and come back again and again.

- Identify and understand what your customer's wants and needs are. Do this by asking questions. Ask your customer what she likes, what she wants, what she needs, and are there any special problems or other considerations? By trying to diagnose the wants and needs of your customer, she feels that you are trying to help her select the correct product and that you do really *care* what she selects.

   You may not be on the same wavelength regarding your customer's wants and needs at all. But you are not there to judge the customer, and you are not going to live with the purchases. The range of wants and needs that you will encounter make this business interesting. It's very boring to mold and influence every customer to go with what you like.

- Show the customer that you do care about her as a person. Act like a friend. If you know that the customer is having a birthday, send a card. If you see a news clipping or magazine article that would interest that person, clip it out and send it to them. Call once in a while just to say hello (not for any other reason). You need not become completely social with that person, but learn to really like *all types* of people. Don't be completely professional all of the time. Be human, warm, and friendly. When you are willing to make that occasional extra effort for your customers, they feel that they are thought of not only as a sale, but as a person whose friendship is valued by you.

- Build trust with your clients. Trust is built between you and your customers by being honest with them. Don't promise them anything that you are doubtful that you can deliver. If you do, you will appear flaky, wishy-washy, and out to promise anything to get the sale. They certainly will not be back, let alone refer you to anyone else. Simply tell them you will try to get it delivered by the proposed delivery date, but you are not able to promise them that date because there are many other variables involved. Keep customers posted on the progress of the order and let them know that you are staying on top of the situation. Should you meet their desired due date, great! If not, they will understand why it wasn't possible and will feel that you did try. They won't let the failure of meeting the desired date hold them back from making future purchases from you.

- Try and do your best. Individual decorating projects are very important to the customer. You of course are doing one after the other. Don't ever project that you are uncaring, nonchalant, or unfeeling with your customer's project. Even if the project comes out beautiful due to your practiced experience, the customer will be worried the whole time that you don't care what they get. After the project is completed those feelings will diminish the quality of the project in their eyes. Act excited and enthusiastic even when you are completely burnt out.

- Be there for your customers. Give your customers access to you. This does not mean give out your home phone number. It does mean checking messages frequently and calling the customer back on the same day. Establish set hours that you are in the store every week. Post these hours on your business card or write them in for every customer. They may want to run in to ask you another question. By providing access, you show the customers that you do care and are available to work with them.

If your customers are satisfied, they will return. If they are upset, they won't. Neither will their friends and neighbors. The business professional knows that her business is dependent on her customers' satisfaction. Satisfied customers will refer business to your business. Never overlook the value of your customers.

Establish a Customer Service Policy

The basis of customer goodwill is the existence of a sound customer relations policy. This policy needs to be practiced and understood by all employees. A well thought out policy will help prevent problems from occurring, and if they do, will deal with them promptly, satisfactorily, and fairly in your customer's view. Create a policy that covers all aspects of your business that directly relate to the customer: advertising, sales promotion, displays, selling methods, returns, pricing, servicing, deliveries, complaints, sales promotions, warranties, and any other special customer services.

Give *all* employees a copy of the policy and if possible review it with them. They need to be familiar with and *willing* to follow the policy that you lay out for your company. Print your policy in your advertisements and display it in your studio. This will remind your customers that they can count on your company to follow through. If the policy is displayed and readily reviewed by employees following a customer's question, misunderstandings are minimized and solved before they occur.

The biggest factor that contributes to dissatisfied customers is that they don't have anyone that seems to care about their problems. All communications with your customer should be handled in a courteous and helpful manner.

Spell out in your policy about how, when, where, and to whom all complaints should be directed. Designate one person in your company to handle complaints and solve problems. This person should be responsible for customer relations and have the ultimate authority to make decisions in this area. In a small company, this will probably be the owner. In a larger firm, this would probably be the business manager with the authority and flexibility to act on behalf of the company in all customer relations matters.

Keep your company policy consistent with applicable federal, state, and local regulations. Be sure that management unfailingly monitors and enforces the outlined policy.

The best policy is to always try to resolve customer complaints in their favor. While you may be within the law in *not* doing so, businesses that don't do the right thing and take care of the customer lose thousands of dollars in lost business from the customer and in all the people they would have referred. Smart businesses even throw in *something extra* for the customer to compensate for the aggravation and frustration.

Complaint Handling Procedures

Implement an easy and effective complaint handling system. This system should get to a solution as quickly as possible. Assure the customer that you do care and that prompt action will be taken to resolve the problem. Have controls set up to ensure that complaints are processed according to your policy and procedures. The controls should ensure prompt handling and settlement of complaints within a reasonable and satisfactory time period. Include the following in your complaint handling procedure.

Logging In:
Record in a master complaint book or on an individual complaint sheet the date a complaint is taken and any pertinent information. Record all complaints received over the phone, in person, or by mail in the complaint book or sheet.

Acknowledgement:
For problems that may not be quickly resolved, acknowledge by letter that the problem is receiving attention and that you will be promptly informing your customer of the decision or steps to be taken to resolve the problem. Try to give the customer a time frame for when the problem will be resolved and completed. Should a further delay arise, keep your customer posted on the progress.

Investigation:

Review all of the facts involved with the problem. Organize all records so complaints may be reviewed and investigated promptly and easily.

Decision:

Base all decisions on an equitable policy (fair and just). Any decision must be consistent with your customer relations policy outlined above.

Response:

Make your response to the complaint very clear and easy to understand for your customer. Address the issues raised in the customer's original complaint. Try to be helpful with any solutions that are suggested. Explain how you arrived at your decision to help preserve customer goodwill towards your company.

Follow-up:

After letting your customer know of your company's response to the complaint, follow up in the near future to see if all was completed to the customer's satisfaction. This is an important step. You will not be able to completely satisfy everyone all of the time. What you will gain is information and feedback from your customers on where you are weak and where they are unhappy, and you will be able to work toward building a better customer service system.

Building a Repeat Customer Relationship

Repeat business is where businesses profit the most. Here are some ideas on how to keep your customers coming back with repeat business again and again.

- Decide where you can find customers that will need to repeatedly use your services. Go after them with your marketing efforts.

- Do your best to provide prospective repeaters with the best service you can provide.

- Try to become friends with prospective repeat customers. If the potential repeater should invite you anywhere or to do anything, go. Call them once in a while just to say hi — not to try to sell them something.

- Be helpful and provide information when your prospective repeaters call you, even if it is not something that you are directly involved in with your business.

- If information or an article in the area of interest of your customer catches your eye, send it to the customer.

- Place potential repeat customers on your mailing list for every mailing you do to market your business.

- If it is a business that may give you repeat business in the future, strive to be friendly with other pertinent personnel, such as secretaries and receptionists.

- Always be very positive, honest, polite, and friendly with all of your customers.

Customer service is a very important element of an interior design or decorating business. In order to be paid in full for the job, to receive referrals from satisfied customers, and to have customers come back again and again, you must provide services and products that *satisfy* your customers.

Part 25

Marketing and Promotion

Create a Company Image

Develop a personality and image for your business that separates your business from the other interior design businesses located in your area.

You create a graphics image of your company by the logo you have designed, the style and type of signs you select, the business information packet you put together, the brochure created to tell about your business, style of yellow page ad, design and layout of letterheads and business cards, store front and displays, the line of products selected, and so on.

Take careful attention with the style of lettering you select for your company's image. Some lettering projects a high-quality feel and promotes consumer desire. Other lettering looks low quality and will alienate prospects.

A logo is the symbolic image for your company. Logos are used on all of your advertisements, business cards, *all* paperwork (both consumer and contractors), the sign out in front of your business, the firm's vans and trucks, etc. The colors used for your logo should be consistent. When you keep your logo consistent, you are creating awareness of your logo and of your company, either consciously or unconsciously.

Note about business cards: Oversized business cards are handy for containing a lot of information, hard-to-read type styles, and they allow you to be "different" from the rest of the competition. Realize, however, that they don't fit into wallets and these fonts are hard to read. Their potential for being misplaced or thrown out is great. Your goal should be for the prospective client to easily pull your card out of their wallet.

Marketing

When planning how you are going to market your business to generate leads and subsequent sales for your business, realize that you are in the problem-solving business. You are there to provide solutions. There are three ways to increase your company's sales:

- Obtain more customers.

- Get past customers to come in more frequently.

- Get all customers (new and old) to spend more money when they do business with your company.

As the total number of customer contacts increases, the number of in-home visits and closings increases. More leads produce higher income.

Company marketing must have a solid foundation from which to work. The foundation of a good marketing plan is the distribution and exposure of your products and services to prospective customers. The marketing supports to achieving success are product quality, packaging or styling character, the right pricing for the current market, and advertising that motivates the customer to contact you. If you don't find out the customer's needs and sell them the benefits, the price will often seem to high to the customer.

Experts say that it is impossible for a business to have all of these three key elements. Instead, a successful business must concentrate on having two out of the three elements. It is considered to be impossible to have all three elements and survive in this competitive business climate. You cannot provide a quality product and great service and pay a fair salary or commission and have the lowest prices in town. Decide which two of the three are the key elements that you will concentrate on with your business.

- Low prices.

- Great service.

- Good quality products.

Marketing studies show:
- Today, consumers spend more than 90 percent of their money on psychological fulfillments.

- A particular product or brand name will be a marketing success if it meets the quality standards of consumers and not just product specialists.

- Packaging includes your "company packaging," product samples, and product information. It is a productive marketing tool (strong psychological factor) if it has both display effectiveness and agreeable psychological undertones.

- Selected company name, colors, "packaging," and slogans will make or break your company.

- Symbols, signs, packages, designs, shapes, and colors are more constructive than words are in motivating customers to buy. People do not have defense mechanisms against symbols. They are not conscious that symbols have an impact on them and, consequently, affect their behavior.

- Marketing experts use words in association with symbols, images, and colors. Customers communicate with words, not symbols.

- Creativity, originality, and unusualness all have value in marketing communication or advertising if they have the ability to influence the prospect to buy.

- Advertising is constructive if it motivates customers to buy without making them conscious that the advertisement is actually selling them.

- *Certain* synonymous words or certain symbols may have the same meaning, but may negatively affect the customer. Use a thesaurus and find quality, simple, positive words for all of your copy.

- *All* people consciously or subconsciously practice sensation transference. They judge a book by its cover, they judge your company by what they see, they judge your decorators by their appearance, etc.

Marketing Mistakes to Avoid

- Not testing marketing tools. This includes pricing, ads, headlines, offers, etc.

- Not determining and cultivating the unique advantages you have over other companies. And not stressing and exploiting these advantages.

- Not planning for continuing sales at the time of the initial sale. Add all customers' names and addresses to your mailing list, whether they are large custom sales or small accessory sales.

- Failing to determine your customer's wants and needs. Determine what specific problem you are solving in your customer's life.

- Not determining your customer's additional/future wants and needs at the time of the initial sale.

- Mixing your features with your benefits. Get a grasp on the difference between them. Place emphasis on the benefits. *What it will do for the customer. What is in it for them.*

- Saying too much in your ads. Do not put too much information into a small space.

- Not asking every customer how he os she heard about your company. Once you establish *exactly* where your customers are coming from, you know where to spend your advertising dollars.

- Not using testimonials from happy customers. Written testimonials should be provided with all of your marketing materials and a list of referrals from happy customers should be offered to every potential customer for him or her to call and verify your work.

- Failing to make customers feel that conducting business with your company is easy and fun.

- Not educating while selling your customers.

- Using conventional ads instead of direct response ads. This type of ad only announces that your company is here — it does not call the customer to action to respond or come in to see you.

- Not focusing on your target market customer when your prepare your advertisements and marketing materials.

- Not reinforcing with your customers what a good deal they received and why you can give it to them at this price.

- Failing to get a prospective customer's attention with your marketing efforts.

- Not sticking with marketing and advertising ideas/ads that work. Use the same ads and ideas until they quit working.

- Using humor in ads. While it may make for a funny ad, funny ads generally won't help you make more sales.

- Not ascertaining the most effective ways to reach your target market.

- Producing your own graphic designs and artwork. Unless you have the education and the experience, leave this area to a professional.

- Trying to reach several markets with the same direct mailing piece. Produce separate mailing pieces for individual markets. To combine and attempt to make an all-purpose mailer to fit all targeted markets will miss the target for all of the markets.

- Being in a big hurry. If you are, you will spend excessive money and make mistakes.

Negative Marketing Signals

When and if any of the negative marketing signals below start to surface, reexamine your current marketing program and immediately implement marketing techniques outlined and discussed throughout this section.

- Sales start slipping.

- External competition and events are unpredictable and uncertain.

- New competition has arrived on the scene.

- Your company is lacking in marketing expertise.

- You are changing the location of your business.

- Your selected line of products/services is changing.

- Your company's management has changed.

- Customer price awareness has changed.

- Your company's long-term plan is deficient.

- Your company is experiencing internal system pressures.

- Signs of uncertain customer direction.

- The interior design industry is changing.

- Evaluation plans need to be implemented.

- Industry technology has changed.

- Periodic review of marketing procedures are required.

What is Your Marketing Strategy?

Consider the following questions to determine marketing decisions. Review the list and consider each question on a regular basis as your business changes and the economic climate changes, for sound marketing decisions.

Marketing:
- Who is your market?

- What are your marketing goals and objectives?

- What are the desired results from your marketing efforts?

- How much can you spend annually on marketing?

- How much can you spend for each sale you make?

- What are your sales goals?

- How much of a market share can you expect?

- What percentage of your market share will be residential? Commercial?

Marketing functions:
- Is the location for the business a good one?

- Will you offer financing? What type? How does the credit plan work?

- What is the primary means of communication with the customer? By telephone, in person, mail, or fax?

- What are your major strengths? What are your competitors' major strengths?

- What are your competitors' major weaknesses? What are your major weaknesses?

- Do you have a written marketing plan that you refer to regularly? A marketing plan directs your marketing plans and activities for a specific period, which can be as short as a few months and as long as several years. A marketing plan directs your marketing thinking for a specific period of time and allows you to perform necessary functions to prepare for the marketing activity during planning periods.

Promotions:

- Do you know the strengths and weaknesses of the different types of promotional vehicles?

- Which types will you use for your firm?

- Which of your products and services can be successfully advertised?

- Which media can most effectively reach your targeted group of customers: radio, newspaper, TV, yellow pages, or flyers?

- Will you use direct mail to get out your message to prospective customers? Do you have a current mailing list?

- Do you know the truth-in-advertising requirements?

- Will your promotional efforts be on a regular basis, or will they be concentrated with the differing seasons?

- Are certain days of the week busier than other days of the week?

- Is there financial or technical assistance available for use in emphasizing your promotional endeavors?

- Will the local TV stations, radio, or newspaper help you with your promotional efforts?

- Do your intended suppliers have cooperative advertising efforts available to split your advertising costs?

- Will you tie in your promotional efforts with your major suppliers' national advertising programs?

- Will you join other area merchants in your advertising efforts?

- Do you know what other competing interior design firms are spending on their promotions?

- Do you closely watch the advertising efforts of other successful businesses in addition to competing interior design-type businesses?

- Do you have a system to measure the response of the various promotional programs that you plan to use?

- What prospective customers can a direct mailing house reach for you?

- How will the customer know of your products and services?

- What information do the customers need? How will this information be provided? What will the message be: sales persuasion, informational, or a reminder message to a personal customer?

- Will you use different techniques depending on the customer?

- Will all of the customers be provided the same information?

- What is the best combination for you to use in advertising, personal selling, promotions, and publicity?

- Will you use mass promotion or individual promotion?

- What medium will you use to get out the message?

- How often should you repeat the message to the customer?

Promotional materials:
- What are your promotional materials?

- Do your promotional materials make a good impression on customers?

- What materials are working better than others?

- What materials aren't working well?

Customer profile:
- What different types of customers do you have?

- Who is your target customer? Who are the people most likely to buy from your business?

- How can you recognize your target customer?

- What goods and services and what will they want to obtain from your firm?

- Who is your typical customer? What is his or her age? Sex? Education level? Income level?

- For commercial customers, what is the usual type of business? How do they usually use your products and services?

- What are your customers' buying attitudes? What are their objectives for using your services and buying your products?

- What are the primary decorating needs and product uses for this customer? Are some of the needs more important than others? Are there other products and lines available that your customer might also consider using to fulfill his or her needs?

- What does the customer consider to be the advantages and disadvantages about the line of products you carry? How does your customer feel about your competitor's line of products?

- Are certain types of customers more dissatisfied than others with your lines of products and the lines of products of your competitors?

- Where does your target market customer live?

- Is the neighborhood changing either for the better or for the worse?

- How do your target customers shop? Do they come in and see your line of products first before asking to have a decorator come out?

- How much do they usually spend when shopping for interior items?

- What do your customers think about your competitors?

- Have you estimated the total interior design market share?

- Would it be better to appeal to the whole market or to only a segment of the market?

- Is a segment of the market large enough to be profitable?

- Do you foresee or know about *any* possible changes in the future amongst your potential customers that could affect business?

- Do the incomes in the area appear to be stable?

- Is the population in the area stable or does it tend to change frequently?

- Will you offer customer incentives such as lower prices, better quality, wider selection, faster service, financing, etc?

- Do you ask for customers' opinions and send them questionnaires on how your business could be better for them?

- Are you open on Saturday, which is a very strong buying day?

- Do you stay abreast of new products and news by belonging to organizations and subscribing to trade journals?

- Do you attend trade shows to view new products and ideas?

Products and services:

- What products are you going to carry and have available? Services?

- How will these items be transported?

- Where will they be stored?

- How will you price your products and services?

- What methods will you use to promote your products and services?

- What are the benefits and features of the selected products and offered services?

- What are the strengths of the selected products and offered services? What are the weaknesses?

- What do you wish you had in the way of products and services?

- Have you drawn up a buying schedule for planned purchases for the different seasons?

- Does the strategy achieve a planned inventory turnover?

- Have you categorized the purchases by merchandise classifications?

- Do you know from whom you will be making the planned purchases?

- Who sells the lines you plan to buy?

- Will you consolidate most of your purchases and buy from two or three main suppliers?

- What type of plan do you have for reviewing new products coming onto the market?

- Will you keep track of the successful purchases in the past to help you with future year's buying decisions?

- Do you have a system for evaluating your supplier's performances?

- Who will be in charge of buying for the firm?

- Are name brands important? Would less-expensive lines of the brand names or alternate brands be acceptable?

- What image are you striving to project with the line of selected merchandise?

- What additional features and accessories would you like to carry and have available?

- Will you buy right from the manufacturer, or from wholesalers and distributors?

- How quickly will the various vendors fill your orders? How quickly will the merchandise be delivered?

- How are the various products packed for shipment? How would your customer prefer them to be packed for shipment? Are instructions available for simple window treatment installations?

- What are the terms of the sale?

- What are the warranties and guarantees for the various products?

- Will the preferred vendors extend you credit?

- Will you make buying trips to design centers? How often?

- What information should you include on your purchase orders?

- Do you need to service any lines of merchandise more than others?

Plan a Promotional Program

You have to attract customers and stay way ahead of your competition. Follow these steps to prepare a powerful and effective promotional program. A "promotion" is a short-lived, intense, and easily measured program.

- Make an evaluation of the situation. For example, the competition is moving in on you.

- Plan your promotional strategy. What are your options?

- Activate your promotional program. Test frequently to see what really works.

- Evaluate your results.

Test Marketing

By the time you decide to start your own business, you are probably aware of *who* your customers are, where they spend their money, and who are the competitors competing for the customers' business. If you are sure that now is the right time to start your interior design firm, you need to test the idea of your new business concept before spending tons of money trying to get it off of the ground, and risking failure. Test customer receptiveness to your idea of a business and find out whether you are correct in your research, that *now* is the opportune time for you to start that business. Depending on the results of your testing, you may find out that you may need to change or adjust some of your plans.

Find out the opinions of people who might require your goods and services in the future. The way to get their opinions is to get your products and services in front of them. Some people, while acting very positive toward your products and services, would not actually buy them. All their praise won't do you a bit of good if they won't actually buy your products and services.

Ask questions to determine if price is a major factor, if certain types of name brands are considerations, and if distinctive styling is of major importance.

Test any mailings you plan to do on a segment of customers to see how the mailing will pull. It is preferable to test several different sale offers to several different groups of people to see which mailing pulls the best. Code the address by adding a dash and a letter (e.g. 475-A) to the street address. When responses come in by mail, the coded street address tells you the source of the lead. Anyone calling over the phone should be quizzed as to how they have heard about your company.

The Baby Boomer Market

In years past, marketing strategies could be planned around predictable buyers. Customers today are different. They are the product of thirty years of social change. The family as a unit has become segmented and variable. Generally, the head of the family puts in long hours on the job. Studies of today's baby boomers (the large group of persons born between 1947 and 1961) show them overall to be:

- Conscious that women's roles are changing.

- Interested in self-fulfillment.

- Highly educated and skilled.

- Sophisticated and refined.

- Dedicated to expressing personal individuality.

- Extremely time conscious (preference for time-saving items).

- Pleasure seeking.

- Suspicious and cautious.

- Hostile to traditional customs, habits, and rituals.

- Committed to change.

- Sometimes jaded and weary.

- *Less* name brand loyal/name brand aware.

- Quality and superior service conscious.

- Youth conscious.

- Health conscious.

- Concerned about child and elder care.

- Concerned that job security is more important than high salaries.

- Saving money for retirement and children's college educations.

Marketing Thoughts and Perceptions

- Many people need direction when it comes to decorating. Tell them why they should do business with your company.

- Call people to action. Tell them what action to take. Ask for the sale, tell them to call this number and come into the studio.

- If you can *double* the response to your ads, you will *double* your income.

- Advertising is nothing more than written salesmanship, intensified.

- Make a *complete argument* for your products and services.

- Manifest *high perceived value* for your products and services.

- Use bonuses to entice prospects. Use bonuses that give value to the prospect that do not cost much. Give free problem evaluations, consultations, booklets, brochures, newsletters, information kits, invitations to seminars, demonstrations, free trials, use of products, gift certificates, coupons, free analysis, free estimates, gifts, etc.

- Use risk *reversal*. Take away the risk of purchasing. Use guarantees.

Psychology of Color in Company Image

When we walk into various environments we are affected by the color and decor of the space on a subconscious level. Color and design are psychological factors that can be used constructively or destructively in business. Not many people are aware that decor, color, and shapes have an effect on their emotions.

If a competitor is using a specific color, you may not want to use that color when planning your company image. Testing the market with color selections is the key to correct color choices.

- Pure hues (colors) that have the *greatest visibility*, attention-getting effectiveness, high memory and recall, are in this order of effectiveness: yellow, yellow-green, yellow-orange, orange, and orange-red. People associate these colors with these feelings: warm, hunger, active, stimulating, strong. In some circumstances, these colors may be considered abrupt, perilous, disturbing, and intimidating.

- Colors that rate *low in visibility*, attention-getting power, and retention are in this order of effectiveness: violet-blue, blue, blue-green, and green. People usually associate these colors with cool, nature, relaxing, calm.

- Warm tints are colors containing yellow-orange, peach, and beige and rate low in visibility.

- Warm tones affect us the same as warm tints do.

- Cool tints containing blue, green-blue, aqua-blue, and aqua-green are considered delicate and calm.

- Cool tones and shades are classified as having the same effects as cool tints.

- Men prefer deeper shades.

- Women prefer delicate tints and tones.

- White reflects light and is associated with purity and cleanliness.

- Black has negative connotations but makes any adjacent color more appealing.

- Gray (a neutral) is a desirable color in combination with a brighter color.

- Consumers with higher incomes prefer brighter hues.

- Use color as a factor in pricing a product for a particular market.

- Colors that have remained popular with consumers through the years are aqua, turquoise, magenta red, and coral red.

As shown in the Psychology of Shapes section, it is important when planning *anything* that you appeal to your customer. **Consider what males recall and prefer and what females recall and prefer. Use the following as a guideline for color planning:**

Customer:	Color:	Visibility:	Preference:	Recall:	Associated with:
Female:	blue	low	low	low	oppressive, authority
	black	low	high	low	elegant, sensuous, lavish
	red	high	high	high	warm, intimate, rich
	pink	low	high	low	feminine, soft, warm
	brown	low	high	low	warm, earthy
Male:	blue	low	high	low	dependable, intelligent
	black	low	high	low	sumptuous, elegant
	red	high	low	high	exciting, danger
	pink	low	low	low	feminine, quiet, soothing
	brown	low	high	low	good quality, opulence
Female/Male:	white	high	low	low	pure, clean, sterile
	orange	high	low	high	healthy, earthy, energy
	yellow	high	low	high	sunny, warm, friendly
	green	low	low	low	relaxing

Note: Some colors have great appeal and favorable associations for women only.

Psychology of Shapes

When planning your logo, ads, image, displays, etc., realize that certain shapes are more pleasing to women than to men. If you are a man, you will react differently to certain shapes than a woman will. Use the following list as a guideline for shape planning.

Note: Shapes do not have to be exactly square, triangular, round, or oval to fall in these categories.

Customer:	Shape:	Visibility:	Preference:	Recall:	Associated With:
Female:	circle	high	high	high	tender, loving, warm
	square	low	low	low	rigid, hard, rough
	triangle	high	low	high	aggressive, strong
Male:	circle	high	low	high	soft, delicate, feminine
	square	low	high	low	solid, anticipate, certain
	triangle	high	low	high	mysterious, forceful
Female/Male:	oval	high	high	high	security, comfort

Note: Images and symbols with sharp points tend to turn women off.

Words and Phrases That Sell

Since this area was covered in *Secrets of Success for Today's Interior Designers and Decorators*, under List of Right Words to Use, we are simply adding to that list.

Advertising terms to use to entice potential customers to call you:

- Accent
- Advice
- Appeal
- Appear, appearance
- A special invitation
- Act now
- Admire
- Appreciate
- Bargain
- Beautiful
- Bonus
- Brighten
- Buy two — get one free
- Classic
- Complete, completion
- Compare
- Complement
- Coordinate
- Combinations, combine
- Create
- Current
- Custom design
- Decor, decorate, decorative
- Deluxe
- Deserve
- Design, designer
- Discover
- Do not delay
- Drape, draped, draping
- Dream
- Dress it up
- Earn
- Effect
- Elegance, elegant
- Ensembles
- Exciting
- Exclusive
- Facts
- Fancy
- Fashion
- Feminine
- Fine

- Flatter
- Frame
- Free
- Free details
- Fresh
- Fullness
- Fun
- Gain
- Get started today
- Gift
- Gorgeous
- Graceful
- Great
- Hand of the fabric
- Helpful
- Here
- Here's news
- High fashion
- How-to
- Ideas
- Imagine, imagination
- Important
- Impress
- Improve, improved, improvement
- Informative
- Inspire
- Interesting
- Introducing
- It's easy
- Judge for yourself
- Last chance
- Latest
- Layer
- Learn
- Like
- Look
- Lovely
- Lush
- Money
- Never before
- New look

- Now
- Offer
- Original idea
- Personalize
- Picture
- Popular
- Prefer
- Professional
- Profit
- Profitable
- Proven results
- Quick
- Refundable
- Reliable
- Romantic
- Safe
- Save time and money
- Select, selection
- Solve, solution
- Soft, soft effect, soft look
- Special
- Stimulate
- Stop
- Style
- Successful
- Tested
- There's no risk or obligation
- Three good reasons
- Timeless
- Top it off
- Transform
- Treatment
- Trial offer
- Trim
- Trust
- Try
- Value
- Wanted
- Warm
- Well dressed
- Your

- Call for an initial appointment.
- Call now for a free initial consultation.
- Call for your free interior analysis.
- Call for your initial, interior planning appointment with one of our consultants.
- Call for your free interior evaluation.
- Call now for your free, no-obligation consultation or in-home appointment.
- Call now for your free estimate.
- Call now to have one of our consultants come out to measure for your needed interior items.

Do not make the potential customer feel intimidated because you are trying to "sell" them something. Use terms such as planning, measuring, consulting, designing, estimating, evaluating, analyzing, and helping when writing ad copy.

- Use a different approach and style when writing ad copy. Use descriptive words.

- Save all advertisements (of all types) that you come across that you feel are great ads. Use similar copy techniques to grab your customers' attention.

- Read and study ad copy from decorating magazines, mail order catalogues, manufacturers' product literature (also check with their ad department), competitors' ads, and department store home sale catalogues. Notice how the writer romances you with the selected words for the copy.

- Check with the advertising department of the medium where you will be placing an ad. Do they have any suggestions or guidance to offer you? Assistance is usually *"free,"* or in other words *included in the price of the ad,* so you should use their help.

- Professional advertising agencies are another alternative for firms that can afford their services, and for individuals who won't attempt to develop their own ad copy style.

Why Advertise?

Your objectives and reasons for advertising are many. An advertisement should have a specific, direct objective aimed at prospective customers to fulfill an area of the marketing plan. Use the following list of objectives to plan your advertising campaign:

- Produce leads, some of which will translate into sales.

- Attract new customers and prospects.

- Produce direct sales of inventory items.

- Help you get your foot in the door.

- Exact advertisements may be reprinted and used as direct mail pieces, and flyers

- Gain access to other markets and territories.

- Advertise business expansions and additions of new stores.

- Cultivate reorders from past customers.

- Show new ideas and ways to use products.

- Reach hard-to-find prospective customers.

- Inform your audience (customers and competition) of your existence.

- Reach prospects who make buying decisions for companies and corporation.

- Remind customers that you are still interested in doing business with them.

- Keep in touch with your customers.

- Reach the upper levels of management without going through other levels first.

- Bring traffic into your store or studio.

- Keep your present customers sold on the brands of products that you carry.

- Increase and promote turnover of inventory.

- Increase sales during slow periods.

- Keep your name current in your prospective and past customers' minds.

- To level out periods when sales are good and when sales are poor.

- So prospective/past customers will demand the products that you carry (and not settle for any other).

- Promote multi-item sales.

- Show and promote your entire line of products and services.

- Promote sales of related items and add-on purchases.

- Trade up customers to the quality of the products and services you have available.

- Announce seminars, demonstrations, or offer a "free" in-home decorator appointment.

- Resell and *find* customers you have lost contact with.

- Discourage competitors by showing that your company is major competition to them.

- Grab your competitors' customers (that are unhappy and dissatisfied).

- Increase uses of a particular product.

- Create new buying habits.

- Encourage customers to buy before they planned to.

- Test an ad's potential, before you roll out a larger ad campaign with the same publication.

- To attract vendors and distributors (and improve the relationship with and receive better discounts), salespeople, and employers who will want to work for and work with your company.

- Inform vendors and distributors about upcoming advertising and promotional campaigns.

- Teach your prospects what they should desire and want.

- Show prospects what are the benefits and features of the advertised product or service.

- Offer limited-time specials, sales, coupon offers.

- Promote premium or special manufacturers' offers for specific products.

- Demonstrate technical information about specific products.

- Stimulation of word-of-mouth advertising.

- Encourage customers to come see interior and window displays of products

- Verify to potential customers that your are a leader in the market.

- Establish prestige.

- Eliminate favoritism of other companies.

- Become known as the "source" of interior design products and services.

- Prevent and eliminate substitution of inferior or other brand products.

- Create a corporate image.

- Increase customer goodwill.

- Gain acceptance from the professional group of potential customers

- Build brand name image.

- Intensify your product and services distinctiveness.

- Protect any company trademarks.

- Reduce decorator and employee turnover.

- Increase decorator and employee loyalty and pride in your company.

- Enhance your company's image.

- If you have reformatted an existing business, to introduce the public to the company's new concept, style, products, and services.

- Improve your relationship with overall community.

- Impress and attract stockholders — both present and future.

- Assure proper and correct use of products.

- Make potential customers feel that their present interior needs a "new look."

- Exploit favorable publicity (press releases and other articles about your business).

- Stress the advantages of doing business with your company rather than with a competitor.

- Conduct research on potential customers and their needs and desires.

- Publicize results of any research.

- Discourage potential competitors from entering the same field.

- Exploit any special advantages of an advertising medium. Running split-runs or short spots on TV.

- If you have lower prices, to announce and inform customers of the available lower pricing.

- Stimulate and promote prospective customers to ask for more information.

- Offer sales information and literature.

- Promote cooperative advertising with related businesses.

- Announce and publicize your company's policies.

- Increase distribution of company literature.

- Inform your audience of success stories about your company and the products you carry.

- Announce promotions or to tell about employees within your company.

What Can Advertising Do For Your Business?

If you are not careful, you can spend and waste (needlessly) lots of money on advertising. You need to evaluate the advertising objectives you are attempting to achieve before you start advertising anywhere. Below is an overview of the various types of advertising and what they can do for your business.

Image advertising:
Image (or awareness) advertising announces that you are here and open for business. The objective is to make potential customers aware of your company and its products and services. Image advertising builds

name recognition. It is also used to announce that you are still in business. If you stop advertising, prospects and past customers may think you are out of business. Use image advertising to tell customers anything new about products, services, terms of doing business, etc.

Action advertising:

The other extremely common advertising method is action advertising. The objective is to get customers to come in or call your business so that you can sell them something. With action advertising, you use a different plan of action than you do with image advertising. Action advertising normally features a coupon, limited-time offers, or a special sale.

Delayed action advertising:

Advertising to stimulate action at a later date, when the product or service is actually needed. With delayed action advertising, you attempt to put a business card and a brochure into a potential customers' hand for reference later, when he or she needs to make interior purchases. You are attempting to keep your name current in the potential customer's mind, so that you will at least be allowed to compete for the job.

The main objective of advertising is not to get your company name and image in print, on TV, or the radio, but to sell your products and services. The ultimate goal with advertising is to lead your prospective customers down the path to where they ultimately buy from you.

Phases customers go through before making buying decisions:

- **Awareness.** The potential customer becomes aware of the products and services provided by your company.

- **Seeks information and becomes interested.** The customer starts to become interested in what you are offering. Show and tell the customer what the product or service does and will do for them. Have literature and brochures available to hand out to customers, to tell all the good points about the individual products and your services.

- **Gathers more information.** The customer gathers and researches the products and services provided by your company and by the competition. The customer starts to get an idea of price. The customer continues to shop competition for different styles and types of the product she is interested in, and compares pricing of various companies.

  As a sales professional, your goal is to move the customer beyond this point, rapidly. You want the potential customer to become interested and want to buy from you and your company. This is achieved by translating features into benefits. *What will it do for the customer?*

  A sales professional *stays* with the customer and keeps working with her in a positive manner that reflects, *"You are my customer and you should buy from me. Because if you buy from someone else, you will not receive the same value that you will if you buy from me."* You must assume the sale to get the sale. Act happy to repeatedly answer objections and provide further information (including pricing of other treatments and styles).

- **Desire.** Get the prospective customer to *want to buy* that product or service. Let him or her feel the carpet or fabric, and show pictures of how the treatment will look. Describe how much nicer and more prestigious his or her home is going to look and feel.

- **The spouse becomes involved in the buying decision.** The prospective customer has narrowed down the selection, and now needs the spouse's approval.

- **Call to action.** Ask for the order. Remind the customer the sale ends Saturday, for example. The prospective customer decides to make the purchase.

Use your advertising as a tool to make this decision-making process part of a smooth buying process. Think about how your customers arrive at a decision to buy from you or your company. How did they arrive at this decision? Advertise in several different advertising media that will hit your target market and will serve to repeatedly reinforce your advertising message.

Decide how you can reach those people that are *most* likely to buy from you. What newspapers and magazines do they read? What radio and TV stations do they tune in to? Create an advertising campaign that will hit your prospective customers from several different directions. Use media such as radio, sale flyers, TV, regional magazines, newspapers, personal referrals, seminars, and mall displays. Decide what media will work to reach your target market and use them as the tools for your ad campaign. The objective is to move your prospective customers from awareness, to seeking information and feeling interested, to desire, and finally action.

According to the studies that have been done, advertising must be directed at a customer twenty-seven times before a prospect will act, actually picking up the phone or making a visit in to see you. **Twenty-seven times!** Most of these times the potential customer never even notices or sees your advertisement. Subconsciously, the prospective customer will notice it some of the time, but not all of the time. Do not make the mistake of repeatedly advertising in a medium and quitting before you do it twenty-seven times. If you are advertising in other media, this also helps to finally get the message across.

Decide what type of advertising you need to use — image advertising, action advertising, or delayed action advertising. You may choose to use several different types of ads at different intervals for your ad campaign. Start with image advertising to create awareness early in the campaign. Image ads will lay the groundwork for your direct sales efforts or subsequent action or delayed action ads.

Familiar Advertising Methods

Interior design businesses usually spend 1.5 percent to 2.5 percent of their gross sales on various advertising methods. Some of the more familiar methods used are yellow page ads, weekly newspapers, radio, direct mail, consumer and decorating magazines, and exterior signs.

Promotional opportunities include open houses, in-store seminars, and educational displays.

Inexpensive techniques you should try are cooperative advertising with manufacturers/vendors and word-of-mouth advertising.

Overview of Advertising Media

Medium	Advantage	Disadvantage
Daily regional newspaper	wide circulation	nonselective readership
Weekly/local newspaper	local customers	limited customer base
Local shopper magazine	local customers	free publication that may not be read
Local magazines	if magazine is carefully selected (consumer interior design magazines), can be ideal	expensive medium, limited audience

Telephone directories	readers are in the market for your goods and services	limited to those who actually look up your category of goods and services
Direct mail	if targeted to right customers a very good medium to use	high price per thousand
Radio	wide coverage — select market group carefully	customer must remember or write down information
Television	wide coverage — select market carefully	very expensive, much production time required
Outdoor signs	frequent exposure, use big signs	may be hard to find places to display signs other than at your business (some locales have very strict rules governing sign size and placement at business sites)
Location of business along public transit routes	frequent, repetitious exposure	narrow audience

Keys to Productive Advertising

The ad is what the customer is actually purchasing. The ad is representing your company, and taking the salesperson's place. It has to do the selling for you.

Creating an effective advertisement can be a very trying task. But if you don't give your ad copy your best, the advertisement may be ignored and money for the advertisement is wasted. Use the following guidelines when preparing all types of advertisements:

- Use persuasive words such as: *save, you, money, new, love, guarantee, results, easy, health, safety, discover, proven, fast, free.* See the section on Words and Phrases That Sell.

- Get the reader's attention.

- KIS — keep it simple (in language and in your layout).

- Use style and reflect your image in the advertisement. Stay consistent with the selected theme for all advertisements, brochures, signage, etc.

- Be timely and up-to-date with your copy style.

- Focus on the right product or service.

- Use imagination.

- Select a logo for easy customer recognition.

- Use easy-to-read and -understand words.

- Be informative.

- Use a simple layout that has easy eye flow. Make the ad easy to see in size.

- For radio, make the advertisement long enough to be heard.

- Stimulate emotions such as desire, fear, hope.

- Be convincing.

- Arouse emotions such as wants, desires, hopes, admiration from others, fear.

- Repeat the advertisement at regular, frequent intervals.

- Time advertising to prepare for the holidays, spring time, etc.

- Display in the ad highly desirable products, styles, or looks.

- Conform to Federal Trade Commission regulations guidelines for honesty.

- Always mail copies of any press releases, articles, and commendations about your company to past and prospective customers.

- Show and tell the customer how to respond by giving a telephone number, an invitation into the studio, an address, etc.

- Always place your company name, address, and telephone number on each mailing piece.

Steps to attracting customers:
- Grab the customer's attention with a benefit-based headline. Base this headline on a basic need or emotion.

- Hold the customer's attention with a believable offer. Use sincere and factual copy.

- Call the customer to action. Create a sense of urgency. Act now and receive an extra bonus, special time-limited price, etc. Give the customer a way to respond by giving a phone number, an address with hours listed, a coupon, etc.

The Interior Design Field

Read everything available on the interior design field. Start with this book and Touch of Design's *Secrets of Success for Today's Interior Designers and Decorators* (ordering information is in the back of this book). These two books are your road map to success in this career. Very little alternative information is available for this career. Read general books on marketing and advertising, printing and graphic arts, accounting and bookkeeping, salesmanship, starting a business, etc.

At your larger local library, review the *Business Periodical Index* and the *Wall Street Journal Index* for magazine articles on the field of interior design and decorating. You will get a feel for where the business is headed nationally for the time period you are contemplating starting your business.

Ask the librarian to direct you to the area of the library that covers small business management. Tell the librarian what you are looking for, and chances are she will try to help you find all available information.

Referrals and Repeat Business

Referrals

This is your best possible lead. A satisfied customer has referred you to a friend, relative, or associate. The referred customer already has a favorable impression of you. You must remind customers at *every* opportunity that you would appreciate being referred. If you don't spell it out to your customers, they may not do it or think of doing it, even though they were extremely satisfied with your quality of work. Let them know that you reward customers who refer with nice future price reductions on products and services.

If you take care of your customers and let them know that you would appreciate them referring you to other friends, acquaintances, and relatives, they will. Let them do the majority of your selling for you. This is the best lead you can get — the referral by a happy customer. The prospect receives information from a satisfied customer that *you* are the one to work with on his or her project. The referred customer will offer you little sales resistance, and will trust you from the beginning.

If you are doing a commercial job and were hired by a particular division, come right out and ask the person you are working with who else in the company might be interested in your products and services. You are in a preferable position as you are already doing a decorating job for another division of the same company. Try to get the prospect's title, mailing address, and phone number from the referrer. Then ask the person who referred you if it is okay to use his or her name. Generally, they'll be happy for you to use their name. Call the potential customer and say, "So and so has referred me to you because you may also need my products and services."

A letter sent out to a possible referrer for prospective customers is also an effective way to pick up referrals. Send a thank-you note for their business and a reminder that you are happy to service the products if the need should arise. Ask for future referrals for business and if they know of anyone (with their company, a friend, relative, or an associate) with immediate decorating needs, or needs in the near future, to please let you know as you would like to contact the person and let him or her know that you just completed a job for the referrer, to please come see it (if this is possible), and to ask the referrer how the job went with your company.

Acknowledge any referral by a thank-you note, a small percentage of the overall sale, a discount coupon on a next purchase, or a small gift. You want to keep your happy customers referring you and by acknowledging your appreciation in this way, it keeps them inspired to refer you again and again.

Other methods of getting referrals:

- Determine which personal contacts can be used to spread the word about your company. Who is in a position to refer customers to you?

- Have customers invite friends and relatives to your open houses and seminars.

- Ask for names of referrals after seminars.

- Ask for names of friends and relatives that would also like to receive your newsletters and direct mail pieces announcing special events and sales.

Referral program:

Give referral money to local stores that carry ready-made products, carpet, flooring, wallpaper, paint, linens, or furniture. Give the person who makes a referral $10 to $20 for each customer that make a purchase from you. Consider giving a small percentage (1 percent — 2 percent) of the gross sale for referring you customers they can't take care of them themselves with their line of products.

Have the salespeople supplied with referral slips they can use to take down the customer's name and telephone number. Have them tell the customer that you will call the customer. The referring salesperson can either drop off the slips to you or call you with the information. They should keep a copy of the referral slip for their records, so they can double check with you to see if the customer made a purchase.

Be very careful to give credit where credit is due. When new employees start working at the various stores, go there and introduce yourself and your program. Once they have gotten a check from you, it is the easiest money they have ever earned and they are going to go out of their way to bring you lots of business. These people start to count on the extra money supplied by you. And they may earn several hundred dollars from you, monthly. The best lead you can get is the referral by another person.

Offer customers a small discount off of future purchases for referrals of friends. Give each interested customer brochures and cards to distribute to their network of family and friends.

Ways to Stimulate Personal Referrals and Recommendations

If you are attempting to maximize the amount of personal referrals or recommendations from your customers, follow these recommendations:

- Your products and your service need to be the best they can be.

- The overall appearance of the business and products, packaging, and literature lends to credibility of the firm.

- Should the amount of customers increase dramatically, be prepared to handle the overflow evenly and proficiently.

- Sell the senses: sight and touch. Display products to their maximum potential. Be sure that the overall image of your business is the best that you can make it.

- Use fair, easy-to-understand pricing. Keep it consistent from one customer to the next.

- Treat everyone, both employees and customers, in a professional, consistently honest manner. Be open to communication.

- Tell your customers you *want* referrals and explain what is unique and superior about your business, products, and services.

- Have an easy-to-find location for your business.

- Offer a satisfaction-guaranteed policy. Make it easy for unhappy customers to return or reject defective merchandise.

- Market regularly and frequently. When you stop marketing the flow of fresh leads stops.

- Should problems arise, customers should feel that their problem will be handled in an equitable manner.

- Have regular sales that new customers can take advantage of.

- Have a current (regularly reviewed and updated) mailing list of your customers. Mail regular sale announcements, promotions, special clients, special offers and correspondence to past customers. Invite them to share the information with friends and acquaintances.

Repeat Business

Repeat business is extremely important. It can make the difference between your showing a profit or sweating it and only sliding by each month.

Repeat business, if you took care of the customer the first time around, is easy for you to pick up. If the customer was satisfied the first time and you treated her right, why would she want to waste her time in shopping around for another decorator or company to work with? You have already "sold" her the first time, you are probably now friends, and all subsequent sales are faster, less stressful (for both of you), and much easier to do. This is the *best sale* you can get — the repeat customer who is happy with you and your company. **These are the ways to keep customers satisfied:**

- Do the best job that you can.

- Keep customers informed of the progress of the job.

- Strive to meet deadlines any way that you can. If you can't, let your customer know in advance that you can't meet the deadline. Don't wait till the night before the day of the proposed delivery to tell her. Your customer may have planned a party or other event around your proposed delivery date.

- Go the extra mile. Give them more service than you told them you would. Don't ever shortchange your customers. Giving more than the expected shows your customers that you care about their job and about retaining them as customers.

- Don't overpromise. Don't lead your customers to believe that you are going to do more than you are actually going to do. Don't exaggerate your expertise and credentials, what the results of the job will be, etc.

- Note everything in writing while working with your prospective customer. Write down conclusions of all items and details discussed. Later, if the customer comes back and says that she is not happy about such and such, pull out your notes and say, "*I recommended doing it this other way and you declined to do it. We went ahead and did it your way.*"

    Simply re-clarify what happened during the planning process. Chances are when you mention it the customer will remember and not be angry anymore, as they now remember that they were the one who opted to do the job that way. If she wants to make changes now, she can, if she doesn't mind paying for it.

- Be easy to work with and get along with. Don't act like a prima donna decorator or designer. If you really want to bond with your customers, you will strive to be a friend. Listen to your prospects ideas and think about where she is coming from, what is her point of view? Try to please customers — give them what they want. They are the ones who will be looking at the interior every day, not you. It is, after all, their money, not yours.

The way to get both referrals and repeat business is by providing quality service. Quality service leads to customer satisfaction. This does not mean that the job has to go in perfectly. What it means is that although there may have been small problems that came up along the way, you kept your customer informed and handled the problems as painlessly as possible for your customer.

Print Advertising

Print advertising is less expensive than direct mail, but it can produce a lower-quality prospect. Print advertising is also fast. Some prospects respond better to print than to a direct mail piece. You may need to buy space in publications whose target demographics are similar to your target market demographics. If you have previously bought mailing lists from a publication that worked well, space ads in that same publication will probably also work favorably. **The use of print advertising is better if:**

- The market is not definitely targeted.

- The target market has not already been defined by mailing lists.

- You need to produce as many inquiries as possible, quickly, practically, and inexpensively.

- You want to test creative strategies.

- You need to create a mailing list of new prospects for direct mail purposes.

Note: The smaller the display ad, the more important it is to place a border around the ad to define and separate it from surrounding material. Borders draw attention to the ad. Or you may opt to place a border around only a portion of the ad.

Make Your Advertising Stand Out

In past times all a company needed to do was to advertise the benefits of a product to sell it. Today, this is not enough. If you use the old methods, you are only adding your advertising piece to the growing pile of nondescript advertising pieces already arriving on everyone's doorstep.

The average consumer is flooded with 500,000 intensively competitive messages that fight each other for attention. Due to the overload of advertising messages, people shut off and will not even see the vast majority of advertisements. The general public's taste changes subtly from year to year. The movement is toward more sophistication. Give the customer a reason to buy your product — a personal advantage that they can secure by purchasing your product.

Some of the advertisements still get through, and they work. Some advertisers advertise more often, more flamboyantly, more offensively, or more attention demanding.

The secret for successful advertising is to advertise something that the customer is interested in. The advertisement stands out from the advertisements competing for attention, and becomes a message of interest to the reader.

Instead of attempting to force your message, dangle a carrot. When the consumer reaches for the carrot, he or she is faced with a message that solves a problem for him or her. This problem-solving technique develops audience interest and creates the desire to move the customer to action.

The problem areas in developing an advertising message include: deciding what your audience is interested in, how to deliver the message to the right group of people, how to make the message appeal to their interests, and how to all of the above efficiently.

Coordinate and use all the resources at your disposal and be far ahead of your competitors. Work with all facts you can get your hands on, a carefully thought out plan of action tailored to your needs, a creatively developed advertisement piece, and a regular review process, to measure just how well your ads are working (and *which* ones are working).

If you implement the above plan, the results will be highly leveraged advertisement pieces that pull in more inquiries, higher response rates with direct mail pieces, attention-getting point-of-purchase materials and ad pieces, and more effective public relations for your company.

Since today's advertising costs are *very expensive*, risk is very real and a major consideration of any advertising campaign. Risk is simply *the degree of unknown* in a situation. By carefully planning your advertising approach, risk is reduced. The approach you should take stands out and the results are measured.

- Carry and provide products that fulfill basic human needs. Products and services must include a unique approach for answering that human need.

- Products and services must appeal to a broad, economically promotable market.

- Products and services must lend themselves to an attention-getting promotional concept.

- Advertising can persuade people to buy inferior products only once.

- If you stop your advertising efforts you will kill your business.

- The higher the prices you place on your products and services, the more the customer perceives its value and the more desirable it becomes to the consumer.

- Offer prospects a special introductory bargain — a *really* special price for a limited time only. Make sure that this is a special price only for new customers.

Ad-a-grams

Ad-a-grams are available to subscribers of *Draperies & Window Coverings* magazine, free of charge. Ad-a-grams are professionally designed and illustrated, contemporary advertisements. If the subscriber desires, the advertisements are mailed every quarter (thirty-six different window covering advertisements yearly) to regular paid subscribers of the magazine. Each Ad-a-gram is unique and features a different window covering product or decorating concept. Pick and choose and adapt each ad for various occasions.

These ads are a *fabulous* perk for the price of subscribing to a high-quality, modestly priced magazine. The ads are professionally designed by experienced advertising and industry professionals. Add your store logo and use the ads as they are, or change the copy, reduce or enlarge the ads, or use only the desired parts of the ads.

Contact Draperies and Window Coverings, P.O. Box 13079, North Palm Beach, FL 33408, for a subscription and Ad-a-gram information. We highly recommend the magazine and ads.

Telephone Book Ads

Ads in the telephone book yellow pages and white pages are expensive but necessary for your interior design business. They will bring you business, but they are expensive. And you must plan well ahead to get an ad published in phone books.

Many different options are available from the telephone company design department; for example, the use of red as an accent color, borders and corners (they have a wide variety to choose from) to make your ad stand out and a variety of sizes and prices. Call the phone company and ask to receive sales information on both the yellow pages and the white pages. After receiving the information, think about what you might want to do and make an appointment for a representative to come out and see you. The price list is hard to decipher until you have used it several times.

If you haven't thought up a name for your company yet, try to pick one that starts with the letter A or B. This places your name right in the beginning of each category that you select to be listed under in the yellow pages. Since there is quite a bit of competition out there, you want potential customers to spot your ad before they see other ads. Include the words, "*Mention this ad and receive an extra $25 off of your order.*" They may call several other competitors, but they are *sure* to call your company.

Magazine Advertising

Advertise in regional magazines and directories — *any publication that your target market is reading.* These ads should be tested — the wording of the ad, the size, shape, and publication in which the ad will run. If the ads are working in a particular publication, keep running them. Remember, the average customer must see an ad twenty-seven times before he or she will decide to act on it.

Make sure your ad is consistent with the needs, desires, and values of your target market and also the newspaper or publication in which you advertise. Try to find out where your competition advertises. If their ads are running month after month, you know they are working or they wouldn't keep running the ads.

Magazine ads are most effective if they are on the back page of the magazine or included within the first fifteen pages of the publication. Attempt to have the ad placed on the right hand page rather than on the less-effective left hand page. An advertising agency that repeatedly does business with the magazine will have more pull than you will have in getting you better placement.

The use of color in magazine ads is not as effective as with newspapers, since magazines contain a lot of color already.

Larger libraries carry *Standard Rate and Data Service* publications that list ad rates for all larger consumer magazines, business magazines, and some regional publications. Or, find a publication that interests you and write for their rate card. Be sure that the section of the magazine where your ad is placed is favorable and listed in a category that clearly spells out what you do; for example, Interior Design and Decorating Services; Window Treatments; Carpeting and Floor Covering.

Newspaper Advertising

Newspapers are the fastest way to test an ad. You can use a coded ad in half of the newspapers and another coded ad in the other half. Change only one major item in the ad and see which one gets the best response. The important items to test are the headline, subhead (the smaller headline), and the offer. Or leave these elements alone and test the price.

Use your imagination when creating newspaper advertisements. A second color can be very effective, since very little color is usually used in newspapers. If you opt to use a second color, the price for the ad will go up at least 20 percent, but your response to the ad will also go up. Test and code the use of color against plain black and white.

Customers are used to the discount look, the designer look (no information included), and the department store look (expensive ad agency) advertising a specific sale. Stand apart and be different. Imaginative ads will give you more leads, and subsequently more sales and profit. If you feel uncomfortable in creating and designing your own advertisements, hire a marketing or advertising agency to help you. **Strive to use these following elements in your ads:**

- Personality.

- Uncommon ad layouts.

- Easy-reading copy.

- Illustrations.

- Attention-getting headlines.

- Stress your company's strong and unique points that are different from your competition. Focus on price (if yours are lower), product mix, available fabrics, brand names, guarantees, other services, reputation, location (if to your benefit), and anything else that makes your company the preferred one to select.

- Sell window beauty. Show different ideas that work.

- Include a coupon with an expiration date to encourage prospects to act now.

Once you have settled on an ad that is working for you, keep using it. You want customers to be familiar with the image and identity you are projecting.

Advertisement Placement

The very best place your advertisement can appear for maximum visibility and maximum readership is on the front page of a section. The second best placement for your ad is on the back page of the newspaper section. Not many people will read an entire newspaper. But everyone who handles the paper will read, or at least glance at, the front and back of each section. Place the same ad within the various newspaper sections and they will only be read by the person who is interested enough to open that section.

Should a reader happen to see an eye-catching ad or an interesting headline, he or she will stop and take a *slightly* closer look. You have got to get the reader to *see* the ad before he or she will *read* the ad.

Make Your Advertisements Look Like News Stories

Make your ad look like a news story. Make it look like an editor got excited about your business and what you had to offer and decided to write a feature article complete with pictures about you and your company. At the end of the feature story, tell the readers how and where they can find you and your company. Have the article typeset to look like it is a part of the newspaper and is simply another story. Tests have shown that editorial material or material that is made to look like editorial material will get 500 percent more readership than material that looks like an advertisement (graphics, line art, reverse type, different type styles, etc.).

While planning your feature story ad, remember to add several boldfaced and large subheadings for your story. While you will have a headline, should the column run vertically down the page of the newspaper, you can catch the eye of the reader further down the column with subheads.

Remnant Space

Buy remnant space whenever possible for your advertisements. Do this by sending material to be published to the newspaper or regional magazine, and make a request with an accompanying letter to hold the ad until they have remnant or surplus space. Enclose an insertion order and a check for half of the going rate for a standby ad for the particular medium.

Space becomes available due to last minute cancellations of scheduled advertisements or because of production problems that arise. Normally when this happens, the newspaper will insert a house ad or a public service ad to fill the spot in the medium. When they do this, they are not paid for the advertisement, but they do it as a public service. When you buy remnant space from a newspaper or magazine, they are able to fill a spot and still make *some* money.

Ask the newspaper or magazine to hold the material and the check *until* such space becomes available. Request a tear sheet (a copy) of the ad to be sent to you when the ad is run. Finalize your letter by asking the newspaper to act on your offer by such and such a time (within one month) or return the check and destroy the ad if they do not want to participate at this time. Give a contact name and number for them to call should there be any questions. *Most* newspapers and regional magazines will take you up on your offer.

Ad Planning

Planning Effective Display Advertisements

When planning a display advertisement, use the following suggestions for success:

- Analyze your competitor's ads. Decide how you could improve their ads and create a better ad for your company.

- Use your nicely designed logo — over time it will become recognized.

- Design the ad to target your ideal customer. Articulate in terms of that customer's wants and needs. Demonstrate precisely how you have the answer to his or her unique problem.

- Most people are used to reading copy set at forty characters wide. Setting the copy wider or narrower will tend to make it *harder to read* for the average person.

- Boldface or italics are great for setting off key sentences and paragraphs.

- Eleven-point fonts are a good size for readability.

- Create an eye-catching headline, which should stress a benefit and be placed above the ad. What do you have to *benefit* the prospect? Try to address the headline to the reader (use "you").

- Use subheads.

- Mention your offer in your headline or subhead.

- Stress benefits.

- Keep the message simple (KIS) and easy to understand and read. Write the ad so it is clear and gets to the point; who you are, what benefits are offered, what your company has to offer, and how to reach you.

- Use the same theme for all of your ads. This is known as using a unique selling proposition.

- Be informative with your message.

- Follow the Federal Trade Commission truth in advertising guidelines.

- Tell the truth.

- Incorporate testimonials into the ad. Use full names and cities instead of just initials in the testimonials.

- Try to convince the reader of the credibility of the ad.

- Be repetitive in your message — repeat the same message worded in a different way.

- Appeal to the customer's emotions (hope, admiration, fear).

- Make the ad large enough to see.

- Make the message long enough to get the message across.

- Use imagination. But remember humorous ads *rarely* make sales.

- Use the most effective timing for the ad placement.

- Display the right product in the ad (sought after and salable).

- If you have a newsletter, publication, or information kit, show a small picture of it in your ad. Give this newsletter, publication, or kit a classy name, such as an information kit, resourse guide, etc.

- If you are trying for those corporate or commercial jobs, include you fax machine number in your ads.

- Test the ad. If you are placing the ad in more than one publication, try a variation on the wording in the various publications to see which one pulls the most response.

- Use the name of your firm's owner in the ad. Invite the prospect to call you.

- Give your address, phone number, coupon, and invitation to look you up in the yellow pages.

- Use a limited-time offer. Offer free information, a free consultation, gift, etc. Describe the "free item." Discuss the high value of the free offer.

- An offer of a premium, sweepstakes, free offer, and low pricing will help build the initial response to the ad.

- Call the customer to action — tell the customer what to do.

- Use a border or corner design (in a different color if possible) to call attention to the ad and separate it from other adjacent ads.

- Once you have developed an effective ad, treat it as the control, and attempt to beat it by varying something every time you use the ad in the future. Try adding devices such as a premium, the use of expiration dates, or adding a personalized cover letter to see if the response increases.

- Keep accurate records of the results of each of your ads for future testing reference.

When your ad finally does start to show less response, it is time to rewrite it. Reuse the original ad later, when it will appear new again.

If your ads are effective, your competition will try to emulate you. Some competitors will copy you closely, give their company a similar name and copying your ads.

Direct Mail

Direct mail can be a very effective marketing tool to use, if you time it right and get the mail in the hands of the right prospect. Instead of taking names and addresses out of a phone book, mail to certain professions or purchase a mailing list. Mailing lists are available for newly closed escrows, marriages, births, and from local professional organizations, etc.

Prepare a package to send out to prospective customers. The package should consist of a one-page letter, a brochure and a reply card (or a reply coupon and small addressed envelope) placed in a #10 envelope. The reply card may be filled out by prospects and mailed back to set up an appointment.

The best months for response are January and October. Time your mail to arrive on a day other than Monday. People are usually flooded with mail on Mondays and your piece may be tossed in the trash, unopened.

Test the letter and brochure by mailing to two hundred prospects. If you generate a fair response (7 to 10 percent), then mail it out in larger quantities. If you do not get any response, rewrite the letter, review your market (who did you send the letters to), and give it another try. When you find a letter that is working for you, keep using it.

Multiply the percentage of return (say 2 percent) of the initial mailing times how many mailings you plan to do each time, to see what your response will be ahead of time. This will give you an accurate idea of what you may expect when you mail out five hundred or one thousand letters. If you need to pick up twenty leads to make ten sales then you need to mail out a specified number of letters to achieve this figure. Proper timing is important. Recessionary periods, the holidays, vacation time, (for consumers, not businesses), etc. must be considered. Generally, you will receive most of the response from you mailings within two to four weeks after you mail them. Remember, third class mail (bulk mail) is the lowest priority mail of the post office. It goes out after all other mail. **Below is the letter format to use when direct mailing your packets of information:**

- Grab their attention with an opening statement written in the second person (place a "you" within the first few words of the opening sentence). You will *get and hold* prospective buyers' attention with this technique. State a strong benefit in the opening sentence. Or state an interesting fact or statistic or ask a question.

- For the next several paragraphs elaborate on a perceived problem that your potential customer may have. Let the customer know what your company has to help solve this "problem."

- Give information about your company and reputation and offer a few quoted testimonial comments that you received from your customers. Tell the prospect why your services are superior and how you are able to solve his or her interior design problems and needs.

- Call for the prospect to act **now**. Do this by offering a free estimate or in-home consultation, a discount on future purchases (enclose a dated coupon), a free newsletter or publication, or a free gift. Ask the prospect to either fill out the enclosed reply card (either stamped or unstamped) or call to make an appointment with you or one of your decorators. The reply card should be rather noncommittal so you do not scare off your prospect. State at the top of the card, beneath your logo, "*Yes, I am interested in finding out more information about the products and services that you have to offer. I am currently interested in_____and in the future may be interested in_____.*"

    Next, have two boxes to check. The first one should read something like this: "*Please call to set up my free, no obligation, in-home consultation, so that I may find out more about your products and services.*" The first box to check is for the immediate need customers. They *realize* that a decorator will call them. Naturally, there will be far fewer customers checking this box than there will be checking the following box.

    The second box should offer the other choice: information. "*Please send me information on the following services and products: _____.*" By checking the second box, the customer is saying, "*I'm somewhat interested. Please send me more information about the services and products, but do not call and apply any pressure.*"

    Of the prospects who check either box, only 10 percent to 27 percent will actually buy from you within the next year or so. Some of the customers were not really that interested and were merely curious. Some may have been interior design students or wishful interior designers who were collecting information for future business ideas. Many of the potential customers looked at your information, got interested, and found a deal elsewhere that they couldn't pass up. Some of the people died, divorced, got married, lost their jobs, or moved. Some wish they could redecorate but haven't and never will. Some of the prospects may have been intimidated by the professionalism of your mailing pieces, and others may have thought they weren't professional enough in appearance. You just cannot please everyone.

High-Impact Direct Mail Marketing Pieces

Direct mail marketing is a successful and effective way to sell products and services for interior design firms. Unfortunately, potential customers receive vast amounts of advertising pieces daily in the mail. To be effective with this marketing method, create direct mail pieces that will stand out, get noticed, and not end up in the trash can. If the direct mail piece does not stand out, it will not get noticed by a consumer who may need your products and services.

Your main goals with your direct mail pieces are to entice potential customers to give you their business. Realize that any direct mail piece presents your company's image on paper to your potential customers. Make them professional looking.

Creating effective direct response pieces takes careful planning and much thought. Every part of the flyer or brochure contributes to the effectiveness of the direct mail piece. The purposes of direct mail pieces are to:

- Attract attention.

- Create interest.

- Call the customer to action.

- Appeal to a customer's emotions, not to his or her intellect. Feelings and emotions are the strong motivators to move a customer to buy or not to buy.

Techniques to use for noticeable direct mail flyers and brochures:

Professional appearance:
Direct mail pieces must have a professional appearance. Your direct mail piece speaks for your company. It relates to the customer whether you are organized, careful, dependable, and neat. Design a quality direct mail piece and create a good first impression.

Logo:
Have a logo designed and created for your company. Logos can be as simple as stylized type to a unique special object or design. People remember logos and are more impressed when you have one than if you don't. Subconsciously people will recognize your logo when they see it again and will automatically read other advertisements that they see with the same logo.

Illustrations:
Drawings and quality photographs are worth a thousand words and will increase your response to your advertising pieces. Readers will immediately see what you are trying to say. Studies indicate a picture of a telephone next to your telephone number will give you a much higher response from readers, than just listing a phone number on the direct response piece. Place captions under illustrations and photographs, since twice as many people read captions than read body copy.

Graphics:
Add graphics to the direct mail piece for style and interest. Clip art books are readily available at art supply stores, and computer graphic programs are readily available at computer and software stores for your use. If you desire hand drawn pictures, have them drawn by a professional artist rather than attempting them on your own and adding a "cheap" feel to your ad piece.

Size:
Plan the size of your direct mail piece for its purpose. If you want the customer to keep it around, plan a fold-up brochure rather than an 8 ½" by 11" flyer that may or may not be read before being tossed in the trash.

Don't overcrowd the direct mail piece:
Less is more. If you overcrowd the direct mail piece, your potential customer will not be able to easily see the information due to the overcrowdedness. Don't place the most important part of your message at the end of your mail piece; place it near the beginning where you are trying to grab and hold the reader's attention. Focus on the strong points that are the most important to the customer.

Use balance:

Incorporate *visual triangles* in your direct mail piece. Triangles draw the eye to the important points in the message. If you lay out all of the information in straight lines, the reader quickly becomes bored. Start with a short heading, add copy and pictures underneath that widen out to the sides in the middle area of the flyer. Visually *invert* another triangle that butts against the top triangle. Continue the copy to the bottom of the triangle, and the bottom of the flyer. Use short lines to end the flyer (and top of the triangle), stating your address, telephone number, and other pertinent information.

Make the offer a financial savings:

Make an offer for your services or products that will save the potential customer money. Introductory offers get the reader's attention. Plan the direct mail piece so that the special offer is at the top of the mail piece to grab attention. Place coupons at the bottom or top to avoid cutting your message in half. Plan coupons so that they do not exceed three inches in height. If you make them larger, you are taking a chance that they take up too much space and the customer won't save them.

Include a personalized letter with the direct mail piece:

To get maximum response, include a personalized letter with your direct mail piece. A letter will increase the response to the direct mail piece, and you are able to describe *how* what you are offering will benefit the potential customer.

Include an incentive:

Get your potential customer to respond early by giving him or her an incentive to do so. Offer a small gift for making the appointment or visiting your studio by a certain date.

Satisfy a need:

Satisfy a need with your product or service. Jot down everything you want to communicate to your customer. Keep customer needs uppermost in your mind. Brainstorm and think of unique ways your product or service may be used.

Lend credibility:

Lend credibility to your company by offering important data about your company in your direct mail pieces. Tell them how many employees you have, how long you have been in business, the number of satisfied customers, size and rate of growth of your company, and include a photograph of the company president and your store or studio. Do not exaggerate your claims.

Testimonials

Testimonials are comments or letters about your company, products, and service from satisfied customers. Put them in your brochures and advertising pieces. If you are not receiving many letters — most people are now too busy to bother — send a note to your satisfied customers *asking* for comments about the services and products that you provided.

At the end of the note, have a place where they may sign and the phrase, *"You have my permission to use my name and comments in ads, brochures, in mailing pieces, and for other promotional efforts for the purpose of marketing your products and services."* By writing a note to customers asking for their comments, you are also asking for feedback on your products and services. The comments may not all be positive. You will get a good idea of the areas that need improving. **Testimonials come in three forms:**

- **The satisfied customer.** Use several one- or two-line endorsements from customers in your brochure.

- **Third-party endorsements.** An expert not associated with your company could present the offer, giving his or her professional opinion about the dependability and quality of the jobs your company provides.

- **Celebrity endorsements.** If you are lucky enough to know any well-known celebrities or dignitaries, a small picture of them, with a one-liner and their autograph endorsing your company, can go a long way in lending credibility to your company.

Validators

Validators are used on direct mail pieces to *appear* that as an afterthought you added a reminder to the prospect to get their attention. The key to their effectiveness is to keep the validator simple. Here are a few examples:

- This offer is only for our preferred customers.

- This is a one-time offer!

- This is a private sale (invitation) for you only.

- Hurry, the supply is limited!

- A personal message from our company president:

- Make your appointment now. The price will be going up next month!

Premiums

Premiums are small "free" gifts that you give prospects and customers as an incentive to get them to come to your place of business, or to set up that appointment. Premiums usually range in price from $1 to $10 and should be imprinted with your logo, company name, address, and telephone number. If you have a company slogan, this is a opportune place to use it. People love to get something free, and premiums make them feel good about your company. If the premium is useful and/or something that will be used frequently by your potential customer, he or she will notice your name every time the item is used. Typical premiums are calendars, coffee mugs, key chains, note pads, pens, pencils, balloons, tote bags, big clip paper clips, etc. The more original and useful the item, the better.

Writing Ad Copy

As long as it is placed in the right medium where it will reach the type of customer who will respond to your ad, your ad copy is what sells your goods and services to your customer. The ad copy you present to the prospective customer will make or break you.

- You cannot bore (with uninteresting ad copy) people into buying from you; you can only interest them in buying from you.

- Use short sentences, short paragraphs, and easy-to-understand words to write your copy.

- Briefly tell your prospects what your firm will do for them and list specific reasons for them to call your company.

- The more particulars and facts you give, the more prospects you will attract to your firm.

- Start your copy with a drop initial (larger first letter) to call attention to it.

- Advertisements with long copy communicate the impression that you have something important to say, whether people go ahead and read the copy or not.

- If you design your ads to look like editorials, you will interest more readers. Experts project that six times more readers will read an advertisement that looks like an editorial than will read one that looks like an advertisement. Set your copy in serif type, thirty-five to forty-five characters wide, in three columns of type. Should the newspaper or magazine insist on labeling your ad with the word "advertisement," set the word in italic caps in reverse (upside down) at the top or bottom of the ad. Not many people will notice or be able to read it.

- Most customers like sales, markdowns, and special offers. On some products, be specific with prices. Customers do not like to ask the price of things.

- Use a testimonial in your copy; doing so will make you appear more credible.

- Use coupons as mini ads. Readers will go right to the coupon to see what you are offering. Design coupons to include your company name, what you are promising, and a small drawing or photo of what you are offering. Keep your prospects motivated by phrases such as: limited editions, limited supply, last time at this price, special price for making appointment by ____, etc.

If you do not think you can write effective copy after reviewing this section, then hire a copywriter to write your advertising copy for you. A good copywriter will be a good investment for you — it is the copy that will bring in the customers.

The headline:

The headline that you select is the most important part of any ad. Appeal to the potential customer's self interest. Design a positive headline that will reach out and grab the reader's attention. If the headline is not dynamic, the reader will probably not even look at the body copy. The headline announces to your reader what you are going to review in your piece. If you have some *news* to tell, tell it in the headline. Try to include your company name in the headline, if possible. If you don't, 80 percent, of the people who read the headline only will not know what company is advertising.

Every word that you use for the headline is very important. Select words that are concise, easy to read and understand, and get right to the point. Suggested words include *now, you, any, today, new, free, and easy.*

Since five times as many people read the headline than read the body copy, unless you are able to sell the customer in the headline, you have wasted 90 percent of your money. The key part of any headline is the "hook." The hook is used to catch the readers' attention and create enough interest for them to want to read further. Unless you grab your reader with an enticing headline, you have wasted your time and money with the piece.

Words frequently used to hook your reader: include *why, how, now, new, this,* and *what.* By designing your headline around these words, your reader or prospective customer wants to know *how* your subject of the headline does what it does, *what* is new or *why* it is what it is. The customer then proceeds to read on and find out *why, what, or how.*

- The headline should be brief and to the point, under ten words).

- Appeal to the customer's self interests. *What can it do for the customer?*

- Write the headline in a positive, "you" point of view.

- Do not put periods at the end of headlines. This causes eyes to subconsciously stop and not want to read further into the copy.

- Give every photograph or illustration a caption.

- Headlines below illustrations or photographs are read by 10 percent more people than are headlines above illustrations and photographs.

- Do not use all capital letters for headlines. All capitals are not as easy to read as a combination of upper- and lowercase letters.

- Do not set the letters too far apart in a headline or subhead. Your reader may not even see it if you do.

- Do not use oversized lettering for the copy. Again, your reader will not even see it. How many times have you searched through an ad looking for vital information that was right before your eyes in too-large letters.

- Do not superimpose headlines on top of medium to deep toned illustrations or photographs.

- The use of solid or screened reverse block backgrounds is a common way to make headlines stand out. Screened backgrounds are more subtle; screen them from 15 percent to 25 percent.

- To create a romantic effect, use a light printed background with a superimposed solid headline on top of the printed background.

Stress benefits to the customer:

Benefits sell. Load your headlines, subheads, and copy with benefits. Stress benefits early in your copy. Keep the customer interested in wanting to know more. What will it do for the customer? Tell the customer what your ideas, products, and services will do for him or her. Consumers buy to satisfy their wants and desires. The purchase needs to fulfil a need, either physical or emotional, before the customer will buy.

- Analyze which benefit will have the most impact on the reader and stress that benefit when writing your ad copy.

- Do not exaggerate or appear to do so in your ad copy. Base any statements on fact.

The lead:

The lead or subhead (boldface smaller headline) of the opening paragraph is the next most important part of your ad piece. The lead is the introduction to the rest of your body copy. Again, the lead needs to compel your reader to want to know more. Create a lead that gets right to the point and does not leave your reader trying to guess what you are trying to say. Unlike the headline, which announces what is to be discussed in the piece, the lead actually discusses the subject at hand. The use of a lead is particularly effective if you are using long copy. Place a two-sentence lead in a smaller type size (between the headline size and copy size). Placing a lead heightens the reader's desire to read the body copy.

Effective leads are one or more questions asked of your reader. A lead that starts this way tells the reader that you are going to discuss the question/questions you have asked. A question lead arouses your reader's curiosity.

Another common lead technique is to review the information that you are about to discuss in depth in the body copy. A lead of this nature describes *who, what, where, when, why, and how.*

Sometimes it is best to expand on the headline and go into more detail. If you continue to hold your reader's attention in the lead, he or she is directed toward reading the rest of the body copy. When writing your lead, focus on the most important features and benefits of the product. Provide information while making the lead interesting to your readers. Lead them to continue to read the rest of your message in your body copy. Create interest and describe the most important benefit or characteristic of your product or service

Body copy:

The body copy of your ad mail piece is the written information part. The body copy should be planned as carefully as the rest of your piece. *Every* word counts, so careful word selection is imperative. Keep it simple and easy to understand with word selection, sentence structure, and use short sentences. It is said that you should strive to write for the general population at a sixth or seventh grade level.

In body copy hold your reader's attention by using high-impact, powerful, attention-getting words such as *free, easy, guaranteed, unique, elegant, proven, value, new, now, secret, latest, today, exciting, limited time, limited supply, latest, and proven.*

Design and organize the body copy so that it can present a complete credible discussion of what you are describing. The body copy should tell the readers how your product or service will solve their problem. The body copy is your chance to appear credible by providing readers with explanations and proof of promised answers to their problem.

The most important area of your body copy is the *call to action.* Tell the potential customer *what* to do, and when. For an effective ad you must direct your readers to act. Let them know *how* they may buy your products and services or get more information. Use a direct request or an appeal to get the reader to act. Buy now! Call now! Limited-time sale! Order today! Send this coupon at once! This type of wording imparts a sense of urgency to your readers and gives them an incentive to act. Give them something free if they will act before a certain time period. Motivate your readers to act at once without delay.

Copy guidelines:

- State a problem or need.

- Present solutions to the problem and needs, stated clearly and credibly.

- Explain your solution and give proof.

- Call the prospective customer to action (tell them how to act)

- Consider a special incentive if the customer will respond quickly (extra $25 savings if the appointment is made by _____).

- The use of a drop initial to start your copy is an effective way to get readers to read the copy.

- Limit the opening paragraph to eleven words.

- After two or three inches of copy, insert a subhead and thereafter throughout the copy. Subheads keep the reader reading the copy. Asking questions in a subhead is an effective way to keep the reader curious about what is to come.

The layout:

Once you have designed your headline and lead and written your body copy, arrange everything on the page in an attractive, simple, and appealing manner so the reader will want to read it. The layout is a very important part of your ad.

Type your text with black ink and white paper for layouts, regardless of the colors used to print. Cut out pictures and move them around on the paper until you have an eye-pleasing arrangement. Do not use more than three different type styles on the same piece. Select type styles that you can consistently use from now on for *all* of your advertising pieces. Think in angles, particularly at the top of the piece and the bottom.

Next, try out different sizes for the fonts for headlines and subheads. This is easily done on a computer with a laser printer that has different size fonts built-in or with a separate computer program that tells the printer to make the selected fonts. Also available are transfer-lettering sheets at art stores.

If you are not computer literate and don't have a computer literate friend, take your rough layout in the original type to a printer to have the flyer professionally typeset in the size fonts desired for the various pieces of copy.

- Have artwork or headlines easily reduced or enlarged at copy shops that have high-quality copiers.

- Lay out your page so the items with the most information are placed from top to bottom. Placing them in this manner leads the reader's eye down the page.

- Some phrases need to be placed in a larger font or other type styles than some of the other phrases.

- Place the headline in a bold, larger type face at the top of the page because this placement grabs the reader's attention.

- Place special incentives, such as what you are offering free, near the center of the page, which will move the reader's eye down the page while giving him or her more information.

- Near the bottom of the page, place your call to action in bold letters. **Sale ends tomorrow.** Placement at the bottom of the page motivates the reader to act now.

- Identify the most important information and place it so that it may be spotted quickly on the page. This information should paint a complete picture for the customer.

- Select an easy-to-read typeface. Use capitals for the first letters of the main words, and lowercase letters for all other letters (all capitals letters for headlines and subhead are hard to read).

- Allow enough white space so your ad does not look overcrowded.

- Remove all smudges, excessive glue and cover-up specks, and unwanted lines with correction fluid.

- Be sure to proofread when you are done with the layout and before you go to print! It is preferable to have someone else proofread as sometimes one can completely overlook the obvious. Be sure that the final layout grabs the reader's interest and invites them to keep reading to see what you have to offer.

Layout supplies:

Glue sticks are a wonderful invention for paste-up. You can pull up the paper strips (as with rubber cement) if you make a mistake. Also, glue sticks seal the paper tighter together than does rubber cement. When you have the ad designed the way you want it, take it to a high-quality print shop that has a paste-up program for its computerized copy machine. All the paper strips lines on the flyer will disappear, and you won't have to use correction fluid to erase them. If the copy shop doesn't have the computerized paste-up program for its copier, then use correction fluid to erase all lines that show up after you make a high-quality copy. It is important to have a high-quality initial copy made, even if it costs somewhat more. Then use the higher-quality copy as the master copy, from which all subsequent copies will be made.

Typography:

Good typography helps people read your copy, while bad topography hinders them. Do not make the mistake of setting headlines in all capital letters. Capitals do not have ascenders or descenders to help you recognize words. Words made up of all capital letters, tend to be read letter-by-letter, not word-by-word. People are used to reading material in lower-case letters. **Follow these topography rules:**

- Make sure that you use easy-to-read fonts in a readable type size. eleven-point type size is easy to real and readily used. Never use a type size smaller than eight point for the smallest type.

- Leading is the amount of space between each line of type. Don't make the lines too close together, or they will be harder to read.

- The easiest to read typefaces are those that people are already used to. These are the serif fonts. These have a curlicue or cross stroke given to Roman typefaces to keep your eye moving. Look closely at the type style you are reading for the tiny hooks on each letter.

- Sans serif faces are also known as Gothic, without serifs or small hooks on the ends of each letter to lead your eye to the next letter. They are very difficult to read. Use sans serif faces only in headlines and in small amounts. Serif fonts help the eye pick up the shape of the letter.

- *Never* use more than two different typefaces in any layout for your printed materials.

- The fancier the typeface, the harder it is to read.

Commercial art/graphic art:

Commercial art is the design and paste-up of camera-ready layouts for your advertising pieces and marketing materials. Commercial artists may be found as free lance commercial artists, at advertising agencies, and through print shops and print brokers. Be sure to balance an overly creative design with its sales ability. Your ultimate goal is to attract as many customers as possible, not to have an award-winning design that doesn't do its sales job.

Borders, corners, graphic designs:

Narrow to wide lines and a wide variety of corner effects help separate ads from one another. These design elements are commonly found in telephone book advertisements, but may be incorporated into the logo of your company and consistently used for all types of printed material. Newspapers and phone book ad providers have a variety of borders, corners, and graphic designs available for use when they help design your ad for their publication.

Clip art books available at graphic arts stores, art stores, and bookstores have all types of lines, borders, corners, and clip art graphic designs available for use. Scan them with a scanner for your computer or copy them and paste them on to your layout.

Balance the use of graphic images wisely to attract attention to your advertisement. Overuse of graphic images and lines can cause your ad to look overcrowded and prevent your reader from having smooth eye flow when reading it.

Newsletters

Self-published newsletters, mailed quarterly to your past customers and potential customers, are another way to keep your name and your company's name current in the minds of customers.

Newsletters can bring you fame, prestige, and personal satisfaction. Poorly done newsletters will also make you look incompetent. Do not proceed with self-published newsletters unless you are an expert and know what you are writing about. Realize that although you may be affiliated with various organizations and have your degree in interior design, you may not be an expert. Do you have the hands-on experience and well-rounded knowledge to go along with the education? Potential customers will read and review your newsletters before hiring you to see if you know what you are doing. They know they don't know how to do the job, but want to make sure that you know how to do the job. When they feel you are an expert, they will become long-term customers and won't settle for another designer to work with them.

Should you decide to publish a newsletter, share your greatest ideas. Don't hold back. By revealing the best you have, you turn the readers into future customers. To sell these potential customers tell them what you know, and make them feel that you will also deliver your best for them should they hire you.

- Send newsletters at regular intervals. Customers will start looking for them and expecting creative decorating ideas and solutions in the mail.

- Print the newsletter on two to four sheets of paper. Have it typeset on a laser printer and have them copied at a high-quality copy shop.

- Provide correct information, tips, suggestions, ideas, and advice relating to your line of products and services.

- Incorporate your company's name in the title of your newsletter.

- If you have a catchy company name, call your newsletter "The (your company name) Quarterly, Digest, Newsletter."

- Readers want to *experience* your personality. Add a unique personality to the newsletter, and some *definite* opinions.

- Include on your mailing list prominent members of the community: local politicians, CEOs of the largest companies in the area, officers of civic and business organizations, and local media including radio and TV personalities and newspaper reporters and editors. mailing list.

- Distribute your newsletter *free* to companies and prospective customers that you would like to do business with.

Direct Mail Postcards

Direct mail postcards need to be written to sell. Consider using inexpensive postcards as a direct mail piece. The customer has thirty seconds to decide to give you a call. Decide what is different about your product and sell those points. Try out different headlines and test each approach in one-month intervals. Track the results. When working with a customer, ask her which features of the sales pitch appealed to her, and *why* she responded to the postcard. These are the key elements of designing a successful direct mail postcard:

- Whatever marketing concepts you use, test it and make changes. Continue to test and make changes. Test each element of the postcard, one at a time, until you find out which one outpulls all others.

- The headline includes the main point of the advertisement. Headlines need to grab your prospects' attention and get them interested to learn more and keep reading.

- Have an eye-catching and appealing logo, in terms of color and design. Use it several times in different sizes both in front and in back of the postcard.

- Use the *AIDA* rules when writing copy for your postcard. Get your customers' *attention*, gain their *interest*, create *desire*, and call them to *action* (call today).

- Write the copy for the postcard on about a seventh- or eighth-grade reading level. Use simpler words for maximum readership and understandability.

- Use words that appeal to customers. Some of the words to use: *discover, announcing, free, new, special, guarantee, no charge, savings, and innovative.*

- Ask short, direct questions. Are you interested in having a *free* decorator consultation? Do you want to *solve* your decorating problems? Are you *interested?* Customers are reminded about their problems, and you are offering a solution.

- When writing copy for postcards, repeat important information that you don't want missed, in different ways, again and again.

- Repeat the name of your company several times. Your objective is to have your name sink in and stay with the customer.

- Use bullets as shown here to list easy-to-follow vital or specific points about your message.

- Customers will read footnotes, so use them. They are the most read part of the postcard. Use a PS or other footnote to support the headline in the postcard (which is probably on the reverse of the postcard). Catch your potential customer's eye with the headline, go into detail in the body of the copy, and then reiterate the information to support the headline. If you use *free* in the headline, then support it in the footnote with words like "no charge." Simply say in another way what you have already said. This is the place to tell them there's a money-back guarantee, the item may be returned within thirty days for a refund, satisfaction is guaranteed, etc.

• Add your signature (have it printed; it is preferable to hand signing each postcard).

Brochures

When starting your own interior design or decorating firm, decide to project a professional appearance immediately for your prospective customers. This is not something that you should put off, until you have plenty of money coming in. Project a professional appearance to get this type of business off of the ground and to keep it growing. Chances are your competition is *not* doing this, which is great! Outshine them from the start.

Design a brochure that reflects the products and services you have to offer. The brochure should tell the customer what you are about, but still leave some information unsaid. You are trying to entice the customer to phone your company, or come in and pay you a visit to find out more.

Create a promotional brochure that offers decorating tips and solutions. Be careful to give the customer tips and solutions that the majority of people can use. If you do, they will save the brochure for future reference — either for themselves or for someone they know with a decorating dilemma. Include information about the services and products that you have available and how the customer may reach you.

Wherever you see bulletin boards, attach several small brochures and business cards.

Large businesses and commercial clients must have a brochure or other sales information about your company before they will buy from you. Sometimes you will not even be allowed to bid on the job unless you appear professional enough with quality sales information. If you supply sales information tailored to your business, and your competition doesn't, who do you think will appear more professional and get the job? People like to pick up the phone and ask for more information to be sent out to them. A brochure helps you establish credibility with your prospective customer.

Outline the brochure to cover key points that are also mentioned during a sales talk. The customer is serviced until he or she is satisfied, you offer a four-week delivery, you take Visa and Mastercard, and list other preferred reasons for the customer to select your company over another.

Sales information and brochures educate customers about the problem that they are faced with. Hand potential customers a brochure about your company and services offered, along with other brochures about the particular products they are considering purchasing. They can now read up on your company, while becoming informed about products they are interested in.

Any sales material requested by your prospects should promptly be sent out by the following day. Keep enough supplies on hand so you do not run out.

Brochure Planning

Create a six-panel brochure with an 8 ½" by 11", letter-size paper by folding the sheet into six panels. Place the paper in front of you with the 8 ½" area laying horizontal. Place two horizontal folds as you would when you place a letter in an envelope. The brochure will come out 3 ⅔" by 8 ½". This is a nice size brochure or booklet.

Create an eight-paneled brochure by folding 8 ½" x 14", legal size paper into eight panels in the same manner, with three horizontal folds. Again, this makes a nice brochure.

Plan a four-panel brochure by creating a six-panel brochure and perforate the last panel, creating a tear-off coupon for your customer to fill out and return to you for extra savings, referrals, or an in-home appointment.

Brochures of this size fit easily into an envelope with a letter for mailing. Plan these brochures to be self-mailers. Self-mailers have one end panel for addressing and mailing. The end panel should *back up* to the return coupon. The reason to back up the coupon to the address panel is that when the customer returns the coupon, you can easily look on your data base and match the original mailed name and address, and record customer response results. Some facts about this size brochure:

- It fits easily into a #10 envelope.
- It is a nice size that fits easily into an envelope.
- One panel can be perforated, torn off, and sent back as a coupon.
- Your copy space is limited, allowing you to keep your brochure to the point and simple.

Formats to Use When Writing Copy for Brochures

List type of format:

This is an easy-to-read way to lay out your brochure. List the reasons *why* you are a great company to deal with and the important features about your services. Arrange the list in the order of importance. Make each point a subhead and follow with a discussion, elaborating on each point made. Always think of the way that it will benefit the customer. *What's in it for them?* How will this solve a problem, make life easier, provide self esteem? Remember to remind the customer about your fabulous reputation.

Question-and-answer dialogue:

Think about the type of questions someone inexperienced in decorating will likely ask you. Write them down and come up with appropriate, complete, positive answers. Organize them in order of the way they would probably be asked. Set off the questions in bold italics, to make them stand out in the brochure. Always have an open-ended question for the last question — how can we get started, what's the next step, etc. Plan an answer to this question that *calls for action*. Have them call for a *free* in-home appointment, stop in to the studio, or return the attached coupon back.

The who, what, where, when, why, and how approach:

This copy approach helps cover all important points. Give benefit statements when describing each topic.

Fact sheets:

You may not want to have a brochure at all, but instead may want to plan a fact sheet. Fact sheets are sheets of paper 8 ½" x 11" (preferably glossy stock) that may be planned in any of the above formats. Fact sheets can be placed with a letter, order forms, etc., and mailed in a 9" x 12" envelope.

Full-size brochures:

Larger-sized brochures will give you even more room. Do you have that much to say? Include illustrations or photographs in the brochure. With a larger brochure, there is more room for copy, allowing further detail on all points. You are given more room to sell the customer. Psychologically, you are making yourself look more substantial, impressive, and more professional.

A full-sized brochure has one page that is either 7" x 10" or 8 ½" x 11". Full-sized brochures may be four, eight, or sixteen pages. Realize that your printer works less expensively with sixteen pages, followed by eight pages (depends on the size of the finished pages). When you are getting into a brochure of this size, it needs to be bound or stapled in some way.

If the brochure is eight or more pages, it qualifies for a fourth-class book rate. This can cost you *substantially less* than it would to mail the same eight pages first class.

Lift Letters

A lift letter is a short testimonial letter enclosed in the information packet or brochure. It can be written by a respected design professional, a well-known member of the community, or a satisfied customer. This letter gives a different point of view and changes the tone of the mailing. The presentation may be completely different, and appeal to a completely separate subgroup of your intended target market group.

The lift letter can lend credibility with an added testimonial, re-emphasize what a great value the offer is, or include an extra consideration about the offer you didn't cover elsewhere. Lift letters will help to strengthen the effectiveness of mailings and give the prospect more encouragement to respond to your offer.

Information packet:

Combine your brochure with a personalized letter and any product brochures that your potential customer has expressed interest in. Tailor the letter and information to your customer's needs. Information packets make a favorable impression on prospective customers. Send information packets to the media with a press release and say that there are identical information packets available for interested customers. **Information to provide in your information packet:**

- A cover letter written in the second person (you) welcoming the potential customer to do business with you.

- A company brochure that describes your company and experience.

- Questions that customers frequently ask, complete with "benefit" answers.

- Include customer testimonials that can be verified by the potential customer.

- A list of completed, prestigious commercial jobs that may be verified and viewed by prospects.

- Reprints of press releases and published articles.

- A fee schedule for services only, if products are not purchased from you. Include terms and conditions. If you have Visa and Mastercard available, say so.

- A return coupon to schedule in-home appointments.

This type of information packet covers all the bases, answering questions that the customer hasn't even thought of yet. You appear very professional and appear to be the company that your customer should select.

Sales kit:

This is a notebook of company brochures, products, reprinted articles, letters from satisfied customers, decorators' education certificates and diplomas, a copy of your company guarantee, a list of other commercial jobs that have been completed, copies of published advertisements, affiliation with interior design organizations, and photographs of beautifully completed jobs that you show prospective customers while on in-home appointments or sales calls.

Have this information available even if your customer is not interested in looking at all of it. She may want to know where she may go to see some of your work. Flip to the appropriate page. *Are you really as qualified and educated as you say you are?* Show her your diploma or certificate and copies of articles that you have written on interior design. *What is the quality of the job you might do?* Show her your testimonial letters.

- Have the three-ring binders imprinted with your company name and logo. They are readily available from print shops, mail order office suppliers, and stationery shops.

- Each item in the sales kit should be put into a clear plastic page.

- Tailor the kit by adding or subtracting appropriate pages to fit the customer you are going to see, particularly if it is a commercial job where this kit will have a large impact.

Planning sales information:

- Create a strong benefit statement for the title for the brochure or fact sheet. The headline is 75 percent of the entire ad. The headline should promise a benefit and entice the prospect to keep reading.

- Use clear, concise language. Words, sentences, and paragraphs should be short and to the point.

- Stress *benefits* rather than features when writing ad copy. Back up the benefits with facts.

- *Use command copy.* Come right out and tell the customer what to do next and how.

- Write the copy in the second person (you need this). Try to place a "you" near the beginning of your sentences.

- Use a call to action. What does the customer do next?

- A complete company name, address, telephone number, and contact name should be listed.

- Plan colors to relate with the rest of your company cards and stationery for a nicer presentation. Half of the time they will end up in the same envelope.

- Decorators should staple business cards to the brochures to make them even more personalized.

- Include customer testimonials.

- Do not attempt to oversell your customer. They do not *usually* want to get that technical and are bored with all the details. Watch for body language signs that they have reached their saturation point on the topic at hand. Move on when you see these signs. *If you provide your prospective customer with the information he or she needs, completely answer all questions, and address other concerns about you or your company and the proposed job, the prospect will buy from you.*

- Limited-time offers speed up customer reaction time while increasing response.

- Continue to run the ads that pull well until they are no longer profitable and/or you have come up with something better.

Effective Envelopes

The outer envelope that contains the information you are sending is extremely important. Design an effective envelope that will *actually be opened*. There are several effective approaches to take in designing envelopes:

- Use a plain #10 envelope designed to look like personal mail without a company name and ad message imprinted on the envelope. This will appear to be personal correspondence rather than direct mail. Use a computer, a typewriter, or handwrite the customer's name and address directly on the envelope, rather than using labels.

- Use the face of the envelope to deliver a sales message that is so captivating that the recipient wants to open it to find out more information. Ask a question or challenge the customer to do something. Make a promise, or briefly state your offer.

- Use the words "personal" or "confidential" on the face of the envelope to ensure that it gets opened.

- Use envelopes of higher-quality stock. The envelopes will appear stylish and important.

- Use odd-shaped or odd-sized envelopes.

- Use an unusual color for the envelope or *on* the envelope.

- Use illustrations on the envelope to attract the reader's attention.

- Create an official-looking envelope. Have the envelope appear to be from a governmental agency or bureau. Do not make it so official looking that once it is open, the recipient is angered by your approach.

- Design an envelope that looks like an overnight express services package. This type of envelope should be created in red, white, and blue and appear similar to the postal service's overnight express mail.

- Have rubber stamps made in your firm's colors, or have brightly colored stickers made up to deliver messages such as, *Information You Have Requested, Preferred Customer, Open Now, or Dated Information.* If you use dull, flat colors, rather than a color that stands out, the reader may just ignore the message.

- Affix postage stamps, even if they are third-class or bulk mail rate, rather than bulk mail indicia or metered tapes for the postage. The use of metered tapes is better than bulk rate indicias.

- Mail first class, rather than third-class bulk rate, if economically feasible.

- Handwrite your name beneath your company's logo and return address in the upper left-hand corner of the envelope. This makes the correspondence appear to be personal correspondence.

Posters:

Print shops can easily and inexpensively take an ad, flyer, business card, etc., and enlarge it to poster size. A poster should deliver your selling promise not only in words but also pictorially. Use large type and have your firm name visible and easy to read from a distance. Use stronger, purer colors. And never use more than three design elements in your layout.

Business and Sales Letters

Business letters should be used for general correspondence to attract new customers, and to make more sales to existing customers. Letters can be used to:

- Reveal new and different products, services, or terms.

- Answer customer inquiries and questions.

- Invite prospective customers into your showroom or studio.

- Stay in contact with customers while they are waiting for deliveries and installations.

- Win over unhappy customers and get them to come back again.

- Increase the size of the orders.

- Introduce you and your company before telemarketing calls and/or in-home visits.

- To expand the use of your products and services with your existing customers.

- Stimulate prospective customers to contact your company to find out more about your products and services.

- Acquire sales leads.

- Encourage prospective customers to call your company.

- Invite prospective and past customers to seminars.

Target a specific segment of your market with personalized letters. These are prospects that can potentially give you very large jobs, or past customers. Tailor the letter to the individual customer and business. What do you specifically have to offer them? How will they be benefitted by hiring your firm and purchasing products from you?

Read the business section of the newspaper and look for new businesses and newly promoted people. Send them a note of congratulations on their new business or promotion. With the use of a computer and a good word processing program, you are able to write a standard letter that may be revised for other prospects.

To get and keep the reader's attention, use the following outline. If you don't feel you can successfully apply the techniques and guidelines below, hire a copywriter to do it for you:

- The success of sales letters depends on copywriting, the offer given, and the selected mailing list.

- Prepare an outline including all of the points you need to cover in the letter.

- Write the letter on 8 ½" x 11" business letterhead.

- Personalize the letter by using the customer's name (spell it correctly). Do not use the customer's name in the letter more than two times. For past customers, refer to their past order, specific ordered items, date, and amount of their last purchase.

- Use one-inch or wider margins.

- Use easy-to-read and -understand words.

- Do not justify the margins in letters; rather, keep them ragged right. Books, such as this one, are often written with justified margins to give a cleaner look. You are trying to make your reader feel you are writing the letter to him or her, personally.

- Try not to hyphenate words at the end of the line. If you can't fit the whole word on the line, place the word on the next line.

- Use correct spelling, grammar, and punctuation.

- Write the letter in the second-person. Place a "you" within the first few words of the first sentence.

- Write the letter based upon the theme, "*What is in it for the customer?*"

- *Emphasize* any offer you are making, including savings, discounts, or sales.

- Use a very positive tone throughout the letter, regardless of the reason for the letter.

- Be very specific and get right to the point of the letter.

- Write the letter in the active voice, rather than the passive voice, to add strength to your statements.

- Use nouns and verbs, rather than adjectives.

- State the facts, be honest, and do not exaggerate.

- Write the letter as you would say the words if you were talking with the customer.

- Use a headline to attract your customer's attention.

- Tell the customer what your letter is *about* in the first paragraph.

- Stress value, not the price of the product or service.

- Stimulate interest by offering something free.

- Give frequent repetition of the offered products/services features and benefits. *They* are what sell.

- If enclosing additional information or literature, pre-sell the customer on the enclosures.

- Try to hold the letter length down to one page, if possible.

- Do not exceed eight or nine lines per paragraph in the body of your letter. Do not make all of your paragraphs the same length. If you do, your letter automatically appears boring and the reader loses interest.

- If the letter is multiple pages, end the pages in midsentence, thus causing your reader to turn to the next page to read more.

- Indent paragraphs from both sides to make them stand out and appear meaningful.

- Create emphasis in other ways by <u>underlining words and phrases</u>, the use of *italics*, **bold words**, ***bold italics***, exclamation points! (one is enough), and the use of CAPITAL LETTERS. Beware of *overdoing* the use of any of these options to create emphasis in your letter.

- Add illustrations to grab and hold readers' interest.

- Read the letter out loud. If it doesn't easily flow, clean it up.

- Ask someone who doesn't know anything about decorating to read your letter to see if she understands the terminology and written information.

- Offer a guarantee. Word the guarantee in a very clear manner so the prospect completely understands what you are saying.

- Provide enough information so the prospect knows all of the facts. If the prospect lacks one piece of important information, he or she will put off calling you for that appointment.

- Keep the process for contacting you for an in-home appointment clear and simple. The fewer actions the prospect has to take, the easier he or she will find it to call you.

- Call the customer to action and encourage him or her to respond now.

- Repeat an important main point in a postscript at the end of the letter.

Additional tips for letters responding to inquiries:
- Highlight the questions the customer wants answered.

- Answer promptly, thus ensuring goodwill with your customer.

- Refer to the date of the original letter the customer sent you.

- Acknowledge the customer's inquiry.

Typography rules for letters:
- Select an easy-to-read typeface size. The older people get, the harder it is to read small type sizes. Select at least an eleven- or twelve-point type size.

- Use larger type size bold faces for headings and subheadings throughout your letters. The use of headings and subheads helps break up the letter copy and keep your reader interested in reading more.

- Serif faces (such as Times Roman, the type style used here) are *easy-to-read* type styles that take up a minimum amount of space and have little hooks on each letter that lead your eye to the next letter.

- Sans-serif typefaces are very clean and crisp and *harder to read*. Because they lack the "hooks" on the letters, your eye will not flow as fast across the letters and the words. Sans-serif typefaces should be used for headings and subheadings *only*.

- Courier is the normal typewriter face. Each letter in Courier takes up the same amount of space, unlike proportional typefaces. If you use Courier as your selected typeface, you will need more room for the same letters you use for other typefaces.

Printing and Typesetting

Typewriters:

Typewriters are a perfectly acceptable medium to use for letters and general correspondence. For any advertising pieces, have your ads typeset or use a computer and laser printer to make your camera-ready copy.

Typesetting:

Print shops will professionally typeset your advertising pieces for you. They have computerized photo-typesetting equipment and capabilities. Costs for typesetting will range from $10 to $50 per page.

Laser printing:

The use of a high-quality laser printer will give a professional typeset appearance, and you can do it yourself! If you do not purchase a laser printer, larger libraries and print shops have them available for use by the hour or by the page. Secretarial services are another resource.

Camera-ready copy:

Camera-ready copy is material that is already typeset or laser printed in high enough quality to reproduce in its original form. If you are supplying typewritten copy or computer printed copy that need fonts of varying sizes added, you will incur extra typesetting or laser printing costs, and it will take extra time before your copy is ready to be printed.

Printing and copying:

Artwork is printed or photographed to make either a quick-print paper master, or a long-running metal plate. Quickprint masters are for shortrun jobs up to three thousand copies. If artwork has lots of solid black design or heavy-line art, copies with quick-print masters may appear gray. For sharper impressions, use metal plates (they cost about $10 each), which last for thousands of copies. The size of the target market and your existing customer mailing list will dictate to you how many copies you need to have printed or photocopied.

What quality do you want to use? Less-expensive photocopies or finer-quality printing? If you use copies, have them made at a copy shop with high-quality machines. Make a sample copy before you commit to the job. If the print is hard to read, try another copy shop.

Printing quality also varies tremendously. Shop around and get several quotes. Every time you go do a reprint or add another advertising piece, shop around. Printers are aware that the average business may shop around the first time, but probably won't thereafter. Prices tend to be higher the second and subsequent times around. If you are not aware of this, you may not realize that you are paying quite a bit more, unless you pull your initial invoice. If you don't make any changes in reprints, the price should actually be less, as you are using the same plates and negatives.

Ask other business associates where they have their printing done, and ask to see samples of their work. Depending on the competition between copy shops and print shops in your area if you want more than one-thousand pieces, printing will probably be less expensive and more professional looking.

Save flyers and direct mail pieces that you think are eye-catching and nicely laid out. Take some inspiration from each of their good points and bad points and use them as guides when you design your direct mail pieces. Decide what makes the flyers appealing or interesting or uninteresting to you. Does it reach out and grab you? Do you feel like you want to keep reading to see what the message is?

Ways to Control Promotional Costs

- Have realistic expectations regarding the amount of response that will probably be generated for your efforts.

- Plan your own copy. You know what you want to say and with a little research, you can say it in ways to entice potential customers.

- Outline key points of what you want the copy to say for advertisements, and then give the outline to your copywriter to cut down his or her time charges.

- Do as much of the writing, layout, and graphic work yourself as possible. This doesn't mean do the final layout. Give the printer an almost finished product to simply perfect for you. Save up to 75 percent of the cost of a graphic artist by doing a rough layout and have the graphic artist refine it for you. Demonstrate exactly what you want from him or her.

- Show the printer or graphic artist samples of typefaces, styles of brochures or other advertisements, or any other information that can give an idea of what you are looking for.

- One ink color for your promotional pieces may just be as effective as two colors.

- Use two-color layouts rather than more expensive four-color layouts. In business publications, four-color ads cost about a third more than black and white. But, four-color layouts attract at least two times as many readers.

- Keep your graphic work simple. Cover designs that require colored reverse copy, close registration, bleeds, complicated screens, hand-lettered type styles, outlining, and full color printing are not necessary to get your message across. The more complex the color arrangement in your cover, the more expensive it will be to separate, strip, and print.

- Creative design can work wonders with two colors of ink. Screened areas of single or blended colors can provide such a variety of hues that the consumer may never even realize that you did not use a four-color process. When dealing with screens created via a computer layout program, have these output directly onto film, and when exact color match is needed, a color key can be made from these film outputs. Separation labs make color keys, service bureaus provide the film.

- A variety of screen tints combined with solid-ink elements can make even a single color look vibrant or interesting. Creative use of design, line art, and high-contrast half-tones can also bypass color to achieve an eye-catching effect. Be sure the half-tones are sharp and have good contrast.

- Use standardized sizes for your brochures and other promotional pieces.

- There is not much difference in price between printing five hundred pieces or one thousand. The price generally jumps up from 1000 to 2000. Get pricing for various quantities before making a decision.

- Realize the more printing you buy in the thousands, the less expensive each piece will be. But do not buy more than you need. Printed matter sitting there is a waste of money, especially if it's dated, and needlessly ties up money that would be better spent elsewhere.

- Become familiar with printing terminology so you can communicate intelligently with your printing suppliers and are able to comfortably shop various printing sources.

- Ask what your options are when problems arise, or when an item seems unnecessarily expensive. Ask how you can cut down the price. Ask the printer to recommend how you might achieve the same results with slight changes.

- Design promotional materials that can be used for several purposes.

- Ask if the supplier has discounts for prepayments or prompt account balances. It may cost less to pay for the printing order on your credit card, and then pay the credit balance in full at the end of the month. Get free credit up to twenty-five days.

- Take advantage of all tax deductions available for your promotional expenses.

- Always test your promotional pieces on a small scale to see if they are going to work before sending out thousands of advertisements.

- Periodically evaluate all promotional costs and find ways to cut expenses.

- Purchase only the quality of paper that you require to get your message across (ask your printer's advice). Paper comes in glossy finish or matte, white or colored, and cover weight and body weight. Very few people are going to notice the difference, unless they are involved in printing and graphic arts. Multiple colors will require a fairly heavy paper.

- Realize that when you have a rush job, your printer may have forty other rush jobs in front of yours. Plan ahead by calling your printer, giving advance notice, and asking to be fit into the schedule for all required rush jobs.

- Allow about a week for simple jobs — printed envelopes, letterhead, business cards. Allow longer periods for brochures, flyers that need to be typeset, interior display signs, etc.

- When planning your printed piece or changing proofs, try to present to the printer or graphic artist copy that is as neat as possible. If it is neat and easy to decipher, it will be easier and quicker for your printer to understand, fewer mistakes or misunderstandings will occur, and the job will go smoother, faster, and be less-expensive. Both you and the printer will be happier with the job.

- When selecting colors for the background and copy that is to sit on the background color, make sure that there is sharp contrast between the two so the copy is legible. Don't make the mistake of using black copy over a deep background color or white or reverse copy (white) against a light background.

- Thin type styles are less legible than thicker type styles.

- Any extra services such as typesetting, graphic artist services, layouts, last-minute changes, or correcting mistakes you have made in the proof stage, etc., will cost you money. Do as much preliminary work as you can if you want to keep your costs to a minimum.

- Printers with computers compatible to yours will be able to work with a computer disk. You may not have the laser or postscript printer, or typesetting machine, but they may have. They can change the font sizes of your document on disk and print in out on their high-quality printer, rather than do paste-up by hand. If you work with your printer on their output devices, you will get high quality output, and save money on the pre-press charges. You will be eliminating the amount of steps that the printer and you have to go through to create a quality product.

- Set copy in black type on white paper. Reverse copy, white type on black copy, will reduce your readership, unless you are preparing slides for a screen.

Printing Procedures

1. **Original copy:** Original ideas and copy are presented to the printer or typesetter.

2. **Typesetting:** The copy is set into type.

3. **Proof:** The proof needs to be reviewed and signed off before the printer prints. Any corrections are made here. If the corrections are the printer's fault, they won't charge for them. If they are your fault, you will be charged per correction made.

4. **Correction cycle:** All corrections are made by the typesetter.

5. **Second proof:** If any corrections were made, review and sign off the second proof.

6. **Layout:** If not already done, the type is laid out for the printed piece. If the piece is very complex, a graphic artist may be needed. You may need to revise, check, and okay the proof before going to print.

7. **Proof artwork:** Any artwork for your printed piece needs to placed on the layout and again proofed for placement.

8. **Printing:** The piece is now ready for printing.

9. **Binding:** Any desired binding is done last.

Proofs

The best way to save money with your printing is to resist changing the copy in the proof stage. If the printer has made the error on the copy, they will fix it free of charge. If you spot an error at this stage that was present in the original copy, you will pay dearly for it in time and money if changes are made at this point. Ask yourself if the error is really that bad and must be changed. You may want to go ahead and correct the error when you reprint later.

Spot errors before you present your original copy to the printer. Proofread all copy and hand it over to someone else to see what has been overlooked (phone number, address, how to contact you, misspellings, punctuation, sentence structure errors, etc.).

The printer is working off of a deadline when presented original copy for printing. You are working off of a deadline regarding *when* you need the printing done. If you do not work in a timely manner with the printer on proof corrections and with the graphic artist and typesetter making required changes and decisions, the printer will be unable to meet his or her projected deadlines.

Bulk Mail

Bulk business mail includes third-class mail, bound printed matter, and small parcels weighing less than sixteen ounces. Letters cannot exceed 3.3067 ounces. Material sent as bulk business mail must contain the same general message aimed at all who receive it, rather than an individualized piece of mail aimed at a particular individual. In other words, all of the pieces must be the same.

There is an annual fee for third-class bulk mail, which enables you to mail at the same post office at the third-class mail rates for one year. Presently the fee is $75 per year.

Each third-class bulk mailing must consist of a minimum of two hundred pieces or fifty pounds. All pieces in the mailing must belong to the same processing category. For example, they must be all letters, all flats, or all machinable parcels.

Bulk mail must be deposited during business hours at the bulk mail acceptance unit at the post office where your permit is held. Bulk mail will not be received at every post office. Select the main post office in the city where you will be doing business.

You may either meter your postage, have your printed matter printed with your permit imprint (which contains your bulk rate permit number), or use stamps (available at the regular customer counter by the roll) to affix postage to your mail. Should you use the printed permit imprint, you will pay the postal worker for the amount of individual pieces or by weight when you drop off the mail.

You will have to pre-sort the mail by zip code if all are in the same zip code areas, or by state (ten or more pieces to the same state must be secured with rubber bands and labeled with a post office label).

The post office will supply you with a book about bulk mail when you sign up for a permit. Bulk mail is the only way to go for two hundred or more pieces of mail — *especially* if each piece weighs more than one ounce (first class). Currently the price for two-hundred or more letters weighing up to 3.3067 ounces is 19.8 cents per piece. Keep in mind that third-class mail get third-class treatment from the post office. It goes out when they get around to it.

Publicity

The definition of publicity is, *"The attention or interest of the public gained, by any method."* Eighty percent of all the stories you see in the newspaper are placed there by people seeking to gain your attention. A story planted about your company gives it credibility and attention. Newspaper and magazine stories will bring you business. A story can build relationships with customers, discuss in depth your available products and services, position you and your company as experts, and remind the public that you are ready for their business.

Design firms need to constantly plan ways to put themselves before the public eye. The best publicity that a design firm can receive is to have photographs of design jobs appear in the local and regional publications, preferably shelter or trade magazines and newspapers. Should a design job get publicity from a publication, reprint and distribute copies of the article to all prospective customers. You or a public relations firm can submit the photographs and accompanying article to area trade publications that place an emphasis on shelter.

If you do a job that has a heavy emphasis on a certain product, send photographs of the product in use to the manufacturer of the product. If the company is interested in using your job in its advertisements, it will have the job professionally photographed, if you haven't already done so. If the manufacturer runs the photographs in shelter magazines with your firm's name, you have achieved invaluable exposure that you could never pay for. While you are not after the whole country for customers, you are able to freely distribute reprints of the advertisement to everyone, and can display large copies of the ad in your studio. Your company will gain *instant* credibility in the eyes of potential customers.

Get Publicity for Your Business

Publicity is the attention you get without paying for. Publicity is letting people know what you do. Normally the media are used to help you get publicity. The media include any form of public communication, from magazines and newspapers to the radio and TV. Any way you can get the word out about your business is publicity, including word-of-mouth. Publicity is proclaiming your accomplishments for all of your prospective customers to hear.

When you start your business you will be faced with the problem of how to let everyone know about your business as quickly, effectively, and inexpensively as you can. You must attract attention, if your company is to survive and grow.

Publicity can help you boost your business out of sales slumps or get your business off of the ground, magnify your company's visibility, create interest in a special sale promotion or seminar you may be having, promote the products and services you have to offer, and create a professional image for both you and your company. Publicity will stimulate your business activity, enhance your profits and increase the public's awareness about your products and services. Use publicity as part of your regular promotional activities, all year around, to keep interest high in your business. You are building your image with the use of publicity.

If you are able to retain a marketing or public relations expert, do so, as the results will outweigh the costs. Newspapers, radios, and television can provide you with free publicity if you use the right methods when approach them.

Advantages of Publicity

Publicity offers several advantages over paid advertisements and other promotional tools:

- **Expense.** As with paid advertising, you are using the media to get your company's message out to the public. Publicity costs much less. If you do all of the legwork yourself, publicity won't cost you more than a few dollars for telephone calls, postage, and printing to mail out press releases.

- **Size of the audience you are able to reach.** You are able to get the message out to vast numbers of people very fast. If the message gets out in several media, your message may be heard or seen again and again by the same prospective customers.

- **You gain credibility.** Publicity appears more credible to the public than paid advertising. The public tends to perceive you as an expert.

- **Publicity subtly persuades prospective customers.** It has the power to mold public and personal opinions in your favor. You are even able to change a negative image into a positive one.

- **Publicity is a tool that you are able to use again and again.** Use any write-ups or quotes about your company to your advantage. Use positive comments from the media in your advertising, brochures, and sales presentations. Show potential customers what has and is being said about your company by the media.

- **Editors and reporters don't care if you have spent advertising dollars with their outlet.** If you have interesting news, they want to get the word out to their audience, whether you advertise with them or not. They are not providing publicity to pay you back for all of your purchased ads.

- **Use publicity to get more publicity.** When attempting to obtain more publicity or to get other media interested in you and your company, show them what others have said about you.

Local Publicity

Take a close look at the various media outlets offered in your community. Note what types of news get reviewed in the local newspapers, magazines, radio, and cable channel. Which businesses are mentioned and why are they mentioned? What type of customer benefits are stressed?

If you offer valuable tips, ideas, and suggestions for decorating problems to the various media, you may just get a feature article about these free ideas. If an article about your company is scheduled to run, this is an ideal time to place a small display ad in the same section of the newspaper or magazine. Some newspapers have expert columnists featured with their solutions for various decorating problems. If your local newspaper doesn't, contact them to see if they would be interested in your providing such a column. You will probably not be paid for your work, but the prestige, benefits, and generated sales for you and your company of being featured as an expert columnist will far outweigh the time and expenses incurred.

Public Relations Opportunities

Quality public relations firms know which marketing activities will lead to the most success for the advertising dollars. Some of these opportunities are:

- Offer a contest for readers and listeners to participate in. Plan events around the various holidays throughout the year.

- The retirement, promotion, or addition of a top employee.

- Announce a special award being received by your firm.

- New store image and seasonal displays.

- Your 5,000th customer.

- Special jobs that you have just completed.

- Donation of custom products for charity and fundraisers.

- Participation in a design house in your area.

- Do local research on buyers' preference and publicize the findings to the media.

- Work on a community relations project.

- Give a special award to an employee or community leader.

- Produce special decorating tips, ideas, and suggestions.

- Write a decorating how-to piece.

- Be interviewed on local TV or radio talk shows.

- Speak before local business organizations or retirement communities.

- Have decorating seminars. Subjects might include how-to, insider tips and suggestions, new product developments, or overview of future trends.

- Hold and announce special promotions, events, or celebrations. These might include a grand opening, anniversary parties for your store, exhibits based on a theme, charity fundraisers, educational seminars for the public, store tours to show various products, open houses, new location open houses.

Local magazine publicity:

If you are fortunate to have local shelter-type magazines in your area, this is an outlet to focus on. Shelter magazines tend to be passed around from friend to friend, and will sit for years in doctors' offices and be read many times by many people.

Study your local magazines (libraries have them saved either on microfiche or save the actual magazine for several years), see who handles the decorating articles, and what type of articles are commonly used. Send press releases to that person. Offer to submit articles free for their magazines. Stress to the editor that you have valuable information to share with his or her readers. You will be promoting yourself as an authority in interior design. If a customer has to choose between working with an interior design business that she has heard of and feels confident about, and another that she hasn't heard of, she will pick the business that she knows *something* about.

Public Relations Firms and Agencies

A cost-effective way to put your new business before the public is by employing a public relations agency. Public relations firms have experience and knowledge about whom to contact with the various media to get your company placed before the public's eye. They use these contacts to obtain the best coverage for your news releases.

Public relations is the art or science of developing mutual goodwill and understanding between an individual, a company or other institution, and the public. Public relations is problem-solving through effective communications. Publicity is only one tool in the public relations practitioner's tool kit.

Public relation agencies range from very sophisticated expensive, to retired, very experienced individuals working out of their homes. Selecting which is right for you is on an individual basis. If you desire to be in front of the media constantly, with frequent large-scale presentations, etc., then the more sophisticated, more expensive operations are probably the right choice for you. They have specialized and experienced staff to plan the right course of action to take. If you are planning a more modest venture, a less-expensive PR agency will probably suffice.

Start by interviewing agencies. Outline what you believe a PR agency should do for your company. You may or may not have a realistic idea of what they may be able to accomplish for you.

Set appointments to interview several agencies. They may want to come to you if they are sufficiently staffed with salespeople, or they may want you to come to their agency for the preliminary interview. Before you set the appointment, ask if the initial consultation is free. If you don't ask, expect to be billed for the preliminary interview.

When you make your selection, be sure you are comfortable with the representative you will be working with. You will be working with this person on a regular basis, and it is important that the relationship is comfortable for the both of you.

During the initial consultation, the representative of the PR agency will want to get a fairly complete overview of your company, your expectations, plans, and marketing program. They need this information to develop a preliminary PR proposal for your consideration. Again, ask if this preliminary proposal is provided to you free or at their cost. Otherwise, expect to be billed at the going rate for their services.

Find an agency that you feel you can work with, that you can afford, and that will work with you on the goals and ideas you have for your company. Use the following guidelines when you are ready to narrow down your selection of a PR agency:

- Review and understand the contract the agencies present to you. Understand what obligations you and the agency have to each other. Have any questions clarified before you sign a contract.

- If you don't pay your bills promptly, you won't get service.

- Let the PR agency do its job. Let it make the contacts, plan the promotions, etc. You are paying for them to do their job, so let them do it.

- Allow the agency to use its regular suppliers. The agency has developed working relationships with quality suppliers of photography, artwork, graphic design services, printers, and caterers with proven track records. Let them do the planning and implement their ideas. If you try to supplement their ideas with your suppliers, the job will not run as smoothly or as professionally, and you will have a lower-quality product. You will also spend more money than if you let the PR agency proceed in the manner it is used to.

- Agencies earn commissions (usually 15 percent) from media outlets for any advertising space/time purchased for clients. Public relations agencies also mark up outside purchases to reflect a 15 percent to 20 percent commission. This is a common practice and is probably spelled out in the contract. You will be using the agency's money or credit to buy outside services. This is a standard repayment policy, in addition to other charges.

- Be a willing participant in the process. The agency needs your support for everything to proceed as planned.

- Be honest with your PR representative. He or she needs accurate facts and figures from you to release to various target markets.

- Treat your public relations agency with respect and you will get better service and treatment.

- Ask for progress reports on a regular basis. Quality PR agencies expect to provide reports to keep their clients informed about the status of projects.

- Be patient. Quality public relations takes time. You want a solid program, which takes time to create and build.

- Not all of the PR plans will work as well as others. This is not a reason to *not* try out different ideas. Sometimes you should keep trying different ideas before settling on the few that really work for your business.

- Public relations agencies can help build your business. This is their area of expertise.

- The very best PR any company can have is to offer the finest product or service possible.

What a Public Relations Firm Can Do For You

- Design business logos and graphics.

- Help with company name selection.

- Design and write direct mail pieces and advertisements.

- Conduct a public poll or survey about your firm and discuss the results.

- Plan and create events to put you before the public's eye, such as open-houses, seminars, workshops, etc.

- Write and distribute news releases.

- Design/produce audio visual shows about your company and jobs you have completed.

Generate Publicity With News Releases

An editor's job is to fill his or her publication with lots of interesting articles that will attract the largest possible audience to the publication. Unfortunately, the editor decides what is news, and even if a story about your company is printed, there are no guarantees about what information is included.

Every time something newsworthy happens, such as your firm receiving a large, well-known project, or there is an event you organize, send out press releases to the local newspapers. They want news. Unfortunately, they want only news and not self-promotion.

A press release is a short news item, feature story, or idea that is sent out to newspaper editors who might be interested. They may want to contact you and write an expanded story. A news release will give you more business than an ad of the same size, because it appears more credible.

Put together a package with the following information that makes it extremely easy for an editor to use your release without too much extra effort. The editor may even publish your news release verbatim. If they want to expand on your story, they can call the sources provided by you in your fact sheet and check out your references.

- Include an 8" x 10" black and white glossy photo of yourself and your studio or storefront to send along with your news release. Doing so will almost assure that the release will at least be reviewed. Be sure to identify every person in any pictures. In the same package include a biography about yourself, including where you went to school, when you graduated, where you have worked, and what important projects you have worked on.

- Include a fact sheet that gives sources and supports any statements made in your news release.

- Send the packet by Federal Express to the editor. Wait two days and then call him or her to make sure the packet arrived. Ask the editor if he or she has any questions. Ask if they are going to use your press release or provided information.

Offer a *free* booklet, information packet, report, or other useful information in the newspaper. In this type of release, announce the availability of the newly published item in the first paragraph. Summarize its contents and mention several items of interest to hook the reader into wanting the information. Close with how the potential customer may receive this information.

Start with an interesting, eye-catching title for your published piece. Enclose a copy of it with the press release to show the valuable, free offering.

Phone or write letters to editors letting them know that you are an expert in the field of interior design. Invite them to call or contact you if they ever need information, help, or an article in the interior design area. In essence, you are offering yourself as a source for them to contact, should the need arise. You will have your name quoted in the article and again you are perceived as an expert to the general public. If you have printed address file cards, this is the time to send them out. The editor can keep this information on hand for when the need arises.

Call attention to your interior design business and let potential customers know about the services you have available by sending out news releases at every opportunity. Unlike advertising, this type of publicity is almost free. The only costs that you will incur are your time putting together a publicity campaign, costs for printing and mailing the news releases or media kits, and follow-up telephone calls.

Newspapers, magazines, radio stations, and cable TV stations will be interested in news of interest to their audience. They want to know about the news before it happens, not after. The media need to fill their pages and air time with news. There are two types of news of interest to the media: hard news and feature news. Hard news is the unusual things that happen — earthquakes, murders, fires, etc. Feature news is the human interest, or people, stories. Try to tailor your news into feature news.

Publicity for your business may be generated in several ways using a variety of techniques. The print media is the easiest for you to break into. You may write a letter, make a phone call, hire publicists, or put together fancy media kits. Your goal with this type of publicity is to generate interest from potential customers that will lead to sales. You must first catch the interest of the targeted editor and then the editor's audience.

Realize that editors and program directors are not interested in giving anyone free advertising and do not owe you anything even though you may be a regular subscriber to their magazine or newspaper. They are interested in providing their audience with news or information that informs, benefits, or entertains their readers and listeners. Whether you will receive free publicity depends on whether your news or information is newsworthy or interesting to the majority of their audience. If it is, you will get publicity; if not, you won't.

The key is not to blatantly make your news or press releases sound or look like an advertisement, but rather, look like news with the human touch. Editors are looking for the hook to hang your news on. The hook can be in almost any direction. Decide what it is about your business that is different from the rest of the interior design businesses in your area. How will this different feature benefit the customer? If what you have to offer is new to the readers and listeners, then it is probably newsworthy. If you are just opening your studio, this is news. If you are offering innovative, new, exciting products that will benefit the public, this is news. If you have just hired a well-known top designer in your area or have received a design award, this is news. If you are offering a free seminar for the public to attend, this is news.

As with all people, what interests one person or editor will not interest others. An important point to remember is if you regularly advertise in the publication or outlet that you are attempting to penetrate with a news release, you will be more successful in acquiring free publicity from them.

Decide what your main goals are before putting together your press release package. Are you trying to generate direct leads from potential customers or are you attempting to put together a mailing list of semi-interested customers that you can send information to.

Do not go all out and try to be fancy. Professional editors are not interested in fancy, but rather in how interesting and "newsy" your news is. Add one color to the release to make it eye-catching so the reviewer will take a second look at it before tossing it into the trash.

Should you get lucky and have your news release printed in the publication, be sure to follow up with a thank-you call and note. You want to keep them interested in doing it again for you in the future. They appreciate your thanks.

News Release Basics

Have a high-quality press release written to introduce your new firm to the media. After reading the press release, editors will then determine whether your story is newsworthy. Some editors will think that what you have to offer is interesting and if a photo is also included, may just run the press release as you wrote it, with the photo. They may want to interview you and write their own story, or they may just rewrite your press release from the information given to them.

Hire a copywriter to write your press release if possible. If not, use the following as a guideline when preparing your press release:

- Let the media know before the event happens. They want the local angle, the "scoop."

- Editors are looking for news, an angle, a hook, or an interesting event to write about. Outline and highlight this information in a press release.

- Make sure that your message is really "news," not just publicity.

- Decide what your objective is before you start writing your news release.

- Make sure you have accurate, complete facts on the subject.

- Remember to use a human interest approach, using a broad appeal for your message.

- Think up an eye-catching headline that grabs the reader's attention.

- Cover who, what, where, when, and why.

- Make your message a "new" message, and time it correctly.

- Briefly describe your new company's image and style. Describe why the opening is news and is of interest to their readers. A news release is not an advertisement.

- Make your message easy to read. Strive for clarity.

- Use correct spelling and grammar.

- Don't start your sentences with verbs, unless it is the name of the event. Avoid the use of adjectives that reflect your opinion. Let the reader decide what kind of event it is. It may be exciting to you, but not to the reader. Just be straightforward and factual. Do not make your sentences sound like they are commands.

- Type and double space the release.

- Use 1 ½" margins on the sides, top, and bottom.

- Print the release on white paper or business letterhead with your logo imprinted.

- Use basic English with crisp words and short sentences.

- Do not use flowery phrases or words like "fantastic" or "unique."

- Write the copy in the third person, to make it sound as if someone else wrote it about you or your company. Writing it this way makes it easy to quote yourself.

- The press doesn't owe you anything, so treat your press contacts like they are doing you a favor. But realize the press does need your "news." They have the option to act on your message.

- Include a photograph of the exterior or interior of your new store, at least 8" x 10", or send a transparency (slide).

- Be available to provide more information to the media, should they need more.

- Generally use 8 ½" by 11" paper, unless you are presenting a combination news release and biography press release. See the section on Biographies.

- When planning and writing a release, think of it as an inverted pyramid. The most important, interesting information should be at the top, within the first few words. You only have five seconds to attract and hold a reader's attention.

- Call the selected media and inquire whom to send your media kit to for a more personalized approach.

- Limit the press release to a maximum of two pages. At the bottom of the first page, center and type the word "-more-."

- On the top of the second page, repeat and center the headline, and add "page 2."

- At the end of the press release (or wherever it ends on the page) use one of these endings, centered — the initials of your company -TD- (as for Touch of Design); ###; 2-2-2; -30-; or -end-.

- Never print press releases on both sides of a single sheet of paper. Place a two-page release on two separate pages.

- Staple a two-page news release together in the left corner with the staple running vertical rather than parallel with the top of the page (more professional in appearance).

- Have your news releases professionally printed, not photocopied. With a laser printer and a serif font you can easily create the effect of typesetting and printing and print each release individually.

- If you are only sending the release to one medium, such as the local newspaper, type the release and type the words "exclusive to (name the publication)." If you use this technique, and it really is exclusive to that medium, you will probably get your news reviewed and covered. If you get caught lying, you won't have any more releases published by that outlet. If you do submit your media kit to more than one person, let the editors know.

- Write a brief cover letter to accompany the news release, thanking the reader for reviewing the news release. Personally sign the cover letter.

- The larger the circulation of the outlet, the less likely that they will find your opening newsworthy for their readers.

- Start with the smaller media in your area and work out from there. If you received good press locally, send copies of the press releases to the larger publications.

- Check your magazine shops for more localized publications that might be interested in your news.

- Look at the *Standard Rate and Data* or *Gale's Directory* at your local library for information on larger magazines and publications.

- Plan your press releases to arrive the day after a holiday. There is generally not enough news to report after a holiday and your chance of your news getting printed is better.

- People find news releases more credible than advertisement copy. If the editor says it, then it must be true.

Information to Include in a News/Press Release

Source information:

Source information gives the media the name and telephone number of whom to contact for more information. Place this information near the top of the release either to the right or to the left side of the page.

Release date:

Type in full capitals, FOR IMMEDIATE RELEASE, on the right hand side of the page, positioned just above the headline. This tells the media that the release may be used immediately or at their earliest available convenience.

Headline:

Type and center the headline in capital letters. Use a headline that summarizes the content of the release. Effective headlines should consist of an abbreviated sentence with a subject plus a verb plus a object. Although the editor will probably use a completely different headline, you must catch the editor's attention to have the release read and acted on. *Stress a benefit for their readers or listeners.*

First paragraph:

Include the most important facts here. Include the who, what, where, when, why, and how of the news you are presenting. If it won't fit in the first paragraph, place the most important facts here and drop the secondary ones into the next paragraph. Keep all paragraphs short and easy to read.

Details and information to include:

Include other information in the release that might prompt a feature story about your business, rather that just a short announcement about your news. Include information such as benefits that potential customers will derive by calling, writing, or coming by your studio, seminar, exhibit, etc. Explain why your business is different.

Additional information:

Include background information that adds color and style to the news. Describe your different products and include decorating tips and ideas. Tell what your company or you have done in the past. Describe your track record. Include comments you have received from prestigious sources (with their permission). Offer free brochures, information, and literature to anyone who is interested in learning more about what your design studio has to offer interested readers and listeners. Editors will list free items as a service to readers.

Last paragraph:

This is the area to include how to get more information about your company and the products and services you are offering. Include your company name and address, along with any available promotional materials. If your promotional material is free, also include where and how to get it.

Tip or fact sheets:

When possible, include a tip sheet about your company along with your releases. Tip sheets should be laid out in an easy-to-read manner. Use bullets to guide the editor's eye to key points about your company.

Biographies:

Biographies are also known as bios. A bio is usually submitted on legal-size paper. You could accompany your news release with a biography about your company and a black and white photograph about your news. Bios tell who your company is and why it is different and of interest to readers and listeners. They read like a article. Editors are able to run the article as it is submitted, with few alterations, and submit it under their byline. A bio can be written by you or by a freelance writer.

Press or media kits:

Put together a press or media kit to submit with your news release. Place the following in a folder: pertinent articles, brochures, pamphlets, business cards, tip or fact sheets, and your company's logo.

Follow-up calls:

Follow up your press kit by calling and asking the editor if he or she received it and ask if he or she needs any more information. Let the editor decide if he or she wants to print the material. Send the material to only one person at each outlet. You will anger an editor if he or she finds out that you sent the same material to another department.

Look for special sections of newspapers and magazines that may be able to use your material. You could try columnists, editorial writers, areas of the paper where longer articles are placed, and the letter to the editor sections.

Weekly newspapers specialize in localized news rather than more general news. They generally come out on Thursdays, so plan to have the material arrive by Monday morning. Do this by mailing the material on Friday or Saturday. News and photographs of local people and businesses is important to weekly papers. Let the weekly paper know what area you live in when you submit the material.

Follow up on news releases sent by calling a few days after the media package has been sent to the editor. In the case of newspapers, avoid calling on their deadline. For morning papers call about 9:30 a.m., when the day shift is just getting underway. With afternoon papers, call midday after the day's edition is completed. Call weekly papers that come out on Thursdays on Thursday or Friday, after the week's issue is completed, to offer more information and encouragement about your submitted material for the following week, if they did not use it in the same week.

Many larger cities have *Finder Binders* available for purchase or through local libraries that contain information on all the local media. Also check *Bacon's Publicity Checker*, which lists various media and their departments in specific targeted geographic areas. Look for the newspaper or regional magazine you are interested in. The names and addresses for the various editors and the areas they cover are neatly listed for you. Examine publications with a home or interior design section. Note who the editor is.

Publicity Don'ts

- Do not say news or press release at the top of the release.

- Do not misspell names — either your employees or the editor's.

- Do not request clippings of the press release. You will have to hire a clipping service or check the media yourself.

- Do not ask for a guarantee that your press release will be used or your news event will be covered.

- Do not get pushy with an editor. Use phrases such as, "*You might want to*"; "*This might be useful to you*"; *I don't know if you would be interested in this or not.*"

- Do not complain later to the editor if your message doesn't appear. Write another press release, and keep trying. Call and make sure that you sent the release to the right person and the right department.

- Do not ask for corrections or retractions for minor errors.

- Do not try to *buy* the editor with gifts or lunches. If it is news, it will stand on its own merits.

- If you do advertise in the medium, do not attempt to use this as leverage for getting your release printed. News really has nothing to do with advertising. This type of pressure will cause the editor to become angry with you, and your release will probably not appear.

- Do not call when the editors and writers are meeting their deadlines for the day, week, or month.

Television

Watch your local cable channels and listen to the local radio stations and see what type of guests are featured, and what is their news hook. Check to see what type of promotional material and literature is offered free at the end of the shows. Come up with fresh ideas for you to also appear on the shows. The use of humor in TV advertising has been proven to be effective. Make a powerful offer to entice prospects to call you. Keep your message simple. Display your telephone number on the screen for a minimum of fifteen seconds.

Television is a visual medium that needs to project activity for the camera. The camera crew takes the pictures and you have to come up with the news hook. Slides can also be used if necessary.

Your news story should be brief and take only about forty-five seconds. Talk directly to your target market. Don't worry about wasting time on anyone else. The prospective customer should feel that you are talking right to him or her so that he or she will listen to your message. To be successful with television, you must get viewers' attention within the first five seconds, and they need to make a decision to contact you within the first minute. Let them know who you are, and that they are your target marketed customer. Hire a professional spokesperson with credibility to get your message out on television. You could opt to use real-life testimonials, your company president, a celebrity, or have an actor discuss and display some jobs and your company reliability and honesty.

Come up with your own ideas to offer about what scenes should be shot regarding your news. Make a list of several points of interest to cover in a short time. Invite the camera crew to your store or studio or the location of the "news hook."

Television stations also broadcast public service announcements (PSAs), from ten to sixty seconds long and are aired without charge during station breaks.

Radio Advertising

Radio advertising is written to get the message out in fifteen to sixty seconds. This type of advertising works well for interior design businesses in the following instances:

- To publicize free seminars.

- To obtain leads for your business, especially if you have an easy-to-remember 800 number to call for free information. Ask the phone company for a number that spells out the name of your business or a design related term.

- To tell customers where and how they may find out more information about your company and any special sale or promotion you may be advertising. You may be running a newspaper or regional magazine display ad. With the use of radio advertising, you can refer the listener to the display ad for specifics about the promotion you are offering.

Radio appearances:
Use press releases and letters to announce you as an authority in your field with radio stations. Mention that a free brochure or information packet is available to listeners who contact you.

Radio stations:
Radio stations require plenty of short news stories that are to the point. Many radio shows can be done over the phone. Come up with an idea, send it in to them either in a news release form or audio tape, and offer to be available for the interview. Should you use the telephone, make sure that you are organized and have your message prepared ahead of time. Use an enthusiastic tone of voice, spoken in a clear manner. Make the message long enough to hear.

Another idea is to go ahead and tape your well-planned, short news message and send it to them to use at their discretion. Make sure that you are direct and to the point. A news message for radio needs to be only twenty to sixty seconds long. They may either use the tape or call you for your interview. Be ready and organized.

You may choose to have your copy read by the radio announcer or another radio professional. Make sure the copy is well written. You will not have any visuals to help you get the message out to prospects. There are firms that specialize in making commercials for radio.

- Invite a radio reporter to the news event you have planned. Do not call a radio station during or right before the news broadcast time. Call right after the news has been broadcast.

- Some local radio stations might be interested in your doing a series of radio programs on interior design, before or after the news.

To be successful with the various news media available, you need to know what they will and won't use. You learn this by researching the various media.

Telemarketing

Telemarketing is a fast-growing industry. It uses the telephone as a means of contacting potential customers. You could set up a phone room, hire professional telemarketers, or set up a recording device to call prospects and inquire if they need any interior design products or services. You can ask if they would be interested in learning more about your services (send out brochures and information) or in a *free* estimate. Set up a telemarketing recorder to do the calling for you as many insurance professionals do. Hire someone to return calls and set up appointments.

You are place in a weakened position by using telemarketing with some customers. You may appear that you are not very busy and need work. Telemarketing is also very annoying to customers. It is always best to get the prospective customer to come to you. But, some potential customers may not know about you, may have been thinking about calling some other company, or were just thinking about doing some redecorating. You are putting your company's name in their mind by calling them. **These are successful telemarketing rules:**

- Work from a prepared script. The telemarketer shouldn't sound as if she is reading the script, but she should use it to control the conversation. Write out a succession of questions and answers that the telemarketer will likely get asked. She now has the correct answers to give to the questions. Cross-index the questions and answers for ease of use.

- The telemarketer should get right to the point. Have several different closes to use written into the script. Place one near the beginning to attempt a fast close.

- Don't use high pressure sales on anyone. If the prospect says no, instruct the telemarketer to accept the answer and move on to the next prospect. Pay your telemarketers a base salary and an incentive bonus, not straight commission; this will ensure lower pressure on the prospect.

Networking

Attract new business through your personal contacts. Attend meetings, luncheons, social events, business lectures, and networking clubs. Join several clubs and associations. The whole purpose of networking is to meet as many people as you can. They may give you their business, or may give you names of friends and associates that may need your business. Networking will give you new contacts and referrals, which translates to business.

Networking with others serves two functions. First, through networking you find customers. Referrals are quality solid leads that will help you build your business. By networking with your own satisfied customers, you ensure their continued loyalty toward your company.

Networking will help you build a base of associates to use for printing, legal advice, photographers, accountants, writers, etc. When you choose to work with a professional that you have contacted through your networking efforts, he or she tends to want to do a superior job for you. You are able to exchange sources of professionals with each other as the need arises.

Always hand out plenty of cards. The person you are handing your card to may turn it over to someone that mentions that they need to redecorate. The face-to-face contact of networking has more impact than advertisements ever will.

Networking referrals can come from people in fields different from yours, or from people working in your own field that offer similar products and services. They may be asked for a product that they do not carry, and are happy to refer the customer to you.

Do not attempt to "sell" your company to your network contacts at the time you meet them. Simply get to know them at this point. Ask your contacts about what they do to get them talking. Follow up the initial contact with a note about how pleasant it was to meet them. Give them another card at this point and an information packet about the business you do. They now have an extra business card to give away. Try to refer your networking contacts to others whenever you can.

Realize that if you expect professional businesspeople to keep referring you to others and help promote your business, you will also need to reciprocate and refer them to other people. Network with people who have something positive to offer your business. Networking with people can help you with the promotion of your business. Talk to everyone you come in contact with about your business. Give them several cards and brochures that they can pass along to others for you.

Network with your own employees. Hand out special-value cards. These value cards should offer certain products at their lowest possible price. Have them sign each value card and ask them to hand out the cards to their friends and acquaintances. Have an employee contest for the most cards to be redeemed. Have a grand prize, a second, and a third prize for everyone participating. Add up the redeemed amounts, not the number of value cards.

Cross Promotions

Cross promoting is networking with other companies and organizations. You supply their customers with coupons or other incentives to call you. Cross promotions make it appear that the company or organization is doing its customers or members a favor by giving them a great value. When cross promoting with other companies and organizations, organize it so you can also supply your customers with their special values. Some of the networking businesses and their customers, members, or employees to approach for cross promoting are:

● Neighborhood businesses to their customers and clients.

● Employers to employees.

● Associations and organizations to their members.

● Chamber of commerce members, downtown merchant association.

● Educational institutions to students and employees.

● Businesses serving other businesses to their customers.

- Special event promoters to their attendees.

- Nonprofit groups to their community supporters.

- Your employees to their friends and acquaintances.

- Your business to your customers.

- News media to their audience.

- Advertising media to their audience.

- Any type of business that will bring you your target market customer.

- In a mall, cross promote with merchants on the other end of the mall.

- Businesses can use your coupon as an extra value inserted in their billing statements. This is an opportunity to show appreciation to their customers by giving them an extra value.

Approach a business that complements yours and say, "I'm the owner of Touch of Design. I would like to offer you the opportunity to provide your customers a way to get more for their money with an added value and a special way for you to say thanks for their business." Then ask the owner/manager if he or she would participate if it costs them nothing.

Ask the owner/manager for a customer count. Invite him to visit your design studio and also encourage him to cross promote with you. Ask for a good-quality company logo (like a logo on their letterhead) to use in designing your literature for cross promotion purposes. Ask him how he would like his company/owner's name to appear on a special thank-you certificate. Ask how many employees work there and offer to bring *buy-one-get-one-free* values for each of them. Imply how much his customers will appreciate being given your special offer by the business.

Design a coupon or special value, with an expiration date, that states, "*Compliments of _____(name of business you are "doing a favor for"*). When you find a business that is interested in doing a cross promotion with you, arrange everything quickly, and get your literature printed before they lose interest. Give the manager, business owner, and employees who will be handing out your offer extra special bonuses such as a buy-one-get-one-free offer.

Join Associations and Organizations

Join trade associations and read trade publications. Contact the trade associations that you would like to belong to and request subscription information and back issues of their publications. Trade associations also have information for sources of useful information. Ask about the services they have to offer. If their fees are not too exorbitant, join their associations. You can always list that you belong to that association in all of your marketing efforts.

Write Articles for Local Publications

If you write articles for a local publication or newspaper, you are getting invaluable publicity for your firm. You may or may not be paid for the article. The national magazines will pay well for your articles, while the local or specialized publications will not. The smaller publications, if they pay anything, will only pay small fees. They realize the reason for your interest in writing articles is to promote yourself and your business. They also realize that the publicity that you will receive from the publication of the article is very valuable to you. You are trading your article for free publicity. Establish yourself as an expert in your field, and customers will flock to you. It would be very expensive to buy the space in advertisements that you will be paid nominally for *if at all*.

The most value you will receive for articles is not when they are published in the publication or newspaper, but when you reprint them to show your prospective and past customers. After the articles have been printed, you are able to use them again and again. Enclose them with a personalized letter with your information packet that you send to prospective customers. Take the articles and form a newsletter with them. Send them out to all of your past customers. Tailor the article reprint to be sent out to the product or service that your client is inquiring about. If your mailing list is quite extensive, consider printing the reprints on more attractive coated (glossy) stock.

- Keep the article short — under fifteen hundred words, so that it may be reprinted as the subject comes up for clients. Plan the article so that it fits on one or two sides of a single 8 ½" x 11" sheet of paper.

- Write the article so that it is in a list format as you see these items listed. Title the list with Tips To, Rules Of, Ways To, etc. Lists are easy to organize, easy to write and set up, and easy to read. They are favored by readers.

- Write about subjects that relate to your business. Show that you are an expert on a subject by writing about it.

- Make sure that your telephone number and address are always listed in every article. Enclose this information at the very end of the article along with a list of your qualifications. If the editor objects to this being added, discuss it with him or her. You are doing editors a favor by writing an article (by an expert) that will interest their readers. You may want to tell the editor to waive the modest fee that they planned to pay you. You need this information intact, if you expect to pick up additional business through your articles.

Make it easy for your prospect to find you. If the editor will not bend on the issue of allowing you to print your address and telephone information, you definitely need to have an ad in the same publication with this information. Try to swap the modest fee that the publication was going to pay you for an ad spot.

Try for the largest ad that you think they may give you. Realize that ad space is very expensive. You may be able to get twice the cost of what they were willing to pay you in an ad spot. Or you may only be able to evenly trade their article fee for the same dollar value in an ad space.

Create a list of article ideas that have wide appeal pertaining to your subject. Contact editors and attempt to sell at least one of the ideas for an article every month. When an editor shows interest in having you write an article, give the title of the article, outline the points you will be covering, and give reasons why this article will interest their readers. Enclose your list of qualifications with the outline. Enclose a self-addressed envelope with the outline and letter. If you are not contacted by the editor within two weeks, follow up with another letter to the editor. If the editor still doesn't follow through with an answer, write another letter stating that you are withdrawing your proposed article from consideration. Next, try again with another publication.

Publications to contact:
- Local weekly and daily newspapers.

- Trade publications that other members of your specialty subscribe to.

- Trade publications read by your prospective customers. These may be within their trade or profession. If you notice that you are attracting people from a certain profession that turn out to be great customers, then advertise where they work, or in what they read.

- Local business publications.

- Local consumer magazines.

- Regional garden and decorating magazines.

- National business magazines.

- National consumer magazines.

- National general interest magazines.

From now on when you read publications, become familiar with their contents and style. Check to see if any of the columns featured rotate with different businesspeople every time they are printed. This is an ideal situation for you to try to get an article of general interest in your specialty published.

Editors would rather get articles from experts in a particular area that will interest their readers, than from a writer who is attempting to research the subject and really has no practical knowledge of the field.

When you have written a successful article, and the editor contacts you to say that he or she liked the article or received positive response from readers, have future article suggestions ready to mention. Later, you may build such a rapport with the editor that when you get an idea, simply call him or her with the proposed article idea. Propose to make your article a regular column in the publication. You will be keeping your name in the forefront in your field.

Consider placing an ad in the publication when your article appears. This will give you double exposure. You may want to wait and see what type of response you receive from your article before you do this. If you received some response, this shows that this may be a good medium for you to advertise in. No response would suggest that you not waste your money advertising here.

Participate in Area Showcase Houses

This is an expensive way to get yourself recognized. You may want to consider participating in a showcase house if you have lots of time and money to devote to the project. Not only will you be working on the project for months, you will have to foot the bill yourself for many of the materials you will need to buy.

Chances are if you network with manufacturers and other retailers, you can "borrow" some of what you need for your assigned room in the showcase house. If you do a room in a showcase house located in some areas you will be given a list of sources that are willing to supply such items as electrical, paint, carpet, some furnishings, and some labor for "free" or a reduced cost to you (as long as they are given credit for the supplied items or labor).

But, if the showcase house is not located anywhere near your business, don't even bother with participating. You will spend tons of time and money and although your room may be a masterpiece, chances are a potential customer won't call you if your business isn't nearby. True, customers do come from miles around. Weigh the pros and cons, and think about lower cost ways to advertise.

Seminars and Public Speaking

Speak before groups of people every opportunity you can about decorating trends, ideas, new products, and the quality services and products that your company carries. Although you probably won't receive pay for the speaking engagements, again, the added sales will far outweigh the "costs" to you.

By holding seminars or speaking before groups of people with a common interest, you are able to easily establish yourself as an expert and make *quite an impressive impact* with a demonstration of your knowledge. You are able to speak with potential customers and answer questions both before and after your talks. Unfortunately, you are not able to reach as many people at a time as you can with published articles. Try to use both means for maximum impact.

You should also consider audiotaping your speeches, and distributing tapes on specific topics to potential customers. Tapes are relatively inexpensive to produce and get a customer's attention. Many customers will listen to your tape while driving around in their cars.

If you have come up with a great article idea, then this idea might be very interesting in a speech too. Hold seminars at your place of business and invite the public to attend. This could include church groups, schools, business groups, real estate boards, and civic groups. Other possible meeting locations include a group or organization's regular meeting location, motels or hotels, banquet rooms, bank meeting rooms, and if you are a lessee of a shopping mall, its meeting room. Once you start holding seminars, you will be invited to speak at luncheon and dinner meetings.

You may be able to hold a "mini" course through the adult education program in your community. This is an opportunity to get paid while you obtain new customers.

Ask for information about the function and the people who will be in attendance. Does the audience include people that are able to purchase interior home fashions? How many people will be attending? What is their profession? Are they homeowners? If they are not qualified customers, reconsider the invitation.

Select a topic that you know very well, that is related to the services and products you have to offer, and that is of high interest to your audience. You should not try to "sell" the audience, but relate to them what you have to offer. Provide them with interesting information on interior design and decorating.

If you are not comfortable with public speaking, enroll in a speech class at your local college and learn how to be an effective speaker. Select possible topics and areas that you might use if you were conducting a seminar. Get some practice on that particular topic before going before a professional audience.

Seminar guidelines:

- Use 11" by 17" self-mailers to mail out and advertise your seminar. This size has proven to be very effective and is also inexpensive.

- Use a large title on both the front and the back of your direct mail piece to announce your seminar. Include an outline of the subject matter of the seminar, written to sell your prospect on attending. Use bullets to cover each area, and place the outline in a separate bordered box on the direct mail piece.

- Advertise and do mailings for seminars eight to nine weeks before the seminar date.

- March through May, and September through November tend to be higher-attendance months to conduct seminars.

- Give the information to the audience at their education level.

- Speak in a relaxed, comfortable manner. Don't be overly long-winded.

- Try not to read your speech to the audience, but deliver it in a relaxed tone.

- Walk around while speaking to the audience.

- Try to plan talks that will last about twenty-five to thirty minutes. Practice and time the speech until you have the talk reasonably perfected, fitting it into your allotted time.

- Stimulate audience interest by adding visual aids to your speech. Visual aids effectively help the message to sink in with the audience. Your manufacturers' and suppliers' advertising departments may be able to provide just the tools required. They also have seminars for all of their reps.

- Provide time at the end of the seminar for questions from the audience.

- Willingly accept criticism and other people's point of view.

If you are a bit "seminar shy," invite manufacturer's reps or other product authorities to come speak and provide the audience their expert point of view, while demonstrating the new products for the public. Select new products to display and demonstrate. Do not make the audience feel that you are there to sell them, but rather to educate them about the new products.

Have handouts and promotional materials of the products discussed to hand out at the seminar. People love handouts. Consider providing an outline of the key points you will be addressing, with a brochure and business card about your business (make sure your address and phone number are on each piece you are handing out). This is an opportune time to hand out those glossy reprinted articles that were published in newspapers and magazines.

Have a table strategically placed at the back of the room, with all types of brochures and information, as well as duplicates of your handouts. Many of the people in attendance will want to look at specific products and get information for friends.

Be sure to get a list of all of the people at the seminar and add them to your mailing list. They are most likely impressed with you, and though they may not be ready to call you now, surely they will need to later.

How to get the word out about your seminar:

- **Word of mouth.** Make a point to tell every customer you come in contact with about the seminar.

- **Direct mail.** Send invitations to the selected audience. Include any interested potential customers, and other current customers who would enjoy attending.

- **Flyers everywhere.** Place flyers in the library, on grocery store bulletin boards, in shop windows, and everywhere else you can think of.

- **Press releases.** Send a press release about the seminar to all local media, inviting interested people to attend.

Fairs and Home Improvement Shows

Shows are another way to reach people that you would have otherwise missed. You are able to expand your business visibility, to practice your public relations skills, to generate new customer leads, and to market unique products. The key to a successful trade show or fair that generates a lot of interest for your studio is to have decorating seminars, before-and-after demonstrations, an exhibit with an audio element. The exhibit needs sound to make it stand out from the other exhibits. Have a microphone for the speaker. Include background music and try to create lively seminars.

Remember that the reason you are there is for customer contact. Get up and talk to as many people who come into your booth as you can. Follow these steps for a well-organized exhibit.

- Plan far enough in advance as you can.

- How many people are expected to attend the event?

- What will you be handing out to the customers to promote business? Make sure that all visitors to your booth leave with something.

- What type of exhibit will you have? Demonstrations? What can you do to make your exhibit stand out?

- What signs do you need to have printed. Remember to contrast them from their background so they will stand out.

- Will you make or buy the basic structure of your exhibit? Who will customize and finish the exhibit?

- Who will work the exhibit? This usually includes working nights and weekends also.

- What products do you plan to promote and show?

- What other treatments do you want to display?

- Will you attempt to sell any products/services during the show? Will you actually provide products at the show (such as accessories) or will you be taking orders? How much product inventory will you need for the show?

- Are you attempting to get sales leads? Who will follow up on the leads after the show? How long after?

Teaching

This is another way to promote yourself and your company. When potential customers hear that you also teach, their reaction usually is quite positive. You *must* know what you are doing, if you can teach it. You will also be paid fairly well for your time.

Write a letter to the head of the interior design or art departments at local community and private colleges. Also consider the state-funded courses, adult education, and community course offerings. The smaller colleges will usually be more interested than the larger universities. Propose a new course idea. List your qualifications and achievements in the design field.

You will also receive referrals from your students and often obtain work for them as well. Teaching will keep you current with the information in your field. You will automatically go out of your way to stay up on new advances in the design field, if you are going to project yourself as an expert while teaching it.

Interior Design 900 Hot Line

Create your own mini-seminars that are called with a 900 number, and generate some capital for your company, while also promoting yourself as an expert.

Purchase a high-quality answering machine, have another line installed at your place of business, and get yourself set up on a 900 number through the phone company. The recorded message may be called twenty-four hours a day, seven days a week. Have the message last about five minutes.

Print a brochure to send out with the press release to make it appear that you haven't just started the hot line. Weekly, change the mini-seminar message that consists of "hot" tips, decorating ideas, information, etc. Every time you change the message, mention what you have scheduled to talk about for the next four or more weeks.

Send out a press releases advertising this available information to all local publications. Also advertise this information in your yellow page ads.

Other Prospecting and Promotion Ideas

- Have your company's flyer inserted in your area newspapers. Select a color ad that will stand out and be noticeable. Having a flyer inserted will cost more than having flyers placed on homes by a neighborhood child or organization. It may also overwhelm you with business. Make sure that your decorators are ready for the surge of business.

- Throwaway advertising circulars are pretty good. You tend to get more ad for the money. Unfortunately, not everyone reads these. You will get the people who may not read the newspaper scanning them, but the average newspaper reader with limited time may not see your ad. Your target market should be the working person who can make a decision and who doesn't have a lot of time to shop around.

- Advertising postcards can be a real business energizer. These are postcards with a message to entice the customer to act now. Again you will be blanketing a large area with your message, and you need to be ready for a surge of business.

- List your company's business services under the newspaper classified sections. This may turn out be a great source of leads and it keeps your company's name current with potential customers.

- Place ads in senior citizens' retirement area newspapers. Included would be nice quality mobile home developments, complexes, retirement homes, etc. As a rule, senior citizens are highly desirable customers. They generally have the money and the desire for custom products. And this is probably the last time they will redecorate so they know what they want. They have usually experienced custom products in the past or want to finally experience them. They will generally not shop you to death as they don't think this is the right thing to do, nor do they have the energy to do it. They will go out of their way to come into your studio and get an idea of prices before having you out to their home. They are also very generous with sharing their life's experience, and consequently a very interesting group of people to work with.

- Churches have directories that may be advertised in for low costs, usually on the back of the weekly agendas. People at the church would rather work with people that go to their church.

- If your neighborhood and/or county has a directory or magazine as retirement communities do, place an ad. People in your same neighborhood would probably prefer to give you their business.

- Do model homes. Most builders will at least pay the cost of doing the job. For possible referrals from other builders, you will have to do the windows at your own expense. If you do this, check treatments regularly to see what shape they are in, and make adjustments as required. They tend to get handled quite a bit. Leave plenty of business cards, brochures, and sale flyers. Have signs made and place them in each room with your company's name, your name, phone number, and address.

- Hospitals, schools, and many other businesses need replacement window coverings every few years. Churches usually have a board to make decisions for the church. Unfortunately, it is very difficult to please a whole group of people and get everyone to agree about anything.

- Attempt to get some commercial accounts such as motels, apartments, buildings, etc. They tend to regularly need replacement carpets, window treatments, and bedspreads. Constant turnover tends to destroy decorating products.

- When doing any commercial project, write in the contract that they agree you can place signs and cards stating that your company is performing the decorating project.

- Visit tract home models. Measure all the windows and plan various basic packages of window coverings (mini blinds, basic satin draperies, etc.). Price out each model for the basic packages. Label each package on a flyer with the model number and information, stating that you do all types of decorating and have many fabrics and products to select from. Distribute the flyers to each home in the housing tract.
  Distribute the same flyers *regularly* — about every couple of weeks. You will not miss new move-ins, and this technique will get your foot in the door. If the customer doesn't like the basic package, upgrade them as they desire to. Price the basic packages reasonably, so if the customer is getting other bids, she will keep coming back to your flyer, which has very attractive prices, and she will call you.

- Work with your local newspaper on putting together a regular question-and-answer column about decorating questions. Your company will gain instant *credibility* if you take the time to do this. You will be the company to call for decorating expertise.

- Join networking groups and exchange lead ideas. Work out co-op advertising ideas you can do together with other members of your network group.

- Distribute brochures and flyers in health clubs and reciprocate by doing the same for them at your place of business.

- Have greeting cards customized with your company logo, have the designer sign them, and mail them out for *all* major holidays.

- Ask competitors to refer any customers that they cannot accommodate (not carrying a desired product, for example).

- Assign neighborhoods for your decorators to work. Have them regularly place sale flyers with their cards attached on homes in their assigned areas. They will get the lead if the customer asks for them when they call. Whenever they are out on a call and they notice a home with shabby draperies, have them stop and place a flyer on the house.

- Tape flyers on large, multiple mail boxes for tract homes.

- Get to know local building contractors. They can earn referral money or you may want to give them special discounts in return for referring you business. They are working with people who are in need of the products you carry. They have just added the room in need or just replaced the windows that are now uncovered. Ask your own subcontractors to refer business your way and pay them for it. Also reciprocate and refer them business.

- Place all salaried people in your business on your referral program. They *love* earning the extra money; in fact, *they start to count on it* as part of their pay every month.

- Work out co-op programs with small businesses by having them insert your advertising piece in the same envelope as their bill and sharing the postage. Work out plans with related businesses to share in advertising together. You will reach twice as many potential customers by sharing advertising this way.

- Set up an exhibit in malls or a high-traffic area that has events to draw customers in.

- Set up a display of beautiful treatments at the local fair or street event. You will want to construct a movable display that you can use regularly to take to these events. There are companies that make these displays for you. Find them in the back of business magazines. You will want to invest in some of your vendors' stand-up displays. Have your decorators work their floor time handing out flyers with coupons, and take names and numbers for mailing lists and possibly set up appointments. You are keeping a high profile in the community this way.

- Anywhere people are forced to stand in line and wait is a great place for exhibits; e.g. banks and lending institutions.

- Place signs in front of homes you are working on that say ,"*This home is in the process of being decorated by Touch of Design.* Make this part of the agreement with the purchaser for the better price you gave him.

- Use placards on your car when working and on your installers' vehicles when they are doing your installations. If you use a van, have the van painted in your company's colors along with your logo. Be sure to add your address and telephone number in large letters.

- Use bus stop benches, billboards, and taxi cab rental signs for low-cost, wide exposure advertising. People drive by in high traffic areas all day and if the bus stop is unoccupied, your ad is staring them in the face.
  Cabs are all over the area and so can your ad be on top of the cab with your company name, telephone number, and address. People will see these ads most of the time on a subconscious level, and your logo and name will become synonymous with decorating on a subconscious level.

- Place interesting, eye-catching items such as furniture pieces outside your store to draw customers into your store.

- Share floor and store space with a card, flower, or accessory shop to draw customers into your store. Decorator shops are intimidating. You need some welcoming features to lower the intimidation level and get customers into your shop.

- Locate your business in a high-traffic area. Use sandwich signs, if they are allowed in your area, to advertise specials.

- Keep window displays fresh and changing. Make your displays dramatic and eye catching. Locations with heavy stop-and-go traffic where potential customers are at a dead stop, staring at your business, are great places for a display, sign, and phone number.

- Promotions of open houses, parties, wine-tastings, displays, and demonstrations of general interest held at your place of business are all going to help you spread the word about your company.

- Get involved in your neighborhood watch program. Hold the meeting at your nicely decorated home. Although only some of the neighbors show up, they will spread the word all over the neighborhood.

- Hold voting at your house — inside your house, if possible. Leave flyers, cards, and brochures for anyone interested to pick up.

- Join the better business bureau and your local chamber of commerce.

- Speak at decorating classes in your area. These people are really interested and may go ahead and give you their business. Only a few students actually continue on and make decorating or design a career. Others take the courses to learn how to decorate. They need sources to buy their products from. Give them student discounts and invite them to visit your studio. Make less profit from them, but allow them to order through your studio. They will also spread the word to others (they love decorating and love to talk about it). Keep local decorating classes supplied with discontinued samples with your company's stickers affixed.

- Go on talk shows and talk about current and future decorating forecasts and trends. This is a subject of interest to just about everyone. Learn a lot about trends by subscribing to trade publication and magazines.

- Have your designers call past customers at least twice a year to follow up on direct mailings, personally invite them to seminars, invite them to lunch, tea, say hello, etc.

- Fabric shops are another great source to post your cards and advertisements. Many people *briefly* consider making their own soft window treatments — that is, until they price the fabric and get an idea of how much work it really is. They are relieved to see your card and ad and are happy to take you up on it.

- Most fabric shops selling interior fabrics probably have a higher retail price than your shop. Consequently, customers will come in wanting to purchase the fabric to make their own draperies. You may or may not want to accommodate these customers. I say sell everything you can, keep this customer happy, and she will be back for other products. She will refer you to friends who wouldn't even consider making their own window treatments and other soft accessories. Why let this customer walk? You will probably still make 100 percent markup on the fabric sale with very little effort on your part. You will not be able to guarantee the fabric, unless you make the draperies. Put this in writing, and make this clear to the customer. Some shops use this rule: As long as we make the drapery portion of the windows, we will sell you the fabric for the top treatment or other decorative accessories in the room.

- Display all of your decorator's and studio coordinator's pictures in the studio for the customers to see. Let the customer see who they will be working with if they should come in when the decorator is out in the field. Pictures also help *tremendously* for customers who have worked with a specific decorator and cannot remember his or her name.

- Place prices were they can clearly be seen on fabrics, sample window treatment displays, carpet and flooring samples, accessories, and furniture. It is a turnoff to the customer to have a decorator look up each and every thing for them. True, they do want your help, but in the first few visits to your studio, they need to feel comfortable with your studio setting before they approach you. Help break the ice.

- Work off of a reverse directory (*Haines*, at the library, shows names and addresses by the street numbers), and mail prospects information about special sales or promotions you are having. Follow up the mailing with a cold call several days later. The customer may be very interested in making an appointment. You've put the idea in her head, then you call and ask if she is interested. Ask if both spouses will be present. It is cost- and time-effective to have your decorators cluster their appointments in the same neighborhoods. It cuts down travel time tremendously.

- Have the solicitor tell the customer that you are having a special promotion — if they are able to make a decision the day the decorator comes to their home they receive an extra $50 off of the price. Your decorators have one thing in mind. Make a sale. This technique really does work very well. Remember, your decorators are on commission. True, they aren't going to close every sale. You will keep them busy and they will sell much more than they would if they aren't out there attempting to make sales. This plan works especially well if you handle Visa, Mastercard, or provide financing. Work out a plan with a local financing company. You will probably get some people with less income in need of your products that you otherwise wouldn't have ever made a sale to. They would not have thought your company was in their realm of possibilities.

- Stay on top of the homes that have just closed escrow at the county recorder's office or sign up for new move-in mailing list services. Review our companion to this book, *Secrets of Success for Today's Interior Designers and Decorators,* where this material and much more is thoroughly covered.

- Have your designers join organizations where they can network and advertise inexpensively in the newsletters.

- Sign up with the welcome wagon. If the new move-in gets a flyer from you in the mail, and the welcome wagon representative comes to see them shortly thereafter, your name is going to appear very familiar and current to them. Be sure to supply coupons for dollars-off of their purchase, in addition to your information packet about your company.

- Donate custom items such as returns of bedspreads and soft accessories to nonprofit organizations and receive publicity as a result. They will list you as the donor in all material they use to announce their auction, free drawings, contests, etc. Donate nicely designed items for a lucky winner to win for fundraisers and charity events. Of course your company name will be mentioned in a prestigious manner, offering positive promotion of your services.

- Require your designers to make a set number of cold calls to commercial businesses and establishments as a field sales representative does every week. Make this an employment requirement. Have them introduce themselves to the CEO and drop of your information packet for information on future company decorating projects. You may also get the CEO as a personal customer that can afford to decorate.

- Offer to decorate free a public building in designer fashion for Christmas (you will have to supply the decorations). Select decorations that can be modified or combined in a different manner for the next year, so you are able to reuse them the next year. Your company will definitely be talked about, written about, and the building photographed and displayed in the media if you do.

Tracking Marketing Efforts

For purposes of tracking how your various advertising and marketing efforts are doing, in addition to tracking the performance of your individual decorators, you need to keep a close eye on your leads.

Record the following information:
- Name, the company that they are representing, address, telephone number, and extension.

- How did they hear about you? Did they call or write to you?

- Consumer or commercial job? What do they seem to be interested in?

- Who went out on the call? What are the results of the call. Did the customer make a purchase? How did the decorator follow up on the call?

- The decorator should show that he or she does want that customer's business by subtly following up regularly with the customer by telephone and by mail. Have them follow up until the customer indicates that she has purchased the items or products somewhere else.

- Be sure to add to your mailing list prospects that have not yet come to a decision or that seem to be the type of customer you would like to have, even if they have bought elsewhere. Keep pursuing them. They may choose another company, but if that company performs like most decorating companies — poor service, taking the customer's money and running, the customer may cancel the order or come back to you on the next purchase.

Interior Design Programs

The following is a list of interior design programs primarily throughout the United States. A few programs outside the United States are also listed. It is possible and highly probable that some of the schools listed may have found it necessary, due to budgetary restraints, to have dropped their interior design programs. Other schools that may offer fine interior design programs may have been omitted unintentionally. Some schools below may go by several names and may have been unintentionally listed twice. We apologize if this is the case.

We would appreciate being informed about any interior design programs not listed or that may have been dropped, so that we can list them or drop them in subsequent reprintings of this book. **The listed programs are in alphabetical order by state, and then in alphabetical order by city. Programs outside the United States follow the U.S. list.**

FIDER Accredited Programs

FIDER (The Foundation for Interior Design Education Research) is an international nonprofit organization that is considered an authority on interior design program curricula and provides accreditation through evaluation of minimum standards of the various program for schools, colleges, and universities in the United States and Canada.

Schools that are accredited with FIDER must maintain minimum standards and are only granted accreditation for a limited period of time. The programs are then periodically reevaluated to make sure the minimum standards are being maintained. If they are, then the accreditation is extended for another limited time period.

FIDER bases its accreditation standards on the requirements of the interior design profession and the public. While FIDER does require minimum standards maintained for a program to qualify for accreditation, it does allow a level of flexibility with its standards of individual programs and curricula. FIDER-based programs allow students to be adequately prepared for employment in the interior design field.

The FIDER organization is recognized by the Council on Post-secondary Accreditation (COPA), the United States Department of Education (ED) and the National Council on Interior Design Qualification (NCIDQ). Members of American Society of Interior Designers (ASID), Institute of Business Designers (IBD), Interior Design Educator Council (IDEC), International Society of Interior Designers (ISID) serve on FIDER's board, committees, and evaluation teams. Addresses for FIDER and other recognized interior design organizations follow the list of Interior Design Programs.

FIDER-accredited programs are marked below their city with *,** and the degree or certificate offered at the school. Many schools listed below are not FIDER-accredited programs but are still fine programs. As a student striving to succeed with the interior design program, you must weigh the pluses of taking a FIDER-accredited program against the negatives of attending an adequate school that may prepare you for employment just as sufficiently, but without the FIDER-designated approval.

Alabama

Auburn University, Main Campus
Interior Design Department of Architecture
104 Dudley Hall
Auburn, AL 36849-3501
***Bachelor of Interior Design

Birmingham Metropolitan Skill Center
216 12th St. S.
Birmingham, AL 35233-1209

Jefferson State Community College
2601 Carson Road
Birmingham, AL 35215-3007

Samford University
800 Lakeshore Dr.
Birmingham, AL 35229-0002

Southern Junior College of Business
2015-2019 Highland
Birmingham, AL 35205-3801

University of Northern Alabama
Florence, AL 35632-0001

George M. Rogers Vocational Center
800 Main St.
Gardendale, AL 35071-2634

Wallace State Community College
801 Main St. N. W.
Hanceville, AL 35077-9080

Southern Junior College of Business
4900 Corporate Dr. N.W.
Huntsville, AL 35805-6202

University of Alabama, Huntsville
4701 University Dr.
Huntsville, AL 35899-0101

Oakwood College
Huntsville, AL 35896-0001

Jacksonville State University
Jacksonville, AL 36265

Judson College
Marion, AL 36756

University of Montevallo
Montevallo, AL 35115-6000

Alabama A & M University
P.O. Box 285
Normal, AL 35762-7501

University of Alabama
Department of Clothing,
Textiles and Interior Design
College of Human
Environmental Sciences
P.O. Box 870158
Tuscaloosa, AL 35487-0158
***Bachelor of Science in
Human Environmental
Science

Tuskegee University
Tuskegee, AL 36088

Alaska

**Anchorage Community
College**
2533 Providence Dr.
Anchorage, AK 99508

Arizona

Northern Arizona University
Flagstaff, AZ 86011-6020

American College
335 Sycamore
Mesa, AZ 85202

Mesa Community College
1833 W. Southern Ave.
Mesa, AZ 85202-4866

Glendale Comm. College
6000 W. Olive Ave.
Glendale, AZ 85302-3090

**College of Business and
Design**
114 Camelback Rd.
Phoenix, AZ 85013-2520

Durham College
4530 N. Central Ave.
Phoenix, AZ 85012

**Metro Technical/Vocational
Institute, Phoenix**
Phoenix, AZ 85015-6051

Phoenix College
1202 W. Thomas Rd.
Phoenix, AZ 85013-4234

**Phoenix Institute of
Technology**
2555 E. University Dr.
Phoenix, AZ 85034-6912

Plaza Three Academy
4343 N. 16th St.
Phoenix, AZ 85016

Yavapai College
1100 E. Sheldon
Prescott, AZ 86301

**Scottsdale Community
College**
9000 E. Chapparel Rd.
Scottsdale, AZ 85256-2699

Arizona State University _50 thousand people per reustr_
School of Design
College of Architecture and
Environmental Design
Tempe, AZ 85287-0605
***Bachelor of Science in
Design

Appollo College
3870 Oracle Rd.
Tucson, AZ 85705-3227

**Pia Community College,
West Campus**
Tucson, AZ 85709-0002

Tucson College of Business
7830 E. Broadway
Tucson, AZ 85710-3923

University of Arizona
Tucson, AZ 86011-6020

Arkansas

**University of Central
Arkansas**
Conway, AR 72032

**University of Arkansas, Main
Campus**
Interior Design and Housing
Department of Home
Economics
College of Agriculture and
Home Economics
118 Home Economics
Fayetteville, AR 72701-1201
***Bachelor of Science in
Home Economics

**South Central Career
College**
2801 Olive Sr.
Pine Bluff, AR 71603-5439

Harding University
Searcy, AR 72143-5599

California

Los Angeles Mission College
1212 San Fernando
Wilmington CA 91340-3212

Chaffey Community College
5885 Haven Ave.
Alta Loma, CA 91701

Balin Institute of Technology
3301 W. Lincoln Ave.
Anaheim, CA 92801

Criss College
1238 E. Katella Ave.
Anaheim, CA 92805

Pacific Union College
Angwin, CA 94508-9797

Cabrillo College
6500 Soquel Dr.
Aptos, CA 95003-3119

Bakersfield College
1801 Panorama Dr.
Bakersfield, CA 93305-1299

College of Notre Dame
1500 Ralston Ave.
Belmont, CA 94002-1997

University of California
Berkeley, CA 94720

Woodbury University
Department of Interior
Design
School of Professional
Design
7500 Glen Oaks Blvd.
P.O. Box 7846
Burbank, CA 91910-7846
***Bachelor of Science

California State University
Chico, CA 95929-1000

Southwestern College
900 Otay Lakes Rd.
Chula Vista, CA 92010-7223

Orange Coast College
2701 Fairview Rd.
Costa Mesa, CA 92628

Fashion Institute of Design
3420 Bristol, S400
Costa Mesa, CA 92626-1923

De Anza College
21250 Stevens Creek
Cupertino, CA 95014-5702

Cypress College
9200 Valley View
Cypress, CA 90630-5897

**University of California,
Davis**
Davis, CA 95616-8585

Grossmont College
8800 Grossmont College
El Cajon, CA 92020-1765

Ohlone College
P.O. Box 3909
Fremont, CA 94539-5884

**California State University,
Fresno**
Interior Design Major
Department of Industrial
Technology
5300 N. Campus Dr.
Fresno, CA 93740-0009
***Bachelor of Arts

Fresno City College
1101 University Ave.
Fresno, CA 93741-0001

**California State University,
Fullerton**
Fullerton, CA 92634-4080

Fullerton College
Fullerton, CA 92632-2095

Glendale Community College
1500 Verdugo Rd.
Glendale, CA 91208-2809

Citrus College
1001 W. Foothill Blvd.
Glendora, CA 91740-1899

Chabot College
25555 Hesperian Blvd.
Hayward, CA 94545-2447

Golden West College
15744 Golden West
Huntington Beach, CA
92647-0592

Marin Community Colleges
College Ave.
Kentfield, CA 94904

Antelope Valley College
3041 W. Avenue K
Lancaster, CA 93534

Las Postias College
3033 Collier Canyon
Livermore, CA 94550-9797

Brooks College
4825 E. Pacific Coast
Highway
Long Beach, CA 90804-9987

**California State University,
Long Beach**
Interior Design Program
Department of Design
School of Fine Arts
1250 Bellflower Blvd.
Long Beach, CA 90840-0001
***Bachelor of Fine Arts in
Interior Design

**California State University,
Long Beach**
Interiors: Environmental
Factors
Home Economics
School of Applied Arts and
Sciences
1250 Bellflower Blvd.
Long Beach, CA 90840-0001
***Bachelor of Arts

Long Beach City College
4901 E. Carson St.
Long Beach, CA 90808-1780

Foothill College
12345 El Monte Rd.
Los Alto Hills, CA 94022-
4504

**American College of Applied
Arts**
1651 Westwood Blvd.
Los Angeles, CA 90024-5603

**California State University,
Los Angeles**
5151 State University Dr.
Los Angeles, CA 90032

**Fashion Institute of Design
& Merchandising**
Interior Design Department
919 S. Grand Ave.
Los Angeles, CA 90017-3407
***Associate of Arts,
Interior Design

Los Angeles City College
855 N. Vermont Ave.
Los Angeles, CA 90029-3500

**Los Angeles Southwest
College**
1600 N. Imperial Highway
Los Angeles, CA 90047

**Otis Parsons School of
Design**
2401 Wilshire Blvd.
Los Angeles, CA 90057-3304

**University of California, Los
Angeles**
405 Hilgard Ave.
Los Angeles, CA 90024-1301

**University of California, Los
Angeles**
Interior and Environmental
Design
Professional Designation
Program
Department of the Arts,
UCLA Extension
10999 Le Conte Ave.
Los Angeles, CA 90024
***Professional Designation
in Interior Design

Yuba College
Department of Vocational
Education
2088 North Beale St.
Marysville, CA 95901-7699

Saddleback College
28000 Marguerite Pky
Mission Viejo, CA 92692-
3601

Modesto Junior College
435 College Ave.
Modesto, CA 95350-5808

Monterey Peninsula College
980 Fremont
Monterey, CA 93940-4799

Moorpark College
7075 Campus Rd.
Moorpark, CA 93021-1600

Interior Designer's Institute
1061 Camelback St.
Newport Beach, CA 92660-
3228

**California State University,
Northridge**
18111 Nordhoff St.
Northridge, CA 91330-0001

Marin Colleges
Indian Valley
1800 Ignacio Blvd.
Novato, CA 94947

**California College of Arts
and Crafts**
5212 Broadway
Oakland, CA 94618-1426
BA Degree Program

Laney College
900 Fallon St.
Oakland, CA 94607-4893

John F. Kennedy University
12 Altarindo Rd.
Orinda, CA 94563-2603

Butte College
3536 Butte Campus Dr.
Oroville, CA 95965-8303

College of the Desert
43-500 Monterey St.
Palm Desert, CA 92260-2499

Pasadena City College
1570 E. Colorado Ave.
Pasadena, CA 91106

**California State Polytechnical
University, Pomona**
3801 W. Temple Ave.
Pomona, CA 91768-2557

Chaffey College
5885 Haven Ave.
Rancho Cucamonga, CA
91701-3002

Marymount College
Rancho Palos Verdes, CA
90274-6299

Shasta College
P.O. Box 496006
Redding, CA 96049-6006

Canada College
4200 Farm Hill Blvd.
Redwood City, CA 94061-
1099

**Kings River Community
College**
995 North Reed
Reedley, CA 93654-2017

University of CA
Riverside, CA 92521

Sierra College
5000 Rocklin Rd.
Rocklin, CA 95677-3397

American River College
Department of Art and
Music
4700 College Oak Dr.
Sacramento, CA 95841-4286

**California State University,
Sacramento**
Interior Design Program
School of Arts and Sciences

Department of Home
Economics
6000 J. St.
Sacramento, CA 95841-4286
***Bachelor of Arts in
Interior Design

Cosumnes River College
8401 Center Parkway
Sacramento, CA 95823

**San Bernardino Valley
College**
701 S. Mount Vernon Ave.
San Bernardino, CA 92410-
2748

American Business College
5952 El Cajon Blvd.
San Diego, CA 92115

**Design Institute of San
Diego**
Interior Design Program
8555 Commerce Ave.
San Diego, CA 92121
***Certificate in Interior
Design
***Bachelor of Fine Arts in
Interior Design

Pt. Loma Nazarene College
3900 Lomaland Dr.
San Diego, CA 92106-2810

San Diego Mesa College
7250 Mesa College Dr.
San Diego, CA 92111-4902

San Diego State University
Interior Design Program
Art Department
College of Professional
Studies and Fine Arts
5300 Campanile Dr.
San Diego, CA 92104
***Bachelor of Arts in
Applied Arts and Science

Academy of Art College
Interior Design Program
2300 Stockton St., Suite 300
San Francisco, CA 94133
***Bachelor of Fine Arts,
Interior Design

**California College of Arts &
Crafts**
Interior Architectural Design
School of Architectural
Studies
1700 17th St.
San Francisco, CA 94103
***Bachelor of Fine Arts

City College, San Francisco
50 Phelan Ave.
San Francisco, CA 94112-1821

Fashion Institute of Design and Merchandising
55 Stockton St., 5th Floor
San Francisco, CA 94108-580

San Francisco State University
1600 Holloway Ave.
San Francisco, CA 94132-1722

Evergreen Valley College
3095 Yerba Buena Rd.
San Jose, CA 95135-1513

Central County Occupational Center
760 Hilldale Ave.
San Jose, CA 95136-1106

Barbizon School, San Jose
3033 Moorpark Ave.
San Jose, CA 95128

San Jose State University
San Jose, CA 95192-0001

California Polytechnic State University
Interior Design Program
Home Economics
Department, MHE 136
San Luis Obispo, CA 93407
***Bachelor of Science in Home Economics

Palomar College
1140 W. Mission Rd.
San Marcos, CA 92069-1487

College of San Mateo
1700 W. Hillsdale Blvd.
San Mateo, CA 94402-3784

Contra Costa College
2600 Mission Bell Dr.
San Pablo, CA 94806-3195

Rancho Santiago College
17th at Bristol
Santa Ana, CA 92706-3398

UC Santa Cruz Extension
740 Front St., Suite 155
Santa Cruz, CA 95060

Santa Monica College
1900 Pico Blvd.
Santa Monica, CA 90405-1644

Santa Rosa Junior College
1501 Mendocino Ave.
Santa Rosa, CA 95401-4332

West Valley College
Interior Design Program
14000 Fruitvale Ave.
Saratoga, CA 95070-5698
***Three-Year Certificate in Interior Design

Fashion Institute of Design & Merchandising
13701 Riverside Dr.
Sherman Oaks CA 91423-2430

San Joaquin Delta College
5151 Pacific Ave.
Stockton, CA 95207-6370

Soland Community College
4000 Suisun Valley Rd.
Suisun City, CA 94585-3197

El Camino College
16007 Crenshaw Blvd.
Torrance, CA 90506-0001

Southern California Regional Occupational Center
2300 Crenshaw Blvd.
Torrance, CA 90501

Los Angeles Valley College
5800 Fulton Ave.
Van Nuys, CA 91401-4062

Ventura College
4667 Telegraph Rd.
Ventura, CA 93003-3899

College of the Sequoias
Mooney Blvd.
Visalia, CA 93277

Mt. San Antonio College
1100 Grand
Walnut, CA 91789-1397

College of the Siskiyous
800 College Ave.
Weed, CA 96094-2899

Los Angeles Harbor College
1111 Figuerora Place
Wilmington, CA 90744-2311

West Valley Occupational Center
6200 Winnetka Ave.
Woodland Hills, CA 91367

Colorado

Interior Design Internship
2960 Diagonal Highway
Boulder, CO 80301

Technical Trades Institute
1955 No. Union Blvd.
Colorado Springs, CO. 80909-6096

Colorado Institute of Art
200 E. 9th Ave.
Denver, CO 80203-2903

Emily Griffith Opportunity School
1250 Weldon St.
Denver, CO 80204

Interior Design Internship
1401 Blake St.
Denver, CO 80202
Three-year professional program

Interior Design Institute of Denver
Interior Design Program
1401 Blake St.
Denver, CO 80202
***Bachelor of Interior Design

University of Colorado at Denver
1200 Larimer
Denver, CO 80204-5310

Colorado State University
Interior Design Program
College of Applied Human Sciences
156 Aylesworth Hall S. E.
Fort Collins, CO 80523-0001
***Bachelor of Science

Arapahoe Community College
2500 W. College Dr.
Littleton, CO 80160-9002

Connecticut

University of Bridgeport
Bridgeport, CT 06601-2449

Paier College of Art
6 Prospect Ct.
Hamden, CT 06517

Silvermine Rd.
New Canaan, CT 06840-4337

Barbizon School of Fashion

Merchandising
26 Sixth St.
Stamford, CT 06905

University of Connecticut, Main Campus
U-58 348 Mansfield
Storrs, CT 06269-2058

Post College
800 Country Club Rd.
Waterbury, CT 06723-2540

University of Hartford
200 Bloomfield Ave.
West Hartford, CT 06601-2449

Delaware

Delaware State College
Dover, DE 19901

University of Delaware
Newark, DE 19716

Kent County Vocational Technical School
P.O. Box 97
Woodside, DE

District of Columbia

Catholic University of America
Washingon, DC 20064

Gallaudet University
7th and Florida Ave. N. E.
Washington, DC 20002-3695

George Washington University
Washington, DC 20052

Howard University
2400 Sixth St. N. W.
Washington, DC 20059-0002

International Institute of Interior Design
2225 R. St. N.W.
Washington, DC 20008

Mount Vernon College
Interior Design Department
2100 Foxhall Rd., N. W.
Washington, DC 20007-1199
***Bachelor of Arts

University of DC, Mt. Vernon Campus
916 G. St. N. W.
Washington, DC 20001

Florida

College of Boca Raton
Boca Raton, FL 33431-5598

Manatee Community College
P.O. Box 1849
Bradenton, FL 34206-7046

St. Petersburg Junior College
2465 Drew St.
Clearwater, FL 33515

Daytona Beach Community College
P.O. Box 2811
Daytona Beach, FL 32115-2811

Broward Community College
3501 S.W. Davie Rd.
Fort Lauderdale, FL 33314

Indian River Community College
3209 Virginia Ave.
Fort Pierce, FL 34981-5541

University of Florida
Interior Design Department
340 Architects Building
College of Architecture
Gainesville, FL 36211-2004
***Bachelor of Design in Interior Design

Florida Community College-Kent Center
3939 Roosevelt Blvd.
Jacksonville, FL 32205-8923

Florida Junior College at Jacksonville
501 W. State St.
Jacksonville, FL 32202

Palm Beach Community College, Central
4200 Congress Ave.
Lake Worth, FL 33461-4705

Central Florida Community College
P.O. Box 1388
Ocala, FL 32678-1388

Florida International University
University Park
Miami, FL 33199-0499

Garces Commercial College
1301 S.W. 1st St.
Miami, FL 33135

Garces Commercial College
5385 N.W. 36th St.
Miami Springs, FL

International Fine Arts College
1737 N. Bayshore Dr.
Miami, FL 33132-2204

Miami Dade Community College, North
11380 N. W. 27th Ave.
Miami, FL 33132-1199

Miami Dade Community College, New World
300 N E 2nd Ave.
Miami, FL 33232-2204

Miami Dade Community College, South
11011 S. W. 104 St.
Miami, FL 33176-3330

Pensacola Junior College
1000 College Blvd.
Pensacola, FL

University of West Florida
Pensacola, FL 32514-5750

Seminole Community College
100 Weldon Blvd.
Sanford, FL 32773-6132

Colson School of Art and Fine Art Tapestries
1666 Hillview
Sarasota, FL 34239

Ringling School of Art and Design
Interior Design and Space Planning
2700 N. Tamiami Tr.
Sarasota, FL 34234-5895
***Certificate in Interior Design

Sarasota Vocational Technical School
4748 Beneva Rd.
Sarasota, FL 33581

St. Petersburg Vocational Technical Inst.
901 34th St., South
St. Petersburg, FL 33711

Florida State University
Interior Design Department
School of Visual Arts
Tallahassee, FL 32306-2051
***Bachelor of Science and Bachelor of Arts in Interior Design

Erwin Vocational Technical Center
2010 E. Hillsborough Ave.
Tampa, FL 33610

Hillsborough Community College
39 Columbia Drive
Tampa, FL 33631-3127

International Academy of Merchandise & Design
211 Mariner Sq. Park
Tampa, FL 33609-3523

Florida College
Temple Terrace, FL 33617-5578

Manatee Community College, South
P.O. Box 8996
Venice, FL 34284-8996

Georgia

American College of Applied Arts
3330 Peachtree N E
Atlanta, GA 30326-1001

Art Institute of Atlanta
3376 Peachtree, N. E.
Atlanta, GA 30326-1018

Atlanta Area Technical School
1560 Stewart Ave., Southwest
Atlanta, GA 30310

Atlanta College of Art
1280 Peachtree, N. E.
Atlanta, GA 30309-3582

Bauder Fashion College
Philips Plaza
3500 Peach Tree Rd. N.E.
Atlanta, GA 30326

Georgia State University
University Plaza
Atlanta, GA 30303-3044

University of Georgia
Interior Design Major
Art Department
Franklin College of Arts & Sciences
Athens, GA 30602
***Bachelor of Fine Arts

Augusta Technical Institute
3116 Dean Bridge Rd.
Augusta, GA 30906

West Georgia College
Carrollton, GA 30118-0001

Middle Georgia College
Cochrna, GA 31014-1599

Mable Bailey Fashion College
1332 13th St.
Columbus, GA 31901

Fort Valley State College
Fort Valley, GA 31030-3298

Brenau College
Gainesville, GA 30501-3697

Berry College
Mount Berry, GA 30149-0001

Savannah College of Art
P.O. Box 3146
Savannah, GA 31402-3146

Georgia Southern College
Statesboro, GA 30460-8034

Middle Georgia Technical Institute
1311 Corder Rd.
Warner Robins, GA 31088

Hawaii

Chaminade University of Honolulu
3140 Waialae Ave.
Honolulu, HI 96816-1510

University of Hawaii, Manoa
2515 Campus Rd.
Honolulu, HI 96822

Idaho

Boise State Univ.
1910 University Drive
Boise, ID 83725-0001

University of Idaho
Moscow, ID 83460-0615

Northwest Nazarene College
Nampa, ID 83686

Idaho State University
Pocatello, ID 83209-0009

Ricks College
Interior Design Program
244-C Clarke Building
Rexburg, ID 83460-0615

***Three-Year Associate in Interior Design

Illinois

Southern Illinois University at Carbondale
Interior Design
Division of Graphic Communications
College of Technical Careers
410 Quigley Hall
Carbondale, IL 62901
***Bachelor of Science

Eastern Illinois University
Charleston, IL 61920

Prairie State College
202 S. Halstead
Chicago Heights, IL 60411-1275

Columbia College
600 S. Michigan
Chicago, IL 60605-2418

Harrington Institute Interior Design
410 S. Michigan Ave.
Chicago, IL 60605-1302
***Associate of Technology in Interior Design

International Academy of Merchandising and Design, LTD
350 N. Orleans St.
Chicago, IL 60654

MacCormac College Downtown Center
327 S. La Salle St.
Chicago, IL 60604

Mundelein College
6363 N. Sheridan Rd.
Chicago, IL 60660-1717

Ray-Vogue School of Design
664 N. Michigan Ave.
Chicago, IL 60611

Northern Illinois University
De Kalb, IL 601115-2883

Illinois Central College
East Peoria, IL 61635-0002

College of Dupage
22nd St. and Lambert Rd.
Glen Ellyn, IL 60137-6599

Joliet Junior College
1216 Houbolt Ave.

Joliet, IL 60436-9352

Olivet Nazarene University
Kankakee, IL 60901-0592

Indiana Vocational Technical College
Kokomo, IL 46901

Western Illinois University
Adams St.
Macomb, IL 61455

Black Hawk College
Moline, IL 61265

Illinois State University
Normal, IL 61761-6901

William Rainey Harper College
Algonzuin and Roselle
Palatin, IL 60067-7398

Bradley University
Peoria, IL 61625-0001

Rosary College
7900 West Div.
River Forest, IL 60305-1099

Ray College of Design
1051 Perimeter Dr.
Schaumburg, IL 60173-5833

University of IL, Urbana Campus
Urbana, IL 61801

Indiana

Indiana University at Bloomington
Interior Design Program
Department of Apparel Merchandising and Interior Design
College of Arts and Sciences
203 Wylie Hall
Bloomington, IN 47405-3201
***Bachelor of Science

Indiana Vocational Technical College
646 Franklin St.
Columbus, IN 47201

Indiana Vocational Technical College — Southwest
3501 First Ave.
Evansville, IN 47710

Indiana University Purdue, Ft Wayne
2101 Coliseum Blvd. E.

Fort Wayne, IN 46805-1445

Goshen College
Goshen, IN 46526-4795

Manchester College
North Manchester, IN 46962-1299

Ball State University
Muncie, IN 47306

Indiana Vocational Technical College — North Central
1534 W. Sample St.
South Bend, IN 46619

Michiana College
1030 E. Jefferson Blvd.
South Bend IN 46617-3123

Indiana State University, Main Campus
Interior Design Department
Terre Haute, IN 47405-3201

Vincennes University Junior College
1002 No. First St.
Vincennes, IN 47591-1504

Purdue University, Main Campus
Consumer Sciences & Retailing
1262 Matthews Hall
West Lafayette, IN 47907

Iowa

Iowa State University of Science & Technology
Interior Design Program
Department of Art and Design
158 College of Design
Ames, IA 50011-0001
***Bachelor of Fine Arts in Interior Design

Scott Community College
500 Belmont Rd.
Bettendorf, IA 52722-5649

Northeast Iowa Technical Institute
P.O. Box 400
Calmar, IA 52132

University of Northern Iowa
Cedar Falls, IA 50614

Kirkwood Community College
P.O. Box 2068

Cedar Rapids, IA 52406-2068

Eastern Iowa Community College
District Scott, Clinton
306 N. River Dr.
Davenport, IA 52801

Drake University
25th St. University
Des Moines, IA 50311

University of Iowa
Iowa City, IA 52242

William Penn College
Oskaloosa, IA 52577-1799

Hawkeye Institute Technology
Box 8015
Waterloo, IA 50704-8015

Kansas

Coffeyville Community College
11th and Willon
Coffeyville, KS 67337-5063

Emporia State University
1200 Commercial St.
Emporia, KS 66801-5087

Garden City Community College
801 Campus Dr.
Garden City, KS 67846-6333

Barton County Community College
Bissells Pt. Rd. R R 3
Great Bend, KS 67530-9803

Fort Hays State University
600 Park St.
Hays, KS 67601-4009

Hutchinson Community College
1300 N. Plum St.
Hutchinson, KS 67501-5831

Independence Community College
P.O. Box 708
Independence, KS 67301-0708

University of Kansas
Lawrence, KS 66045-1630

Kansas State University
Interior Design Option

Department of Clothing, Textiles, and Interior Design
College of Human Ecology
Manhattan, KS 66506
***Bachelor of Science

Kansas State University
Department of Interior Architecture
College of Architecture and Design
Manhattan, KS 66506
***Bachelor of Interior Architecture

McPherson College
McPherson, KS 67460-3899

Bethel College
North Newton, KS 67117

Johnson County Community College
12345 College Blvd.
Overland Park, KS 66210-1283

Pittsburg State University
Pittsburg, KS 66762-5880

Sterling College
Sterling, KS 67579

Patricia Stevens Career College
2823 E. Douglas
Wichita, KS 67211

Vocational-Technical Center
301 S. Grove
Wichita, KS 67211-2021

Kentucky

Berea College
Berea, KY 40404-0002

Bowling Green St. Vo/Tech School
P.O. Box 6000
Bowling Green, KY 42101-2678

Western Kentucky University
Bowling Green, KY 42101

Georgetown College
Georgetown, KY 40324-1620

University of Kentucky
Interior Design Program
Department of Human Environment:Design/Textiles
College of Home Economics
Lexington, KY 40506-0054

***Bachelor of Arts in Interior Design

Kentucky Polytechnic Institute
7410 La Grange Rd.
Louisville, KY 40222

Louisville Technical Institute
3901 Atkinson Dr.
Louisville, KY 40218-4519

University of Louisville
Louisville, KY 40292

Midway College
Stephens St.
Midway, KY 40347-9731

Morehead State University
Morehead, KY 40351-1680

Murray State University
Murray KY 42071-3311

Eastern Kentucky University
Richmond, KY 40475

Louisiana

Baton Rouge Schools Computers
9255 Interline Ave.
Baton Rouge, LA 70809-1908

Louisiana State University
Department of Interior Design
402 Design Building
Baton Rouge, LA 70803
***Bachelor of Interior Design

Southern University A M C, Main Campus
Baton Rouge, LA 70813

Southeastern Louisiana University
Hammond, LA 70402

University of Southwestern Louisiana
Interior Design Program
Department of Architecture
School of Art and Architecture
P.O. Box 43850
Joel L. Fletcher Hall, Rm. 102
Lafayette, LA 70504
***Bachelor of Interior Design

McNeese State University
Lake Charles, LA 70609

Northeast Louisiana University
Monroe, LA 71209

Northwestern State University of Louisiana
Natchitoches, LA 71497

Delgado Community College, City Park
615 City Park Ave.
New Orleans, LA 70119-4326

Tulane University of Louisiana
New Orleans, LA 70118

Louisiana Tech University
Interior Design Option
Art and Architecture Department
College of Arts and Sciences
P.O. Box 3175 Tech Station
Ruston, LA 71272-0001
***Bachelor of Interior Design

Nicholls State University
Thibodaux, LA 70310-2001

Maryland

Le Millet Private Art School
2415 St. Paul St.
Baltimore, MD 21218

Maryland Institute College of Art
1300 Mt. Royal Ave.
Baltimore, MD 21217-4134

Harford Community College
401 Thomas Run Rd.
Bel Air, MD 21014-1627

Catonsville Community College
800 S. Rolling Rd.
Catonsville, MD 21228-5317

University of Maryland
Department of Housing & Design
1401 Marie Mount Hall
College Park, MD 20742-7525

Hood College
Frederick, MD 21701-8575

Charles County Community College

La Plata, MD 20646

Patrica Stevens Fashion
11301 Rockville Pike
North Bethesda, MD 20895-1021

University of Maryland, Eastern Shore
Princess Anne, MD 21853

Montgomery College, Rockville
51 Mannakee
Rockville, MD 20850-1101

Maine

University of Maine at Farmington
Farmington, ME 04938

University of Maine at Orono
Merrill Hall
Orono, ME 04469

Massachusetts

University of Massachusetts, Amherst Campus
Interior Design Concentration
Design Area
Fine Arts Center 351
Amherst, MA 01003
***Bachelor of Fine Arts in Design

Endicott College
Beverly, MA 01915

North Shore Community College
3 Essex St.
Beverly, MA 01915

Boston Architectural Center
Boston, MA 02115

Boston University
725 Commonwealth Ave.
Boston, MA 02215-13401

Chamberlayne Junior College
128 Commonwealth Ave.
Boston, MA 02116

Chamberlain School of Retailing
90 Marlborough St.
Boston, MA 02116

John Robert Powers Finishing and Modeling School
9 Newbury St.
Boston, MA 02116

Newbury College
921 Boylston St.
Boston, MA 02115

The New England School of Art & Design
Interior/Environmental Design
28 Newbury St.
Boston, MA 02116-3276
***Diploma of Interior/Environmental Design

Wentworth Institute of Technology
Interior Design Program
Interior Design and Facilities Management
College of Design and Construction
550 Huntington Ave.
Boston, MA 02115-5998
***Bachelor of Science

Bridgewater State College
Bridgewater, MA 02324-2699

Harvard Graduate School of Design
Gund Hall
Cambridge, MA 02138

Massachusetts Institute of Technology
77 Massachusetts Ave.
Cambridge, MA 02139-4307

Pine Manor College
400 Heath St.
Chestnut Hill, MA 02167-2332

Diman Regional Technical Institute
Stonehaven Rd.
Fall River, MA 02723

Framingham State College
Framingham, MA 01701-2471

Dean Junior College
99 Main St.
Franklin, MA 02038-1994

Bay Path College
588 Longmeadow St.
LongMeadow, MA 01106-2212

University of Massachusetts
Art Department
Fine Arts Center
Louisiana Tech University,
Amherst MA 01003

Mount Ida College
777 Dedham St.
Newton Centre, MA 02159-3310

Anna Maria College
Paxton, MA 01612-1198

Massachusetts Bay Community College
50 Oakland St.
Wellesley Hills, MA 02181

Becker College
P.O. Box 15071
Worcester, MA 01615-0071

Michigan

Adrian College
Adrian, MI 49221-2575

Michigan Technical Institute
611 Church St.
P.O. Box 8200
Ann Arbor, MI 48107

Grand Valley State University
1 Campus Drive
Allendale, MI 49401-9401

University of Michigan, Main Campus
Ann Arbor, MI 48109-2069

Andrews University
Berrien Springs, MI 49104-0001

Cranbrook Academy of Art
Box 801
Bloomfield Hills, MI 48013-4299

Henry Ford Community College
5101 Evergreen Road
Dearborn, MI 48128-1495

Center of Creative Studies
245 Kirby
Detriot, MI 48202-4013

Wayne County Community College
801 W. Fort St.
Detriot, MI 48226

Wayne State University
150 Art
Detriot, MI 48202

Michigan State University
Interior Design Program
Human Environment & Design
204 Human Ecology
East Lansing, MI 48824-1030
***Bachelor of Arts with a Major in Interior Design

Baker College
1050 W. Bristol Rd.
Flint, MI 48507

Fashion Institute of America
P.O. Box 624
Franklin, MI 48025-0624

Grand Rapids Junior College
143 Bostwick Ave., N. E.
Grand Rapids, MI 49503-3201

Kendall College of Art and Design
Division of Design Studies:
Interior Design
111 Division Ave. North
Grand Rapids, MI 49503
***Bachelor of Fine Arts

Hope College
Holland, MI 49423-3698

Western Michigan University
Kalamazoo, MI 49008-3804

Lansing Community College
Lansing, MI 48914

Madonna College
36600 Schoolcraft Rd.
Livonia, MI 48150-1173

Northern Michigan University
Marquette, MI 49855-5310

Central Michigan University
Mount Pleasant, MI 48859

Baker College
1020 S. Washington St.
Owosso, MI 48824-1020

Saint Clair College
323 Erie St.
Pt. Huron, MI 48060

Lawrence Technological University
Interior Architecture/Design
21000 W. Ten Mile Rd.

Southfield, MI 48075-6170
***Bachelor of Science

John Robert Powers Career School
16250 Northland Dr.
Southfield, MI 48075

Delta College
University Center, MI 48202

Eastern Michigan University
Interior Design Program
Department of Human Environmental and Consumer Resources
Roosevelt Hall, Rm. 206
Ypsilanti, MI 48197-2207
***Bachelor of Science

Minnesota

Alexandria Technical College
Department of Interior Design
1600 Jefferson St.
Alexandria, MN 56308-2796
***Associate of Interior Design

Anoka Vocational-Technical Institute
Anoka, MN 55303

College of St. Scholastica
1200 Kenwood Ave.
Duluth, MN 55811-4199

University of Minnesota, Duluth
Duluth, MN 55812

Mankato State University
Mankato, MN. 55811-4199

Mankato Technical College
Box 1920
Mankato, MN 56001

Lowthian College
821 Marquette Ave.
Minneapolis, MN 55402-2935

Minneapolis College of Art & Design
2501 Stevens Ave. Sth.
Minneapolis, MN 55404-4347

Minnesota University of Twin Cities
Twin Cities Campus
Minneapolis, MN 55455

Pillsbury Baptist Bible College
Owatonna, MN 55060

Dakota County Technical College
Interior Design and Sales
1300-145th St. E.
Rosemount, MN 55068
***Two-Year Diploma

College of Saint Benedict
St. Joseph, MN 56374-2099

College of St. Catherine
2004 Randolph Ave.
St. Paul, MN 55105-1750

University of Minnesota, St. Paul
Department of Design,
Housing & Apparel
College of Human Ecology
1985 Buford Ave.
St. Paul MN 55108-1013
***Bachelor of Science

Lakewood Community College
3401 Century Ave.
White Bear Lake, MN 55110

Winona State University
Winona, MN 55987-3288

Mississippi

Blue Mountain College
Blue Mountain, MS 38610

Northeast Mississippi Community College
Booneville, MS 38829

Delta State University
Cleveland, MS 38733-0001

Mississippi College
Clinton, MS 39058-0001

Mississipi University for Women
Columbus, MS 39701

Jones County Junior College
Ellisville MS, 39437

University of Southern Mississippi
Interior Design Program
School of Home Economics
College of Health and
Human Sciences
Southern Station Box 5035-
USM

Hattiesburg, MS 39406-5035
***Bachelor of Science

Hinds Junior College
University Center
1855 Eastover Dr.
Jackson, MS 39211-6435

Alcorn State University
Lorman, MS 39096

Mississippi State University
Mississippi ST, MS 39762-5765

Mississippi Delta Junior College
Moorhead, MS 38761

Mississippi Gulf Coast Junior College
Perkinston Campus
P.O. Box 47
Perkinston, MS 39573

University of Mississippi, Main Campus
University, MS 38677

Missouri

Southwest Baptist University
Bolivar MO 65211

Cape Girardeau Vocational-Technical School
301 N. Clark
Cape Girardeau, MO 63701-5105

Southeast Missouri State University
Cape Girardeau, MO 63701

University of Missouri, Columbia
Interior Design Program
Department of
Environmental Design
College of Human
Environmental Sciences
137 Stanley Hall
Columbia, MO 65211
***Bachelor of Science

William Woods College
200 West 12th St.
Fulton, MO 65251-1098

Kansas City Technical Education
301 E. Armour Blvd.
Kansas City, MO 64111-1252

Northeast Missouri State University
Kirksville, MO 63701

Northwest Missouri State University
Maryville, MO 64468-6001

Southwest Missouri State Univ.
901 S. National
Springfield, MO 65804-0027

Saint Louis Tech
4144 Cypress
St. Ann, MO 63074-1521

Platt College
3131 Frederick Ave.
St. Joseph, MO 64506-2911

Fontbonne College
6800 Wydown Blvd.
St. Louis, MO 63141-7299

Patricia Stevens College
1831 Chestnut S400
St. Louis, MO 63141-7299

Maryville University of St. Louis
Interior Design Program/Art
Division
13550 Conway Rd.
St. Louis, MO 63141-7299
***Bachelor of Fine Arts

St. Louis Community College, Meramec
11333 Big Ben Blvd.
St. Louis, MO 63122-5720

Central Missouri State University
Warrensburg, MO 64093

Montana

Montana State University
Bozeman, MT 59717-0002

University of Montana
Missoula, MT 59812

Nebraska

Chadron State College
1000 Main St.
Chadron, NE 69337-2666

Central Community College-Platte
P.O. Box 1027

Columbus, NE 68602-1027

Kearny State College
Kearny, NE 68849-0001

University of Nebraska, East Campus
Interiors Option
Department of Textiles,
Clothing and Design
Lincoln, NE 68583-0802
***Bachelor of Science

McCook Community College
1205 E. Third St.
McCook, NE 69001

Metropolitan Community College, Elkhorn
204th and W. Dodge Rd.
Omaha, NE 68103

Patricia Stevens Fashion and Secretarial College
117 N. 32nd Ave.
Omaha, NE 68131

University of Nebraska at Omaha
Arts & Science Hall #108
Omaha, NE 68182-0214

Nebraska Western College
1601 E. 27th St., Northeast
Scottsbluff, NE 69361

Wayne State College
Wayne, NE 68787-1486

New Hamphire

University of New Hampshire, Keene State College
229 Main St.
Keene, NH 03431-4101

Hesser College
25 Lowell St.
Manchester, NH 03101

New Jersey

College of St. Elizabeth
Convent Station, NJ 07961

Glassboro State College
Glassboro, NJ 08028-1701

Jersey City State College
2039 Kennedy Blvd.
Jersey City, NJ 07305-1537

Centenary College
Jefferson St.
Hackettstown, NJ 07840

Brookdale Community College
765 Newman Springs Rd.
Lincroft, NJ 07738-1543

Commercial Technical Institute
1500 Cardinal Dr.
Little Falls, NJ 07424

The Plaza School
Bergen Mall
Paramus, NJ 07652

Roberts-Walsh Business School
Summit, NJ 07901-2707

Ocean County Area Vocational Tech. Schools
Toms River, NJ 08753

Mercer County Community College
P.O. Box B
Trenton, NJ 08608

Trenton State College
Interior Design Program
Art Department
Hillwood Lakes, CN-4700
Trenton, NJ 08650-4700
***Bachelor of Fine Arts

Kean College of New Jersey
Union, NJ 07083

Roberts-Walsh Business School
2343 Morris Ave.
Union, NJ 07083

Star Technical Institute
Vineland, NJ 08360-6210

Berkeley School of Bergen
100 W. Prospect St.
Waldwick, NJ 07463

William Paterson College
300 Pompton Rd.
Wayne, NJ 07470-2103

Interior Design Institute
39 Clairmont
Woodcliff Lake, NJ 07675

New York

Sage Junior College
140 New Scotland Ave.

Albany, NY 12208-3425

S U N Y College of Technology, Alfred
Alfred, NY 14802-1196

Broome Community College
Upper Front St.
Binghamton, NY 13902

Pratt Institute
Department of Interior Design
Pratt Studios 24
200 Willoughby Ave.
Brooklyn, NY 11205
***Bachelor of Fine Arts

Syrit Computer School System
1760 53rd St.
Brooklyn, NY 11204-1524

Bryant Stratton Business Institute
1028 Main St.
Buffalo, NY 14202-1193

Buffalo State College
1300 Elmwood Ave.
Buffalo, NY 14222-1095

J'advance Model and Career Center
310 Delaware Ave.
Buffalo, NY 14202

John Robert Powers School
310 Delaware Ave.
Buffalo, NY 14202

Villa Maria College, Buffalo
240 Pine Ridge Rd.
Buffalo, NY 14225-3999

Cazenovia College
Cazenovia, NY 13035-1084

C U N Y Queens College
Flushing, NY 11367-0904

Cornell University, Main Campus
Interior Design Program
Department of Design and
Environmental Analysis
NYS College of Human Ecology
Van Rensselaer Hall
Ithaca, NY 14853-4401
***Bachelor of Science

Willsey Institute of Interior Design
380 N. Broadway
Jericho, NY 11753

Western Piedmont Community College
1001 Barkemont Ave.
Morgantown, NY 28655

American Academy in Rome
Fellowships Coordinator
41 E. 65th St.
New York, NY 10021
***Associate of Applied Science in Interior Design

C U N Y City College
Convent Ave at 138th
New York, NY 10031

Fashion Institute of Technology
Interior Design Department
227 W. 27th St.
New York, NY 10001-5902

Mayer School of Fashion Design
70 W. 36th St.
New York, NY 10018

New York Institute of Technology, Metropolitan
1855 Broadway
New York, NY 10023-7602

New York School of Interior Design
155 E. 56th St.
New York, NY 100222708
***Bachelor of Fine Arts
***Diploma in Interior Design

New York University
New York, NY 10003-6687

Parsons School of Design
66 Fifth Ave.
New York, NY 10011-8802

School of Visual Arts
209 East 23rd St.
New York, NY 10010-5689

Sheffield School of Interior Design
Home Study
211 East 43 St
New York, NY 10017

Traphagen School of Fashion
686 Broadway
New York, NY 10012-7304

New York Institute of Technology
Interior Design Program
Old Westbury, NY 11568
***Bachelor of Fine Arts

S U N Y College at Oneonta
Oneonta, NY 13820-9318

Metropolitan Institute of Interior Design
15 Newtown Rd.
Plainview, NY 11803

S U N Y College, Plattsburgh
Plattsburgh, NY 12901

Pace University Pleasantville, Briarcliff
861 Bedford Rd.,
Paton House
Pleasantville, NY 10570-2799

Barbizon School, Rego Park
95-20 63rd Rd
Rego Park, NY 11374

Suffolk Community College Campus
Speonk Riverhead Rd.
Riverhead, NY 11901-3499

Rochester Institute of Technology
Rochester, NY 14623-0887

Suffolk Community College
533 College Rd.
Selden, NY 11784-288

Onondaga Community College
Onondaga Hill
Syracuse, NY 13215-7901

Syracuse University
Interior Design Program
Department of Design
336 Smith Hall
Syracuse, NY 13244-0002
***Bachelor of Fine Arts

Syracuse University
Environmental Design —
Interiors
Department of
Environmental Arts,
Consumer Studies and
Retailing
224 Slocum Hall
Syracuse, NY 13244-1250
***Bachelor of Science
Environmental Design —
Interiors

Marymount College
100 Marymount Ave.
Tarrytown, NY 10591-3796

North Dakota

North Dakota State University, Main Campus
Department of Apparel, Textiles, and Interior Design
College of Home Economics
Home Economics 178
Box 5057
Fargo, ND 58105
***Bachelor of Arts in Home Economics/Bachelor of Science in Home Economics

University of North Dakota, Main Campus
Grand Forks, ND 58202-8273

Minot State University
500 University Ave. W.
Minot, ND 58702-5002

University of North Dakota, Williston Center
Williston, ND 58801

Nevada

Ikenobo Floral Arts
2162 N. Lamb
Las Vegas, NV 898110

Interior Design Institute, School of Interior Design
4225 S. Eastern #3
Las Vegas, NV 89119

University of Nevada, Las Vegas
4505 Maryland Pkwy
Las Vegas, NV 89154-0001

University of Nevada, Reno
Reno, NV 89557-0002

North Carolina

Randolph Community College
P.O. Box 1009
Asheboro, NC 27204-1009

Randolph Tech
P.O. Box 1009
Asheboro, NC 27203

Appalachian State University
Boone, NC 28608

Campbell University
Buies Creek, NC 27506-6001

American Business and Fashion Institute
1515 Mockingbird, Rm. 600
Charlotte, NC 28209-3236

Central Piedmont Community College
Elizabeth at N. Kings
Charlotte, NC 28235

Western Carolina University
Cullowhee, NC 28723-9646

Bennett College
900 E. Washington
Greensboro, NC 27401-3298

North Carolina Agriculture, Technical State University
1601 E. Market St.
Greensboro, NC 27411-0002

East Carolina University
Greenville, NC 27858-4353

North Carolina University
Greenville, NC 27858-4353

University of North Carolina at Greensboro
1000 Spring Garden
Greensboro, NC 27412-0001

High Point College
High Point, NC 27261-1949

Mars Hill College
Mars Hill, NC 28754

Carteret Community College
3505 Arendell St.
Morehead City, NC 28557-2989

Western Piedmont Community College
1001 Burkemont Ave.
Morganton, NC 28655-4504

John Robert Powers School
3522 Haworth Dr.
Raleigh, NC 27609

Meredith College
3800 Hillsborough St.
Raleigh, NC 27607-5298

Peace College
Raleigh, NC 27604-1194

Saint Augustine's College
1315 Oakwood Ave.
Raleigh, NC 27611-9299

Halifax Community College
P.O. Drawer 809

Weldon, NC 27890-0809

Ohio

University of Akron
Akron, OH 44325

Ashland University
401 College Ave.
Ashland, OH 44805-3702

Ohio University, Main Campus
Department of Interior Design
School of Home Economics
108 Tupper Hall
Athens, OH 45701-2979
***Bachelor of Science in Home Economics

Ohio Hi-Point Joint Vocational
2280 State St.
Bellefontaine, OH 43311

Bluffton College
Bluffton, OH 45817-1198

Bowling Green State University, Main Campus
Bowling Green, OH 43403-0001

Baldwin-Wallace College
Berea, OH 44017-2088

Antonelli Institute of Art & Photography
124 E. 77th St.
Cincinnati, OH 45202-2592

God's Bible School
1810 Young St.
Cincinnati, OH 45210-1599

Southern Ohio College
1055 Laidlaw Ave.
Cincinnati, OH 45237

University of Cincinnati, Main Campus
5-Year Program in Interior Design
Interior Design Department
School of Architecture & Interior Design
College of Design, Architecture and Art
Cincinnati, OH 45221-0016
***Bachelor of Science in Design

Cleveland Institute of Art
11141 East Blvd.

Cleveland, OH 44106-1710

Cuyahoga Community College
2900 Community College Ave.
Cleveland, OH 44115

Virginia Marti College of Fashion and Art
11724 Detriot Ave.
Cleveland, OH 44107

Columbus College of Art and Design
Columbus, OH 43215

Interior Design Institute, Inc.
4100 N. High St., Suite 301
Columbus, OH 43214

Ohio State University, Main Campus
Interior Space Design
Department of Industrial Design
College of the Arts
380 Hopkins Hall
128 N. Oval Mall
Columbus, OH 43210-1318
***Bachelor of Science in Industrial Design

Sinclair Community College
444 W. Third St.
Dayton, OH 45402-1421

University of Dayton
300 College Park
Dayton, OH 45469-0001

Southern Ohio College
4641 Bach Lane
Fairfield, OH 45014-1900

Kent State University, Main Campus
Interior Design Program
School of Family and Consumer Studies
College of Fine and Professional Arts
Kent, OH 44242-0001
***Bachelor of Arts

Virginia Marti College of Fashion
11724 Detriot Ave.
Lakewood, OH 44107-3002

Mt. Vernon Nazarene College
800 Martinsburg Rd.
Mt. Vernon, OH 43050-9500

Kent State Stark County, Regional Campus
6000 Frank Rd. N.W.
North Canton, OH 44720-7548

Miami University, Main Campus
Housing and Interior Design
Department of Family and
Consumer Sciences
260 McGuffey Hall
Oxford, OH 45056
***Bachelor of Science in
Family and Consumer
Science

Ursuline College
2500 Lander Rd.
Pepper Pike, OH 44124-4318

Wittenberg University
Springfield, OH 45501

College of Mount St. Joseph
St. Joseph, OH 45051

Davis College
4747 Monroe St.
Toledo, OH 45505

Strautzenberger College
5355 Southwyck Blvd.
Toledo, OH 43614-1561

University of Toledo
2801 W. Bancroft
Toledo, OH 43606-3391

Cuyahoga Community College, Eastern
4250 Richmond Rd.
Warrenville TWS, OH 44122-6104

Otterbein College
Westerville, OH 43081-2006

Central State University
Wilberforce, OH 45384

Penn-Ohio College
3517 Market St.
Youngstown, OH 44507

Oklahoma

East Central University
Ada, OK 74820-6899

Northwestern Oklahoma State University
Alva, OK 73717

Tri-County Technical School
P.O. Box 3428, Eastside
Station
Bartlesville, OK 74003

Southern Nazarene University
6729 N.W. 39 Expressway
Bethany, OK 73008-2694

University of Science and Arts
U.S.A.O. Box 82478
Chickasha, OK 73018-0001

Rogers State College
College Hill
Claremore, OK 74017-2099

Southeastern Oklahoma State University
Station A. Box 4203
Durant, OK 74701

University of Central Oklahoma
100 N. University Dr.
Edmond, OK 73034-0101

Panhandle State University
Goodwell, OK 73939-0430

Cameron University
2800 Gore Blvd.
Lawton, OK 73505-6320

Northeastern Oklahoma A&M Tech
Second & 1 Sts, N E
Miami, OK 74354-6208

University of Oklahoma, Main Campus
Division of Interior Design
College of Architecture
830 VanVlett Oval, Rm. 162
Norman, OK 73019-0265
***Bachelor of Interior
Design

Oklahoma Christian College
P.O. Box 11000
Oklahoma City, OK 73136-1100

Platt College
6125 West Reno
Oklahoma City, OK 73127-6589

Pioneer Area Vocational-Technical School
2101 No. Ash St.
Ponca City, OK 74601-1106

Oklahoma State University, Main Campus
Interior Design Program
Department of Design,
Housing and Merchandising
Home Economics Building
#449
West Stillwater, OK 74078
***Bachelor of Science

Northwestern State University
Tahlequah, OK 74464-7098

Northern Oklahoma College
Tonkawa, OK 74653

Platt College
4821 S. 72nd., East Ave.
Tulsa, OK 74145-6502

Tulsa Junior College
10300 E. 81st St.
Tulsa, OK 74133-4500

Southwestern Oklahoma State University
100 Campus Dr.
Weatherford, OK 73096-3001

New Mexico

New Mexico State University, Main Campus
Las Cruces, NM 88003-0001

Eastern New Mexico Univerity, Main Campus
Portales, NM 88130-7402

Oregon

Oregon State University
Corvallis, OR 97331-6407

University of Oregon
Department of
Architecture/Interior Design
Program
School of Architecture and
Allied Arts
Eugene, OR 97403-1206
***Bachelor of Interior
Design

George Fox College
Newberg, OR 97132-2697

Bassist College
2000 S.W. Fifth Ave.
Portland, OR 97201-4907

John Robert Powers School
203 S.W. 9th Ave.
Portland, OR 97205

Portland Community College
P.O. Box 19000
Portland, OR 27219-0990

Pennsylvania

Northampton Community College
3835 Green Pond Rd.
Bethlehem, PA 18017-7568

Harcum Junior College
Bryn Mawr, PA 19010

Cheyney University
Cheyney, PA 19319

Mercyhurst College
Glenwood Hills
Erie, PA 16546-0001

Beaver College
Glenside, PA 19038-3293

Messiah College
Grantham, PA 17027

Seton Hill College
Greensburg, PA 15601-1599

Grove City College
Grove City, PA 16127-2104

Indiana University of Pennsylvania, Main Campus
Indiana, PA 15705-1087

Mansfield University
Mansfield, PA 16933

Pennsylvania School of the Arts
264 W. Market St.
Marietta, PA 17547

Williamson Free School
Middletown Rd.
Media, PA 19063

Oakbridge Academy of Arts
401 Ninth St.
New Kensington, PA 15068-6425

American Institute of Design
1616 Orthodox St.
Philadelphia, PA 19124-3799

Art Institute of Philadelphia
1622 Chestnut St.
Philadelphia, PA 19103-5119

Drexel University
Interior Design Program
Nesbitt College of Design
Arts
Interior and Graphics Study
Department
32 and Chestnut St.
Philadelphia, PA 19104-2875
***Bachelor of Science

Moore College of Art and Design
Interior Design Department
20th and Race St.
Philadelphia, PA 19103-1179
***Bachelor of Fine Arts

Philadelphia College of Textiles and Science
Schlhse Lane and Henry
Philadelphia, PA 19144-5494

Spring Garden College
7500 Germantown Ave.
Philadelphia, PA 19119-1651

Art Institute of Pittsburg
526 Penn. Ave.
Pittsburgh, PA 15222

Carnegie Mellon University
5000 Forbes Ave.
Pittsburgh, PA 15213-3890

La Roche College
Interior Design Department
Division of Graphics, Design,
and Communication
9000 Babcock Blvd.
Pittsburgh, PA 15237-5898
***Bachelor of Science

Pittsburgh Technical Institute
635 Smithfield St.
Pittsburgh, PA 15222-2560

Antonelli Institute of Art
2910 Jolly Rd.
Plymouth Meeting, PA 19462

Albright College
P.O. Box 15234
Reading, PA 19612-5234

Marywood College
Scranton, PA 18509-1598

Bradley Academy of Visual Arts
625 E. Philadelphia
York, PA 17403-1625

York Academy of Arts
625 E. Philadelphia St.
York, PA 17403

Rhode Island

University of Rhode Island
Kingston, RI 02881-0809

Hall Institute of Technology
120 High St.
Pawtucket, RI 02860-2151

Rhode Island School of Design
Five-Year Professional
Degree Program
Department of Interior
Architectural Studies
2 College St.
Providence, RI 02903-2707
***Bachelor of Interior
Architecture

Community College of Rhode Island
400 East Ave.
Warwick, RI 02886-1805

Puerto Rico

Catholic University of Puerto Rico
Ponce, PR 00731

University of Puerto Rico, Rio Piedras
Rio Piedras, PR 00931

South Carolina

Anderson College
316 Boulevard
Anderson, SC 29621-4035

Forrest College
601 E. River St.
Anderson, SC 29624-2498

Clemson University, Main Campus
Clemson, SC 29634

University of South Carolina, Main Campus
Columbia, SC 29208

Bob Jones University
Greenville, SC 29614-0001

Greenville Technical Education Center
Station B, Box 5616
Greenville, SC 29606

Lander College
Greenwood, SC 29649-2099

Stratford College
38 New Orleans Rd.
Hilton Head Island, SC
29928

Lexington County Vocational Education Center
2421 Augusta Highway
Lexington, SC 29072-2215

South Carolina State University
Orangeburg, SC 29117

Winthrop College
Interior Design Program
Department of Art and
Design
School for Visual and
Performing Arts
Rock Hill, SC 29733-0001
***Bachelor of Fine Arts

Converse College
Interior Design Program
Department of Art
580 E. Main St.
Spartanburg, SC 29302-0006
***Bachelor of Fine Arts

South Dakota

South Dakota University
Brookings, SD 57007-2218

Tennessee

Tennessee Temple University
Chattanooga, TN 37404-3588

University of Tennessee, Chattanooga
615 McCallie Ave.
Chattanooga, TN 37403-2504

Tennessee Technological University
Cookeville, TN 38505

State Area Vocational-Technical School
715 N. Miller Box 2959
Crossville, TN 38555-4381

O'More College of Design
Interior Design Program
423 S. Margin St.
P.O. Box 908
Franklin, TN 37065-0908
***Bachelor of Interior
Design

Lambuth College
Jackson, TN 38301-5296

Carson Newman College
Russell Ave.
Jefferson City, TN 37760

East Tennessee State University
Johnson City, TN 37614-0002

University of Tennessee, Knoxville
Interior Design Program
Textiles, Retailing and
Interior Design
230 Jessie Harris Building
Knoxville, TN 37996-1900
***Bachelor of Science in
Interior Design

Hiwassee College
Madisonville College
Madisonville, TN 37354-9497

University of Tennessee at Martin
Martin, TN 38238

Memphis City Schools-Adult Vocational Education
2597 Avery Ave.
Memphis, TN 38112

Memphis College of Art
Overton Park
Memphis, TN 38112-5498

Memphis State University
Memphis, TN 38152

Middle Tennessee State University
Murfreesboro, TN 37132

Tennessee State University
3500 J. A. Merritt Blvd.
Nashville, TN 37209-1561

Watkins Institute
Sixth Ave. at Church St.
Nashville, TN 37219

Texas

Abilene Christian University
Acu Station, Box 8155
Abilene, TX 79699-8155

Texas State Technical Institute, Amarillo
Interior Design Technology
Program
Box 11197
Amarillo, TX 79111-0003
***Assoc. of Applied Arts
ith a Professional Certificate

Bauder Fashion College
508 South Center St.
Arlington, TX 76010

University of Texas at Arlington
Interior Design Program
School of Architecture
800 S. Cooper St.
Arlington, TX 76019-0108
***Bachelor of Science in Interior Design

University of Texas at Austin
Interior Design Program
Department of Home Economics
College of Natural Sciences
115 Gearing Hall
Austin, TX 78712-1097
***Bachelor of Science in Home Economics

Lamar University
Beaumont, TX 77710

University of Mary Hardin Baylor
P.O. Box 8019
Belton, TX 76513-2599

Ambassador College
Big Sandy, TX 75755

Texas A & M University
College Station, TX 77843-0100

Art Institute of Dallas
8080 Park Lane
Dallas, TX 75231-5919

El Centro College
Interior Design Department
Main and Lamar
Dallas, TX 75202-3698
***Certificate in Interior Design

Miss Wades Fashion College
P.O. Box 58643
Dallas, TX 75258

Texas Woman's University
Interior Design Program
School of Visual Arts
P.O. Box 22995, TWU Station
Denton, TX 76204-1995
BA Degree Program

University of North Texas
Interior Design Program
Art Department-Interior Design
College of Art and Sciences

P.O. Box 5098
Denton, TX 76203-0098
***Bachelor of Fine Arts

Stephen F. Austin State University
Interior Design Program
Department of Home Economics
P.O. Box 13014, SFA Station
Nacogdoches, TX 75962-3014
***Bachelor of Science in Home Economics

El Paso Community College
P.O. Box 20500
El Paso, TX 79998-0500

Mannequin Manor Fashion Career School
9611 Acer Ave. 79925
El Paso, TX 79925

Southwest Institute of Merchandising & Design
9611 Acer Ave.
El Paso, TX 79925-6709

Texas Christian University
Interior Design Program
Department of Design and Fashion
P.O. Box 32869
Fort Worth, TX 76129-0001
***Bachelor of Science

Hill College
P.O. Box 619
Hillsboro, TX 76645-0619

Art Institute of Houston
3600 Yoakum Blvd.
Houston, TX 77006

Houston Community College
P.O. Box 7849
Houston, TX 78203

North Harris County College
2700 W. W. Thorne Dr.
Houston TX 77073

Texas Southern University
3100 Cleburne St.
Houston, TX 77204

University of Houston, University Park
4800 Calhoun
Houston, TX 77204

Sam Houston State University
Huntsville, TX 77341-2177

North Harris County College, East
2000 Kingwood Dr.
Kingwood, TX 77339-3801

Texas A and I University
Santa Gertrudis
Kingsville, TX 78363-3479

Lubbock Christian University
5601 W. 19th
Lubbock, TX 79407-2099

Texas Tech University
Interior Design Program
College of Home Economics
MEDCE, P.O. Box 41162
Lubbock, TX 79409-1162
***Bachelor of Interior Design

San Jacinto College, Central Campus
8060 Spencer Highway
Pasadena, TX 77505-5903

Angelo State University
San Angelo, TX 76909

Incarnate Word College
4301 Broadway
San Antonio, TX 78209-6398

San Antonio College
1300 San Pedro Ave.
San Antonio, TX 78284

St Philip's College
2111 Nevada St.
San Antonio, TX 78203-2047

Trinity University.
715 Stadium Dr.
San Antonio, TX 78212-3104

University of Texas, San Antonio
6700 N. FM. 1604 West
San Antonio, TX 78285-0616

Southwest Texas State University
Interior Design Program
219 Home Economics Building
San Marcos, TX 78666-4605
***Bachelor of Science in Home Economics

Tarleton State University
Tarleton Station
Stephenville, TX 76402-0001

Baylor University, Main Campus
Waco, TX 76798

Utah

Southern Utah State College
Cedar City, UT 84720-2498

Snow College
Ephraim, UT 84627-1299

Utah State University
Logan, UT 84322-0001

Weber State College
Ogden, UT 84408-1503

College of Eastern Utah
Price, UT 84602-1019

Brigham Young University
Brimhall Building
Provo, UT 84602-1019

Dixie College
Saint George, UT 84770-3876

Latter Day Saints Business College
411 E. South Temple
Salt Lake City, UT 84111-1302

University of Utah
228 Alfred C. Emery
Salt Lake City, UT 84112

Virginia

Virginia Highlands Community College
Abingdon, VA 24210

Northern Virginia Community College
4001 Wakefield Chapel Rd.
Annandale, VA 22003

Marymount University
Interior Design Program
2807 N. Glebe Rd.
Arlington, VA 22207-4299
***Bachelor of Arts in Interior Design

Mountain Empire Community College
Drawer 700
Big Stone Gap, VA 24219-0700

Virginia Polytechnical Institute and State University
Interior Design Program
Department of Housing, Interior Design and Resource Management

College of Human Resources
366 Wallis Hall
Blacksburg, VA 24061-0424
***Bachelor of Science

Bridgewater College
Bridgewater, VA 22812-1599

Southern Seminary College
Buena Vista, VA 24416

University of Virginia
Charlottesville, VA 22903

Tidewater Community College
1428 Cedar Rd.
Chesapeake, VA 23320-7108

John Tyler Community College
Chester, VA 23831

Longwood College
Farmville, VA 23901-1895

Hampton University
Hampton, VA 23668-0101

James Madison University
Harrisonburg, VA 22807-0002

Liberty University
Lynchburg, VA 24506-8001

Lord Fairfax Community College
Middletown, VA 22645

Norfolk State University
2401 Corprew Ave.
Norfolk, VA 23504-03907

Virginia State University
Petersburg, VA 23803-2095

Radford University
Radford, VA 24142

J. Sargeant Reynolds Community College
P.O. Box C-3240
Richmond, VA 23261-2040

Virginia Commonwealth University
Department of Interior Design
School of the Arts
325 N. Harrison St.
P.O. Box 2526
Richmond VA 23284-2519
***Bachelor of Fine Arts

Hollins College
Roanoke, VA 24020-4410

Mary Baldwin College
Staunton, VA 24401

North Virginia Community College, Loudoun
1000 H. Flood Byrd Highway
Sterling, VA 22170

Blue Ridge Community College
P.O. Box 80
Weyers Cave, VA 24486

College of William and Mary
Williamsburg, VA 23185

Vermont

University of Vermont
Burlington, VT 05405

Washington

Bellevue Community College
3000 Landerholm Cr.
Bellevue, WA 98009-6484

Western Washington University
Department of Home Economics
516 High St.
Bellingham, WA 98225-5946

Highline Community College
Department of Occupational Education
P.O. Box 98000
Des Moines, WA 98198-9800

Central Washington University
Department of Home Economics
Ellensburg, WA 98926

Everett Community College
Department of Community/Performing Arts
801 Wetmore
Everett, WA 98201-1390

Clover Park Vocational Technical Institute
4500 Stellacoom Blvd., S. W.
Lakewood Center, WA 98499

Columbia Basin College
2600 N. 20th Ave.
Pasco, WA 99301-3397

Northwest College of Art
17791 Ford Dr., N. E.
Poulsbo, WA 98370

Washington State University
Interior Design Program
Department of Apparel/Merchandising/Interior Design
White Hall 202B
Pullman, WA 99164-2020
***Bachelor of Arts in Interior Design

Renton Vocational Technical Institute
3000 N.E. 4th St.
Renton, WA 98055

Art Institute of Seattle
2323 Elliot Ave.
Seattle, WA 98121-1633

Cornish College of Arts
&10 East Roy
Seattle, WA 98102-4604

Seattle Pacific University
3307 3rd. Ave. West
Seattle, WA 98119-1940

Seattle School of Interior Design
419 Occidental Ave. S. #201
Seattle, WA 98104

Spokane Falls Community College
Department of Vocational Education
W. 3410 Ft. George Wright
Spokane, WA 99204-5288

West Virginia

Beckley College
P.O. Box A G
Beckley, WV 25802-2800

West Virginia Wesleyan College
Buckhannon, WV 26201-2998

University of Charleston
23400 Mac Corkle S. E.
Charleston, WV 25304-1045

Fairmont State College
Fairmont, WV 26554-2489

Marshall University, Main Campus
Huntington, WV 25701-2460

West Virginia University
Morgantown, WV 26506-6122

Shepherd College
Shepherdstown, WV 25443-1569

Wisconsin

Fox Valley Vocational Technical and Adult Education
1825 N. Blue Mound Dr.
P.O. Box 2277
Appleton, WI 54913

Gateway Technical College
P.O. Box 1486
Kenosha, WI 53141-1690

Western Wisconsin Tech College
6th and Vine
La Crosse, WI 54602-0908

Madison Area Technical College
3550 Anderson Street
Madison, WI 53704-2599

University of Wisconsin at Madison
Interior Design Major
Environment, Textiles and Design Department
School of Family Resouces & Consumer Sciences
1300 Linden Dr.
Madison, WI 53706-1524
***Bachelor of Science

University of Wisconsin, Stout
Menomonie, WI 54751

Milwaukee Area Technical, North
5555 West Highland
Mequon, WI 53092-1143

Milwaukee Institute of Art & Design
342 N. Water St.
Milwaukee, WI 53202-5715

Mount Mary College
Interior Design Program
2900 N. Menomonee River Pkwy.
Milwaukee, WI 53222-4597
***Bachelor of Arts

Patricia Steven's Career

Patricia Steven's Career College
161 W. Wisconsin Ave.
Milwaukee, WI 53203-2602

Stratton College
1300 N. Jackson St.
Milwaukee, WI 53202

University of Wisconsin, Milwaukee
Milwaukee, WI 53201

University of Wisconsin, Stevens Point
Stevens Point, WI 54481-3897

Wyoming

Casper College
125 College Dr.
Casper, WY 82601-4699

University of Wyoming
P.O. Box 3354
Laramie, WY 82071-3354

Northwest College
Powell, WY 82435

Canada

Fanshawe College
1460 Oxford Street East
London, Ontario, CAN N5W 5H1

Dawson College
Interior Design Department
Penwater Campus
3040 Sherbrooke St. W.
Montreal, Quebec, CAN H3Z 1A4
***Diplome d'Etudes Collegiales

Ryerson Polytechnical Institute
School of Interior Design
Faculty of Applied Arts
350 Victoria St.
Toronto, Ontario, CAN M5B 2K3
***Bachelor of Applied Arts

University of Manitoba
Department of Interior Design
Faculty of Architecture
Winnipeg, Manitoba, CAN R3T 2N2
***Bachelor of Interior Design

Great Britian

Edinburg College of Art
Lauriston Place
Edinburgh EH 3 9DF

Japan

Osaka University of Arts
469 Higashiyama, Kanan-cho
Minakani-Kawachi-Gun
Osaka 58

Professional Organizations

Allied Board of Trade
555 Mamaroneck Ave.
Harrison, NY 10528
(212) 473-3877

American Association of Wholesale Showrooms
P.O. Box 218
Beverly Hills, CA 90213
(213) 936-1414

American Furniture Manufacturers Association
P.O. Box HP-7
High Point, NC 27261
(919) 884-5000

American Hardware Manufacturers Association
931 N. Plum Grove Rd.
Schaumburg, IL 60173-4796
(708) 605-1025

American Institute of Architects (AIA)
1130 Connecticut N.W. Ste. 625
Washington DC 20036
(202) 828-0993
* Professional organization for registered architects

American Lighting Association
435 North Michigan Ave. #1717
Chicago, IL 60611
(312) 644-0828

American Society for Testing & Materials
1916 Race
Philadelphia, PA 19103
(215) 299-5400

American Society of Furniture Designers (ASFD)
521 Hamilton
High Point, NC 27261
(919) 884-4074
* Professional organization for furniture designers

American Society of Interior Designers (ASID)
608 Massachusetts Ave. N.E.
Washington, DC 20002
(202) 546-3480

* Worldwide professional organization for interior designers

American Society of Landscape Designers (ASLA)
4401 Connecticut Ave., N.W.
Washington, DC 20008
(202) 686-2752
* Professional organization for Landscape Designers

American Textile Manufacturers Institute
1801 K St N.W., Ste 900
Washington, D.C. 20006
(202) 862-0552

American Window Covering Manufacturers Association (AWCMA)
355 Lexington Ave.
New York, NY 10017
(212) 661-4261
* Represents leading mfg./suppliers of hard window coverings.

Architectural Woodwork Institute
2310 South Walter Reed Dr.
Arlington, VA 22206
(703) 671-9100

Art Deco Society of Los Angeles
P.O. Box 972
Hollywood, CA 90078
(213) 659-DECO

Art Deco Society of New York
90 West St.
New York, NY 10006
(212) 925-4946

Art & Antique Dealers League of America
1020 Madison Ave.
New York, NY 10006
(212) 879-7558

Associated Landscape Contractors of America
405 North Washington St.
Falls Church, VA 22046
(703) 241-4004

* Association of Landscape Contractors

Association of Registered Interior Designers of Ontario
168 N Bedford Rd.
Toronto, ON M5R 2K9
(416) 921-2127

Association of University Interior Designers
Miami University
Cook Place
Oxford, OH 45056
(513) 529-3730

Better Fabric Testing Bureau, Inc.
101 West 31st. St.
New York, NY 10001
(212) 868-7090

Business & Institutional Furniture Manufactureres' Association (BIFMA)
2335 Burton, S.E.
Grand Rapids, MI 49506
(616) 243-1681

California Redwood Association
405 Enfrente Dr. #200
Novato, CA 94949
(415) 382-0662

The Carpet and Rug Institute
P.O. Box 2048
Dalton, GA 30722
(706) 278-3176
(404) 278-3176
(202) 429-6629
* National trade association for the carpet and rug industry.

Carpet Manufacturers Association of the West
100 North Citrus St. #235
West Covina, CA 91791
(818) 967-5268

Center for Fire Research
National Institute of Standards & Technology
A247 Polymers Bldg.
Gaithersburg, MD 20899
(301) 975-6850

Ceramic Tile Institute
700 North Virgil Ave.
Los Angeles, CA 90029
(213) 660-1911

Color Association of the United States
409 W. 44th St.
New York, NY 10036
(212) 582-6884
* Publishes annual color forecast for interior colors.

The Color Marketing Group (CMG)
4001 N. 9th St., Ste. 102
Arlington, VA 22203
(703) 528-7666
* A professional organization that forcasts colors two years ahead.

Contract Furnishings Council
1190 Merchandise Mart
Chicago, IL 60654
(312) 321-0563
* Full service contract dealer association

Cultured Marble Institute
435 North Michigan Ave.
Chicago, IL 60611
(312) 644-0828

Decorative Window Coverings Association (DWCA)
1050 N. Lindbergh Blvd.
St. Louis, MO 63132-2994
(314) 991-3470
* Non-profit association of fabricators/distributors

Design International
3748 22nd St.
San Francisco, CA 94114
(415) 647-4700

Designers' Saturday, Inc.
A & D Building
150 E. 58th St.
New York, NY 10155
(212) 826-3155
* Trade association of New York contract and residential furnishing firms.

Drapery Manufacturers Association of California
P.O. Box 6611
Orange, CA 92665
(714) 636-7382
* California association of drapery manufacturers

Interior Designers of Canada (IDC)
160 Pears Ave.
Toronto, Ontario
CAN M5R 1TZ

The Foundation for Interior Design Education Research (FIDER)
60 Monroe Center, N.W.
Grand Rapids, MI 49503
(616) 458-0400
* Accredits interior design programs in U.S. and Canada

Home Fashion Information Network
557 S. Duncan
Clearwater, FL 34616
(813) 443-2702
(800) 875-9255
* Publishes and provides information to the wall coverings industry.

Home Fashion Products Association (HFPA)
355 Lexington Ave.
New York, NY 10017-6603
(212) 661-4261
* Professional organization of manufacturers/suppliers of soft window treatments and home furnishings.

Illuminating Engineering Society of North America
345 East 47th St.
New York, NY 10017
(212) 705-7926

Indian Arts and Crafts Association
4215 Lead, S.E.
Albuquerque, NM 87018
(505) 265-9149

Industrial Designers Society of America
1142-E Walker Rd.
Great Falls, VA 22066
(703) 759-0100

Institute of Business Designers (IBD)
341 Merchandise Mart
Chicago, IL 60654
(312) 467-1950

* Contract interior designer's professional association.

Institute of Store Designers
25 North Broadway
Tarrytown, NY 10591
(914) 332-1806

Interior Design Educator Council (IDEC)
14252 Culver Dr.
Irvine, CA 92714
(312) 467-1950

Interior Plantscape Association
11800 Sunrise Valley Dr.
Reston, VA 22091
(703) 771-7044

International Association of Lighting Designers
18 East 16th St.
New York, NY 10003
(212) 206-1281

International Furnishings and Design Association (IFDA)
107 World Trade Center
P.O. Box 58045
Dallas, TX 75258
(214) 747-2406
* Non-profit organization that promotes interior design education and networking among leaders in the industry.

International Linen Promotion Commission
200 Lexington Ave. #225
New York, NY 10016
(212) 685-0424

International Society of Interior Designers (ISID)
433 S. Spring St., Ste. 6-D
Los Angeles, CA 90013
(213) 680-4240
* Educational organization for interior designers and members of the trade.

Marble Institute of America
33505 State St.
Farmington, MI 48335
(313) 476-5558

National Art Dealer Association
5669 Friendship Station
Washington, DC 20016
(202) 537-1000

National Association of Display Industries
470 Park Ave. S.
New York, NY 10016
(212) 213-2662

National Association of Store Fixture Manufacturers
5975 West Sunrise Blvd.
Sunrise, FL 33313
(305) 587-9190

National Council on Interior Design Qualification (NCIDQ)
118 E. 25th St.
New York, NY 10010
(212) 473-1199

National Decorating Products Association (NDPA)
1050 N. Lindbergh Blvd.
St. Louis, MO 63132
(314) 991-3470
* Trade association for retailers of decorative products.

National Fire Protection Association
Batterymarch Park
Quincy, MA 02269
(617) 770-3000

National Home Fashion League
107 World Trade Center
Dallas, TX 75207
(214) 747-2406

National Kitchen and Bath Association
124 Main St.
Hackettstown, NJ 07840
(201) 852-0033

National Institute of Governmental Purchasing
115 Hillwood Ave.
Falls Church, VA 22046
(703) 533-7300

National Oak Flooring Manufacturing Association Oak Flooring Institute
P.O. Box 3009
Memphis, TN 38173
(901) 526-5016
* Trade association for flooring manufacturers.

National Office Products Association (NOPA)
301 N. Fairfax St.
Alexandria, VA 22314

(703) 549-9040

National Paint and Coatings Association
1500 Rhode Island Ave., N.W.
Washington, DC 20001
(202) 462-6272

National Restaurant Association
1200 17th St., N. W.
Washington, DC 20036
(202) 331-5900

National Trust for Historic Preservation
1785 Massachusetts Ave., N.W.
Washington, DC 20036
(202) 673-4000

National Wholesale Furniture Association
209 South Main St. #M-1412
High Point, NC 27261
(919) 889-6411

Professional Picture Framers Association
P.O. Box 7655
Richmond, VA 23231
(804) 226-0430

Resilent Floor Covering Institute
966 Hungerford Dr., Ste. 12-B
Rockville, MD 20850
(301) 340-8580
* Trade association for manufacturers of resilent tile & sheet vinyl products.

Resource Council Inc.
979 Third Ave. #902N
New York, NY 10022
(212) 752-9040

Society for Marketing Professional Services
99 Canal Center Plaza
Alexandria, VA 22314
(703) 549-6117

The Society of Environmental Graphic Designers
47 Third St
Cambridge, MA 02141
(617) 577-8225

Tile Council of America
P.O. Box 326
Princeton, NJ 08542-0326
(609) 921-7050

Upholstered Furniture Action Council (UFAC)
P.O. Box 2436
High Point, NC 27261
(919) 885-5065

Wall Upholstery Guild of America
201 E. 28th St.
New York, NY 10016
(212) 532-2449

Wallcovering Association (WMA)
355 Lexington Ave.
New York, NY 10016
(312) 644-6610
* Wallcovering association for manufacturers, distributors and suppliers.

Wallcovering Information Bureau
66 Morris Ave.
Springfield, NJ 07081
(201) 379-1100

Window Coverings Association of America (WCAA)
1050 N. Lindbergh Blvd.
St. Louis, MO 63132
(314) 997-0558
* Window covering retailer's trade association.

Wood Moulding & Millwork Producers Association
1730 S.W. Skyline Blvd.
P.O. Box 25278
Portland, OR 97225
(503) 292-9288

The Wool Bureau
360 Lexington Ave.
New York, NY 10017
(212) 986-6222
* Non-profit organization engaged in promoting wool products.

Industry Magazines, Trade Journals, Book Clubs, and Other Related Magazines

American Woman
1700 Broadway
New York, NY 10019

Architects and Designers Book Service
333 E. 38th St.
New York, NY 10016

Architects and Planners Book Service
866 Third Ave.
New York, NY 10022

Architectural Digest
P.O. Box 7192
Red Oak, IA 51591-2192

Architects Book Club
11 W. 19th St. 4th Fl.
New York, NY 10011

At Home
680 Eighth St.
San Francisco, CA 94103

Azure Magazine
135 Boon Ave.
Toronto Ontario CAN
M6E 326

Better Homes and Gardens
1716 Locust St.
Des Moines, IA 50309

Better Homes and Gardens Special Interest Publications
750 Third Ave.
New York, NY 10017

Business and Professional Woman
95 Leeward Glenway, Unit 121
Don Mills, Ontario CAN
M3C 226

California Homes & Lifestyle
17911 Sky Park Circle Ste. D
Irvine, CA 92714

Canada Interiors LTD
777 Bay St.
Toronto, Ontario CAN
M5W 1A7

Canadian House and Home
60 St. Clair Ave. E. Ste. 304

Toronto, Ontario CAN M4T
1NS

Canadian Interior/County & Country Home
MaClean-Hunter LTD, Bus.
77 Bay St.
Toronto, Ontario CAN M5W
1A7

Career Woman
44 Broadway
Greenlawn, NY 11740

Century Home
Bluestone House
12 Mill St. S
Port Hope, Ontario CAN
L1A 255

Chatelaine
777 Bay St.
Toronto, Ontario CAN MSW
1A7

Colonial Homes
P.O. Box 7140
Red Oak, IA 51591-2140

Country Accents
P.O. Box 471
Mount Morris, IL 61054-7924

Country Decorating Ideas
1115 Broadway
New York, NY 10160-0397

Country Home Magazine
1716 Locust Street
P.O. Box 10635
Des Moines, IA 50380-0635

Country Homes and Interiors
King's Reach Tower
London ENG SE1 9LS

Country Living
224 W. 57th St.
New York, NY 10019

Custom Kitchen Planner
110 Fifth Ave.
New York, NY 10011

Decor
408 Olive St.
St. Louis, MO 63102

Decorating Ambiance
3117 St. Catherine E., Ste.1
Montreal, Quebec CAN
H1W 2C1

Decorating and Design Sourcebook
1300 Yonge St. Ste. 500
Toronto, Ontario CAN M4T
1X3

Decorating Remodeling
110 Fifth Ave.
New York, NY 10011

Decorating Retailer
National Decorating
Products Assn.
1050 N. Lindbergh Blvd.
St. Louis, MO 63132

Decorative Products World
Chilton CO.
1 Chilton Way
Radnor PA 19089

Design Solutions
P.O. Box 1550
13924 Braddock Rd, Ste. 100
Centreville, VA 22020

Design Source
220 Fifth Ave., 7th Fl.
New York, NY 10001

Design Times
715 Boyston
Boston, MA 02116

The Designer/Designer Specifier
401 N. Broad St.
Philadelphia, PA 19108

Designer's Illustrated
4410 El Camino Real, Ste. 111
Los Altos, CA 94022
Resource Guide

Designer's West/Designer's World
8914 Santa Monica Blvd Fl 3
Los Angeles, CA 90069

Designs
C.P. 692, Gsucc. Place
D'Armes

Montreal, Quebec CAN H2Y
3H8

Digest for Home Furnishers
Minnesota 300
300 Prairie Center Dr. Ste. 210
Eden Prairie, MN 55344

Distinguished Home Plans and Products/
Custom Home Plans Guides
89 E Jericho Turnpike
Mineola, NY 11501

Draperies and Window Coverings
840 U.S. Highway 1
North Palm Beach, FL 33408

Drapery and Window Coverings
1050 N. Lindberg Blvd.
St. Louis, MO 63132

ELLEDECOR
P.O. Box 51914
Boulder, CO 80323-1914

Entenpreneur Magazine
2392 Morse Ave.
Irvine, CA 92714-6234

Entenprenurial Woman
2392 Morse St.
Irvine, CA 92714

Executive Female
P.O. Box 1510
Clearwater, FL 34617

Family Circle
110 Fifth Ave.
New York, NY 10011

Family Circle Great Ideas
488 Madison Ave.
New York, NY 10022

Fine Homebuilding
Taunton Press
52 Church Hill Rd. Box 355
Newtown, CT 06470

First for Women
Bauer Publishing Company
270 Sylavan Ave.
Englewood Cliffs, NJ 07632

Floorcovering News
777 Bay St.
Toronto, Ontario CAN M5W
1A7

Floorcovering Weekly
60 E. 42nd St., Ste. 2341
New York, NY 10165

Flooring
757 Third Ave.
New York, NY 10017

Flooring Magazine
7500 Old Oak Blvd.
Cleveland, OH 44130

Forcast for Home Economics
Scholastic, Inc.
730 Broadway
New York, NY 10003

GardenDesign
P.O. Box 55455
Boulder CO 80323-5455

Haut Decor
3290 N.E. 12th Ave.
Oakland Park, FL 33334

**HFD-The Weekly Home
Furnishings
Newspaper**
Fairchild Publishing, Inc.
7E. 12th St.
New York, NY 10003

Home
1633 Broadway, 41st Fl.
New York, NY 10019

**Home Economics Educators
Association, Newsletter/
Journal of Home Economics**
2010 Massachusetts Ave,
N.W.
Washington, DC 20036

Home Economics Journal
151 Staler St., Rm. 901
Ottawa Ontario, CAN

Home Fashions Magazine
7 W. 34th St.
New York, NY 10001

Home Furnishings Review
South West Home
Furnishings Association
110 World Trade Center
P.O. Box 581207
Dallas, TX 75258

Home Goods Retailing
Maclean-Hunter Building
777 Bay St.

Toronto, Ontario CAN M5W
1A7

Home Journal
Communication
Management. Ltd.
Hong Kong Plaza #1811
188 Connaright Rd. W.
Wanchai Hongkong

Home Magazine
5900 Wilshire Blvd.
Los Angeles, CA 90036

Home Textiles Today
200 S. Main St.
High Point NC 27261

**Homes and Gardens King's
Reach Tower**
Stamford, St.
London ENG SE1 9LS

House and Garden
P.O. Box 51466
Boulder, CO 80321-1466

House and Home
60 St. Clair Ave. E, Ste. 304
Toronto, Ontario M4T 1NS
CAN

House Beautiful
1700 Broadway
New York, NY 10019-5905

**House Beautiful's Specialized
Decorating Magazines**
1700 Broadway
New York, NY 10019

I.D.E.A.S.
Dodi Publishing Corp., Inc.
P.O. Box 343392
Coral Gables, FL 33114

**ID: International Design
Magazine**
Design Publications, Inc.
330 W. 42nd St.
New York, NY 10036

Ideal Home
King's Reach Tower
Stamford St.
London SE1 9LS England

Ideas for Better Living
Boulevard Publications
1755 Northwest Blvd.
Columbus, OH 43312

**Interior Decorator's
Handbook**
Columbia Communications,
Inc.

370 Lexington Ave.
New York, NY 10017

Interior Design
249 W. 17th St.
New York, NY 10011

**Interior Design Buyer's
Guide**
249 W. 17th St.
New York, NY 10011

Interior Design Ontario
Designers of Ontario
168 Bedford Rd.
Toronto, Ontario M5R 2K9
CAN

Interior Designer
Rosen Publishing Group, Inc.
29 E. 21 St.
New York, NY 10010

Interior Designers
William Morrow and Co.
105 Madison Ave.
New York, NY 10016

Interior Textiles
Columbia Communications,
Inc.
370 Lexington Ave.
New York, NY 10017

Interiors
1515 Broadway
New York, NY 10036

Interiors and Sources
450 Skokie Blvd., Ste. 507
Northbrook, IL 60062

**Interiors: Home Fashions
Magazine**
7W. 34th St.
New York, NY 10001

**International Collection of
Interior Design**
Chickshack St.
London ENG WC1X 9HD

LDB Interior Textiles
370 Lexington Ave.
New York, NY 10017

Lifestyles Magazine
110-2103 Airport Rd.
Saskatoon, Sask.
S7L 6WZ, CAN

The Magazine Antiques
P.O. Box 1975
Marion, OH 43306-2075

Martha Stewart, Living
Rochefeller Center
New York, NY 10020-1393

Metropolis
177 E. 87th St.
New York, NY 10128

Metropolitan Home
1716 Locust Street
P.O. Box AC
Des Moines, IA 50380-0009

**National Home Fashion
League**
P.O. Box 58045
Dallas, TX 75258

Progressive Architecture
Rheinhold Publg.
600 Summer St.
P.O. Box 1361
Stamford, CT 06904

Qualified Remodeler
Q.R. Inc
8 S. Michigan Ave. Suite
1616
Chicago, IL 60603

Remodeled Homes
275 Washington St.
Newton, MA 02158-1630

Renovator's Supply
Renovator's Supply, Inc.
Book Reviewer
Millers Falls, MA 01349

Select Home and Food
Advertising Manager
50 Holly St.
Toronto, Ontario M45 3B3
CAN

Select Homes
Planners Plus
382 W. Broadway
Vancouver, B.C. VSY 1R2

Southern Accents
P.O. Box 822
Birmingham, AL 35282-9710

Southern Homes
3146 Reps Miller St.
Norcross, GA 30071

**Southern Prestigious Homes
and Interiors**
P.O. Box 306
Mt Pleasant, SC 29465

Success
342 Madison Ave.
New York, NY 10173

Textile World
McGraw-Hill, Inc.
1221 Ave. of the Americas
New York, NY 10020

Toronto Life Homes
Advertising Manager
59 Front St. E
Toronto, Ontario M5E 1B3
CAN

Town and Country
P.O. Box 7180
Red Oak, IA 51591-2180

Traditional Home Magazine
P.O. Box 2954
Boulder, CO 80329-2945

Victoria
P.O. Box 7148
Red Oak, IA 51591-2148

Victorian Homes
Vintage Pub.
Millers Falls, MA 01349

Victorian Sampler
P.O. Box 344
Mt. Morris, IL 61054-7930

W
P.O. Box 56182
Boulder, CO 80321-6182

Wallcoverings, Windows and Interior Fashions
15 Bank St.
Stamford, CT 069901

The Wallpaper
570 7th Ave., Ste 500
New York, NY 10018-1696

Window Fashions Magazine
6th West 5th Street, Suite 300
St. Paul, MN 55102

Woman & Home
King's Reach Tower
Stamford St.
London SE1 9LS England

Woman's Day Special Interest Publication
1633 Broadway
New York, NY 10019

Woman's Enterprise
Box 3100
Agoura Hills, CA 91301

Woman's World
270 Sylvan Ave.
Englewood Cliffs, NJ 07632

Women in Business
9100 Ward Parkway
Kansas City, MO 64114

Working Woman
342 Madison Ave.
New York, NY 10173

The World of Interiors
234 King's Rd.
London SW3 SUA England

Your Home
Pvt. Bay 15 New Market
Auckland New Zealand

1,001 Decorating Ideas
3 Park Ave.
New York, NY 10016

Index

Books by *Touch of Design* ®

Secrets of Success for Today's Interior Designers and Decorators

Discover Touch of Design's secrets of success. This is your guide to accurate planning and measuring as well as selling the job and keeping the customers coming back for more. This book provides a <u>wealth</u> of knowledge, experience, and benefits for *all* interior designers and decorators. Whether you are new to the interior design field or are very experienced, *everyone* gains knowledge and experience from this book. Improve your sales ability, design planning and measuring skills, and fabric selection expertise. Determine what will and won't work for the particular situation, and gain an overall increased knowledge in the field of interior design. The realm of alternate and fabric window treatments is thoroughly covered. Follow the advice, use the information, and become a window treatment expert. Complete explanations and extensive professional advice are included. Learn methods for getting better leads, proven marketing and advertising techniques, how to eliminate your competition, and how to be financially successful in this career. Buy this book if you want to *increase* your sales and profits and eliminate problems. You get a reference <u>packed with information to ensure your</u> <u>success.</u> 336 pages (8¼" x 11").

Start Your Own Interior Design Business and Keep it Growing!

Here are even more Touch of Design secrets. You'll find a complete business plan covering *everything* you need to know from A to Z to start and grow a successful interior design business. You get many more prospecting, marketing, and advertising secrets. Don't start an interior design business without this book. This is *your* guide to business success. This book is *filled* with successful, useful, practical, helpful, and profitable ideas for *anyone* starting or attempting to grow an interior design business. A <u>must</u> for interior design businesses just starting up — *but* should be read by *all* interior design business owners who want to flourish and earn more money in today's business climate. *All* will benefit from this new book. <u>Extremely comprehensive and complete.</u> 384 pages (8¼" x 11").

The Apple Chart

Save fabric backorders, lost orders, time, and money! This is the expanded and updated decorative fabric reference source book. Your cross-reference guide to finding required fabrics from *other* vendors. A vital and necessary tool for anyone who works with and sells interior fabrics. <u>Don't try to sell fabrics without this reference source book.</u> Available through Touch of Design. **Please note:** Since we buy *The Apple Chart* directly from the publisher, this book is a *nonreturnable* item, is *not* available by phone order, and is *only* available by check or money order.

Yes, I want to make an investment in my future. **Please send me:**   Number of copies

Secrets of Success for Today's Interior Designers and Decorators $39.99 _____ _____
Start Your Own Interior Design Business and Keep it Growing!   39.99 _____ _____
The Apple Chart (sorry, this book is nonreturnable)   31.99 _____ _____
           California residents must add sales tax —   7¼% _____
Shipping and handling, one book $3.45, two books $4.95, three books $6.45   Shipping _____
      Send for pricing information on multiple book orders.   Total _____

I understand that I may return *Secrets of Success for Today's Interior Designers and Decorators* and *Start Your Own Interior Design Business and Keep It Growing!* in *resalable* condition within 30 days for a refund if I am not completely satisfied.

Only prepaid orders will be accepted. Use a check, money order, Visa, or Mastercard for ordering.

Name_____ Firm_____

Address_____ City_____ State_____ Zip_____

Signature_____ Card Number_____ Expiration_____
Type of credit card: ☐Visa ☐Mastercard   (No Visa or Mastercard orders for *The Apple Chart*)

Mail to: *Touch of Design* ®

Dept. 9E, 475 College Boulevard, Suite 6290, Oceanside, CA 92057, or phone order (800) 247-6553
      Are you on our mailing list? If you did not purchase this book directly from Touch of Design, send us your name and address for future notification of available books by Touch of Design.
Please tell your friends and associates in the interior design field about these books.